Press

United States Army
Medals, Badges and Insignia

By
Colonel Frank C. Foster
US Army Ret.

Dedicated to my father
Captain Frank C. Foster, USAR,
a World War II veteran and my
son **Captain Lee B. Fost**er, ANG
and all the other fathers and sons
and the mothers and daughters
of our great country who have so
unselfishly served their country in
the
United States Army.

Library of Congress Catalog Card Number - 2019942030
Hardcover Edition ISBN - 978-1-884452-62-8
Softcover Edition ISBN - 978-1-884452-61-1

Copyright 2019 by MOA Press

Published by:

MOA Press (Medals of America Press)
114 Southchase Blvd. • Fountain Inn, SC 29644
Telephone: (800) 308-0849
www.moapress.com • www.usmedals.com

About the Author

COLONEL
FRANK FOSTER

COL. FRANK C. FOSTER *(Ret.)*, obtained his BS from The Citadel, MBA from the University of Georgia and is a graduate of the Army's Command and General Staff College and War College. He saw service as a Battery Commander in Germany and served in Vietnam with the 173rd Airborne Brigade and USARV General Staff.

In the Adjutant General's Corps, he served as the Adjutant General of the Central Army Group, the 4th Infantry Division and was the Commandant and Chief of the Army's Adjutant General's Corps from 1986 to 1990. His military service provided him a unique understanding of the Armed Forces Awards System. He currently operates Medals of America Press and is the author of the Military Medals of America, several books on the Air Force, Marines and Navy awards and coauthor of The Decorations and Medals of the Republic of Vietnam. He and his wife Linda, who was decorated with the Army Commander's Medal in 1990 for service to the Army, live in Greenville, South Carolina.

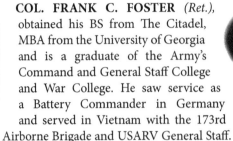

Grateful Acknowledgements

The author wish to express his deepest appreciation to the following individuals for their invaluable contributions. Without their unselfish efforts, this book would have ended as an unfilled dream.

- The Medals of America team with special thanks to: Mrs. Linda Foster for the splendid job in editing this book, Mrs. Lois Owens for custom mounting, Mr. Kirk Stotzer Art Director and Ms. "Buz" Buswell - Pre Press.
- The Medals of America review team of Master Chief (Ret.) Jerry Dantzler and First Sgt. (Ret.) Keith Taylor.
- Col. (Ret.) Charles Mugno, Director of the Institute of Heraldry.
- COL. (Ret.) F. P. Anthony and Mrs. Charlene Rose formerly of the U.S. Marine Corps Military Awards Branch.
- Ms. Phyllis Dula, U.S. Coast Guard Military Personnel Management Specialist and her predecessor, Ms. Diane E. Porter.

- Mr. James "Jim" Thompson for Marine guidance.
- Mr. John Sylvester, for Vietnamese awards.
- Major Peter Morgan for great insignia advice.
- Dr.. Steve Hines and Mrs. Terri Hines for their techinical assistance in getting the book on different production platforms.
- Mr. Bryan Scott Johnson for his references on Medals of the Revolution and readiness to lend a helping hand.
- CDR Jerome Mahar (USN Ret.) - Awards Policy J1 (Personnel) DOD Joint Staff.
- Mr. Clinton Foster for the generous use of his fine photographs of early numbered U.S. Military Medals.
- Mr. Augusto Meneses, Design Director of ADDMedia Creatives for his most excellent work in preparing this book.

MEDALS of AMERICA

Press

✨✨✨ Table of Contents ✨✨✨

"Of the 28 million American citizens who have served in the Armed Forces of the United States since World War II, the majority served in the United States Army. This book tells the story of the honors they won, the skills they developed and the military Insignia they served under."

Growing up in a southern family that has seen military service since the Revolution, the Army has long been a part of our family heritage.

After retirement from the Army, I looked for a way to express my appreciation to all the men and women who have so unselfishly served our Army for the past 235 years. The decision was to honor them with a book which explores the honors and insignias our grateful country has used to recognize her soldiers. I hope that future generations will understand the significance of these unique symbols of service. These honors, in the form of decorations, medals, ribbons, badges and insignia, symbolize the valor, bravery, dedication, patriotism, skills and devotion to duty that millions of loyal Americans have so nobly demonstrated while protecting their nation and their fellow countrymen.

World War II represents the United States Army's greatest victory. It also saw the major expansion of the Army's current awards system and development of most of the uniform insignia we know today. This clearly makes World War II the place a special focus this book especially on the medals the WW II veterans earned but seldom received.

Of the 28 million American citizens who have served in the United States Armed Forces since World War II, the majority served in the United States Army. This book tells the story of the honors they won, the skills they developed and the military insignia they served under.

The book is not just for veterans of World War II, Korea, Vietnam, the Gulf War, Kosovo, the Liberation of Iraq, Afghanistan and dozens of other skirmishes and expeditions, but also for veterans' families. When all is said and done it is more important for a soldier's family to gain an appreciation for the dedication and skill which goes into earning these awards.

We will tell the story of our Army over the past 200 plus years through its symbols of valor, professional skill and identification. Every effort has been made to provide the criteria and background for each medal and badge. However, when it came to the area of shoulder sleeve insignia or patches, we could only try to address the major units involved in each war (for the enthusiast, Major Peter Morgan has done a superb job of covering the wide variety of shoulder sleeve insignia in his book, *The United States Military Patch Guide*). Additionally, the area of unit crest and distinctive unit insignia is so vast that it could only be touched upon very briefly.

Finally, as hard as we try, we know there will be mistakes in this book. Therefore please send all comments, suggestions and corrections in care of the publisher. Thank you for using this book. In so doing, you honor the memory of great Americans, our Army veterans. *"Let no veteran be forgotten!"*

Colonel Frank Foster, U.S. Army, Retired

A Short History of Military Medals, Badges and Insignia

Armillae

Torques

Phalerae

Set of Roman Amillae found in Germany and displayed in the Lauersfort Phalera, Burg Linn Museum Center, Krefeld, Germany.

The Roman Legion was the first to have a very organized award system to honor soldiers for bravery and service.

The Roman soldiers wore these decorations in battle, in parades and displayed them in their homes after their military service. If an entire Roman legion was cited for valor a decoration was added to the Legion's eagle standard.

Over 2000 years ago the ancient Roman historian Polybius wrote: *"If there was any fight, and some soldiers distinguish themselves by bravery, the legion commander would bring his troops together and call forward those to be decorated. The Roman commander would call out the merits, deeds and heroic actions for which the Roman soldier was to be decorated and present the legionnaire with a necklace, armbands or set of disks. During the ceremony the commander would often tie the item to Legionnaire's armor,"* just as today's commander pins a military medal on the chest of a soldier.

By the time of the Empire the Roman army had established a series of decorations for military bravery. The most common decoration for bravery was a golden circle necklet called torques. Torques were worn around the necks of Celtic Warriors and their award originally represented the defeat of an enemy in single combat. Over time the Torques became an award for bravery. A second type of valor award for all ranks were Armillae, a pair of embossed or plain armbands. Another highly coveted award was the embossed discs called Phalerae sometimes awarded in sets and worn on a leather harness over the legionnaire's armor. These discs were presented in bronze, silver and gold and there was no limit to the number a soldier could be awarded.

Above these three awards were various crowns such as the Corona Aurea *(Golden Crown)* presented to Centurions for victorious personal combat and the Corona Vallaris *(Fortification)* crown awarded to the first Legionaries or Centurion over the walls of an enemy fortification. A very high honor was to be awarded

the Corona Civia, a crown of oak leaves for saving the life of a fellow Roman citizen during battle. Over time its award allowed winners to enter the Roman Senate. The one distinction between Roman army awards and today is the Romans only decorated living soldiers. There were no posthumous honors for their fallen.

The symbols from the Roman standard pictured can be seen in the decorations and awards of Napoleon and United States Army hat badge insignia as early as 1812. So as we begin the history of United States Army Decorations and Awards, it is clear that early designs of the eagle, lightning, victory wreaths of laurel and oak came from the ancient Legions of Rome.

After the Roman Empire, the first major military medal that was not an order of chivalry but a recognition of merit for all was established in 1802 when Napoleon Bonaparte created the Legion of Honor *(Légion d'Honneur)*. Napoleon awarded it on the basis of bravery or merit to soldiers and civilians of any rank or profession.

The degrees of the French Legion of Honor were generally structured like a Roman legion, with legionnaires, officers, commanders etc. It is interesting to note that Napoleon patterned the institution of the Legion of Honor after the Roman legions and the United States patterned its Legion of Merit after the French Légion d'Honneur. The Army's highest award, the Medal of Honor, is embossed with the head of Minerva, the Roman goddess of war. Perhaps it is true in military awards and decorations – as in many other things that all roads lead to Rome.

Revolutionary War (1775-1782)

Red Epaulette for a Sergeant

Silver Epaulette for Officers

At the outbreak of the Revolutionary War, the uniforms and insignia of the Army were basically the same as the Colonial regiments that fought in the French and Indian Wars. Pennsylvania troops wore green uniforms, New Jersey troops and South Carolina troops wore blue uniforms, while Connecticut soldiers wore red uniform coats. In 1775, Congress ordered all continental troops to wear brown uniforms but, by 1779 the standard was blue with different colored facings for New England, the southern and the central states.

Aside from uniform color, during the early years of the Revolution the only real distinctive United States Army insignia were pewter buttons with the initials U.S.A. intertwined. Later, towards the end of the war, some officers began to wear a small pewter or silver eagle in the center of their hat's black cockade.

Insignia of rank consisted of a green epaulet on the right shoulder for a corporal and a red epaulet for a sergeant. Officers often wore gold lace on their hats or silver epaulets, Generals wore gold epaulets on both shoulders, sometimes with a star to indicate Brigadier General or Major General. General Washington also directed that key officers wear colored ribbons across their chests for identification.

Early in the American Revolution, Congress voted to award gold medals to outstanding military leaders. The first such medal was struck to honor George Washington for his service in driving the British from Boston in 1776. Similar medals were bestowed upon General Horatio Gates for his victory at the Battle of Saratoga and Captain John Paul Jones after his famous naval engagement with the Serapis in 1779. Unlike present practice, however, these were large, presentation medals not designed to be worn on the military uniform although General Gates portrait shows the medal hanging on a neck ribbon. Interestingly, once the dies were cut for these medals, many copies were manufactured and distributed by the mint as commemorative medals to instill patriotic pride in the new country's victories. Many of these early commemorative medallions are still being struck and offered for sale by the U. S. Mint.

The Continental Congress issued 11 medals for 7 battles:

The Siege of Boston, March 1776 *(one medal)*

The Battle of Saratoga in October 1777 *(one medal)*

The Battle of Stony Point in July 1779 *(three medals)*

The Battle of Paulus Hook August 1779 *(one medal)*

The Battle of Flamborough Head September 1779 *(one medal)*

The Battle of Cowpens January 1781 *(three medals)*

The Battle of the Eutaw Springs September 1781*(one medal)*

Col David Humpreys

"Few inventions could be more happily calculated to diffuse the knowledge and preserve the memory of illustrious characters and splendid events, than medals." wrote Col David Humpreys in 1787 while corresponding for Gen. Washington at Mount Vernon.

The Battle of Boston

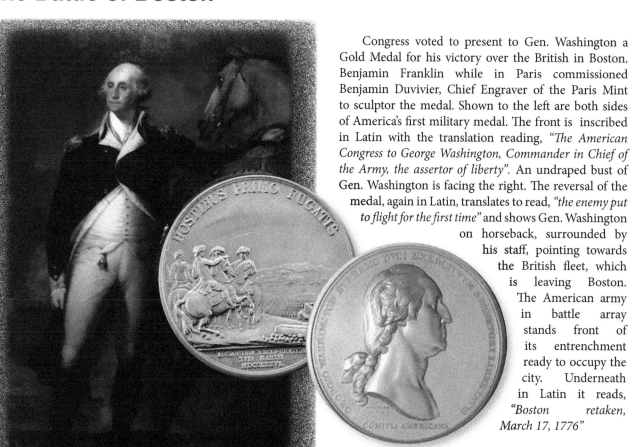

Congress voted to present to Gen. Washington a Gold Medal for his victory over the British in Boston. Benjamin Franklin while in Paris commissioned Benjamin Duvivier, Chief Engraver of the Paris Mint to sculptor the medal. Shown to the left are both sides of America's first military medal. The front is inscribed in Latin with the translation reading, *"The American Congress to George Washington, Commander in Chief of the Army, the assertor of liberty"*. An undraped bust of Gen. Washington is facing the right. The reversal of the medal, again in Latin, translates to read, *"the enemy put to flight for the first time"* and shows Gen. Washington on horseback, surrounded by his staff, pointing towards the British fleet, which is leaving Boston. The American army in battle array stands front of its entrenchment ready to occupy the city. Underneath in Latin it reads, *"Boston retaken, March 17, 1776"*

Gold medal struck to honor George Washington for his service in driving the British from Boston in 1776.

The Battle of Saratoga

The Congress awarded a gold medal to Major Gen. Horatio Gates for his victory at Saratoga. The front of the Gates' medal is inscribed in Latin and reads: "The American Congress to Horatio Gates, a valiant General." On the front a bust of General Gates in uniform faces to the left. The French engraver was Nicolas-Marie Gautteaux, who was the French graveur des médailles du Roi. The reverse of the medal shows Lieut. Gen. Burgoyne surrendering his sword to Gen. Gates. In the background, the vanquished troops of Great Britain are grounding their arms and standards. On the right is a victorious American army, in order of battle with colors flying. The Latin inscription reads: *"The safety of The northern regions. The enemy surrendered at Saratoga on 17 October, 1777."*

The Horatio Gates Medal is now an award of the US Army Adjutant General Regimental Association of the Army Regimental Program.

Major Gen.
Horatio Gates

Reverse of General Gates's Gold Medal. Note the ring attached at the top so the General could wear the medal.

The Battle of Stony Point

The storming of Stony Point should be remembered as the beginning of the end of the American Revolution. The significance of the battle was not lost on Congress.

Three of the gallant officers that led the attack were awarded special "congressional medals". They were the Marquis de Fleury, Colonel John Stewart and General Anthony Wayne, each received one. Considering that Congress only awarded 11 such medals during the entire eight years of war, awarding three for one battle was significant.

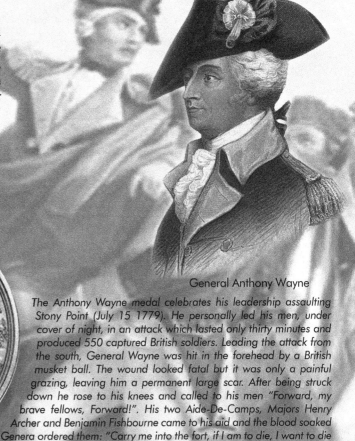

General Anthony Wayne

The Anthony Wayne medal celebrates his leadership assaulting Stony Point (July 15 1779). He personally led his men, under cover of night, in an attack which lasted only thirty minutes and produced 550 captured British soldiers. Leading the attack from the south, General Wayne was hit in the forehead by a British musket ball. The wound looked fatal but it was only a painful grazing, leaving him a permanent large scar. After being struck down he rose to his knees and called to his men "Forward, my brave fellows, Forward!". His two Aide-De-Camps, Majors Henry Archer and Benjamin Fishbourne came to his aid and the blood soaked Genera ordered them: "Carry me into the fort, if I am to die, I want to die at the head of the column."

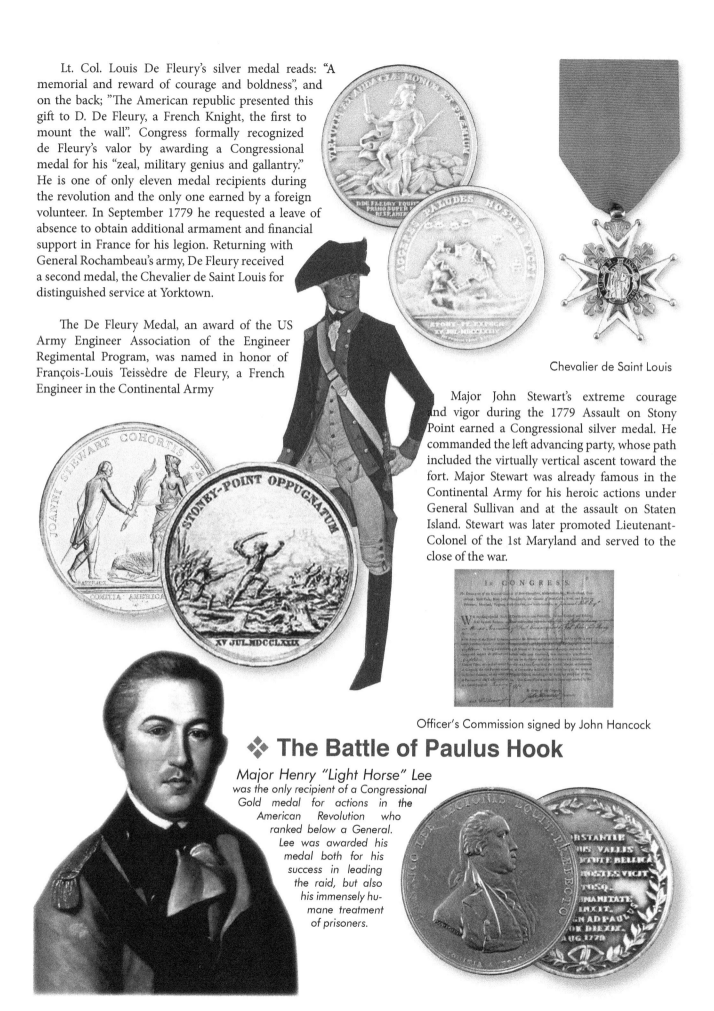

Lt. Col. Louis De Fleury's silver medal reads: "A memorial and reward of courage and boldness", and on the back; "The American republic presented this gift to D. De Fleury, a French Knight, the first to mount the wall". Congress formally recognized de Fleury's valor by awarding a Congressional medal for his "zeal, military genius and gallantry." He is one of only eleven medal recipients during the revolution and the only one earned by a foreign volunteer. In September 1779 he requested a leave of absence to obtain additional armament and financial support in France for his legion. Returning with General Rochambeau's army, De Fleury received a second medal, the Chevalier de Saint Louis for distinguished service at Yorktown.

The De Fleury Medal, an award of the US Army Engineer Association of the Engineer Regimental Program, was named in honor of François-Louis Teissèdre de Fleury, a French Engineer in the Continental Army

Chevalier de Saint Louis

Major John Stewart's extreme courage and vigor during the 1779 Assault on Stony Point earned a Congressional silver medal. He commanded the left advancing party, whose path included the virtually vertical ascent toward the fort. Major Stewart was already famous in the Continental Army for his heroic actions under General Sullivan and at the assault on Staten Island. Stewart was later promoted Lieutenant-Colonel of the 1st Maryland and served to the close of the war.

Officer's Commission signed by John Hancock

❖ The Battle of Paulus Hook

Major Henry "Light Horse" Lee *was the only recipient of a Congressional Gold medal for actions in the American Revolution who ranked below a General. Lee was awarded his medal both for his success in leading the raid, but also his immensely humane treatment of prisoners.*

❖ The Battle of Cowpens

With the war in the north grinding towards a stalemate the British decided on a new Southern strategy. In 1780 the British decided to turn their war efforts to the south with their major focus on South Carolina. This led to more revolutionary war battles in the state of South Carolina than any other state.

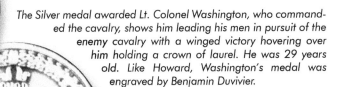

The medal designed by Augustin Dupre is considered the finest artistic creation of the entire series of 11 medals. The front shows an Indian Princess placing a crown on General Daniel Morgan. The back captures the powerful motion of Gen. Morgan on horseback leading his troops in the attack on the British forces. The Latin translates : "Victory, the vindicator of liberty" at the top and on the bottom "The enemy put to flight, taken, or slain at the Cowpens, January 17, 1781.

The Silver medal awarded Lt. Colonel Washington, who commanded the cavalry, shows him leading his men in pursuit of the enemy cavalry with a winged victory hovering over him holding a crown of laurel. He was 29 years old. Like Howard, Washington's medal was engraved by Benjamin Duvivier.

The Silver medal awarded Lt. Colonel John Edgar Howard, who commanded a regiment of infantry shows him in pursuit of an enemy soldier carrying away a flag. A winged victory hovers over him holding a crown of laurel and a palm branch. He also was 29 years old at the time of the battle and suffered seven sword wounds in the battle. The inscription on the back states: "Because in vigorously pursuing the enemy with a handful of soldiers he gave a noble example of innate courage at the battle of the Cowpens, January 17, 1781". Benjamin Duvivier, Chief Engraver of the Paris Mint prepared the dies but they are not of his normal high quality.

Lt. Colonel John Edgar Howard

❖ The Battle of Eutaw Springs

By 1781, General Nathanael Greene had begun a steady push to drive the British out of the south. After a series of battles, General Greene's troops attacked the British at their camp at Eutaw Springs. While both sides claimed victory it was the final battle for the British in the Carolinas. General Greene's leadership was inspirational for six years of continuous fighting during which he did not take a day of leave and his actions inspired the patriot forces in the Carolinas.

His gold medal reads: *"The American Congress to Nathaniel Greene, a distinguished general."* The back of the medal reads: *"The safety of the southern regions"* and *"The enemy vanquished at Eutaw on the 8th of September, 1781."*

The back of the medal shows winged Victory holding a crown of laurel in her right hand and a palm branch in her left: one foot is resting on a trophy of arms and flags of conquered enemies. The medal is by the French medalist Augustin Dupré. In 1787 the medal was finally presented to Greene's widow, the General having died in 1786.

General Nathanael Greene's Gold Medal for Eutaw Springs.

Benjamin Franklin's Famous Victory Medal - Libertas Americana

Benjamin Franklin

While stationed in France during the American Revolutionary War, Benjamin Franklin was sent a detailed after action report of the Yorktown victory and asked to establish a monument in its honor. Instead he proposed a medal, depicting the United States as the infant Hercules in cradle, strangling the two serpents sent by Hera *(the snakes representing the Battle of Saratoga and the Siege of Yorktown)*. Above him France personified as Athena *(Minerva)* would act as his nurse and mentor. The design on the medal's reverse was developed by the French painter Esprit-Antoine Gibelin and engraver Augustin Dupré, who made sure that France would be seen as the protector of the infant by fighting the British Lion who is pouncing at the child. Minerva's shield is decked with the lilies of France. The final Latin inscription reads, *"The courageous child was aided by the gods"* and dated October 1777/1781.

The front of the medal shows the Head of Liberty with flowing hair as if she is running to announce America's victories to the entire world. A spear of liberty surmounted by the Phrygian cap rest on her right shoulder with the date 4 July 1776. Records indicated 300 medals were struck in gold, silver and bronze, many of which were personally presented by Franklin to celebrate the new Republic. The first 2 gold medals were presented by Franklin to the King and Queen of France.

France personified as Athena (Minerva) acting as Americas nurse and mentor.

This was indeed the most famous of the Revolutionary War medals and when time came to design the Medal of Honor in 1861 it is clear where the designers went for inspiration. Minerva holding a shield banishes Discord *(the south)* who holds two snakes. Even today's Army Medal of Honor features the head of Minerva, Goddess of War.

By 7 August 1782, hostilities had ended and peace talks were under way in Paris. That day, George Washington's thoughts were with his men camped nearby at New Windsor. They had suffered appalling privations for over six years. His officers were on the verge of mutiny because of lack of pay, rations and supplies withheld by a corrupt and negligent Congress. Worse, Congress had taken away the authority of his general officers to recognize their soldiers' courage and leadership by awarding commissions in the field. Congress simply could not afford to pay their existing officers let alone any new ones. As a result, faithful service and outstanding acts of bravery went unrecognized and unrewarded. George Washington was determined to end that. So from his headquarters perched 80 feet above the Hudson, he issued a general order establishing the *"Badge of Distinction"* and *"Badge of Merit."*:

Patriots John Paulding, Isaac Van Wart and David Williams were the recipients of the Andre medal

The *"Andre"* medal broke the custom of restricting the award of medals to successful senior officers and is doubly unique in that it was designed for wear around the neck. The medal was presented by Congress in 1780 to the three enlisted men who captured British Major John Andre with the plans of the West Point fortifications in his boot. Patriots John Paulding, Isaac Van Wart and David Williams were the recipients of the Andre medal and as time passed were additionally authorized a lifetime pension.

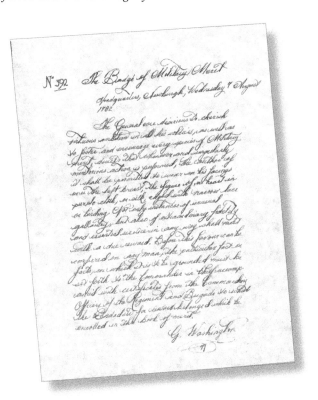

Major Andre, the captured British officer, was hung as a spy.

Actually General George Washington devised two new badges of distinction for enlisted men and noncommissioned officers. To signify loyal military service, he ordered a chevron to be worn on the left sleeve of the uniform coat for the rank and file who had completed three years of duty *"with bravery, fidelity, and good conduct"*; two chevrons signified six years of service. The second badge, for *"any singularly meritorious Action,"* was the *"Figure of a Heart in Purple Cloth or Silk edged with narrow Lace or Binding."* This device, the Badge of Military Merit, was affixed to the uniform coat above the left breast and permitted its wearer to pass guards and sentinels without challenge and to have his name and regiment inscribed in a Book of Merit. The Badge specifically honored the lower ranks, where decorations were unknown in contemporary European Armies. As Washington intended, the road to glory in a patriot army is thus open to all.

1782 Badge of Military Merit

The Badge of Military Merit was the first U.S. decoration which had general application to all enlisted men and one which General George Washington hoped would start a permanent awards system. At the same time, he expressed his fundamental awards philosophy when he issued an order from his headquarters at Newburgh, New York, which read:

"The General, ever desirous to cherish a virtuous ambition in his soldiers, as well as to foster and encourage every species of military merit, directs that, whenever any singularly meritorious action is performed, the author of it shall be permitted to wear on his facings, over his left breast, the figure of a heart in purple cloth or silk, edged with narrow lace or binding. Not only instances of unusual gallantry, but also of extraordinary fidelity, and essential service in any way, shall meet with a due reward...the road to glory in a patriot army and a free country is thus opened to all. This order is also to have retrospect to the earliest days of the war, and to be considered a permanent one."

Although special and commemorative medals had been awarded previously, until this point no decoration had been established which honored the private soldier with a reward for special merit. The wording of the order is worth careful study. The object was *"to cherish a virtuous ambition"* and *"to foster and encourage every species of military merit."* Note also, that Washington appreciated that every kind of service was important by proposing to reward, *"not only instances of unusual gallantry, but also of extraordinary fidelity and essential service in any way."* And finally, the wonderfully democratic sentence, *"the road to glory in a patriotic army and free country is thus opened to all."*

Coming as it did, almost a year after Cornwallis' surrender at Yorktown, the message was never given widespread distribution and, as a result, there were only three known recipients of this badge, Sergeants Elijah Churchill, William Brown and Daniel Bissell. Unfortunately, after the Revolution, the award fell into disuse and disappeared for 150 years.

On the 200th anniversary of Washington's birth, February 22, 1932, the War Department announced that:

"By order of the President of the United States, the Purple Heart, established by Gen. George Washington at Newburgh, New York... is hereby revived out of respect to his memory and military achievements."

Washington's *"figure of a heart in purple"* was retained as the medal's central theme and embellished with Washington's likeness and his coat of arms. The words *"For Military Merit"* appear on the reverse as a respectful reference to its worthy predecessor.

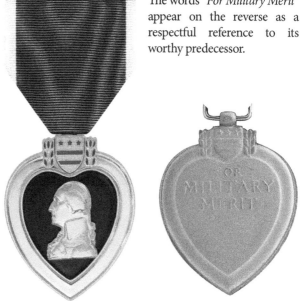

1932 Purple Heart

❖ War of 1812 (1812-1815)

The War of 1812 saw the wide spread introduction of the American bald eagle as the Army's national symbol on flags, hats, breastplates and belt buckles. Infantry shakos used the eagle on the front while officers wore a small silver eagle in the black cockade of their hat.

Additionally, the markings "U.S." began to appear on pieces of equipment for identification. Insignia of rank remained the silver and gold epaulets for officers and colored epaulets for noncommissioned officers. Military Awards and Decorations were extremely few compared to today. Generally only high ranking officer were honored for heroic efforts and victory. Congress had 3 ceremonial accolades reserved for senior officers of victorious battles. All of these awards had to be approved by congress. The most prestigious award was a "Congressional Gold Medal" minted and engraved for a specific action or event. Next, was the "Ceremonial Sword," custom made to recognize a spectacular achievement. However, the most common reward for a highly distinguished officer was a "Letter of Thanks" from the congress.

The Congress retained the custom of commissioning large presentation medals to victorious commanding officers managing to more than double the Gold Medals from 11 during the Revolution to 14 for Naval Officers and 13 for Army Generals in the much shorter war of 1812.

As an example, shown below, is a medal presented to Major General Alexander Macomb for his victory at the Battle of Plattsburgh in 1814.

Line Officer
1813-1816

Major General Alexander Macomb. In recognition of the "gallantry and good conduct" of Major General Alexander Macomb, and the officers and men under his command, in defeating a veteran British Army at Plattsburg on September 11, 1814.

Major General
Alexander Macomb
Medal

Nation Building 1816-1843 – In Florida the Army fought the Spanish often taking areas like Pensacola but returning them in later negotiations until Florida became a U.S. territory in 1821. By 1823 the Army was ordered across the Mississippi to begin action against the western Indians. The Army also fought a series of wars with the Seminole Indians, the Blackhawks and the Creeks through 1842.

Early shako badges featured the national Eagle or Hunting Horn as the symbol of the Infantry.

Some Milita shako badges featured the National Eagle or the Eagle and hunting horn as the symbol of the Infantry.

Infantry Shako Eagle pattern 1821 used 1820 -1851.

Sword belt buckles featured the National Eagle and are still worn by Honor Guards today.

1819 Regulation U.S. shoulder Eagle breast plate worn by soldiers from the early up through the Civil War.

Infantry Sgt. 1827

❖ The Mexican War (1844-1848) and the Beginning of Change

By the time of the Mexican War, many of the U.S. Army insignia that we know today were appearing on the uniform although. The eagle remained the centerpiece on hats and shakos. The large gold and silver epaulets disappeared except on dress uniforms and were replaced for everyday wear with simple shoulder straps for officers and chevrons for noncommissioned offices.

Large Congressional Gold Medal awarded to Major General Winfield Scott for his service as the Army Commander in Chief during the Mexican War of 1847.

Gold and Silver South Carolina Palmetto Regiment Medals

Silver New York Regiment Medal (unnamed)

Two stripes were used for Corporal and three stripes for Sergeant. Some units wore chevrons pointed down while some units wore the point up. The Infantry insignia was the hunting horn; artillery wore crossed cannons while the engineer castle appeared on the hat of enlisted engineers. Color often designated branch with the cavalry wearing yellow and artillery red trim on the uniform. The U.S. insignia began to appear in more places; belt buckles, cartridge boxes, breastplates and canteen covers. In general, the eagle and letters "U.S." became the logo of the United States Army.

During the time of the Mexican War and thereafter the Federal Government still showed a great reluctance to strike medals for soldiers and sailors but continued the award of Congressional Gold Medals. However, various states such as South Carolina and New York showed no such resistance. For example, the state of South Carolina struck 1000 silver medals for members of the Volunteer Palmetto Regiment who served in the Mexican War. Each large silver medal was engraved with the name of the soldier and individually presented to the soldier or next of kin. Officers received Gold Medals. Some cities such as Charleston, South Carolina also commissioned medals specifically for their local company. It is interesting to note that the South Carolina medals were designed for table top display but veterans immediately took to drilling a small hole in the top of the medal and wearing them as watch fobs or hanging them from their coat lapel on patriotic occasions.

❖ Certificate of Merit (1905)

No 169

The Certificate of Merit was established by the Army in 1847 to reward soldiers who distinguished themselves in battle, but this was not translated into medal form until 1905.

Colonel Charles C. Warren wearing the Aztec Club and other Society medals on his uniform for an official portrait.

Aztec Club Medal

"Gen Winfield Scott Enters Plaza de la consitution after the fall of Mexico City."

❖ CIVIL WAR (1861-1865)

By the Civil War, Army officer shoulder strap ranks had almost evolved into today's symbols for lieutenant, captain, major, lieutenant colonel, colonel and general rank. However, as rebel marksmen concentrated on federal officers easily identifiable by their shoulder straps, some officers removed their insignia and begin to wear pin-on rank during combat.

The eagle insignia continued to be worn on some broad brim hats and officer belt buckles. The U.S. insignia became standard on enlisted belt buckles and breastplates. Each branch of the service began to wear its own symbols on hats. A hunting horn on hats symbolize the infantry, crossed sabers the cavalry and crossed cannons the artillery. Enlisted rank continued to be shown by chevrons with each branch using different colors; light blue stripes for infantry, red stripes for artillery, yellow stripes for the cavalry.

The Civil War also saw the first United States military decorations; a Medal of Honor for heroic service to be presented only to enlisted men but as the war continued, the award of the Medal of Honor was extended to include Army officers.

1862 Army Medal
of Honor

Grand Army of the
Republic Reunion Medal

Following the Civil War, there was an absolute explosion of veteran's commemorative medals and reunion medals. Grand Army of the Republic Reunion medals began to so closely resemble the Medals of Honor that Congress was eventually forced to change the Medal of Honor design and patent it.

Union Officers began creating unit medals as early as 1862 when the officers of General Kearny's division ordered a gold medal after the General's death to commemorate serving under his command. The next Division commander ordered a bronze cross for award to enlisted men of the division. Other private medals were the Gilmore Medal struck by General Gilmore for his troops around Charleston, SC and the Butler Medal for colored troops in the Battle of Newmarket Heights in

Butler medal for colored troops
in the Battle of Newmarket
Heights in 1864.

1864. Most of these were paid for by the commanders and had limited use.

Civil War Campaign Medal (Army)

Service: Army **Instituted:** 1905
Dates: 1861-1866
Criteria: Active Federal service between April 1861 and April 1865 or service in Texas between April 1861 and August 1866.
Devices: ⭐

(88)

Civil War Service Medal (Navy)

Service: Navy, Marine Corps.
Instituted: 1908   **Dates:** 1861-1865
Criteria: Active service in the Union Navy or Marine Corps afloat or ashore between April 1861 and April 1865.

The Civil War Campaign Medal is chronologically the first campaign service medal and was authorized in 1905 on the fortieth anniversary of the end of the Civil War. The ribbon from 1905 to 1913 had 2 sets of red, white and blue stripes of equal width separated by a narrow white stripe. The colors were selected to represent the national colors of both sides. The second blue and gray ribbon reflects the uniform colors of both Federal and Confederate soldiers. The Army Civil War Campaign Medal required that a soldier had to serve between 1861 and 1866 when President Johnson signed a Proclamation officially ending the war. The Navy and Marine Civil War Medal was established June 27, 1908.

The front of the Army Civil War Campaign Medal displayed a bust of Abraham Lincoln while the Navy and Marine Corps versions depicted the USS Monitor and CSS Virginia's battle in Hampton Roads. The reverse of the medal displays "The Civil War 1861-1865" encircled by a wreath.

The medal was first established as a badge due to costs. The award was intended from the outset to be for both Union and Confederate soldiers. When it was pointed out the qualifications included the words "active Federal Service", a Congressional Act in 1945 had those words removed. In 1956, some 90 years after the Civil War, Congress provided for the government to provide the medal to all Civil War qualified veterans (whether they were Union or Confederate).

In the center the bronze medal is the head of Lincoln encircled by inscription, WITH MALICE TOWARD NONE WITH CHARITY FOR ALL.

The back of the medal is inscribed THE CIVIL WAR over a bar, under which appear the dates 1861-1865; surrounded by a wreath composed of a branch of oak on the left and a branch of laurel on the right, joined at the base by a bow. The oak representing the strength of the United States and the laurel representing its victory.

The Navy and Marine Corps versions have different backs as shown above. The medal was designed by Francis D. Millet, a noted sculptor who perished on the RMS Titanic in 1912. Confederate soldiers, sailors, and marines who fought in the Civil War, were made U.S. Veterans by an act of Congress in 1957. U.S. Public Law 85-425 May 23, 1958 (H.R. 358) (Attached & Link Below)

This made the Confederate Army, Navy, and Marine Veterans equal to U.S. Veterans. Additionally, under U.S. Public Law 810 (Link Below), approved by the 17th Congress on 26 Feb 1929, The War Department was directed to erect headstones and recognize Confederate grave sites as U.S. War grave sites. **US. Public Law 85-425 May 23, 1958 (H.R. 358)**

"(e) For the purpose of this section, and section 433, the term 'veteran' includes a person who served in the military or naval forces of the Confederate States of America during the Civil War, and the term 'active, military or naval service' includes active service in such forces. The Act of Congress can be founded at:

http://uscode.house.gov/statutes/pl/85/425.pdf
http://uscode.house.gov/statutes/pl/85/810.pdf

10th Corps   2d Corps

8th Corps   5th Corps

6th Corps   7th Corps

Civil War Campaign Medal
front and Reverse

The Civil War also saw the establishment of unit insignia for the first time. Different devices such as diamonds, shamrocks and other distinctive symbols were selected for various divisions and corps within the Grand Army of the Republic. One corps symbol, a red diamond, is still used as the division shoulder sleeve insignia of the Fifth Infantry Division *(mechanized)*.

Identification badges also made their appearance in The Civil War when combat soldiers started writing their names on paper and pinning the paper to their uniforms so their bodies could be identified. Enterprising sutlers began to make silver or metal badges about the size of a quarter with soldiers' names and units on them. These were pinned on the soldiers tunics and were the forerunner of our current dog tags and identification badges.

In 1905, President Roosevelt authorized campaign medals back to the Civil War. The Civil War Campaign Medal *(Army)* was issued for any Federal Army service between April 15,1861 and April 9,1865 *(the period was extended for service in Texas through August 20,1866)*. The front of the medal has a bust of Abraham Lincoln with the words *"With malice towards none; with charity for all"*. The reverse of the medal is inscribed *"Civil War, 1861-1865"*. The first medals had red, white and blue ribbons which were changed in 1913 to match the blue and grey Navy and Marine Civil War Medal ribbon.

There were no Confederate States medals. Prior to the 1905 United States Civil War medal, Confederate soldiers only received recognition from the hands of the United Daughters of the Confederacy *(UDC)* who designed and struck a handsome Southern Cross of Honor. The design is a Maltese Cross with the battle flag of the Confederate forces on the face, surrounded by a reef of laurel with the inscription, "United Daughters of the Confederacy to the U.C.V." The reverse of the cross has the Latin motto of the Confederate States' "Deo Vindice" *(God our Vindicator)* with the dates 1861-1865. On the four arms of the cross are the words "Southern Cross of Honor". Beginning in 1900 approximately 80,000 crosses were awarded, with the last Cross of Honor presented posthumously in 1959 to Confederate Rear Admiral and Brigadier General Raphael Semmes.

Southern Cross of Honor

A Commemorative Stonewall Brigade Medal was commissioned in Paris, France in 1863 and sent back to the south through the Federal blockade. However, the medals never left the warehouse and were never presented to the Brigade soldiers. Today they are used by a Georgia Chapter of the United Daughters of the Confederacy as special gifts.

The Stonewall
Jackson Medal

❖ The Indian Campaign Medal (1865-1891)

Service	Army
Instituted	1905
Dates	1865-1891
Criteria	Service during the above years in campaigns in the Western United States against hostile indian tribes.
Devices	Silver Star **(88)**

Between 1865 and 1891 the United States Army conducted a series of running battles against the Indians in the Western portion of the United States. The Indian Campaign Medal was established by War Department General Orders on 21 January, 1907 and was authorized for military service in any campaign against any tribe during certain periods and locations. In 1918 the Indian Campaign Medal was retroactively authorized a small five pointed silver star, 3/16 of an inch in diameter for gallantry in action during the Indian Wars. These rarely awarded stars were referred to as Citation Stars and were attached to the center of the medal's ribbon. The Indian Campaign Medal was a one-time decoration and there were no devices or service stars authorized for those who had participated in multiple actions. The only attachment authorized to the medal was the silver citation star, awarded for meritorious or heroic conduct. The silver citation star was the predecessor of the Silver Star and was awarded to eleven soldiers between 1865 and 1891.

Service in any of the following campaigns authorized award of the Indian Campaign Medal:

Southern Oregon, Idaho, northern California, and Nevada between 1865 and 1868.

Against the Comanches and confederate tribes in Kansas, Colorado, Texas, New Mexico, and Indian Territory between 1867 and 1875.

Modoc War between 1872 and 1873.

Against the Apaches in Arizona in 1873.

Against the Northern Cheyennes and Sioux between 1876 and 1877.

Nez Perce War in 1877.

Bannock War in 1878.

Against the Northern Cheyennes between 1878 and 1879.

Against the Sheep-Eaters, Piutes, and Bannocks between June and October, 1879.

Against the Utes in Colorado and Utah between September 1879 and November 1880.

Against the Apaches in Arizona and New Mexico between 1885 and 1886.

Against the Sioux in South Dakota between November 1890 and January 1891.

Against hostile Indians in any other action in which United States troops were killed or wounded between 1865 and 1891

❖ Military Society Medals (1865-1913)

Up until the Spanish American War no Army or Navy in the world was so little decorated as the United States. The simplicity of uniforms were set off by no medals or ribbons. After the Civil War, Congress under pressure from veteran's organizations permitted officers and enlisted men to wear their Corps and Division badge. For nearly twenty years, the Medal of Honor remained the sole American military award of any kind. Although the Navy had authorized the first Good Conduct Badge in 1869, clearly the officers and enlisted personnel of the Army and Navy wanted to have medals like their counterparts around the world.

Their solution was to have Congress approve the wearing of the military society medals such as The Aztec club which consisted of officers who served in Mexico in 1847, the Grand Army of the Republic, the Loyal Legion, Army and Navy Union of the United States of America, and the Military Order of the Dragon, commemorating the China relief expedition were just a few. The point was the professional officer corps wanted an awards system to recognize service and if the government was not going to create one they would. The post civil war Congress contained a large number of veterans so approval to wear these society medals on uniforms was not difficult. In regard to Military Society medals a subject that often comes up is a question of wearing certain military society medals on military uniforms. Title X of United States code, section 1123 (a) states:

"A member of the Army, Navy, Air Force or Marine Corps who is a member of a military society originally composed of men who served in the Armed Forces of the United States during the Revolutionary War, the War of 1812, the Mexican War, the Civil War, the Spanish-American War, the Philippine Insurrection, or the Chinese Relief Expedition may wear, on certain occasions of ceremony, the distinctive badges adopted by that society."

General Sherdian in his offical portrait wearing a chest full of Military Society medals.

Basically this can be interpreted that a member of the Armed Forces who is a member of one of the societies listed below can wear these medals on their uniform. The Society of the Cincinnati, the General Society of the War of 1812, the Aztec Club, the Military Order of the Loyola Legion of the United States, the Naval order of the United States and the medals of the Veterans of Foreign Wars since the original founders of the VFW were veterans of the Spanish American war, the Philippine Insurrection and the Chinese Relief Expedition of 1900.

While there may be an occasion when one would wear Society medals or ribbons on their active duty uniform it is seldom to my knowledge actually done. However, the occasion does occur, that veterans wearing miniature medals on formal occasions could wear their society medals after *(at the end)* of their military decorations and service medals.

Society of the Cincinnati

Aztec Club of 1847

General Society of the War of 1812

Grand Army of the Republic Society medal

Jeweled Grand Army of the Republic Society Medal

Military Order of the Loyal Legion

Military Order of the Dragon 1900

❖ War with Spain (1898-1899)

The Spanish-American War 1898

The Spanish-American War was a period of transition for U.S. Army insignia and military medals. The traditional U.S. insignia and branch of service insignia moved to the collar of the uniform. Metal pin-on officer rank insignia moved to the epaulette. The National eagle became the official dress hat emblem for officers. On the enlisted side, branch insignia also moved to the collar and the rank chevrons begin to take on the look we know today.

For nearly forty years, the Medal of Honor had remained the sole American military award of any kind. The *"Bully Little War" (four months of military action)* changed the situation and produced a host of medals to commemorate the events surrounding the Spanish-American War.

The Spanish Campaign Medal *(Army)* was authorized for service in Cuba between May 11 and July 17 and Puerto Rico between July 24 and August 16, 1898. Additionally the Spanish War Service Medal was created in 1918 to honor Spanish American War volunteers who were not eligible for the Spanish Campaign Medal. The first occupation medals were struck to honor soldiers who occupied Cuba and Puerto Rico in 1898 after the war

When Theodore Roosevelt, an ardent supporter of the military, became President, he legislated the creation of medals to honor all those who had served in America's previous conflicts. By 1908, the U.S. had authorized campaign medals, some retroactive, for the Civil War, Indian Wars, War with Spain, Philippine Insurrection and China Relief Expedition of 1900-01. While the services used the same ribbons, different medals were struck. During this time frame the custom of wearing service ribbons on the tunic was adopted with the Army and Navy using different precedences. Thus, the services managed to establish the principle of independence in the creation and wearing of awards that is virtually unchanged today.

Spanish Campaign Medal (1st Ribbon)

Service	Army Instituted 1905
Date	1898
Criteria	Services ashore or en route to any of the following areas: Cuba: May-July 1898; Puerto Rico: July-Aug 1898; Philippine Islands: June-Aug 1898.
Devices	Silver Star

The original ribbon colors were taken from the Spanish Man-of-War flag but changed because the colors might be offensive to Spain, then a friendly foreign power. The second ribbon is gold with a blue stripe inside each edge representing Spain (Gold) and the United States (blue).

The center of the medal is a castle with two small round towers at the corners. The castle with two small round towers at the corners, is said to be a modification of the castle that appears on the Royal Army of Spain, the round towers possibly referring to the two Morro Castles, at Havana and Santiago de Cuba. At the top around the outside edge of the medal is the inscription "WAR WITH SPAIN". At the bottom is the date "1898", to the left of the date is a branch of tobacco plant, and to the right, a stalk of sugar cane.

On the back a spread eagle on a trophy consisting of a cannon, six rifles and four standards, an Indian shield, quiver of arrows and three spears, a Cuban machete and a Sulu kris. Below the trophy are the words "FOR SERVICE". The whole is surrounded by a circle composed of the words "UNITED STATES ARMY" in the upper half and thirteen stars in the lower half.

Spanish War Service Medal

Service	Army Instituted 1918
Date	1898
Criteria	Awarded to all regular or volunteer army personnel who served during the above period but did not qualify for the Spanish Campaign Medal.

The Spanish War Service Medal was awarded for military service of ninety days or more between April 20, 1898, and April 11, 1899. It was originally intended for National Guard troops mobilized during the Spanish-American War but were not eligible for the Spanish Campaign Medal. In the center of the medallion is a sheathed Roman sword hanging on a taablet inscribed FOR SERVICE IN THE SPANISH WAR. The tablet is surrounded by a laurel wreath representing achievement . The Roman sword symbolizes war or military strength; its being sheathed indicates National Guard service within the United States, rather than service in combat.

On the back is the Coat of Arms of the United States surrounded by a wreath displaying crossed rifles; crossed sabers, and crossed cannon. The Arms of the United States denote service to the United States as opposed to state service.

❖ War with Spain Medals

Army of Cuban Occupation Medal

Service	Army
Instituted	1915
Dates	1898-1902
Criteria	Service by Army personnel who participated in the occupation of Cuba during the above dates at the end of the War with Spain.

In the center is the Cuban coat of arms with the dates 1898 and 1902; surrounded by the words ARMY OF OCCUPATION MILITARY GOVERNMENT OF CUBA in raised letters. The coat of arms rests on a fasces and flanked by sprays of oak and laurel. The fasces represents justice; the sprays of oak allude to strength and the laurel represents achievement.

On the back is a trophy of an eagle perched on a cannon

supported by five standards. With the standards are rifles, an Indian shield, a spear and quiver of arrows, a Cuban machete, and a sulu kriss. The standards represent the five great wars of the United States as of 1905: the Revolution; the War of 1812; the Mexican War; the Spanish-American War; and the Philippine Insurrection. The weapons suggest the armed resistance offered by the opponents in those wars. The eagle is the American bald eagle and represents the United States, and the thirteen stars allude the original colonies and symbolize unity. About 14,000 medals were issued.

Army of Occupation of Puerto Rico Medal

Service	Army
Instituted	1919
Date	1898
Criteria	Service during the occupation of Puerto Rico between 14 August and 10 December, 1898.

The Puerto Rican Occupation Medal was awarded to all who served in the Army of Occupation in Porto Rico, between the cessation of hostilities, on August 13, and the signing of the Treaty of Peace with Spain, December 10, 1898, by the terms of which treaty Porto Rico became a possession of the United States. The design is the same as that of the Spanish Campaign

Medal, with an appropriate change of inscription, and the colors of the ribbon are the reverse of those of the Cuban Occupation ribbon. The Puerto Rican Occupation Medal was based on the design of the Spanish Campaign Medal by Francis D. Millet *(1846-1912)*.

In the interest of saving time and money, the design of the Spanish Campaign Medal was used but with a different wording. The wording and dates distinguish the two medals from one another and indicate what they commemorate. Only 3,000 medals were issued

❖ Philippines, China and Central America (1900-1917)

By the time the final peace treaty with Spain was ratified in March 1899, the Philippine Insurrection had already broken out and the majority of regular army and volunteer troops were in the Philippines fighting against insurrectionists, Philippine nationalists and Muslim fundamentalists, a conflict which was to rage from 1899 to 1913. Between 1900 and the 1930s, American soldiers, sailors and marines were dispatched to such areas as China in 1900, Cuba in 1906, Mexico in 1911, Nicaragua in 1912, Haiti in 1915, and the Dominican Republic in 1916, to quell rebellions and deal with civil unrest. As was their earlier custom, the Army and the Navy designed and authorized their own medals to commemorate these events. The Marine Corps, although under the overall command of the Navy, preserved their uniqueness by using the Navy medals with the special Marine Corps design on the reverse.

In 1905, the Army's Philippine Campaign Medal was issued followed in 1908 by a Navy version. The silver Citation Star was retroactively authorized in 1918 for wear on the medal for Army personnel who had performed feats of heroism or bravery.

Soon after the Spanish-American War and the Philippine Campaign, the Army grew from 64,000 to well over 120,000 regular and volunteer troops spread halfway around the world. The Navy was also covering the West Indies, Caribbean and projecting its power as far as China. In 1900, when fanatical Chinese called "Boxers", a rough English translation of the *"Righteous Fists of Fire Society,"* attacked American nationals and other foreigners in the International Legations in Peking, China, the United States sent more than 5,000 soldiers and a battalion of Marines to join a multinational relief force.

The final action just prior to World War I was the Mexican Campaign which took place between the years 1911 and 1917. Once again, civil disobedience, this time in the form of large-scale military activities by well-armed revolutionaries, caused the United States to mount a Punitive Expedition into Mexico to bring peace to the region. In the aftermath of the conflict, the Army Mexican Service Medal was awarded to approximately 15,000 soldiers. For those Army members who had been cited for gallantry in combat, the Citation Star was retroactively authorized in 1918 as a device to the Mexican Service Medal but no devices were authorized for the Navy's medal. Early versions of the Campaign medals of this period were issued with serial numbers stamped on the bottom rim of the medal or engraved on the reverse side with the date of service. This practice was discontinued on later replacement medals.

Philippine Campaign Medal

Service	Army
Instituted	1905
Criteria	Awarded to Army personnel who served in campaigns ashore during the above dates to quell the Philippine Insurrection.
Devices	Silver star

In the center of the medallion is a palm tree bearing coconuts which was often used on Roman coins and medals to record their conquests on the southern Mediterranean shores, the palm tree is the central theme on the medal (alluding to American conquest in the Pacific) and represents the tropical character of the Philippines. To the left of the palm tree there is a Roman lamp, and to its right, a scale. These symbols are encircled by the words PHILIPPINE INSURRECTION in raised letters, and the date 1898 (which appears between two bullets at the base of the medal). The lamp denotes enlightenment.

The scales allude to justice, thus the bringing of enlightenment and justice to the Philippines. The date is the year the Philippine Insurrection began

On the back is a trophy with an eagle perched on a cannon supported by five standards. With the standards are rifles, an Indian shield, a spear and quiver of arrows, a Cuban machete, and a sulu kriss. Below the trophy are the words FOR SERVICE in raised letters. The whole is enclosed by the words, UNITED STATES ARMY in the upper half, and thirteen stars in the lower half. The weapons suggest the armed resistance offered by the opponents. The eagle is the American bald eagle and represents the United States, and the thirteen stars allude the original colonies and symbolize unity.

Philippine Congressional Medal

Service	Army
Instituted	1906
Dates	1899-1902
Criteria	Awarded to Army personnel who volunteered to serve beyond their discharge date and were ashore in the Philippine Islands during above dates.

Awarded to soldiers who enlisted to serve during the Spanish-American War and remained on active duty beyond their enlistment to help suppress the Philippine insurrection *(February 4, 1899 - July 4, 1902)* and received an honorable discharge.

On the front is a military formation of a color bearer holding the United States flag accompanied by two soldiers with rifles on their shoulders, all three facing the viewer's left. The flag extends between the words PHILIPPINE INSURRECTION. The date ·1898· is shown between two bullets.

On the back, the inscription reads FOR / PATRIOTISM / FORTITUDE / AND / LOYALTY centered within a wreath of pine on the left and palm on the right tied at the base with a bow. This medal was given to both Regular Army and Volunteers and therefore has a distinctive reverse *(to distinguish it from medals given only to members of the Regular Army)*. The highly distinctive wreath alludes to the Philippines *(palm)* and the to goals of autonomy and self-determination *(pine)*. About 7,000 medals were issued.

China Campaign Medal

Service	Army
Instituted	1905
Dates	1900-1901
Criteria	Service ashore with the Peking Relief Expedition during the Boxer Rebellion between 20 June 1900 and 27 May 1901.
Devices	Silver Star

The medal was awarded to all officers and men who took part in the international expedition which marched to Peking to relieve the legations during the Boxer trouble of 1900 was awarded to all officers and men who took part.

In the center of the medallion is a Chinese five-toed dragon in the full face position, encircled by the words CHINA RELIEF EXPEDITION 1900 - 1901, the words separated from the dates by bullets. This favorite Chinese design was chosen to symbolize the location and identity of the opponent in this campaign.

The back is the same as the other Regular Army campaign medals; a trophy composed of an eagle perched on a cannon supported by five standards. About 2,400 medals were issued.

Army of Cuban Pacification Medal

Service	Army
Instituted	1909
Dates	1906-1909
Criteria	Awarded to all Army personnel who served in Cuba between October 1906 and April 1909 to assist the new government during the insurrection.

In the center of the medallion is the coat of arms of Cuba, supported on either side by a soldier in khaki uniform; at the top of the medal, the words CUBAN PACIFICATION and at the bottom, the dates 1906-1909. The Cuban coat of arms represents an occupied country and the two soldiers supporting it are American troops dressed in the uniform of the early 1900s. Their stance at parade rest suggests a pacification rather than open and direct combat. The dates are the official dates of the period of the pacification.

The back is the same as other period campaign medals showing a trophy composed of an eagle perched on a cannon supported by five standards. With the standards are rifles, an Indian shield, a spear and quiver of arrows, a Cuban machete, and a sulu kriss. Below the trophy the words FOR SERVICE appear in raised letters. It is enclosed by the words, UNITED STATES ARMY in the upper half, and thirteen stars in the lower half. Approximately 7,000 medals were issued from the orginial strikes.

Mexican Service Medal

Service	Army
Instituted	1917
Dates	1914-1919
Criteria	Awarded to Army personnel who participated in engagements or expeditions in Mexico during 10 specfic periods from April 1914 to June, 1919.

In the center of the medallion is a Yucca plant is shown in full bloom, with mountains in the background. Above the plant are the words MEXICAN SERVICE and beneath it, the dates 1911-1914. The Yucca plant symbolizes the geographic area of the campaign, and

its thorny, spear-like leaves also allude to the nature of the raids carried out by Mexican bandits. The mountains in the background represent the type of terrain on which engagements were fought and the elusive, mysterious nature of the enemy. The wording and dates describe the campaign and time during which it was conducted. Mexican Service Medal No. 1 was issued to General John J. Pershing. The Silver Citation Star could be worn on the ribbon of the Mexican Service Medal. A total of 43 Silver Citation Stars were retroactively awarded to 38 recipients for gallantry in action during the campaign on the Mexican border. Approximately 15,000 medals were issued. The back is the same as other period campaign medals showing a trophy composed of an eagle perched on a cannon supported by five standards.

Mexican Border Service Medal

Service	Army
Instituted	1918
Dates	1916-1917
Criteria	Awarded to Army and National Guard troops who served on the Mexican border between January 1916 and April 1917.

The Mexican Border Service Medal was first authorized for members of the National Guard who served on the Mexican border during 1916 and 1917.

It was later extended to members of the Regular Army and

Federalized Guardsmen for service on the Mexican border between May 9, 1916 and March 24, 1917 or with the Mexican Border Patrol between January 1, 1916 and April 6, 1917. It was authorized for persons not eligible for the Mexican Service Medal.

The design is the same as the Spanish War Service Medal with the wording changed to read *"For Service on the Mexican Border"*. Approximately 41,000 medals were issued.

Texas Cavalry Congressional Medal

Service	Army
Instituted	1924
Dates	1917-1918
Criteria	Awarded to two Texas Cavalry Brigades used to relieve Regular Army units then serving on the Texas-Mexican Border.

The Texas Cavalry Service Medal was established by Act of Congress on April 16, 1924, as a Federal commemorative medal and not a medal produced by the State of Texas.

The Medal com-memorates service on the Mexican border during the First World War. It was

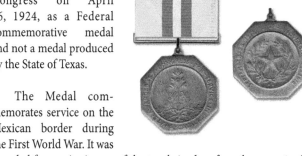

awarded for service in one of the two brigades of cavalry organized by Texas under authority of the War Department between December 8, 1917, and November 11, 1918 *(members of these units were not eligible for the World War I Victory Medal)*. In the center is a bronze octagon with a bluebonnet *(plant)* surrounded by a raised circle. Surrounding the circle, the words AWARDED BY CONGRESS FOR SERVICE IN TEXAS CAVALRY The bluebonnet is the State flower of Texas and represents service within that State.

On the back there is a five-pointed star in the center of a wreath of live oak and olive with the inscription SEPTEMBER 25, 1918 - DECEMBER 8, 1918. The central theme (the star and wreath) is the Seal of the State of Texas *(the "Lone Star" State)*. The inscription denotes the service dates for which the medal was awarded

❖ World War I (1917-1918)

Army Distinguished
Service Cross
First Version

Army Distinguished
Service Medal

At the time of the U.S. entry into World War I, the Medal of Honor, Certificate of Merit and Navy/Marine Corps Good Conduct Medals still represented America's entire inventory of personal decorations. This presented the twin dangers that the Medal of Honor might be cheapened by being awarded too often and that other deeds of valor might go unrecognized. By 1918, popular agitation forced the authorization of two new awards, the Army's Distinguished Service Cross and Distinguished Service Medal, created by Executive Order in 1918. In the same year, the traditional U.S. refusal to permit the armed forces to accept foreign decorations was rescinded, allowing military personnel to accept awards from the grateful Allied governments. In 1919, the Navy created the Navy Cross and its own Distinguished Service Medal for Navy and Marine Corps personnel.

The issuance of the World War I Victory Medal established another precedent, that of wearing clasps with the names of individual battles on the suspension ribbon of a general campaign medal. This was an ongoing practice in many countries, most notably Britain and France, since the 19th Century. When the ribbon bar alone was worn, each clasp was represented by a small (3/16" diameter) bronze star. Fourteen such clasps were adopted along with five clasps to denote service in specific countries. However, the latter were issued only if no campaign clasp was earned. Only one service clasp could be issued to any individual and they were not represented by a small bronze star on the ribbon bar.

During this period, the Army introduced the Citation Star which was established by Congress on July 9, 1918. This award, a 3/16 inch diameter silver star device, was originally authorized to be worn on the World War I Victory Medal to denote those who had been cited for extreme heroism or valor. The device, which evolved into the Silver Star Medal in 1932, was soon made retroactive as an attachment to the Army service medals for the Civil War, Indian, Spanish, China and Mexican Campaigns. The Citation Star was strictly a U.S. Army device. Bronze oak leaf clusters were also introduced to indicate a second award of the Medal of Honor or other decoration in lieu of a second medal.

This 16 foot stain glass window at the Army War College displays all of the Army fighting Division Patches (Marine Regiments served in the Army's 2d Infantry Division).

❖ World War I Victory Medal

Regulation Ribbon Bar

WW I Style Ribbon with Silver Star

Service	Army
Instituted	1917
Criteria	Awarded to all military personnel who served in the Continental United States or overseas between April, 1917 and April, 1920.
Devices	Bronze Star, Silver Star

Bronze

Medal Reverse

Service Clasp

Battle Clasp

Known until 1947 simply as the "Victory Medal", the World War I Victory Medal was awarded to any member of the U.S. military who had served in the armed forces between the following dates in the following locations:6 April 1917 to 11 November 1918 for any military service.12 November 1918 to 5 August 1919 for service in European Russia and 23 November 1918 to 1 April 1920 for service with the American Expeditionary Force Siberia.

Unlike the Army, the Navy only allowed one clasp of any type to be worn on the ribbon. Members of the Marines or Medical Corps who served in France but were not eligible for a battle clasp would receive a bronze Maltese across on their ribbons.

The 14 Allied Nations decided on a single ribbon, but pendant design was left up to each Nation. Mr. James E. Fraser was the designer of the U.S. Victory Medal. The bronze medal front shows a Winged Victory holding a shield and sword. The back of the medal reads"The Great War For Civilization" curved along the top of the medal. On the bottom of the back of the medal are six stars, three on either side of the center column of seven Roman staffs wrapped in a cord. The top of the staff has a round ball on top and is winged on the side. The staff overlays a shield saying "U" on the left side of the staff and "S"

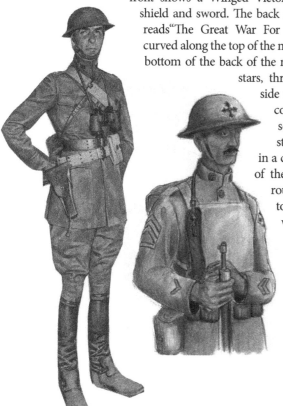

on the right side. Left of the staff are listed World War I Allied countries: France, Italy, Serbia, Japan, Montenegro, Russia, and Greece. On the right side of the staff are: Great Britain, Belgium, Brazil, Portugal, Rumania (now spelled Romania), and China.

A 3/16 inch Silver Citation Star was authorized to be worn on the ribbon of the Victory Medal by any member of the U.S. Army who had been cited for gallantry in action between 1917 and 1920. In 1932, the Silver Citation Star was redesigned as the Silver Star and, upon application, any holder of the Silver Citation Star could have it converted to a Silver Star decoration. Only one bronze star was authorized for wear on the ribbon regardless of the number of campaign bars earned. The Navy Commendation Star to the World War I Victory Medal was authorized to any person who had been commended by the Secretary of the Navy for performance of duty during the First World War. A 3/16 inch silver star was worn on the World War I Victory Medal, identical in appearance to the Army's Citation Star. Unlike the Army's version, however, the Navy Commendation Star could not be upgraded to the Silver Star medal. Marines and Navy Medical Corps personnel attached to the Army in France earned, and were authorized to wear any Army clasps authorized by their parent command.

For sea-related war duty, the Navy issued operational clasps, which were worn on the World War I Victory Medal and inscribed with the name of the duty type which had been performed.

❖ World War I Commemorative Medals

Upon the return of troops to the United States after World War I, many county, state and federal organizations rushed to produce Commemorative medals to honor their returning soldiers. The quality of medal design and strike was quite good and the local commemorative medals were highly prized by veterans and their families. Almost a thousand different WW I Commemorative Medals were presented to their returning veterans by city, county, state and fraternal organizations A beautiful example is South Carolina's Greenville County medal shown directly below with other examples.

Army of Occupation of Germany Medal (Army)

Service: Army   **Instituted:** 1942
Dates: 1918-1923
Criteria: Awarded to Army personnel who served in the occupation of Germany or Austria-Hungary between November, 1918 and July, 1923. Navy personnel on shore duty were also eligible.

WW I, Greenville, S.C.
Commemorative

The Army of Occupation of Germany Medal was created by the (55 Stat. 781) act of the United States Congress on November 21, 1941. The medal recognizes those members of the United States military who served in the European occupation force following the close of World War I.

The medal is retroactive by design and is awarded to any service member who performed occupation garrison duty in either Germany, or the former Austria-Hungary, between the dates of November 12, 1918 and July 11, 1923. The medal was primarily created due to the rising tension with Germany, between 1939 and 1941, and also as a means to honor the World War I service of General of the Armies John J. Pershing, whose likeness appears on the actual medal. Initially the blue edge stripe was wavy, to signify the Rhine River, but that proved impractical to mass-produce and was changed to a straight line.

World War I Commemorative Certicate presented to wounded America soldiers.

The first Army of Occupation of Germany Medal was presented to General of the Armies Pershing, with retroactive presentations made to any service member upon application to the United States War Department. Less than three weeks after the medal was first authorized, the United States was attacked at Pearl Harbor which led to another full-scale war with Germany, now allied with Japan.

❖ World War II Insignia

Between World War I and World War II more skill badges were introduced especially in the military aviation field with different wings for pilots, observers, and balloon pilots. New marksmanship badges were introduced to emphasize the premium that the Army put on good marksmanship with pistols and rifles.

Unit crests or distinctive unit insignia were introduced for most flag carrying units and these enamel unit crest were normally worn on the center of the epaulet. Branch insignia were attached to the lapels of officer uniforms in combination with the national U.S.

Enlisted rank divided into two categories; command and technical with the technical rank usually having the letter T underneath the chevrons. The Army General Staff Identification badge also made its appearance prior to World War II.

Combat Infantryman Badge

During World War II three of the Army's most prestigious badges were authorized. The Combat Infantryman Badge was authorized in 1943 retroactive to 7 December 1941 to recognize the skill and heroism of American Infantrymen. The Combat Medical Badge was established in 1945 and retroactively awarded back to 1941 to recognize the devotion and skill of front line medical personnel. The Parachute and Glider Badge was created at the beginning of World War II to identify and recognize the Army's new airborne soldiers.

Combat Medical Badge

Glider and Parachutists Badge

The Women's Army Corps was issued a special hat brass and button design.

Good Conduct Medal

Following the long established lead of the Navy and the Marine Corps, the Army introduced the Good Conduct Medal for enlisted personnel in 1941. Normally awarded for three years service, the qualifying period was reduced to one year during WW II.

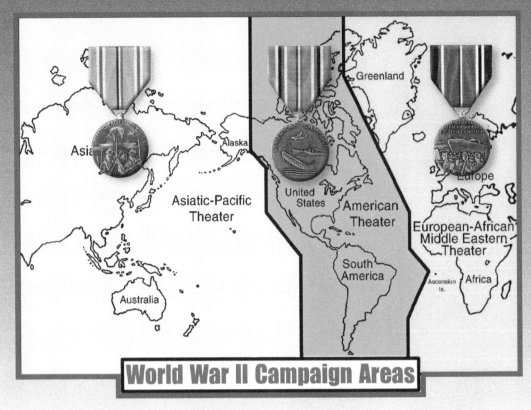

World War II Campaign Areas

American Defense
Service Medal

American
Campaign Medal

Asiaitic-Pacific
Campaign Medal

European African
Middle Eastern
Campaign Medal

Victory
Medal

Occupation
Medal

❖ World War II (1941-1945)

On September 8, 1939, in response to the growing threat of involvement in World War II, the President proclaimed a National Emergency in order to increase the size of U.S. military forces. For the first time, a peacetime service award, the American Defense Service Medal, was authorized for wear by those personnel who served during this period of National Emergency prior to the attack on Pearl Harbor on December 7, 1941.

America's participation in World War II saw a significant increase in both personal decorations and campaign medals. Since U.S. forces were serving all over the world, a campaign medal was designed for each major *(and carefully defined)* area. The three medals for the American, Asiatic-Pacific and European-African-Middle Eastern Campaigns encompassed the globe. However, the World War I practice of using campaign bars was discarded in favor of 3/16" bronze stars that could denote each designated military campaign from a major invasion to a submarine war patrol.

WAC Medal

(Croix de Guerre)

World War II also introduced the first *(and only!)* service medal unique to female military personnel. Known as the Women's Army Corps Service Medal, it was authorized for service in both the W.A.C. and its predecessor, the Women's Army Auxiliary Corps. The war also saw the large scale award of foreign medals and decorations to American servicemen. The Philippine Government, for one, authorized awards to commemorate the Defense and Liberation of their island country. The first foreign **award** designed strictly for units, the Philippine Presidential Unit Citation, patterned after a similar American award, was also approved for wear by American forces. In the European

Theater, France and Belgium made many presentations of their War Crosses *(Croix de Guerre)* to U.S. military personnel.

The end of World War II saw the introduction of two counterparts of previous World War I awards, the Victory and Occupation Medals. This time, no bars or clasps were authorized for the Victory Medal, but bars were issued with the Occupation Medal to denote the recipient's area of service. The Prisoner of War Medal and the Philippine Independence Medal are other examples of medals approved after the war.

The displays below show the basic medals awarded to soldiers who served in one, two or all three theaters.

Occupation Medal, Army

POW Medal

Europe, Middle East, Africa Medals

| American Campaign Medal | Europe-Africa-Middle East | Victory Medal WWII | Occupation Medal, Army |

American Theater Medals

| American Defense Service if serving before 7 Dec. 1941 | American Campaign Medal | Victory Medal WW II |

Asiatic Pacific Medals

| American Campaign Medal | Asiatic Pacific Campaign | Victory Medal WWII | Occupation Medal, Army |

U.S. Veteran's Philippine Medals

| Philippine Defense Medal | Philippine Liberation Medal | Philippine Independence Medal | Philippine Presidential Unit Citation |

But Where Were The World War II Veterans's Medals?

During World War II generally only decorations such as the Distinguished Service Cross, Silver Star, Distinguished Flying Cross and Purple Heart were manufactured. Brass was restricted to the manufacture of munitions so campaign medals were mainly issued as ribbon bars and soldiers, sailors, marines and airmen were not given medals but only ribbon bars to pin on their uniforms. In fact most of the campaign medals were unavailable to veterans until several years after the war. By then most service personnel had been discharged from the Armed Forces and returned to civilian life.

The photograph to the right is a good example of what was available for veterans to wear home. His two campaign ribbons (European-African-Middle Eastern and Asiatic Pacific Campaigns) are 1/2 inch high old style ribbons missing his campaign stars while his Victory ribbon and Good Conduct Medal are the standard 3/8 inch height of the Army and Air Force World War II ribbons. Unless the veteran went through the process of writing the government and asking for their medals, World War II veterans never received their actual campaign or Victory medals. In fact a number of World War II awards were not approved until several years after the war. The approval of the Bronze Star Medal for meritorious service to combat infantrymen and combat medics was not authorized until almost the end of 1947. The Victory and Occupation Medals were not manufactured until mid 1946 by which time many of the personnel authorized them had long since left the Armed Forces.

That is the reason you seldom see WW II veterans wearing their medals or displaying them. Not that they weren't proud of their service for they were very, but you can't wear medals you did not have.

❖ The Cold War (1945 -1991)

The Cold War lasted over 40 years with conflict, tension, and competition beginning in 1946 between the Western World under the leadership of the United States and the Soviet Union and its satellites. From the mid-1940s to the early 1990s, both sides tried to gain advantage using weapons development, military coalitions, espionage, invasions, propaganda and competitive technology, including the famous space race. The Cold War produced massive defense spending on conventional forces and nuclear arms and multiple proxy wars but no actual combat between the USA and USSR. Millions of Americans served in the Armed Forces often in tense and dangerous situations during this period.

In 1998, Congress authorized the Secretary of Defense to award a Cold War Victory Medal to all veterans of the Cold War. However, to date the Secretary of Defense has only authorized a Cold War Recognition Certificate to all members of the armed forces and qualified federal government civilian personnel who served during the Cold War, 2 September, 1945 to 26 December, 1991. The Department of Defense has stated that it will not create a Cold War Service medal nor authorize any commemorative medals made by private vendors for wear on the military uniform. The DOD position is that manufacturing the medal would be too expensive, a surprising position, since processing and mailing the certificate cost about the same as supplying a medal. However, Cold War Victory Commemorative Medals are perhaps one of the most popular and frequently purchased military medals today.

They are not official nor can they be worn on active duty uniforms but they continue the tradition going back to the Revolution of veterans filling their own needs.

The Army runs the Cold War Recognition Certificate program and Cold War veterans can write to the address below for a certificate. Response can be over a month. Write:

U.S. Army Human Resources Cmd
Cold War Recognition Program
ATTN: AHRC-PDP-A Dept 480
1600 Spearhead Division Ave.
Fort Knox, Ky 40122-5408

❖ Korea (1950-1954)

Good Conduct Medal

National Defense Service Medal

US Korean Service Medal

Korea Defense Service Medal

UN Korean Service Medal

ROK War Service Medal

Korean Presidential Unit Citation

The Korean Conflict, fought under the United Nations banner, saw the creation of two new medals for service. The first was the Korean Service Medal, which continued the practice of using 3/16" bronze stars on the ribbon to denote major campaigns. The second, the National Defense Service Medal, was established to recognize the contribution of all military personnel to national defense during a period of armed hostility. Some outstanding units were also awarded the Republic of Korea Presidential Unit Citation and all participants were awarded the United Nations Service Medal. By order of the Korean government, the award was also retroactively authorized to every unit of the United States Army which had deployed to Korea between 1950 and 1954.

In the 1950s, the Republic of Korea (ROK) asked the United States Government for approval to present the Korean War Service Medal to the U.S. troops who served in the Korean conflict, but the award was turned down by the U.S. Government. However as the fiftieth Anniversary of the Korean War approached, veterans groups placed more and more pressure on their congressional representatives and in 1999 the medal was approved for Korean War veterans. The late approval results in the Korean War Service Medal's order of precedence being after the Kuwait Liberation Medal instead of the normal chronological order for foreign awards.

The Korea Defense Service Medal (KDSM) was instituted in 2003 and made retroactive to 1954. The medal is awarded to members of the Armed Forces who have served in the Republic of Korea or adjacent waters since the Korean War to uphold the armistice between South and North Korea. A service member must have at least thirty consecutive days service in the Korean theater to qualify for the KDSM. The medal is also granted for 60 non-consecutive days of service for reservists on annual training in Korea. All Korean War veterans who served 30 days in Korea after 27 July 1954 are eligible for Korea Defense Service Medal. The Korea Defense Service Medal is retroactive to the end of the Korean War and is granted to any service performed after July 28, 1954.

In addition to campaign and service medals normally awarded to a veteran of the Korean War, most Services approved the award of the Good Conduct Medal for a period of one year when service was in Korea. During the Korean War, the Air Force, a separate service since 1947, still used many Army awards. As a results Air Force veterans who earned the Good Conduct Medal during the conflict were awarded the Army Good Conduct Medal.

Good Conduct Medal

National Defense
Service Medal

Armed Forces
Expeditionary
Medal

U.S. Vietnam
Service Medal

RVN Campaign
Medal

❖ Vietnam (1961-1973)

RVN Gallantry
Cross Unit
Citation

The first American advisors in the Republic of South Vietnam were awarded the new Armed Forces Expeditionary Medal which was created in 1961 to cover campaigns for which no specific medal was instituted. However, as the U.S. involvement in the Vietnamese conflict grew, a unique award, the Vietnam Service Medal was authorized, thus giving previous recipients of the Expeditionary Medal the option of which medal to accept. The Government also authorized the acceptance of the Republic of Vietnam Campaign Medal by all who served for six months in-country, or in the surrounding waters or the air after 1960. Towards the end of the war a blanket general order authorized the RVN Gallantry Cross Unit Citation for all those who served in Vietnam.

The most notable change in medal policy occurred during the Vietnam War when the Department of Defense authorized the large scale acceptance of South Vietnamese awards. The South Vietnamese Armed Forces had a comprehensive awards system built to reflect their past as a former French colony. Since a large number of American military advisors and special forces worked with the South Vietnamese Armed Forces for over 15 years, (many serving multiple tours) numerous medals for valor and service were presented to U.S. personnel. Some of the most awarded were the Vietnamese Cross of Gallantry (for valor), the Civil Actions Medal and the Armed Forces Honor Medal (meritorious service). The last two medals are unusual since they were in two different degrees; first class for officers and second class for enlisted personnel. All foreign medals awarded to members of the U.S. Armed Forces were either furnished by the foreign government or purchased by the recipient since the United States government does not provide foreign medals to members of the Armed Forces.

After Vietnam, many new decorations, medals and ribbons came into being as the Department of Defense

and the individual Services developed a complete structure to reward performance from the newest enlistee to the most senior Joint Staff officer. Some of the awards, such as the Army Service Ribbon have no medal but reward the young recruits for successfully completing their transition from civilian to a ready member of the Armed Forces. Achievement and Commendation Medals provide a powerful means for a field commander to recognize younger individuals for outstanding performance.

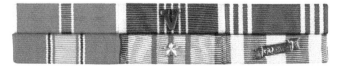

Vietnamese Cross of
Gallantry (for valor)

Armed Forces
Honor Medal

Civil Actions Medal
(Foreign Decoration)

❖ Rebuilding the Army (1975-1990)

After Vietnam the Army begin a decade of rebuilding itself into a modern all volunteer force to meet the United States worldwide missions as leader of the free world. The post Vietnam combat trained officer and noncommissioned officer corps focused on reshaping the American Army to a modern highly trained professional fighting force and awards and insignia played an important role.

 In the early 1980's, the Army went to the "whole branch regiment concept" which basically meant that every active duty soldier would belong to a regiment. Combat arms soldiers became members of numbered flag bearing regiments, while combat support and combat service support soldiers belong to regiments designated as whole branch regiments. For example, Adjutant General Corps soldiers belong to the Adjutant General Corps Regiment, Signal Corps soldiers belong to the Signal Corps Regiment. Each whole branch regiment was officially activated complete with its own flag and crest. Army regulations now specify that soldiers wear their regimental crest over their right pocket as a means of increased esprit de corps.

After Vietnam, many new decorations, medals and ribbons were established as the Department of Defense and the individual Services developed a highly structured awards system to reward performance from the newest enlistee to the most senior Pentagon staffer. Some of the awards, such as the Army Service Ribbon, were created to reward young soldiers and officers for successfully completing initial entry training. Conversely, the Achievement and Commendation Medals provide a useful means for a field commander to recognize younger individuals for outstanding performance.

The diagram below details the location and wear of awards and insignia on the Army green uniform beginning in 1958.

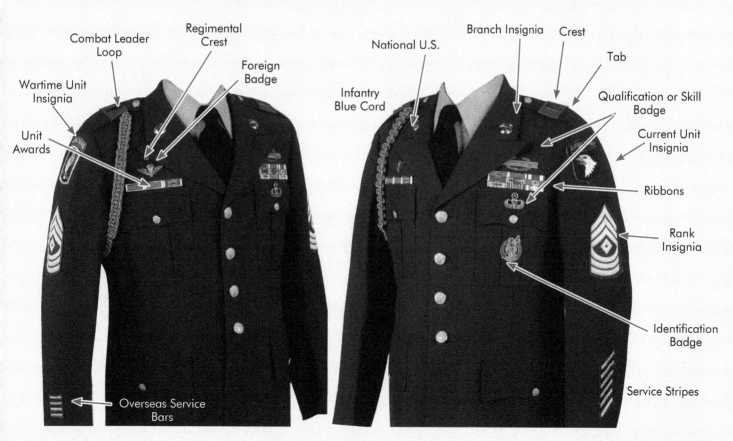

❖ Gulf War (1991-1995)

The conflict in the Persian Gulf, as previously noted, saw the reinstitution of the National Defense Service Medal (this time it also covered the Reserves) and the creation of the Southwest Asia Service Medal for the personnel in Iraq, Kuwait, Saudi Arabia, Oman, Bahrain, Qatar and United Arab Emirates. Between January 17, 1991 and November 30, 1995, service members who performed duty "in support of" the Persian Gulf War are eligible to receive the Southwest Asia Service Medal if duty was performed in either Israel, Egypt, Turkey, Syria or Jordan. The Southwest Asia Service Medal is authorized four campaign stars for service, but only a maximum of three campaign stars can be awarded with the medal. Each recipient of the medal must wear at least one campaign star.

The Department of Defense also approved the wear of the Saudi Arabian Medal for the Liberation of Kuwait, which probably wins the award as the "Most Colorful Medal" authorized American military personnel. Later the Department of Defense also authorized the Kuwait Medal for the Liberation of Kuwait.

❖ NATO Medals (1998 to Present)

Since the Liberation of Kuwait, the Army has become involved more and more as a world police force. Forces have been deployed to Panama, Grenada, Somalia and Bosnia et al. to the extent that soldiers are now receiving United Nations medals, NATO medals and even a United States Army Campaign Medal for peace keeping duties in Kosovo. In the Army, NATO medals authorized for wear include the NATO Medal for Former Yugoslavia, the NATO Medal for Kosovo Service, both of the Article 5 Medals, the Non-Article 5 medals for the Balkans and Afghanistan International Security and Assistance Force (ISAF) and service in Iraq.

The idea is some what similar to the U.S. Joint Service awards which are used to reward joint staff service outside of a service members normal branch of service (i.e. Army, Navy, Air Force, Marines or Coast Guard). For U.S. Forces, service stars indicate additional awards to the NATO Medal. In the USA, NATO medals authorized for wear include the NATO Medal for Former Yugoslavia, the NATO Medal for Kosovo Service, both of the Article 5 Medals, the Non-Article 5 medals for the Balkans and Afghanistan International Security and Assistance Force (ISAF), The NATO Meritorious Service Medal and the Macedonia NATO Medal and the Non-Article 5 Medal for service in Iraq.

National Defense Service Medal

Southwest Asia Service Medal

Saudi Arabian Medal for the Liberation of Kuwait

Kuwait Medal for the Liberation of Kuwait.

Former Yugoslavia

NATO Medal (Kosovo)

NATO Article 5 Medal

NATO Article 5 medal

NATO Non Article 5 Medal

NATO ISAF Medal

❖ The Global War on Terrorism and The Liberation of Afghanistan and Iraq *(2001 to Present)*

The cruel and cowardly terrorist hijacking and attack on the World Trade Center led to a vigorous series of counter attacks on terrorists and their supporters. To recognize these efforts, the National Defense Service Medal was reauthorized in 2001 and two new awards, the Global War on Terrorism Expeditionary and Service Medals were authorized. A White House spokesman said the medals recognize the "sacrifices and contributions" military members make in the global war on terror.

Following the liberation of Afghanistan, an Afghanistan Campaign Medal was created on November 29, 2004 retroactive to October 24, 2001 to acknowledge service there. A similar medal, known as the Iraq Campaign Medal was authorized for service during the same period within the borders of Iraq and is retroactive to March 19, 2003. The two medals may be awarded with the Army's Arrowhead device for assault/parachute landings. These medals replace the Global War on Terrorism Expeditionary Medal for service in Afghanistan and Iraq and military personnel can not receive both for the same period of service. In 2016 a new medal, the Inherent Resolve Campaign Medal, was added for continued conflict in the middle east.

Afghanistan Campaign Medal	Iraq Campaign Medal	Inherent Resolve Campaign Medal	Global War on Terrorism Expeditionary Medal	Global War on Terrorism Service Medal

US Army Photo

❖ Army of the 21st Century

The Army standard green dress uniform under went a change in 2008 when dark blue was chosen to replace it. All soldiers adopted the dark blue uniform by 2014. President Washington chose dark blue as the national color of Continental Army in 1779 and the new Army uniforms reflects the Continental blue color. Changes to the uniform replaced the combat patch worn on the right sleeve of the class A green uniform with a metal combat unit service identification badge worn on the lower right side of the blue uniform. Combat service bars are authorized on the sleeve for both enlisted and officers. Enlisted Soldiers can wear both overseas combat service bars and service stripes on the new blue jacket. Officers and corporals and above will wear gold braid on their trousers to indicate leadership roles.

 The American Army awards and recognition program developed over two centuries of ever more complex missions. In the beginning the country relied on citizens militia and rejected a professional Army. Today we rely on a highly trained professional Army made up of volunteers. If there is criticism that this complete and comprehensive award system is too complex and too involved, then the critic should fully recognize the missions and tasks facing today's American soldiers are the most complex and demanding in our history. In a great republic depending on volunteers it is vitally important to have a complete and comprehensive system to reward and identify our soldiers professional military skills and accomplishments.

The Army award system is the culmination of over 230 years of tradition and service. It comes from the Revolution, where a soldier had little to honor his service, to today's pyramid of honor. Awards and insignia try to recognize a soldier's accomplishments with a complete array of badges, ribbons and medals. Today, a young noncommissioned officer wears many more ribbons than a World War II NCO. There is a clear reason for that. There are now ribbons and awards for almost every level of achievement and every special type of duty assignment. The expansion of awards recognizes the fact that much is expected of today's volunteer soldiers in mastering complex systems and being willing to serve long periods in far away and dangerous lands.

All the decorations, service medals, ribbons, badges and insignia provide a unique and handsome way for the United States to honor her Army veterans for valor and faithful service. These awards also have another important purpose. The display on a soldier's uniform can quickly tell a commander, members of the Armed Forces and veterans the level of experience and performance of the wearer.

From the soldiers viewpoint military awards recognize and reward devotion to duty, performance, valor and service in a way no other manner can. The Army's medals and ribbons reflect how our country has recognizes hundreds of years of unbroken dedicated service and valor going back to the birth of the Republic.

❖ Seals and Emblems

The Insignia of the United States Army is rich with tradition, history and symbolism. The first Army seal and later the Army emblem can all be traced back to the early days of our revolution.

Department of the Army Seal

The traditional War Office seal used since the Revolution was designated as the Department of the Army Seal by the National Security Act of 1947. The date "MDCCLXXVIII" and the designation "War Office" are from the seal. The date *(1778)* refers to the year of its adoption. The term "Board of War and Ordnance, United States of America" was used during the Revolution, later shortened to "United States of America, War Office" and was always associated with the Headquarters of the Army since the Navy had its own seal.

The center of the seal is a Roman cuirass below a vertical unsheathed sword, point up, with the pommel resting on the neck opening of the cuirass and a Phrygian cap *(the emblem of freedom during that period)* supported on the sword point. The entire central device is a group of military trophies. Over this is a serpent holding in its mouth a scroll inscribed "This We'll Defend". Beneath the trophies are the Roman numerals for 1778.

Department of the Army Emblem

The Army seal is traditionally used to authenticate documents and is not authorized for display. To create an official Army emblem the Secretary of the Army approved the design on 29 January 1974. The Army emblem was developed from the Army seal but differs in a number of ways. The emblem is displayed in color and includes the inscription, "Department of the Army", instead of "War Office."

The American flag is on the viewer's left and the Army flag pattern has been added to the other flag. The Roman numerals "MDCCLXXVIII" *(1778)* for the date the Army seal was adopted, are replaced with the date "1775" for the date the Army was established.

The colors are those traditionally associated with the Army. The flags are in proper colors. Blue for loyalty, vigilance, perseverance and truth. Red for courage, zeal and fortitude. White for purity of purpose and black for determination and constancy. Gold represents achievement, dignity and honor.

Great Seal of The United States

The current officers eagle hat insignia came into use around 1902-03 and was derived from the 1782 Great Seal of the United States. The major difference from earlier eagles used as hat insignia is this contained the glory or breaking through a cloud, proper and surrounding thirteen stars, forming a constellation. The constellation denotes a new state taking its place among other sovereign powers. The thirteen stars represents the separate colonies joined together supporting a chief who unites the whole.

Army National Guard Seal and Emblem

The Army National Guard Seal and Emblem features the famous "minute man" of Revolutionary War fame sculpted by Daniel C. French in 1873. The statue symbolizes the citizen soldiers of the Army National Guard's ability to respond at a moment's notice to events in their areas of responsibility.

The emblem is different for the National Guard Bureau Seal since the Bureau represents both the Air Guard and the Army Guard. The National Guard Bureau is the federal instrument responsible for the administration of the National Guard. Established by Congress as a Joint Bureau of the Departments of the Army and the Air Force, it holds a unique status as both a staff and operational agency. Throughout its more than 80-year history, the National Guard Bureau has repeatedly proven that the National Guard can effectively perform its duties, with its own personnel, at a high level of professionalism.

Emblem of The Army Reserve

The Army Reserve Seal and Emblem features the profile of a Revolutionary War patriot, symbolizing the readiness of citizen soldiers of the Army Reserve to respond quickly to mobilization requirements.

❖ Hat Badges, Buttons and Lapel Pins

Army Officers Hat Insignia

In 1895, the Army moved from branch insignia on the officers cap to the national eagle. The all gilt eagle, which is the coat of arms of the United States, became the official hat insignia for all officers in 1903. The glory with 13 stars is over the eagles head and the right claw offers an olive branch while the left grasps 13 arrows.

Army Female Officers Hat Insignia

In 1943, the Women's Army Auxiliary Corps became the Women's Army Corps and the Army replaced their "walking eagle" insignia with the same style hat insignia as male officers, the gold gilt national eagle. The women's officer hat insignia changed color in 1951 to an antique bronze when a new taupe uniform was introduced for the WAC. The introduction of the Army blue uniform and Army green uniform caused the hat insignia to return to its original gold color in 1964. The current female Army officer hat insignia is about 1 1/2 inches wide, slightly smaller than their male counterparts, but identical in every other aspect.

Army Warrant Officers Hat Insignia

(Current) Warrant Officers initially wore enlisted cap devices until 1921 when they wore a black metal eagle of the design created by the Fine Arts Commission. The insignia became obsolete in 2004. This insignia was also worn by Pilot Warrant Officers during World War II.

West Point Cadets Hat Insignia

(Current) United States military academy hat brass. The military hat insignia worn by West Point cadets is the coat of arms of the Military Academy. It has the shield the United States, bearing the helmet of Pallas over a Greek sword and surmounted by an eagle, displays a scroll with the motto, Duty, Honor, Country, West Point MDCCCV USMA, all in a gold color.

Reserve Officers Training Corps Hat and collar Insignia

While there are numerous variations of the Reserve Officer Training Corps hat brass, this is the most common. The ROTC initials are surrounded by a laurel wreath in a gilt color. The use of the national eagle with the letters ROTC is not authorized but is used by some schools.

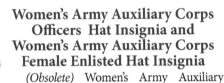

Army Air Corps Cadet Hat Insignia

(Obsolete) Army Air Corps Cadet hat insignia (World War Two) consisted of a double blade airplane propeller in silver superimposed over a set of gold color wings. This same insignia on a slightly smaller scale was used as a branch insignia of the Army Air Corps in World War II.

Women's Army Auxiliary Corps Officers Hat Insignia and Women's Army Auxiliary Corps Female Enlisted Hat Insignia

(Obsolete) Women's Army Auxiliary Corps hat device was unaffectionately called "walking eagle". The Women's Army Auxiliary Corps was initially not part of the Army and therefore required a separate officers hat insignia. This insignia only lasted about a year when the Women's Army Auxiliary Corps changed to the Women's Army Corps and replaced their "walking eagle" insignia with the same style hat insignia as male officers. The walking eagle was also used as a lapel insignia for the WAAC branch.

Army Transport Service Officers Hat Insignia

(Obsolete) Army Transport Service hat brass was part of the special and unique uniforms and insignia developed for the Army Transport Service, which was the Army seagoing transport arm during World War II and until 1949. The most common insignia was introduced in the 1930s and consisted of a 1 2/3 inch gilt Eagle with spread wings and a colored shield mounted on top of a pair of crossed anchors. After World War II, the insignia was modified to include a red enamel shield bearing the Transportation Corps device.

Army Harbor Boat Service Officers Hat Insignia

(Obsolete) The Harbor Boat Service hat insignia was used during World War II although the Harbor Boat Service officers were supposed to use the same hat insignia as the Army Transport Service officers beginning in 1942.

Army Specialist Corps Officers Hat Insignia

(Obsolete) Army Specialists Corps (World War II) was created to provide technical, professional, scientific and administrative personnel in order to release military men for combat. Officers appointed had a special uniform authorized by the War Department. The regular Army officer's hat brass was replaced with a United States Eagle holding a bolt of arrows. The Army Specialists Corps was disbanded midway through World War II.

❖ Hat Badges, Buttons and Lapel Pins

Sergeant Major of the Army Hat Insignia

A special hat insignia for the Sergeant Major of the Army is the national Eagle as worn by officers surrounded by a laurel wreath to symbolize achievement. The Sgt. Major of the Army is the only soldier authorized to wear this hat insignia.

Army Enlisted Hat Insignia

The Enlisted Hat Insignia was originally introduced in World War I. The insignia consist of a gold colored disk with the national coat of arms eagle mounted directly in the center. In 1952, a blue plastic disk, 1 3/4 inches wide was authorized to the worn by enlisted infantrymen to enhance their prestige and morale. Other branches have produced branch colored rims to go around their hat brass but all of these are non regulation. Only the infantry enlisted soldier is authorized to wear blue trim behind his hat insignia.

Army Female Enlisted Hat Insignia

Enlisted women's hat insignia consist of a gold colored circle with the national code of arms eagle mounted directly in the center. It is the same as enlisted men except the coat of arms of the United States Eagle rest in a gilt colored circle while the male insignia is mounted on a disk.

Army Bandsman's Hat Insignia

Army band member's hat brass approved in 1943 consisted of a gilt lyre, with the letters U.S. imposed on the lyre all of which was surrounded by a gilt wreath. A new design shown here was introduced in 1968 which is much more elaborate.

U.S. Letters for Officers and Enlisted

The letters U. S. are probably the oldest and most common United States Army markings going back to the original buttons used in the Revolution.

Army Button in the Revolution

Army Button World War I

Current Army Uniform Button

The Army officer and enlisted buttons are gold plated with the Coat of Arms of the United States superimposed. Optional white gold anodized aluminum buttons are no longer authorized.

Army Engineer Corps Officers Button

The Corps of Engineers officer buttons are of a unique and distinct design not worn by the rest of the Army. The button consists of an Eagle holding the motto "Essayons" *(Let Us Try)* over a base surrounded by water and a rising sun. The design reflects early Corps of Engineers duties, which included the building of Harbor fortifications.

American Expeditionary Force WW I

Button is authorized retired members of the U.S. Army American Expeditionary Forces in World War I.

Honorable Service Lapel Button

(World War II) Affectionately referred to by veterans as the ruptured duck, this gold colored lapel button consists of an eagle perched within a ring composed of a chief and thirteen vertical stripes.

Army Lapel Button

Is a gratuitous issue item made up of a minute man in gold color on a red enamel disk surrounded by 16-pointed gold rays. It is awarded for honorable service after 1984.

U.S. Army Retired Lapel

Button Is authorized retired members of the U.S. Army.

Gold Star Lapel Button

The Gold Star Lapel pin is awarded to widows, widowers, parents, and next-of-kin of members of the Armed Forces who lost their lives in WW I, WW II, Korea, or any conflict after 1958. It is a gold star on a purple background surrounded by a gold laurel wreath. On the back is "United States of America, Act of Congress, August 1966" with a place for the initials of the recipient.

❖ Origin of Officer Rank Insignia

Army Adopted National Symbol 1832

The origin of the military ranks and titles used today probably began with the Greek and Roman forces and gradually evolved over the centuries. Most of the rank names evolved from Latin, therefore the origin of our rank system can generally be traced to the evolution of the Roman legions.

In 1775, there were no standard uniforms in the Continental Army to distinguish the officers. Officers wore old military uniforms and enlisted men wore work or hunting clothes. General George Washington ordered a rank system his men could recognize throughout the Army. Corporals wore a green cloth epaulet on the right shoulder, and sergeants a red epaulet. Officers wore different colored cockades in their hats, and silver epaulets, while senior officers wore different colored ribbons diagonally across their chest. The officer rank insignia we use today evolved when Brigadier Generals were designated with one star on each epaulet, Major Generals by two stars and by 1799 three stars for the rank of Lieutenant General. In 1832, the Army adopted the national symbol of the eagle with shield, arrows and olives leaves for Colonel's rank.

One of the first questions every new soldier asks is why silver takes precedence over gold for officer's insignia of grade. Beginning in 1780, the grade of general officers was indicated by silver stars embroidered on their epaulets. This established silver as the first color used for officers grade insignia. In 1832, silver epaulets were specified for the infantry while all other branches wore gold epaulets. To make sure that rank insignia would be easily recognized, they were the opposite color of the officer's epaulet. Infantry colonels wore gold eagles on silver epaulets and all other colonels had silver eagles on gold epaulets. At that time the only rank insignia were stars for general's and eagles for colonels. Epaulets for lieutenants, captains, majors and lieutenant colonels had no insignia; the length and thickness of the fringe on the epaulet indicated the different grades.

Embroidered shoulder straps began replacing epaulets for field duty about 1836-37 with specific insignia designated for each grade. The order creating the rank of lieutenant colonel specified a gold oak leaf if the strap border was gold and a silver leaf if the border was infantry silver. Majors used the same leaf insignia except they wore a gold leaf with a gold border or a silver leaf with a silver border. (*Gold and silver leafs were used for both ranks.*) Captains were designated

with twin gold bars and first lieutenants were identified with one gold bar. There was no insignia for second lieutenants except an empty shoulder strap.

In 1851, the Army decided to use only one color for colonels insignia and since the majority of colonels wore silver insignia, that was the color selected (additionally influenced by the fact that General officer's stars were silver). Lieutenant colonels were authorized a silver leaf and majors a gold leaf with all shoulder strap borders remaining gold.

During the Civil War, captain's and first lieutenant's bars remained gold. It was not until after the Civil War in 1866 that Congress created the rank of four star general for General Grant.

In 1872, officers' epaulets were abolished and replaced with shoulder knots for the dress uniform. Since the shoulder knot had no fringe, the insignia on the dress uniform needed to be changed in order to distinguish majors from second lieutenants. The gold leaf from the major shoulder strap was a natural insignia for continued use. At the same time, the bars for captains and first lieutenants were changed from gold to the same silver color of all officers but majors.

Metal insignia began appearing on the uniform after the Civil War and was formalized on the Khaki blouse by 1902. World War I saw the second lieutenant finally receive a gold bar as a rank insignia while 1st lieutenant remained silver. There were proposals for second lieutenants to have one bar, first lieutenants two bars and captains three bars but resistance to adopting Confederate style rank insignia and continuing the policy of making as few changes as possible resulted in a gold bar being adopted in 1917. This followed the precedent previously established with the major's rank insignia.

Warrant officers for the Mine Planter Service were provided with insignia beginning in 1921. In 1941, Congress established grades for Chief Warrant officers and junior warrant officers and a flight officer warrant grade was also authorized from 1942 until 1945.

After World War I, the title of "General of the Armies of the United States" was created and conferred upon General John J. Pershing but no special insignia was designated until 1944 when General of the Army was established by Congress with a circle of five stars below the gold colored Coat of Arms of the United States. In 1976 Congress posthumously raised George Washington to the rank of General of the Armies of the United States with rank and precedence above all of the Army, past or present.

While silver outranks gold in the Army officer insignia of grade, gold can still be considered to outrank silver for decorations and medals. The order of precedence in establishing medals is the same dating back to antiquity, i.e. gold, silver and bronze.

❖ U.S. Army Commissioned Rank Insignia

With the exception of the warrant officer grades, the present Army officer rank is the same design as used in World War II. The difference today is the adoption of slide-on soft cloth rank epaulets and a simplified mess dress rank design. The four basic versions (*i.e. metal, cloth, embroidered, epaulet-style*) for officer rank are shown on this and the next page.

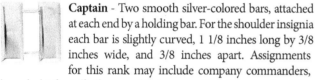

Second Lieutenant - One gold-colored bar of the same type as for a first lieutenant 1 by 3/8 inch. Typically, the entry level commissioned officer rank. Second lieutenants normally spend six months of their time in a training status, preparing for the first assignment in their specialty. Lieutenant comes from the French word lieu *(place)* tenant *(holding)*. An officer who acts in the place of another, the lieutenant's duty is often to be his superior officer's deputy. By use, it has come to mean the officer who is a subordinate of a captain. This most junior officer rank was created in the British Navy in the 16th century to provide an officer ready and able to take command should the captain be absent or unable to command.

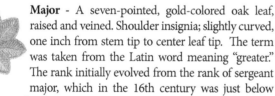

First Lieutenant - One silver-colored bar of the same type as for a captain. Increased responsibility assignments as Executive officers of a company and junior staff officers, are typical of this rank. In the 17th century, the lieutenant rank in Great Britain was given to those noblemen in training to become captains. The bar rank is 1inch by 3/8 inches in regular size.

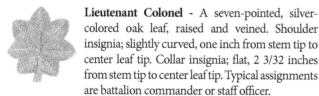

Captain - Two smooth silver-colored bars, attached at each end by a holding bar. For the shoulder insignia each bar is slightly curved, 1 1/8 inches long by 3/8 inches wide, and 3/8 inches apart. Assignments for this rank may include company commanders, branch chiefs, staff officers, and instructors. Captain comes from the Latin word "caput", meaning head and of the Latin word capitaneus *(chief)*. Although a Captain could be the head of any organization *(for example the Spanish; Captain General)*, the rank is associated with officers commanding a company, battery or troop.

Major - A seven-pointed, gold-colored oak leaf, raised and veined. Shoulder insignia; slightly curved, one inch from stem tip to center leaf tip. The term was taken from the Latin word meaning "greater." The rank initially evolved from the rank of sergeant major, which in the 16th century was just below lieutenant colonel. In succeeding centuries, the rank became "major" as the "sergeant" portion was dropped. Typical assignments are battalion executive officer or staff officer.

Lieutenant Colonel - A seven-pointed, silver-colored oak leaf, raised and veined. Shoulder insignia; slightly curved, one inch from stem tip to center leaf tip. Collar insignia; flat, 2 3/32 inches from stem tip to center leaf tip. Typical assignments are battalion commander or staff officer.

Colonel - A silver-colored spread eagle, made in pairs, right and left, talons of one foot grasping an olive branch, the other, a bundle of 13 arrows. Shoulder insignia; slightly curved, with 1 1/2 inch wing span. The term evolved in the 16th century from the Spanish king, Ferdinand, who called the commander of his columns "cabo de colunela" which later became colonel in the French and British armies. The current pronunciation of "kernel" was established by the British. *(Colonel may come from the Italian word colonello meaning little column, an officer commanding a 'column' of soldiers or may come from the word column, a column, or corona, a crown.)* The head of the eagle is worn facing forward.

Brigadier General - One silver-colored star, 1 inch in height. General originally meant to be of similar 'birth' or 'class' with the sovereign; the more recent use is to be familiar with all facets of the army, no longer a specialist in one area, and a "general officer". In summary, any officer in general command of all troops. Original General ranks were: Captain General, Lieutenant General, Sergeant Major General and Brigadier General *(A corporal in French is a Brigadier)*. This explains why a Lieutenant General out ranks a Major General. Major General was originally Sergeant Major General.

Major General - Two silver-colored stars of the same type and arranged in the same manner as for a lieutenant general. A Major General normally commands a Division, large military post, a branch of the service *(i.e. Armor Branch)* or a high level staff branch.

Lieutenant General - Three silver-colored stars, of the same type and arranged in the same manner as for a general, except the distance between centers of adjacent shoulder stars is one inch. Normally commands a corps or a major division of the Army staff.

General - Four silver-colored, five-pointed, pyramid-shaped stars. Shoulder stars are one inch in diameter and are either fastened together on a metal holding bar or placed individually with one point of each star in the same line; distance between the centers of adjacent stars is 3/4 inch. Normally commands an Army, a major command of the Army, or serves as Chief of Staff or Vice Chief of Staff of the Army.

General of the Army - Five silver stars at each of five points, joined together in a pentagonal pattern. For other than metal insignia the National Coat of Arms in gold is displayed above the stars. General George Washington was appointed to this grade by Congress retroactive to 1775 so that he outranks all previous Generals of the Army.

❖ U.S. Army Commissioned Rank Insignia

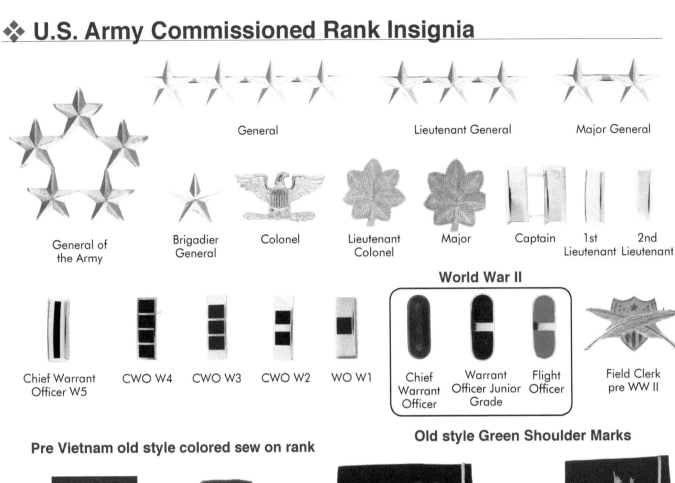

General

Lieutenant General

Major General

General of the Army

Brigadier General

Colonel

Lieutenant Colonel

Major

Captain

1st Lieutenant

2nd Lieutenant

Chief Warrant Officer W5

CWO W4

CWO W3

CWO W2

WO W1

World War II

Chief Warrant Officer

Warrant Officer Junior Grade

Flight Officer

Field Clerk pre WW II

Pre Vietnam old style colored sew on rank

Old style Green Shoulder Marks

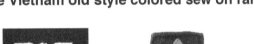

New style subdued sew on rank

Shirt

Sweater

New style subdued pin on rank

New Style Black Shoulder Marks

Civil War Shoulder Straps

Current Full Dress Shoulder Straps

Officer Mess Dress Shoulder Knots

Gen. Grant's 1866 Rank

Colonel, Infantry Lieut. Col. and 2d Lieutenant shoulder straps

Current AGC Branch Colonel

Artillery Branch Captain

Warrant Officer Rank

❖ Warrant Officer's Insignia of Rank

The warrant officer rank was created to fill special positions requiring greater technical skill and responsibility than a noncommissioned officer but without the responsibility of command. The military grade of warrant officer originated several hundred years ago during the early period of the British Navy. The less experienced officers of the Royal Navy relied heavily on the technical expertise, knowledge, and allegiance of senior sailors who were rewarded with a Royal Warrant. The Royal Warrant designation clearly distinguished them from the other sailors while maintaining the strict class system of the period.

Army Field Clerk Insignia

The predecessor of the warrant officer was the Army Field Clerk and the Field Clerk, QMC, both authorized in August 1916. The rank and grade of warrant officer was officially established July, 1918, as the Army Mine Planter Service in the regular Army Coast Artillery Corps. Each mine planter was authorized one master, one first mate, one second mate, one chief engineer, one second assistant, as warrant officers. A sleeve insignia with a three-bladed propeller or foul anchor above the braid was authorized to identify the warrant officer job specialties in January, 1920. This insignia was abolished with the Mine Planter Service in June, 1947.

Chief Engineer   Master   Assistant Engineer

The Army Field Clerks and the Field Clerks, QMC, were designated as warrant officers in June, 1920. They wore the same uniform as the Army Mine Planter Service without sleeve braid until 1921 when they received a special insignia.

Congress authorized two warrant officer grades in August 21, 1941 for other than the Army Mine Planter Service. The insignia for chief warrant officer was a gold bar 3/8 inch wide and 1 inch long with rounded ends, brown enamel on top with a center gold stripe 1/8 inch wide. Junior grade insignia was a 3/8 inch wide gold bar, 1 inch long, rounded at the ends with brown enamel on top and a gold center 1/8 inch wide. In November 1942, the War Department established a flight officer with the same insignia as the warrant officer junior grade except for blue enamel in place of brown. In May of 1945, a peak of almost 57,000 warrant officers were on active duty in both the U.S. Army and U.S. Army Air Force. The rank of Flight Officer was abolished in 1945.

Chief Warrant Officer   Warrant Officer Junior Grade   Flight Officer

In May, 1947, the War Department sought to authorize four grades of Army warrant officers. The insignias were four gold with brown enamel bars for Chief Warrant Officer, three bars for Senior Warrant Officer, two bars for Warrant Officer First Class, and one bar for Warrant Officer. Title changes to Chief Warrant Officer, Warrant Officer First Class, Warrant Officer Second class and Warrant Officer Third Class were approved in October, 1949; however, the insignia was not implemented.

Chief Warrant Officer   Warrant Officer First Class   Warrant Officer Second Class   Warrant Officer Third Class

In September, 1956, with the other Military Services concurrence, four new warrant officer insignia were approved for use across the services. The only differences were that each service used its own unique color on the bar. The first two grades in the Army were gold and brown while the two senior grades were silver and brown.

Chief Warrant Officer W4   Chief Warrant Officer W3   Chief Warrant Officer W2   Chief Warrant Officer W1

New, easier to identify insignia were approved in June, 1970 for wear as of July 1, 1972. Based on the anticipated addition of two warrant grades, new insignia for W5 and W6 were developed but never authorized for wear.

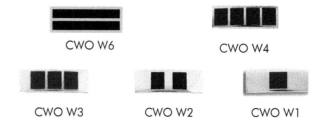

CWO W6   CWO W4

CWO W3   CWO W2   CWO W1

The Chief of Staff approved Master Warrant Officer (W4) insignia on April 8, 1988 designating certain CWO W4 as master warrants. Master Warrant Officer appointment required completion of the Warrant Officer school at Fort Rucker. The first class graduated on December 5, 1991, establishing the grade of CW5. On 9 July 2004, Master Warrant Officer W5 was approved for continued use.

Chief Warrant Officer W5

❖ Reserve Officer's Training Corps

Current

Army ROTC *(Reserve Officers' Training Corps)* is part of many college curricula. During classes, leadership labs, physical training and field training exercises, students learn what it takes to lead others, motivate groups and conduct missions as an Officer in the Army. Upon graduation from Army ROTC, they are commissioned a Second Lieutenant into the Active Army, Army Reserve or Army National Guard. ROTC cadets wear the standard Army uniform with the ROTC insignia and cadet rank insignia according to the position in the ROTC unit.

Old Style

Insignia of Grade for Cadet Officers

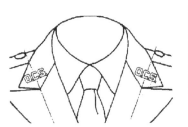

Cadet Colonel

Cadet Lieutenant Colonel

Cadet Major

Cadet Captain

Cadet First Lieutenant

Cadet Second Lieutenant

Insignia of Grade for Cadet Enlisted Personnel

Cadet Command Sergeant Major

Cadet Sergeant Major

Cadet First Sergeant

Cadet Master Sergeant

Cadet Sergeant First Class

ROTC Metal Rank Insignia

Cadet Staff Sergeant

Cadet Sergeant

Cadet Corporal

Cadet Private First Class

Cadet Private

OCS Old Shoulder Insignia

OCS Current Shoulder Insignia

Officer & Warrant Officer Candidate School Insignia

O.C.S.

OCS Collar Insignia

Officer Candidate School *(OCS)* and Warrant Officer Candidate School are schools for enlisted personnel to qualify for appointment as Commissioned Officers or Warrant Officers in the United States Army Reserve for both Active Army and Reserve service. The OCS and WOC insignia is worn in place of the U.S. insignia on the class A uniform lapels or on the shirt collar.

W.O.C.

Warrant Officer Candidate Collar Insignia

❖ Background and Development of Enlisted Ranks

The use of the term private as a military designation began in the 1500s and meant a private man, rather than officer or officeholder. There are also those who say it comes from the Greek citizen soldier who furnished his own weapons and went into battle as a private citizen of his city-state. Following the end of the feudal system, it stood for a private contract of military service, rather than forced service. It is a soldier with no title or rank, a "private soldier".

Corporal comes directly from the Italian "capo di squadra", squad (square) leader. Companies were formed into a defensive square at the head of which was a seasoned veteran called the "capo di squadra" or head of the square. Americans obtained the rank corporal from the French word "caporal".

Sergeant comes directly from the Latin "servire", meaning to serve. During the age of chivalry, serviens were warriors and men at arms who were superior in caste and skill to the common soldier, yet did not have the wealth to become a knight.

When General Washington formed the United States Army the lack of uniforms and insignia required an easy means for new soldiers to identify noncommissioned officers. A General order issued from Army Headquarters at Cambridge stated "Sergeants may be distinguished by an epaulet or stripe of red cloth, sewed upon the right shoulder; the Corporals by one of green."

By 1821, chevrons were adopted as rank insignia for both officers and noncommissioned officers after being introduced for West Point cadets in 1802. Chevron is a heraldry term used as a badge of honor for the main supporters of the clan head or "top of the house" and is seen in coats of arms as an emblem of rank for knights and men-at-arms since the 1100s. One legend is that the chevron was awarded to a knight to show he had taken part in capturing a castle, town or other building. Chevrons were an easily recognized symbol of honor thus resulted in their use as an insignia of grade and honor by the military. Americans picked up the use of chevrons from French soldiers who wore cloth chevrons with the points up on their coat sleeves in 1777 as length of service and good conduct badges.

By 1840s, the British were using chevrons with the points down as rank insignia for both officers and NCOs. Sergeants wore three and Corporals two white chevrons, Lieutenants wore one gold, while a general wore eight gold lace chevrons. Since 1832, only noncommissioned officers have worn chevrons with the exception of cadets at essential military schools such as The Citadel and West Point.

Sgt Major 1847

During the Civil War, many new NCO designations came into being. The new list included: Sergeant majors, quartermaster sergeants, commissary sergeants, leaders of bands, principal or chief musicians, chief buglers, medical cadets, ordnance sergeants, hospital stewards, regimental hospital stewards, battalion sergeant majors, battalion quartermaster sergeants, battalion hospital stewards, battalion saddler sergeants, battalion commissary

sergeants, battalion veterinary sergeants, first sergeants, company quartermaster sergeants, sergeants, corporals, buglers, musicians, farriers and blacksmiths, artificers, saddlers, master wagoners, wagoners, privates, and enlisted men of ordnance.

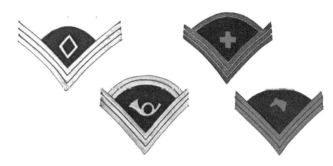

Chevrons were sewn point down on the uniform sleeves from about 1820 to 1905. In 1905 to assure uniformity, the Army ordered all points of the chevrons to be worn point up. It also provided for branch colors: Artillery - scarlet, Cavalry - yellow, Engineers - scarlet piped with orange, Hospital Corps - maroon piped with white; Infantry - light blue, Ordnance - black piped with scarlet, Post QM Sgt - buff and Signal Corps - orange piped with white. The designs and titles varied by branch and there were 45 different insignia descriptions with different colors for the various branches.

A wide variety of insignia was created in 1907. Specific pay grades were not yet in use by the Army and their pay rate was based on title. The pay scale approved in 1908 ranged from $13 for a private in the engineers to $75 for a master signal electrician. The system identified the job assignment of the individual, e.g. cooks, mechanics, etc. By the end of World War I, there were 128 different insignia designs in the supply system. Due to confusion, supply problems and an almost uncontrollable number of combination rank and skill insignia, the number of insignia was reduced to seven and six pay grades were established. Chevrons were worn on the left sleeve, point up. The designs and titles were :

	Master Sergeant (First Grade): Three chevrons with an arc of three bars.
	Technical Sergeant (Second Grade): Three chevrons, and an arc of two bars.
	First Sergeant (Second Grade): Three chevrons and an arc of two bars, with a lozenge (diamond) in the center. The lozenge or diamond, indicating a first sergeant is a mark of distinction and in heraldry, indicates achievement.
	Staff Sergeant (Third Grade): Three chevrons and an arc.
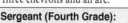	**Sergeant (Fourth Grade):** Three Chevrons.
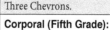	**Corporal (Fifth Grade):** Two Chevrons.
	Privates First Class (Sixth Grade): One Chevron

❖ Background and Development of Enlisted Ranks

In World War II, the grades of technician in the third, fourth and fifth grades were added in January 1942. A letter "T" was added just under the chevrons for grades three, four and five.

The first sergeant was designated first grade from the second grade in 1942, changing to three chevrons and arc of three bars, and a hollow lozenge in the center. This change also included the material as khaki chevrons, arcs, T's and lozenge on dark blue cotton background or olive-drab wool chevrons, arcs, T's and lozenge on a dark blue wool background.

In 1948, sergeant 4th grade was discontinued and recruit was added as the 7th grade. The new insignia was smaller and the colors changed with combat personnel wearing gold color background with dark blue chevrons, arcs and lozenges. Noncombatant personnel wore dark blue with gold color chevrons, arcs, and lozenge. Technicians were also deleted from the rank structure.

The size of the chevrons was changed from 2 inches wide to 3 1/8 inches wide for male personnel in 1951 and pay grades reversed with master sergeant becoming E7. The insignia continued to remain two inches wide for female personnel. The insignia was authorized to be manufactured in one color: a dark blue background with olive-drab chevrons, arcs, and lozenges.

In 1955, after the Korean War, new rank titles were authorized: Master Sergeant E-7 (1st Sgt. was an occupational title) & Master Specialist, Sergeant lst Class, Specialist lst Class E-6, Sergeant, Specialist 2d Class E5, Corporal, Specialist 3d Class E-4, Private First Class E-3, Private E2, E-2, Private El, E-1.

The rank insignia background color changed in 1956 to Army Green (the new uniform color) or Army Blue with the gold chevrons, arc, lozenge and eagle. The new specialists insignia had an embroidered eagle device on a two inch wide arched background with chevrons on top of the eagle:

The specialist insignia was part of an effort to differentiate between the Army's technical or support specialists who were not NCOs and the NCOs. Grades E-8 and E9 were added in June 1958. The specialist insignia was enlarged for males and remained the same size for female personnel. The new insignia were:

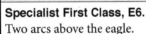

Master Specialist, E7.	
Three arcs above the eagle.	
Specialist First Class, E6.	
Two arcs above the eagle.	
Specialist Second Class, E-5.	
One arc above the eagle.	
Specialist Third Class, E4.	
Eagle device only.	

Sergeant Major, E9.
Three chevrons above three arcs with a five pointed star in the center.
Specialist Nine, E9.
Three arcs above the eagle and two chevrons below.
First Sergeant, E8.
Three chevrons above three arcs with a lozenge in the center.

For morale purposes, the old chevrons and titles for E5, E6 and E7 were authorized for wear until the individual was promoted or demoted.

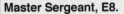

Master Sergeant, E8.
Three chevrons above three arcs.
Specialist Eight, E8.
Three arcs above the eagle and one chevron below.
Platoon Sergeant or Sergeant first class, E7.
Three chevrons above two arcs.
Specialist Seven, E7.
Three arcs above the eagle device.
Staff Sergeant, E6.
Three chevrons above one arc.
Specialist Six, E6.
Two arcs above the eagle device.
Sergeant, E5.
Three chevrons.
Specialist Five, E5.
One arc above the eagle device.
Corporal, E4.
Two chevrons.
Specialist Four, E4.
Eagle device only.
Private First Class.
One chevron.

Specialist Eight and Specialist Nine grades were discontinued in 1965. Subdued black metal insignia was authorized for wear on the collar of the work uniforms in 1967.

1968 saw the Command Sergeant Major insignia authorized, changing the large star in the center to a smaller star with a wreath around the star. The single chevron previously authorized for private first class, was authorized for private E2 while a new insignia of one chevron above and one arc below was authorized for private first class.

Shiny brass metal insignia was authorized for wear on the overcoat, raincoat and windbreaker in 1975. Specialist Seven was discontinued in 1978. A Sergeant Major of the Army insignia of three chevrons above three arcs with two stars centered was established in 1979. Shoulder marks for corporal and higher for wear on the green shirts and black sweater was approved in 1981.

The grades Specialist Five and Specialist Six were discontinued in October 1985. Sergeant Major of the Army insignia changed in 1994 adding the United States coat of arms between the two stars in the center. The male and female sizes of chevrons were changed to large and small insignia in 1996.

❖ US Army Enlisted Rank Insignia

Description	Rank	Current
Sergeant Major/E-9 (SGM): The senior NCO rank. Specialist E9 was dropped in 1965. Since 1968, the senior SGM for a Battalion or higher is designated as a Command Sergeant Major (CSM). Authorized in 1979, the Senior Noncommissioned officer in the Army is designated the Sergeant Major of the Army (SMA) and works directly for the Chief of Staff of the Army. The first rank insignia had two stars in the center.	**E-9**	SMA CSM SGM SP9
First Sergeant/E-8 (1SG): Senior Noncommissioned officer in charge of an entire Company, Battery or Troop. Works directly for the commander in the care and administration of the company soldiers. **Master Sergeant/E-8 (MSG):** Same pay grade as First Sergeant, but less responsibility. May be in charge of more than one platoon/section. Can be acting First Sergeant. Specialist E8 (SP8) was dropped in 1965.	**E-8**	1SG MSG SP8
Platoon Sergeant/Sergeant First Class/E-7(SFC): The first of the senior enlisted ranks, usually in charge of a platoon/section. Can be an acting First Sergeant. **Specialist E7** (SP7) was dropped in 1978.	**E-7**	SFC SP7
Staff Sergeant/E-6 (SSgt.): Given more responsibility than sergeant. Can be given charge of a platoon/section, or administrative duties. Must be technically proficient in his job, an expert. **Specialist E6** (SP6) was dropped in 1985.	**E-6**	SSG SP6
Sergeant/E-5 (Sgt.): Takes responsibility in day to day care of soldiers, training, and discipline. Normally serves three years before considered for promotion, but can be considered early with a waiver, or recommendation. Accrues points for promotion by going to college, taking correspondence courses, military schools, and awards and accommodations. Accrual of points begins at Private/E-1. **Specialist E5** (SP5) was dropped in 1985.	**E-5**	SGT SP5
Corporal/E-4 (CPL.): First Non-Commissioned Officer rank, has responsibility for lower enlisted. Can be put in charge of other enlisted men of lower rank. Must serve two years and go to Primary Leadership Development Course school to get this promotion. **Specialist/E-4 (Spc.):** Same pay grade as Corporal, but no command responsibility. Does not have to go to Primary Leadership Development Course school to get this promotion.	**E-4**	CPL SPC
Private first class/E-3 (PFC): Addressed as Private. E-2 can be promoted to E-3 after one year, earlier upon request by a supervisor.	**E-3**	PFC
Private/E-2 (Pvt2): Same name, but one pay grade up. E-1 is promoted to E-2 automatically after 1 year if there is no negative conduct. Insignia: 1 chevron on each collar of a shirt or uniform sleeve.	**E-2**	PVT

❖ US Army Enlisted Rank Insignia

SMA
Sgt. Major of
the Army

CSM
Cmd. Sgt.
Major

SGM
Sgt. Major

1SG
First Sgt.

MSG
Master Sgt.

SFC
Platoon Sgt./
Sgt. First Class

SSG
Staff Sgt.

SGT
Sergeant

CPL
Corporal

SPC
Specialist 4

PFC
Private First Class

PVT
Private

Overseas
Stripes

Reenlistment
Stripes

Metal Pin On Rank

Sew on CSM

 CSM   SGM   1SG   MSG   SFC   SSG   SGT   CPL   SPC PFC PVT

World War II Enlisted Rank

1st Sgt
1st Grade

Master Sgt
1st Grade

Technical Sgt
2nd Grade

Staff Sgt
3rd Grade

Tech 3rd
Grade

Sergeant
4th Grade

Tech 4th
Grade

Corporal
5th Grade

Tech 5th
Grade

Private 1st Class
6th Grade

Small 1950s Stripes

Vietnam Era Stripes

Tech 5th Grade

Specialist Five

Technical Sergeant
Second Grade WW2

Sergeant First Class
Platoon Sergeant 1950s

Sergeant First Class
Platoon Sergeant Current

SFC

Spec 6
Subdued

SFC Shoulder
Marks

From the time of the Revolution, the Army has been organized into traditional European branches of service such as Infantry, Artillery, Cavalry, Ordnance, Adjutant General, Medical, etc.

Since World War II, the Army branches have become identified in three groups - Combat Arms, Combat Support and Combat Service Support. There are several branches or detailed branches which technically do not fit in any of these categories but for the purpose of this book, they are considered Combat Service Support. There are currently 29 branches in the Army depending on how you count them.

The Combat Arms branches are: Infantry, Field Artillery, Air Defense Artillery, Armor, Aviation, Special Forces, and Corps of Engineers.

The Combat Support branches are: Signal Corps, Military Police, Chemical Corps, and Military Intelligence Corps.

The Combat Service Support branches are: Adjutant General Corps, Acquisition Corps, Chaplain Corps, Cyber, Finance Corps, Judge Advocate General's Corps, Logistics, Ordnance Corps, Psychological Operations, Quartermaster Corps, Transportation Corps, Medical Corps, Dental Corps, Veterinary Corps, Medical Service Corps, Army Nurse Corps, Army Medical Specialist Corps and Army Bands.

The Combat Arms are trained and responsible for actual combat against enemy forces. The Combat Support arms provide operational and technical support to the combat arms and must be prepared to engage in combat if necessary. The Combat Service Support forces main mission is to provide administrative and logistical support to the entire force. These branches normally are not expected to engage in combat but since many soldiers in these branches such as the Adjutant Generals Corps, Transportation Corps and Ordnance Corps plus others can be assigned to combat arms units, they must be trained in combat operations.

Additionally there are detailed special branches such as the General Staff and Inspector General to which select officers are assigned for periods of duty. The U.S. Army Reserve has two branches; Civil Affairs and Staff Specialist *(which folds into other branches upon mobilization).*

Also shown are the branches which have disappeared since World War II. These are: Coast Artillery *(consolidated with the Field Artillery)*, Military Intelligence, USAR and Army Security *(merged with MI in 1962)*, Bureau of Insular Affairs *(transferred in 1939)*, and Women Army Corps *(disestablished in 1978).*

Collar Insignia: A gold color metal device 1 inch in overall height consisting of the Alpha and Omega interlaced, superimposed by an eagle's head, all enclosed around the top with a gold tripartite scroll inscribed "INNOVATION" "EXCELLENCE" "DEDICATION" in incised letters; around the bottom entwined by the scroll ends are two laurel branches crossed at base all gold.

The Greek letters, "Alpha" and "Omega" are interlaced to indicate the intricate and continuous acquisition process. The eagle, our National symbol, represents vigilance and military preparedness. Gold is emblematic of excellence and high ideals. Laurel symbolizes honor and achievement.

Regimental Insignia: A gold color metal and black enameled device 1 1/8 inches consisting of a black disc bearing the Alpha and Omega interlaced between two laurel branches crossed with a sword superimposed on each entwined by a riband, an eagle's head. Attached across the bottom is a black scroll doubled and inscribed with "PACTUM EXCELLO" in gold.

Black and gold are the dominant colors of the U.S. Army Acquisition Corps emblem. The Greek "Alpha" and "Omega" are adapted from the organization's emblem and symbolize the intricate continuous acquisition process and mission.

Acquisition Corps ★

Collar Insignia   Regimental Insignia

The eagle, our National symbol, represents vigilance and military preparedness. Black alludes to dependability and solidarity, while gold signifies excellence and high ideals. Laurel symbolizes honor and high achievement and the swords represent protection, service and support to mission accomplishment. "Pactum Excello" is latin for "Contracting Excellence" and refers to acquisition soldiers performing contracting operations and functions in support of the soldier.

Background: The insignia was authorized on 8 January 2008. The collar insignia is worn by enlisted personnel only. The regimental insignia may be worn by soldiers awarded Military Occupational Specialty *(MOS)* 51C.

⭐ Adjutant General's Corps

| Old red, white and blue enamel Insignia | Branch Insignia Current | Enlisted Insignia | Branch Plaque | Regimental Insignia |

Branch Insignia: A silver metal and enamel shield 1 inch in height on which are thirteen vertical stripes, 7 silver and 6 red; on a blue chief 1 large and 12 small silver stars.

The basic design, the shield from the Coat of Arms of the United States, was adopted in 1872 as a solid shield of silver, bearing thirteen stars. In 1924, this design was authorized to be made in gold metal with the colors red, white, and blue in enamel. In December 1964, the insignia was changed to silver base metal with silver stars and silver and red enamel stripes.

Branch Plaque: The plaque design has the branch insignia in proper colors on a white background and the branch designation in silver letters. The rim is gold.

Regimental Insignia: A silver color metal and enamel device 1 1/8 inches in height consisting of a shield blazoned: Azure (*dark blue*) within a border Gules, an inescutcheon paly of thirteen Argent and Gules, on a chief Azure a mullet Argent between a pattern of twelve of the like (*as on The Adjutant General's insignia of branch*), and enclosed in base by two laurel branches. Attached above the shield a silver scroll inscribed with the numerals "1775" in red and attached below the shield a silver triparted scroll inscribed "DEFEND AND SERVE" in dark blue. The Regimental Insignia

was approved on 23 December 1986. Original design by Col. Frank Foster and SGM Eddie Bass.

Symbolism of Regimental Insignia: Dark blue and scarlet are branch colors of The Adjutant General's Corps. The inner white border signifies unity and the good conscience of those who have done their duty. The inner red, white and blue shield is the insignia of The Adjutant General's Corps and the gold laurel wreath around its base stands for excellence in accomplishing the mission. The "1775" in the crest is the year The Adjutant General's Corps was created. The color red symbolizes valor and the blood shed in our war for independence.

Branch Colors: Dark blue piped with Scarlet. Dark Blue - 65012 cloth; 67126 yarn; PMS 539. Scarlet - 65006 cloth; 67111 yarn; PMS 200.

The blue used in the branch insignia is ultramarine blue rather than the branch color.

Birthday: 16 June 1775. The post of Adjutant General was established 16 June 1775 and has been continuously in operation since that time. The Adjutant General's Department, by that name, was established by the act of 3 March 1813 and was redesignated The Adjutant General's Corps in 1950.

⭐ Air Defense Artillery

| Branch Insignia | Enlisted | Branch Plaque |

(Each ADA Regiment has its own regimental insignia and coat of arms)

Branch Insignia: A missile surmounting two crossed field guns, all of gold colored metal, 1 1/8 inches in height.

Crossed cannons (*field guns*) for Artillery has been in continuous use since 1834, when they were placed on regimental colors, knapsacks, and as part of the cap insignia for Artillery officers.

An Act of Congress, 2 February 1901, divided the Artillery arm into Coast and Field Artillery and the insignia was modified by the addition of a plain scarlet oval at the intersection of the crossed cannons. On 17 July 1902, the Coast Artillery insignia was created by the addition of a gold projectile on the red oval. Concurrently, the Field Artillery insignia was created by the addition of a gold wheel on the red oval; this insignia was replaced by two crossed field guns (*a lighter form of cannon*), the design of which was approved on 4 April 1907.

The Army Organization Act of 1950 consolidated Coast and

Field Artillery to form the Artillery Arm, and the crossed field guns were redesignated as the Artillery branch insignia on 19 December 1950. This insignia was superseded on 2 January 1957 by a new insignia consisting of crossed field guns surmounted by a missile, all gold.

On 20 June 1968, Air Defense Artillery was established as a basic branch of the Army and on 1 December 1968, the ADA branch was authorized to retain the former Artillery insignia, crossed field guns with missile.

Branch Plaque: The plaque design has the branch insignia, letters and border in gold. The background is scarlet.

Regimental Insignia: Personnel assigned to the Air Defense Artillery branch affiliate with a specific regiment and wear the insignia of the affiliated regiment.

Branch Colors: Scarlet. 65006 cloth; 67111 yarn; 200 PMS.

The uniform for the Corps of Artillery, which was formed in 1777, included red trimmings. The plume on the hat was also red. Except for a short period at the beginning of the 1800's when yellow was combined with it, scarlet has been the color of the Artillery throughout the history of the branch. Scarlet has been used by the Coast, Field, and Air Defense Artillery.

Birthday: 17 November 1775. The Continental Congress unanimously elected Henry Knox "Colonel of the Regiment of Artillery" on 17 November 1775. The regiment formally entered service on 1 January 1776. Although Field Artillery and Air Defense Artillery are separate branches, both inherit the traditions of the Artillery branch.

Branch Insignia: The front view of an M-26 tank, gun slightly raised, superimposed on two crossed cavalry sabers in scabbards, cutting edge up, 13/16 inch in height overall, of gold color metal.

The Armor insignia, approved in 1950, consists of the traditional crossed sabers (*originally adopted for the cavalry in 1851*) on which the M-26 tank is superimposed. The design symbolizes the traditional and current roles of armor.

Regimental Insignia: Personnel assigned to the Armor branch affiliate with a specific regiment and wear the insignia of the affiliated regiment.

Branch Colors: Yellow. 65002 cloth; 67108 yarn; 123 PMS.

In March 1855, two regiments of cavalry were created and their trimmings were to be of "yellow". In 1861, the designation of dragoon and mounted rifleman disappeared, all becoming Cavalry with "yellow" as their colors. Armor was assigned the colors green and white by circular 49 on 21 February 1947. When the Cavalry

Branch Insignia

Enlisted

branch was abolished, the present Armor was assigned the former Cavalry color yellow by SR 600-60-1 dated 26 October 1951.

Birthday: 12 December 1775. The Armor branch traces its origin to the Cavalry. A regiment of cavalry was authorized to be raised by the Continental Congress Resolve of 12 December 1775. Although mounted units were raised at various times after the Revolution, the first unit in continuous service was the United States Regiment of Dragoons, organized in 1833. The Tank Service was formed 5 March 1918. The Armored Force was formed on 10 July 1940 and became a permanent branch of the Army in 1950.

Armor and Tank *(Obsolete)*

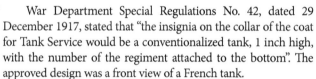 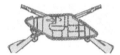 

War Department Special Regulations No. 42, dated 29 December 1917, stated that "the insignia on the collar of the coat for Tank Service would be a conventionalized tank, 1 inch high, with the number of the regiment attached to the bottom". The approved design was a front view of a French tank.

The insignia approved in 1917 was not well received and a new design was announced for the Tank Corps on 7 May 1918. The new design showed the side view of a Mark VIII Tank above two stylized dragons breathing fire over a wreath. War Department Circular 72, dated 16 Mar 1921, eliminated the insignia of the Tank Corps.

On 21 March 1922, The Adjutant General approved a new design for Infantry (*Tanks*). The 1922 change prescribed the insignia for Infantry (*Tanks*) to be "The Infantry insignia with tank superimposed. This insignia was rescinded on 22 August

1933. Change 15, AR 600-35, dated 13 March 1943, added the insignia for Tank Destroyer Forces. This change specified the design was a "75-mm gun, motor carriage M3, in gold color metal." The insignia was rescinded by Change 2, AR 600-35, dated 28 November 1944.

A new insignia for the Armored Forces was authorized by War Department Circular in 1942. This insignia was the side-view of the Mark VIII Tank used in World War I. The insignia was continued in use until the Armor Branch was established in February 1951. The new insignia was the result of the Army Reorganization Act of 1950 when the Armored Forces and Cavalry were combined into a single branch called Armor. The Armored Forces insignia was no longer used; however, the Cavalry was continued in use as a collar insignia for personnel assigned to Cavalry Units.

Branch colors: Green and white

Aviation *(Army Air Force became USAF in 1947)*

Army Air Force Branch Insignia

Army Air Force Enlisted Insignia

Branch Insignia

Enlisted Insignia

(Each Aviation Regiment has its own regimental insignia and coat of arms)

Branch Insignia: A silver propeller in a vertical position between two gold wings in a horizontal position, 1 1/8 inches in width.

The Army Aviation branch was established as a basic branch of the Army effective 12 April 1983. The wings are modified and

differ from the designs used for Army Air Force insignia of WW II. The insignia draws upon the original insignia for historical and symbolic purposes, but was deliberately modified to signify a new chapter in Army aviation history.

(continued on next page)

Regimental Insignia: Personnel assigned to the Aviation branch affiliate with a specific regiment and wear the insignia of the affiliated regiment.

Branch Colors: Ultramarine blue piped with Golden Orange. Ultramarine Blue - 65010 cloth; 67118 yarn; Reflex blue PMS. Golden Orange - 65003 cloth; 67109 yarn; PMS 1375.

The branch colors for aviation were approved with the branch insignia on 7 August 1983 by the Chief of Staff Army. These colors were used by the Army Air Corps during its existence.

Birthday: 12 April 1983. The Army first used light aircraft for artillery forward observation and reconnaissance in June 1942. Following the establishment of the US Air Force as a separate service in 1947, the Army began to further develop its own aviation assets *(light planes and rotary wing aircraft)* in support of ground operations. The Korean War gave this drive impetus, and the war in Vietnam saw its fruition, as Army aviation units performed a variety of missions, including reconnaissance, transport, and fire support. After the war in Vietnam, the role of armed helicopters as tank destroyers received new emphasis. In recognition of the grown importance of aviation in Army doctrine and operations, Aviation became a separate branch on 12 April 1983.

⭐ Army Security, USAR (Obsolete)

Officer   Enlisted

Army Intelligence and Security Branch
(See Military Intelligence on page 39.)

Branch Insignia: A gold colored lightning bolt superimposed by two double web keys, saltirewise, with wards up and out. The insignia was authorized on 1 February 1954 as a result of the Reserve Army Security Branch being created by General Order 110 dated 15 December 1952. The lightning bolt signifies communications and the crossed keys represent secrecy, authority, and guardianship.

Branch Colors: Teal blue and white. The Army Security branch USAR was merged with the newly established Army Intelligence and Security Branch on 1 July 1962. The branch was subsequently redesignated to the Military Intelligence Branch on 1 July 1967.

⭐ Army Band (Enlisted Only)

Enlisted

Branch Insignia: A lyre, on a one inch disk, all in gold color metal. Enlisted only. In 1950, Special Services *(including bands)* became a responsibility of The Adjutant General. On June 28, 1984, the Army established the Office of Chief, Army Bands at Fort Benjamin Harrison, Indiana. The Chief of Army Bands was relocated to Fort Jackson, SC in 2000. Commissioned and warrant officers serving in Army Bands wear Adjutant General Insignia.

Branch Colors: Old Glory Blue.

⭐ Cavalry

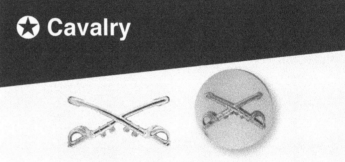

Collar Insignia   Enlisted

Collar Insignia: Two crossed sabers in scabbards, cutting edge up, 11/16 inch in height, of gold color metal.

The cavalry insignia was adopted in 1851. Today, officers and enlisted personnel assigned to cavalry regiments, cavalry squadrons or separate cavalry troops are authorized to wear the cavalry collar insignia in lieu of their insignia of branch when approved by the Major Army commander. Some of the armor and aviation units are designated cavalry units.

Regimental Insignia: Personnel assigned to cavalry units affiliate with a specific regiment of their branch or cavalry unit and wear the insignia of the affiliated regiment.

Regimental Coat of Arms: Each cavalry regiment has its own coat of arms that is displayed on the breast of a displayed eagle. The background of all cavalry flags is yellow.

Colors: Although cavalry is not a branch, yellow is used as a branch color for personnel assigned to cavalry units. In March 1855, two regiments of cavalry were created and their trimmings were to be "yellow." In 1861, the designation of dragoon and mounted rifleman disappeared, all becoming cavalry with "yellow" as their colors.

Yellow was continued as the color for cavalry units subsequent to abolishment as a branch. Although the regimental flags for cavalry units are yellow, the troop guidons are red and white without an insignia on the guidon.

Christian

Jewish

Buddhist

Muslim   Chaplain Canidate

Enlisted Chaplains Assistant

Branch Insignia: Christian Faith: A silver color Latin Cross, one inch in height. The insignia was adopted in 1898.

Jewish Faith: A double tablet bearing Hebrew characters from 1 to 10 surmounted by The Star of David, all of silver color, one inch in height. The insignia for chaplains of the Jewish faith was adopted in 1918 and had Roman numerals on the tablet *(page 112)*. The Roman numerals were changed to Hebrew characters on 9 November 1981.

Buddhist Faith: A silver color dharma chakra, one inch in height. The insignia was adopted in 1990.

Muslim Faith: A silver color crescent, one-inch in height. The insignia was approved on 8 January 1993.

Regimental Insignia: A gold color metal and enamel device 1-1/4 inches in height consisting of a shield, crest and motto blazoned: Azure (oriental blue) issuant in chief a demi-sun radiant to base or and in chief overall a dove, wings outstretched Argent, beak to base holding a sprig of olive Vert an open book of the second. Attached below the shield a blue scroll inscribed "PRO DEO ET PATRIA" in gold. The crest is blazoned: On a wreath of the colors Or and Azure *(oriental blue),* issuant in base a shepherd's crook between the numerals "17" and "75," all of the first in front of an expanse of the heavens Proper issuing to base rays of gold, all enclosed by two palm branches of the first.

The regimental insignia was approved on 4 June 1986 and revised on 11 February 1993 to add the motto on the book in lieu of the Christian and Jewish insignia.

Regimental Insignia

Regimental Coat of Arms: A coat of arms is not authorized for the Chaplain Corps. The regimental flag consists of the regimental insignia on a dark blue background with yellow fringe. Below the insignia is a yellow scroll doubled and inscribed "CHAPLAIN CORPS" in oriental blue.

Symbolism of Regimental Insignia: The sun and rays allude to the provision and presence of God in nature. The dove with olive branch, a traditional symbol of peace, embodies the Corps' mission in the Army to deter war and strive for peace. The pages of the open Bible represent the primacy of God's Word. The blue is representative of the heavens and alludes to the spiritual nature of the mission of the Chaplain Corps. The rays represent universal truth and the surrounding palm branches spiritual victory. The shepherd's crook is emblematic of pastoral ministry and was the first symbol used to identify Chaplains in the Army. The numerals "1775" commemorate the date of the establishment of the Army Chaplain Corps. The motto "PRO DEO ET PATRIA" translates FOR GOD AND COUNTRY.

Branch Colors: Black - cloth 65018; yarn 67138, PMS Black. Chaplains have used black since 1835. In regulations dated that year, a black coat was prescribed for Chaplains.

Birthday: 29 July 1775.

⭐ Chemical Corps

Branch Insignia

Enlisted Insignia

Regimental Insignia

Regimental Coat of Arms

Branch Insignia: A benzene ring of cobalt blue enamel superimposed in the center of crossed gold color retorts, 1/2 inch in height and 1-13/16 inches in width overall. The insignia (in bronze metal) was originally adopted in 1917 for the Chemical Service. In 1921, this insignia was approved for the Chemical Warfare Service. In 1924, the ring was changed to cobalt blue enamel. The benzene ring is the starting point for the method of indicating diagrammatically a molecular composition of the composition of the chemical combination. It has six points, one for each atom of carbon and hydrogen since the formula for benzene is C_6H_6. The retort is the basic container other than the test tube, for laboratory experiments.

Regimental Insignia: The Chemical Corps regimental insignia was approved on 2 May 1986. The insignia consists of a 1.2 inch shield of gold and blue emblazoned with a dragon and a tree. The shield is enclosed by a blue ribbon with Elementis Regamus Proelium in gold lettering.which translates to: "Let us (or may we) rule the battle by means of the elements". Gold and blue, are the colors of the Chemical Corps, while the tree's trunk is battle scarred, a reference to the, battered tree trunks that were often the only reference points that chemical mortar teams had across no man's land during World War I. The mythical chlorine breathing green dragon symbolizes the first use of chemical weapons in warfare *(chlorine).*

Birthday: 28 June 1918.

Branch Insignia   Enlisted Insignia

Branch Insignia: On a globe 5/8 inch in diameter, a torch of liberty 1 inch in height surmounted by a scroll and a sword crossed in saltire, all of gold color.

In 1955, The Civil Affairs and Military Government Branch, USAR, was established. On 30 April 1956, the Office of Civil Affairs and Military Government gave concurrence in the design (gold global background with gold torch, sword and scroll superimposed thereon). The Department of the Army General Staff approved the design on 1 June 1956. The branch was redesignated to Civil Affairs USAR on 2 October 1959. The globe indicates the worldwide areas of Civil Affairs operations. The torch is from the Statue of Liberty, a symbol associated with the spirit of the United States. It also represents the enlightened performance of duty. The scroll and sword depict the civil and military aspects of the organization's mission. The insignia was authorized for wear by all personnel assigned to Regular Army Civil Affairs TOE units on 13 October 1961.

Regimental Insignia: A silver and gold color metal and enamel device 1 3/16 inches in height consisting of a shield, crest and motto. The insignia is blazoned as follows: Purpure, a scroll and sword saltirewise and overall a torch palewise or; a bordure argent. Attached below the shield, a silver scroll inscribed "SECURE THE VICTORY" in black letters. The crest above the shield: On a wreath of the colors (Or and Purpure), a globe Celeste grid lined Argent superimposed by a dexter gauntlet argent holding a balance scale Or. The Regimental Insignia was approved on 14 April 1989.

Regimental Coat of Arms: The coat of arms appears on the breast of a displayed eagle on the regimental flag. The coat of arms is: Purpure, a scroll and sword saltirewise, and overall a torch palewise Or; a bordure Argent. Crest: On a wreath of the colors (Or and Purpure) a globe Celeste grid lined Argent superimposed by a dexter gauntlet Proper holding a balance scale Or. The regimental flag has a purple background and white fringe.

Symbolism of Regimental Insignia: Purple and white are the colors traditionally associated with Civil Affairs. Gold is emblematic of honor and achievement. The scroll, sword and torch are adapted from the Civil Affairs branch insignia and denote the branch-wide scope and application of the design. The scroll and sword depict the civil and military aspects of the organization. The torch refers to the Statue of Liberty, a symbol associated with the spirit of democracy of the United States. The border emphasizes unity, continuity and the whole regimental concept. Crest: The scales represent balance and normality; the gauntlet denotes the military's role in establishing, administering and protecting the equilibrium. The globe signifies the extensive scope of the mission of the Civil Affairs Regiment.

Branch Colors: Purple piped with white. Purple - 65009 cloth; 67115 yarn; PMS 267. White - 65005 cloth; 67101 yarn; PMS white. The colors were approved for civil affairs units in June 1956.

Birthday: 17 August 1955.

⭐ Coast Artillery *(Obsolete)*

Branch Insignia   Enlisted   Army Mine Planter Service

Branch Insignia: Two crossed field guns, gold colored metal, with a scarlet oval with a gold projectile at the intersection of the field guns, thirteen-sixteenths of an inch in height overall.

Crossed cannons *(field guns)* for Artillery have been in continuous use since 1834, when they were placed on regimental colors, knapsacks, and as part of the cap insignia for Artillery officers. In 1901, the Artillery was divided into Coast and Field Artillery and the branch insignia was modified by the addition of a plain scarlet oval at the intersection of the cannons. The Field Artillery insignia approved on 17 July 1902 had a gold wheel on the red oval and the Coast Artillery had a gold projectile on the red oval. The Army Mine Planter Service was authorized to wear this insignia with a mine case below the insignia by War Department Circular 25, dated 17 January 1920. The Army Reorganization Act of 1950 consolidated the Coast and Field Artillery to form the Artillery Arm and the crossed cannons were designated its insignia on 19 December 1950.

Branch Colors: Scarlet

Branch Insignia

Enlisted Insignia

Branch Insignia: A gold color triple turreted castle eleven-sixteenth inch in height.

The triple turreted castle has been in use by the Corps of Engineers since it was adopted in 1840. Prior to that time a similar insignia was worn on the uniforms of the United States Military Academy Cadets since they were under the direction of the Chief of Engineers. Selection of the turreted castle as the Engineer insignia followed the first major construction undertaken by the Corps of Engineers - the building of a system of castle-like fortifications for the protection of Atlantic Coast harbors. These fortifications, many of which are still standing, were in fact called "castles". By 1924, the insignia had evolved into its current design and gold color.

Regimental Insignia: A silver color metal and enamel device 1 1/16 inches in height consisting of a scarlet shield with silver border and gold castle at center and attached below a scarlet scroll inscribed "ESSAYONS" (*Let Us Try*) in silver. The regimental insignia was approved on 11 April 1986.

Regimental Coat of Arms: The coat of arms appears on the breast of a displayed eagle on the regimental flag. The coat of arms is: Gules, within a diminished bordure Argent a castle affronte, Or. The background of the flag is scarlet and the fringe is white. The motto "ESSAYONS" is on the scroll at the eagle's beak and the scroll below the eagle has the designation "CORPS OF ENGINEERS".

Symbolism of Regimental Insignia: Scarlet and white are the colors of the Corps of Engineers. The castle and the motto "ESSAYONS" traditionally have been associated with the Corps.

Branch Colors: Scarlet piped with white. Scarlet - 65006 cloth; 67111 yarn; PMS 200. White - 65005 cloth; 67101 yarn; PMS white.

Scarlet and white were established as the Corps of Engineers colors in 1872. Before that date, several other colors had been associated with the Engineers.

Birthday: 16 June 1775. Continental Congress authority for a "Chief of Engineer for the Army" dates from 16 June 1775. A Corps of Engineers for the United States was authorized by the Congress on 11 March 1779. The Corps of Engineers, as it is known today, came into being on 16 March 1802, when the President was authorized to "organize and establish a Corps of Engineers... that the said Corps...shall be stationed at West Point in the State of New York and shall constitute a Military Academy." A Corps of Topographical Engineers, authorized on 4 July 1838, was merged with the Corps of Engineers on 3 March 1963.

The Cyber Branch is the newest branch of the United States Army.

Cyber Warfare

Branch Insignia: Cyber branch insignia has crossed lightning bolts over a vertical sword. It is a maneuver branch with the mission to conduct defensive and offensive cyberspace operations. It is the only branch designed to directly engage threats within the cyberspace domain.

Regimental Insignia: A silver and black color metal and enamel device 1 1/16 inches in height consisting of a shield with silver border and gold sword at center and attached below a scarlet scroll inscribed "Defend, Attack, Exploit. Authorized on 1 December 2015 and amended five months later to reflect a new motto, the Cyber Corps RDI features a shield quartered into black and white sections which reflect the strategic capabilities of the electronic warfare aspects of the Regiment. An upright gold dagger symbolizes the Corps' preparedness and readiness to prevent cyber attacks, intrusions, and disruptions anywhere on the globe and the shield's gray border denotes the Cyber Regiment's

Branch Insignia

Enlisted Insignia

ability to contain cyber-attacks that may threaten to escalate and threaten the U.S. or other nations.

Branch Colors: Steel Gray with Black Piping.

Birthday: It was established on 1 September 2014 by then-Secretary of the Army, John McHugh

Branch Insignia

Enlisted Insignia

Branch Insignia: The Electronic Warfare insignia is designated for noncommissioned officers and warrant officers but not for EW officers *(29A)* as they are in a Functional Area and continue to wear their basic branch insignia. The EW colors are U.S. Army Golden Yellow and Black. Golden Yellow signifies the need to maintain control of an asset of inestimable value, the electromagnetic spectrum. Black represents the mission to blind and confuse enemies; it is also the color of the raven, alluding to the first EW personnel who served during World War II and were referred to as "Ravens."

The collar insignia consist of a shield, a key, and a lightning bolt. The shield symbolizes the need to protect the ability to operate within the EMS. The key symbolizes the importance of accessing adversary and safekeeping friendly capabilities and information. The lightning bolt represents the intent to rapidly, decisively, and precisely strike at adversaries.

The US Army's new Cyber Branch as of 2018 was divided between Cyber Operations *(Military Occupational Specialties 17A, 170A, 17C)* and Electronic Warfare *(MOS 17B, 170B, 17E)*.

★ Field Artillery

Branch Insignia

Enlisted

(Each Field Artillery Regiment has its own regimental insignia and coat of arms)

Branch Insignia: Two crossed field guns, gold color metal, thirteen-sixteenth inch in height.

Crossed cannons *(field guns)* for Artillery have been in continuous use since 1834 when they were placed on regimental colors, knapsacks, and as part of the cap insignia for Artillery officers. In 1901, the Artillery was divided into Coast and Field Artillery and the branch insignia was modified by the addition of a plain scarlet oval at the intersection of the cannons. The Field Artillery insignia approved on 17 July 1902 had a gold wheel on the red oval and the Coast Artillery had a gold projectile on the red oval. This red oval and wheel was replaced on 4 April 1907 by two field guns. It was superseded in 1957 by the consolidated Artillery insignia consisting of the crossed field guns surmounted by a missile. In 1968, when the Air Defense Artillery and the Field Artillery were authorized to have separate insignia, the former Field Artillery insignia was reinstated.

Regimental Insignia: Personnel assigned to the Field Artillery branch affiliate with a specific regiment and wear the insignia of the affiliated regiment.

Regimental Coat of Arms: There is no standard Field Artillery regimental flag to represent all of the Field Artillery regiments. Each regiment of Field Artillery has its own coat of arms that appears on the breast of a displayed eagle. The background of all the Field Artillery regimental flags is scarlet with yellow fringe.

Branch Colors: Scarlet - 65006 cloth; 67111 yarn; PMS 200.

The uniform for the Corps of Artillery, which was formed in 1777, included red trimmings. The plume on the hat was also red. Except for a short period at the beginning of the 1800's when yellow was combined with it, scarlet has been the color of the Artillery throughout the history of the branch. Scarlet has been used by the Coast Artillery, Air Defense Artillery and Field Artillery.

Birthday: 17 November 1775. The Continental Congress unanimously elected Henry Knox "Colonel of the Regiment of Artillery" on 17 November 1775. The regiment formally entered service on 1 January 1776. Although Field Artillery and Air Defense Artillery are separate branches, both inherit the traditions of the Artillery branch.

Branch Insignia: A gold color diamond, 1 inch by 3/4 inch, short axis vertical. In 1896, the diamond design (*embroidered in silver or made of silver metal*) was approved as the insignia of the Pay Department. **Branch Plaque:** The plaque design has the branch insignia, letters, and rim in gold. The background is silver gray.

Regimental Insignia: A gold color metal and enamel device 1 1/8 inch in height consisting of the shield adapted from the coat of arms and blazoned: Argent (*Silver Gray*), a globe Azure grid

lined Or, overall in saltire a sword with point to sinister base Argent hilted Or and a quill Argent, superimposed at fess point a representation of the Finance Corps branch insignia Proper. Attached below a gold scroll inscribed with the words "TO SUPPORT AND SERVE" in blue letters. The insignia was originally approved on 8 September 1986 but the design was changed on 1 June 1988 to change the diamond from yellow enamel to a separate device in gold.

Symbolism of Regimental Insignia: Silver gray and golden yellow are the colors associated with the Finance Corps and are universally symbolic of the treasury and monetary matters. The globe denotes the worldwide scope of the Corps' mission. The

Branch Insignia

Enlisted Insignia

sword and quill represent the Corps' combat service support role. The diamond shape symbolizes the public monies entrusted to the Corps. The motto "TO SUPPORT AND SERVE" refers to the Corps' mission. The gold gryphon in the crest represents treasure or money and in Greek mythology is the guardian of gold and treasure, thus symbolizing the vigilance of the Finance Corps in safeguarding the public funds entrusted to it.

Branch Colors: Silver gray piped with golden yellow. Silver gray - 65008 cloth; 67137 yarn; PMS 422. Golden Yellow - 65001 cloth; 67104 yarn; PMS 116. Silver gray piped with golden yellow was prescribed for the Finance Corps in 1920.

Birthday: 16 June 1775. The Finance Corps is the successor to the old Pay Department, which was created in June 1775. The Finance Department was created by law on 1 July 1920 and became the Finance Corps in 1950.

Branch Insignia: The coat of arms of the United States, 5/8 inch in height, of gold color metal superimposed on a five-pointed silver color star, 1 inch in circumscribing diameter. The shield to be in enamel stripes of white and red, chief of blue and the glory blue.

The Chief of Staff of the Army, approved the design of the General Staff insignia to take effect 1 July 1904. The device has been in continual use since that date. The insignia was originally worn only by officers, in the grade of captain and above, detailed to the General Staff Corps. Authority for its wear was later extended to officers detailed to General Staff Corps with troops.

General Staff Detail ⭐

When the Department of the Army became the legal successor to the War Department, the word "Corps" in the title of branch officers detailed to the General Staff Corps was dropped. The device is now worn by officers detailed in orders to the Army General Staff and to General Staff with troops.

The star is symbolic of the highest level in the Army and the Arms of the United States allude to the mission of the General Staff which is to exercise General Staff supervision over the management of the land forces of the United States.

Branch Colors: No color assigned.

Immaterial and Command Sergeant Major ⭐

Sgt. Major of the JCS

Branch Immaterial Device

Sgt. Major of the Army

Collar Insignia: The Coat of Arms of the United States on a 1 inch disk, all gold color metal.

The Coat of Arms was first authorized for wear as a collar insignia by officers not assigned to a branch in March 1918. It was authorized for wear and designated as the insignia for the Detached Enlisted Men's in March 1921. The insignia was discontinued as an officer collar insignia in 1948. The name

was changed to "Unassigned to Branch" for enlisted personnel in April 1953. The name was changed to Branch Immaterial in 1976 and Command Sergeants Major were the only enlisted personnel to wear the insignia. The collar insignia changed to "Command Sergeant Major" in September 1992.

The Sergeant Major of the Army is authorized a special collar insignia which incorporates the shield of the Chief of Staff of the Army. The Sergeant Major to the Chairman of the Joints Chiefs is authorized a special collar insignia which incorporates the shield of the Chairman of the Joints Chiefs.

Branch Immaterial Flag Device: The device is used as the insignia for guidons and flags of organizations that are not branch specific. When used on the flag of branch immaterial units, the device is teal blue and yellow.

Branch Immaterial Colors: Teal blue and yellow.

★ Infantry

Branch Insignia

Enlisted Insignia

Infantry with blue backing disk

(Each Infantry Regiment has its own regimental insignia and coat of arms)

Infantry has been the "Queen of Battle" since the days of the Romans. The first Infantry insignia used in the American Army was a brass hunting horn designated for Rifle Regiments.

Branch Insignia: Two gold color crossed vintage 1795 Springfield muskets, 3/4 inch in height.

Crossed muskets were first introduced into the Army as the insignia of officers and enlisted men of the Infantry on 19 November 1875 to take effect 1 June 1876. Numerous attempts in the earlier years were made to keep the insignia current with the ever changing styles of rifles being introduced into the Army. However, in 1924 the branch insignia was standardized by the adoption of crossed 1795 model Springfield Arsenal muskets. This was the first official United States shoulder arm made in a government arsenal with interchangeable parts, caliber .69, flint lock, smooth bore, muzzle loader. The standardized musket insignia now in use was first suggested by Major General Charles S. Farnsworth, U.S. Army, while Chief of Infantry and approved by General Pershing, Chief of Staff in 1922. The device adopted in 1922 has been in continual use since 1924. There

have been slight modifications in the size of the insignia over the years; however, the basic design has remained unchanged.

Regimental Insignia: Personnel assigned to the Infantry branch affiliate with a specific regiment and wear the insignia of the affiliated regiment.

Regimental Coat of Arms: There is no standard infantry regimental flag to represent all of the infantry regiments. Each regiment of infantry has its own coat of arms which appears on the breast of a displayed eagle. The background of all the infantry regimental flags is flag blue with yellow fringe.

Branch Colors: Light blue - 65014 cloth; 67120 yarn; PMS 5415. The infantry color is light blue; however, infantry regimental flags and guidons have been National Flag blue since 1835. White is used as a secondary color on the guidons for letters, numbers and insignia.

Birthday: 14 June 1775. The Infantry is the oldest branch in the Army. Ten companies of riflemen were authorized by the Continental Congress Resolve of 14 June 1775. However, the oldest Regular Army Infantry Regiment, the 3d Infantry, was constituted on 3 June 1784 as the First American Regiment.

★ Inspector General

Branch Insignia

Enlisted Insignia

Branch Insignia: A sword and fasces 3/4 inch in height, crossed and wreathed in gold color metal with the inscription "DROIT ET AVANT" *(Right and Forward)* in blue enamel on the upper part of the wreath.

On 26 February 1890, the Inspector General's insignia

was approved by the Secretary of War. It consists of a crossed sword and fasces with wreath. The fasces, composed of an axe in a bundle of rods, was a symbol of authority of Roman magistrates.

Branch Colors: Dark Blue piped with light blue. Dark blue - 65012 cloth; 67126 yarn; PMS 539; Light blue - 65014 cloth; 67120 yarn; PMS 5415

The Inspector General's Department in 1851 had pompons of buff with upper one third in scarlet. In 1915, specifications established the facings as dark blue. The 14 October 1921 regulation established the colors as dark blue piped with white. Circular #70, dated 18 October 1936, announced the exchange of colors with the Judge Advocate General's Department that resulted in the present colors.

★ Bureau of Insular Affairs *(Obsolete)*

Branch Insignia: A bunch of seven arrows, points up, superimposed on a pair of wings, all gold.

The Division of Customs and Insular Affairs was organized on 13 December 1898. This Division was responsible for the administration of U.S. possessions and islands under military occupation. The War Department managed some

of the possessions and the State Department managed some of the affairs.

In 1902, the Bureau was established with the War Department responsible for all of the possessions. The insignia was authorized on 31 December 1902 in General Regulations and amended by General Orders No. 132 on the same date. The Bureau was transferred from the War Department to the Department of Interior in 1939.

Branch Colors: Dark Blue

Branch Insignia

Enlisted Insignia

Branch Insignia: A gold color sword and pen crossed and superimposed on a laurel wreath 11/16 inches in height.

In May 1890, "a sword and pen crossed and wreathed embroidered in silver" was originally adopted for wear by officers of the Judge Advocate General's Department. In 1899, the color was changed to gold. The pen represents the recording of testimony and the sword symbolizes the military character of the Corps. The wreath is symbolic of honor. The enlisted branch of service insignia was authorized on 4 August 1967.

Regimental Insignia. A silver color metal and enamel device 1 1/8 inches in height consisting of a shield blazoned as follows: Argent, an escutcheon Azure *(dark blue)* charged with a wreath of laurel surmounted by a sword point to base in bend surmounted by a quill in bend sinister all gold. Attached below the shield is a dark blue scroll doubled and inscribed with the numerals "1775" in silver. The regimental insignia for the Judge Advocate General's Corps was approved 22 August 1986.

Regimental Coat of Arms: The coat of arms appears on the breast of a displayed eagle on the regimental flag. The coat of arms is: Azure *(dark blue),* a wreath of laurel surmounted by a quill in bend sinister all gold. Attached below the shield is a dark blue scroll doubled and inscribed with the numerals "1775" in silver.

Symbolism of the Regimental Insignia: The quill and sword symbolize the mission of the Corps, to advise the Secretary of the Army and supervise the system of military justice throughout the Army. Dark blue and silver *(white)* are the colors associated with the Corps. Gold is for excellence. The motto indicates the anniversary of the Corps.

Branch colors: Dark blue piped with white. Dark blue - 65012 cloth; 67126 yarn; PMS 539.

Birthday: 29 July 1775. The Office of Judge Advocate of the Army is deemed to have been created on 29 July 1775.

Branch Insignia: A diagonally crossed cannon, muzzle up and key, ward down and pointing in, surmounted by a ship's steering wheel, all in gold colored metal; bearing on the hub a stylized star and inscribed on the ship's wheel in Latin, above "SUSTINENDUM" and below "VICTORIAM" all in soldier red. Overall dimension is 1 inch in height.

Soldier red is the Logistics branch color. The logistics mission of planning, integrating and executing sustainment activities is represented by elements from the Quartermaster (key) and Transportation *(ship's wheel)* branch insignia, Ordnance regimental insignia (cannon) and Combined Arms Support Command distinctive unit insignia *(stylized star).* The key represents the Quartermaster Corps' mission to provide supplies and services; the ship's wheel denotes the Transportation Corps' responsibilities for the movement of troops, supplies and equipment; the cannon represents the Ordnance Corps' responsibilities of maintenance and munitions; the stylized star represents the unity and integration of logistics functions. The motto translates to "Sustaining Victory."

Regimental Insignia: There is no regimental insignia for Logistics. Officers wear the regimental insignia of their assigned functional area of expertise *(secondary specialty)* within the Logistics branch of Transportation, Ordnance or Quartermaster.

Flag and Guidons: There are no logistic units and accordingly, there are no flags or guidons.

Branch Insignia

Branch Colors: Soldier Red piped with bronze. Soldier Red - 80095 cloth; 67157 yarn; PMS 209. Bronze - 80111 cloth; 67147 yarn; PMS 874.

Birthday: 1 January 2008. Department of the Army General Orders No. 6, dated 27 November 2007, established Logistics as a basic branch of the Army effective 1 January 2008. This changed the functional area 90 *(multifunctional logistician)* program into a branch of the Army. All Ordnance, Quartermaster and Transportation Corps basic branch officers of all components *(Active, Reserve and National Guard),* in the rank of Captain or above, who have graduated from the Combined Logistics Captains Career Course *(or its earlier equivalent called the Combined Logistics Officer Advanced Course)* or any Ordnance, Quartermaster or Transportation Corps Reserve Component Captains Career Course now wear the Logistics branch insignia.

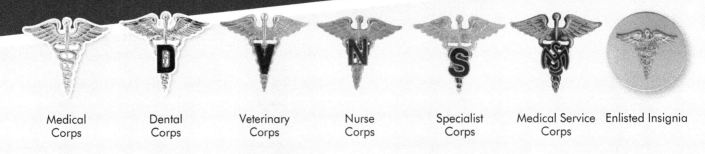

| Medical Corps | Dental Corps | Veterinary Corps | Nurse Corps | Specialist Corps | Medical Service Corps | Enlisted Insignia |

Army Medical Department (Rescinded)

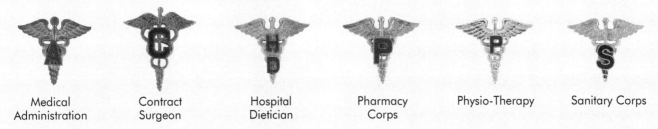

| Medical Administration | Contract Surgeon | Hospital Dietician | Pharmacy Corps | Physio-Therapy | Sanitary Corps |

Branch Insignia: A gold color medal caduceus, 1 inch in height. *(With the exception of the basic Medical Corps, each Corps is identified by black enamel letters centered on the caduceus indicative of their Corps.)* The insignia for Medical Service Corps is silver.

In 1851, "a caduceus embroidered in yellow silk on a half chevron of emerald green silk" was worn by Hospital Stewards of the Medical Department. The caduceus in its present form was approved in 1902. Rooted in mythology, the caduceus, historically an emblem of physicians, symbolizes knowledge, wisdom, promptness and various aspects of medical skill.

Regimental Insignia: A silver color metal and enamel device 1 inch in height overall consisting of a shield blazoned as follows: Per pale: to dexter, paly of thirteen Gules and Argent, on a chief Azure 20 mullets in four rows of five each of the Second; to sinister, Argent, a staff entwined with a serpent Vert; attached below the shield a blue scroll inscribed "TO CONSERVE FIGHTING STRENGTH" in silver. The insignia was originally approved on 17 April 1986 but the size was changed from 1 1/4 inch to 1 inch on 28 August 1986.

Regimental Coat of Arms: The coat of arms is displayed on the breast of a displayed eagle on the regimental flag. The coat of arms is: Per pale: to dexter, paly of thirteen Gules and Argent, on a chief Azure twenty mullets in four rows of five each of the second; to sinister, Argent, a staff entwined with a serpent Vert. The crest *(On a wreath of the colors Argent and Gules, a cross below an arc of seven mullets all within a wreath of laurel, all Argent)* is displayed above the eagle's head. The flag is maroon and the fringe is white. The coat of arms was approved on 17 April 1986.

 **Symbolism of Regimental Insignia:** The design of the shield is based on the shield of a historical heraldic device probably first used in 1818 by the Army Medical Department. The white stars on a blue background and the red and white stripes represents the United States flag of 1818. The green staff entwined with the serpent, originating in mythology, is symbolic of medicine and healing. Green was the color associated with the Corps during the last half of the nineteenth century. Symbology of the crest of the coat of arms: The colors Argent and Gules are those associated with the Army Medical Department. The cross and the wreath are adapted from devices authorized for hospital stewards and other enlisted men when the Hospital Corps was established in 1887. The seven stars emphasize the elements of the organization: Medical Corps, Army Nurse Corps, Dental Corps, Veterinary Corps, Medical Service Corps, Army Specialist Corps and the Enlisted Medical Specialist. The motto "TO CONSERVE FIGHTING STRENGTH" reflects the medical mission.

Branch Colors: Maroon piped with white. Maroon-65017 cloth; 67114 yarn; PMS 504.

Green was prescribed as the first Medical Department color in 1847 when the sash for Medical Officers was described. The green was established in the insignia of the Hospital Stewards uniform on 31 October 1851 and in 1857 the green was piped with yellow and the pompon was topped with medium or emerald green. Later the pompom was green piped with white until 1902 when the maroon color was adopted. In 1903 the Hospital Corps chevrons were maroon piped with white. Maroon and white were established for all branches of the Medical Department by the uniform specifications dated October 1916.

Birthday: 27 July 1775. Army Medical Department and the Medical Corps trace their origins to 27 July 1775, when the Continental Congress established the Army hospital headed by a "Director General and Chief Physician." The Army Nurse Corps dates from 1901, the Dental Corps from 1911, the Veterinary Corps from 1916, the Medical Service Corps from 1917 and the Army Medical Specialist Corps from 1947. The Army Organization Act of 1950 renamed the Medical Department as the Army Medical Service. On 4 June 1968, the Army Medical Service was redesignated the Army Medical Department.

Branch Insignia

Enlisted Insignia

Regimental Coat of Arms

Branch Insignia: On a gold color metal dagger, point up, 1 1/4 inches overall in height, a gold color metal heraldic sun composed of four straight and four wavy alternating rays surmounted by a gold heraldic rose, the petals dark blue enamel.

The insignia was originally approved in 1962 for the Army Intelligence and Security Branch and redesignated to the Military Intelligence Branch on 1 July 1967. The sun, composed of four straight and four wavy alternating rays, is the symbol of Helios who, as God of the Sun, could see and hear everything. The four straight rays of the sun symbol also allude to the four points of the compass and the worldwide mission of the Military Intelligence Branch. The placement of the sun symbol beneath the rose *(an ancient symbol of secrecy)* refers to the operations and activities being conducted under circumstances forbidding disclosure. The partially concealed unsheathed dagger alludes to the aggressive and protective requirements and the element of physical danger inherent in the mission. The color gold signifies successful accomplishment and the dark blue signifies vigilance and loyalty.

Regimental Insignia: A gold color metal and enamel device 1 1/8 inches in height overall consisting of a shield blazoned as follows: Azure *(oriental blue)* a lightning flash and a key, ward up, saltirewise, superimposed by a sphinx Or; attached below the shield a gold scroll inscribed "ALWAYS OUT FRONT" in black letters. The regimental insignia was originally approved on 28 July 1986 but was revised on 24 March 1987 to change the sphinx from enamel to recessed and gold plated.

Regimental Coat of Arms: The coat of arms appears on the breast of a displayed eagle on the regimental flag. The coat of arms is: Azure *(oriental blue)*, a key bendwise sinister in saltire with a lightning flash Argent, in fess point overall a sphinx Or. Displayed above the eagle's head is the Crest. On a wreath of the colors Argent and Azure *(oriental blue)* a torch Or enflamed Proper in front of two swords in saltire with hilts gold and blades of the first. The background of the flag is oriental blue and the fringe is silver gray.

Symbolism of Regimental Insignia: Oriental blue and silver gray are the colors associated with the Military Intelligence Corps. The key, flash and sphinx symbolize the three basic categories of intelligence: human, signal, and tactical. The flaming torch between the crossed swords of the crest suggests the illumination as provided by Intelligence upon the field of battle. The motto "ALWAYS OUT FRONT" reflects the forward location in gathering intelligence information.

Branch Colors: Oriental blue piped with silver gray. Oriental blue - 80176 cloth; 67172 yarn; PMS 285. Silver gray - 65008 cloth; 67137 yarn; PMS 422.

Birthday: 1 July 1962. Historically, intelligence always has been an essential element of Army operations during war as well as during so-called periods of peace. In the past, requirements were met by personnel from the Army Intelligence and Army Security Reserve branches. To meet the Army's increased requirements for national and tactical intelligence, an Intelligence and Security Branch was established in the Army effective 1 July 1962 by GO 38, 3 July 1962. On 1 July 1967, the branch was redesignated as Military Intelligence.

Military Intelligence, USAR *(Obsolete)* ⭐

Branch Insignia: A gold colored eared shield bearing a circle connected with the border by 13 radial ribs, within the circle a sphinx in profile couchant.

The insignia was authorized on 30 July 1923. The thirteen stripes on the shield converge toward a common point at the center where sits the sphinx, the symbol of wisdom and strength, thus symbolizing the collection of information by the Military Intelligence; and conversely from the center after evaluation, the military information is disseminated.

The Military Intelligence Branch, USAR, was merged

Officer

Enlisted

with the newly established Army Intelligence and Security Branch on 1 July 1962 and the insignia was cancelled.

Branch Color: Golden yellow and purple.

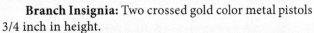

Branch Insignia   Enlisted Insignia

Branch Insignia: Two crossed gold color metal pistols 3/4 inch in height.

The insignia was approved in 1922. The old type pistol sometimes referred to as the Harper's Ferry Pistol *(made at the Harper's Ferry Arsenal)*, was selected since it is the first American Military pistol and remained the Army model for many years. The parts of this weapon were standardized and interchangeable, thereby marking an advance in arms.

Regimental Insignia: A gold color metal and enamel device 1 3/16 inches in height consisting of a shield blazoned as follows: Vert, a fasces palewise, axe Or and rods Proper *(brown)*, therefore in fess a balance and in saltire overall a key with bow in sinister base and a sword with hilt in dexter base all of the second. The shield is enclosed at bottom and sides by a gold scroll of three folds inscribed "ASSIST PROTECT DEFEND" in green letters and surmounted at the top by two crossed gold pistols. The regimental insignia was approved on 3 July 1986.

Regimental Coat of Arms: The coat of arms appears on the breast of a displayed eagle on the regimental flag. The coat of arms is: Vert, a fasces palewise, axe Or and rods Proper *(brown)*; therefore in fess a balance and in saltire overall a key with bow in sinister base and a sword with hilt in dexter base all of the second. The crest *(On a wreath of the colors Or and Vert)* a pair of crossed pistols are displayed above the eagle's head. The background

color of the flag is green and the fringe is yellow. The coat of arms was approved on 2 May 1986.

Symbolism of Regimental Insignia: Green and yellow are the colors associated with the Military Police Corps. The fasces is an ancient symbol of authority related to a Roman magistrate. The balance is symbolic of equal justice under law and the key signifies security. The sword represents the military. The crossed pistols are the symbol of the Military Police Corps mission: to uphold the law and to keep order. The motto "ASSIST PROTECT AND DEFEND" reflects the mission.

Branch Colors: Green piped with yellow. Green - 65007 cloth; 67129 yarn; PMS 357. Yellow - 65002 cloth; 67108 yarn; PMS 123.

The color yellow piped with green was assigned to the Military Police by AR 600-35 dated 20 April 1922. With the establishment of yellow for the Armor and the use of green for the insignia on the Armor flag, the colors for the Military Police were reversed. The current colors, green piped with yellow, were assigned by regulation 600-60-1 dated 26 October 1951.

Birthday: 26 September 1941. The Provost Marshal General's Office and Corps of Military Police were established in 1941. Prior to that time, except during the Civil War and World War I, there was no regularly appointed Provost Marshal General or regularly constituted Military Police Corps, although a "Provost Marshal" can be found as early as January 1776, and a Provost Corps as early as 1778.

✪ National Guard Bureau

Branch Insignia: Two crossed gold color metal fasces superimposed on an eagle displayed with wings reversed, 1 inch in height.

On 12 July 1920, the Commission of Fine Arts was requested by the War Department to render assistance in the design of an insignia for the Militia Bureau. The citizen-soldier is represented by the fasces, denoting the unity of the States, and the eagle represented the Federal Government. The original design and model were made by Anthony de Francisci, the Sculptor, and were approved

by the Commission. In a memorandum from the Chief of Staff to the Quartermaster General, under date of 12 May 1921, the design and model submitted by the Commission of Fine Arts, was approved. The symbolism of the design, as expressed by the Commission of Fine Arts, was adopted and has remained the basic symbolism since 12 May 1921.

The Militia Bureau was redesignated as the National Guard Bureau on 15 June 1933, in accordance with Public Law No. 64, 73d Congress, and the name of the branch insignia was changed accordingly.

Branch Colors: Dark Blue.

Branch Insignia: A gold color metal shell and flame 1 inch in height.

The use of the "shell and flame" by the Ordnance Corps dates back to 1832; it is considered to be the oldest branch insignia of the Army. Similar insignia had been used by the British Army. After its adoption by the American Army, the design was used by the Artillery as well as the Ordnance until 1834 when the crossed cannon was adopted by the Artillery. In 1835, the shell and flame was used on a button for members of the Ordnance Corps and the design had been used in various items worn on the uniform since it was first adopted. The simplicity of the shell and flame harmonizes with the armament of days gone by, while the action it connotes is applicable with equal force to the weapons of today.

Regimental Insignia: A gold color metal and enamel device 1 1/8 inches in height overall consisting of two gray antique cannons in saltire on a white disc behind an encircling scroll in the form of a buckle red belt with, between the intersecting cannons and the belt, a black antique bomb, its scarlet flames issuing at the top of the device from behind the belt, which bears the inscription "ORDNANCE CORPS U.S.A." in gold letters. The regimental insignia for the Ordnance Corps was approved on 25 March 1986.

Regimental Coat of Arms: There is no coat of arms approved for Ordnance Corps Regiment. The regimental insignia *(all in yellow except the letters on the insignia are crimson)* is displayed above a yellow scroll inscribed "ARMAMENT FOR PEACE" in crimson. The background of the flag is crimson and the fringe is yellow.

Symbolism of Regimental Insignia: The crossed cannons

Branch Insignia   Enlisted Insignia

are representative of the Ordnance Corps' early relationship to the Artillery. The flaming bomb, also known as the shell and flame, represents the armament of days gone by, while the energy it connotes is applicable to the weapons of our own day. The cannoneer's belt, which encircles the flaming bomb and crossed cannons, is embossed with the words "ORDNANCE CORPS U.S.A." and represents the traditional association between munitions and armament. The white background symbolizes the Ordnance Corps' motto, "ARMAMENT FOR PEACE."

Branch Colors: Crimson piped with yellow. Crimson - 65013 cloth; 67112 yarn; PMS 220. Yellow - 65002 cloth; 67108 yarn; PMS 123.

In 1835, the Ordnance Corps had a red plume - the same as Artillery. Crimson was prescribed as the Ordnance color in 1851. In 1902, it was changed to black and scarlet. Crimson and yellow were established as the branch colors on 14 October 1921.

Birthday: 14 May 1812. The Ordnance Department was established by the act of 14 May 1812. During the Revolutionary War, ordnance material was under supervision of the Board of War and Ordnance. Numerous shifts in duties and responsibilities have occurred in the Ordnance Corps since colonial times. It acquired its present designation in 1950.

Psychological Operations ⭐

Collar Insignia   Collar Insignia
Officer   Enlisted

Collar Insignia: On a gold color disk, crossed daggers with blade forming a lightning bolt, superimposed by a knight chess piece.

Approved as a branch on 16 October 2006. The knight chess piece is a traditional symbol of special operations and signifies the ability to influence all types of warfare. The lightning bolts represent the psychological operations ability

to strike anywhere with speed and the two swords represent the combat capabilities.

Symbolism of Regimental Insignia. Silver gray, white and black represent the three types of Psychological Operations; white represents the overt processes, black is for the covert and gray for the hidden. The center device is adapted from the Psychological Operations collar insignia. The chess knight represents the ability to act obliquely and influence all types of warfare. The lightning bolt swords denote speed and the ability to strike anywhere.

Plaque: The plaque design has the Psychological Operations collar insignia, letters and rim in gold. The background is bottle green.

Colors: Bottle green has traditionally been used as the primary color on the Psychological Operations flags and guidons. The secondary color is silver gray.

Enlisted Collar Insignia

Collar Insignia: A vertical broadsword set against a cross quill with pen and a lightning bolt.

Authorized on 26 October 1989 for wear by enlisted personnel assigned to the Public Affairs career management field *(CMF 46)*. The quill identifies the functional area of public affairs and journalism. It crosses a lightning flash symbolizing speed and the transmittal or broadcasting of information. They are combined with a broadsword, underscoring the tactical value and impact that dissemination of information has in total military preparedness and in combat readiness. Officers assigned to public affairs continue to wear their basic branch insignia.

Plaque: The plaque design has the Public Affairs collar insignia, letters, and rim in gold. The background is teal blue.

Regimental Insignia: There is no regimental insignia for Public Affairs. Personnel assigned to Public Affairs are affiliated based on their assigned branch.

Flag and Guidons: There are no battalion size public affairs units. Accordingly, there are no flags for public affairs units. The public affairs collar insignia is used on the guidons for public affairs detachments.

Colors: Since the public affairs functions are multi-branch, teal blue *(branch unassigned)* is the color used on the plaque and guidons. Yellow is used as the secondary color for the insignia and numbers on guidons.

Quartermaster Corps

Branch Insignia: A gold color eagle with wings spread perched on a wheel with a blue felloe set with thirteen gold stars, having thirteen gold spokes and the hub white with a red center; superimposed on the wheel a gold sword and key crossed diagonally hilt and bow up. The insignia is 3/4 inches in height.

The insignia of the Quartermaster Department was approved in 1895. The design was retained when the Corps was established in 1912. After World War I, the earlier design, with the eagle's head superimposed on one wing, was changed to depict the head above the wings. The wagon wheel is symbolic of transportation and symbolize the original colonies and the origin of the Corps during the Revolutionary War. The sword, indicative of the military forces, and the key, alluding to storekeeping functions, symbolizes the control of military supplies by the Quartermaster Corps. The eagle symbolizes our nation; red, white, and blue are the national colors.

Regimental Insignia: A gold color metal and enamel device 1 inch in height consisting of a gold eagle with wings spread and head lowered looking to his right and standing upon a wheel with a blue felloe set with thirteen gold stars, having thirteen gold spokes and the hub white with a red center; superimposed on the wheel a gold sword and key crossed diagonally hilt and bow up, all on a black background and resting upon a wreath of green laurel terminating at either side below the eagle's wings at the upper end of the sword and key. Attached below the device is a gold scroll inscribed "SUPPORTING VICTORY" in black. The original regimental insignia was all gold and approved on 31 March 1986. The design was changed on 7 June 1994 to add color to the insignia.

Branch Insignia   Enlisted Insignia

Regimental Coat of Arms: The coat of arms appears on the breast of a displayed eagle on the regimental flag. The coat of arms is: Buff, a chevron Azure between a short sword point down bendwise sinister surmounted by a helmet contourne Argent, a bundle of arrows Sable surmounted by a garb Or, and a quill bendwise of the third surmounted by a key wards to base bendwise sinister of the fifth. Displayed above the eagle's head is the crest *(on a wreath of the colors Or and buff, the device from the Quartermaster Corps Regimental Insignia Proper)*. The Coat of Arms was approved on 16 June 1994.

Symbolism of Regimental Insignia: The device utilizes the traditional Quartermaster Corps branch insignia with the eagle in a slightly different configuration known historically as the "Regimental Eagle". The eagle symbolizes our nation; the wagon wheel is symbolic of transportation and delivery of supplies. The stars and spokes of the wheel symbolize the original colonies. The sword, indicative of the military forces, and the key, alluding to the storekeeping functions, symbolize the control of military supplies by the Quartermaster Corps. The wreath signifies honor and achievement.

(continued on next page)

Quartermaster Corps... *continued*

Symbolism of the Regimental Coat of Arms: Buff is the primary color traditionally associated with the Quartermaster Corps. The dark blue chevron represents valor and alludes to the fact that the Quartermaster Corps is the foundation of logistics. The Spartan helmet and short sword symbolize the Corps' warrior spirit — warriors supporting warriors. The shock of wheat superimposed over the spray of arrows represents the diversity of vital supplies the Quartermaster Corps provides. The arrows symbolize the defensive mission of the Corps. The wheat symbolizes the life-giving sustenance the Corps provides all soldiers.

The key and quill represents the Quartermaster's control of military supplies and attests to the sound business practices and professionalism of the Corps.

Branch Colors: Buff - 65015 cloth; 67135 yarn; PMS 46

Light or saxony blue was used for the Quartermaster Department. In 1884, the color buff was adopted which is presently used. Light blue is still used as the secondary color on flags for Quartermaster units.

Birthday: 16 June 1775. The Quartermaster Corps, originally designated the Quartermaster Department, was established on 16 June 1775. While numerous additions, deletions and changes of functions have occurred, its basic supply and service support functions have continued in existence.

Signal Corps ✪

Branch Insignia   Enlisted Insignia

Branch Insignia: Two signal flags crossed, dexter flag white with a red center, the sinister flag red with a white center, staffs gold, with a flaming torch of gold color metal upright at center of crossed flags; 7/8 inch in height.

"Crossed flags" have been used by the Signal Corps since 1868, when they were prescribed for wear on the uniform coat by enlisted men of the Signal Corps. In 1884, a burning torch was added to the insignia and the present design adopted on 1 July 1884. The flags and torch are symbolic of signaling or communication.

 Regimental Insignia: A gold color metal and enamel device 1 3/16 inches in height consisting of a gold eagle grasping a horizontal baton from which is suspended a red signal flag with a white center, enclosing the flag from a star at the bottom, a wreath of laurel all gold and a top left and right a white scroll inscribed "PRO PATRIA" at left and "VIGILANS" at right in gold. The regimental insignia was approved on 20 Mar 1986.

Regimental Coat of Arms: The coat of arms appears on the breast of a displayed eagle on the regimental flag. The coat of arms is: Argent, within a bordure Tenne a baton fesswise Or and suspended there from a signal flag Gules charged at center with a square of the first, in chief a mullet bronze. Displayed above the eagle's head is the crest: On a wreath of the Argent and Tenne, a dexter hand couped at the wrist, clenched, palm affronte, grasping three forked lightning flashes, all Proper, flashes Argent.

Symbolism of Regimental Insignia: The gold eagle holds in his talons a golden baton, from which descends a signal flag. The design originated in 1865 from a meeting of Signal Corps officers, led by Major Albert Myer, the Chief Signal Officer, in Washington, DC. The badge was a symbol of faithful service and good fellowship for those who served together in war and was called the "Order of the Signal Corps." The motto "PRO PATRIA VIGILANS" was adopted from the Signal School insignia and serves to portray the cohesiveness of Signal soldiers and their affiliation with their regimental home. The gold laurel wreath depicts the myriad of achievements through strength made by the Corps since its inception. The battle star centered on the wreath represents formal recognition for participation in combat. It adorned a Signal flag and was first awarded to Signal Corps soldiers in 1862. The battle star typifies the close operational relationship between the combined arms and the Signal Corps.

Symbolism of Regimental Coat of Arms: The Coat of Arms has the Signal flag suspended from a baton, which was adopted from the badge that originated in 1865 and was called the "Order of the Signal Corps." The bronze battle star represents formal recognition for participation in combat; it adorned a signal flag and was first awarded to Signal Corps soldiers in 1862. Orange and white are the traditional colors of the Signal Corps. The hand on the crest personifying the Corps has grasped the lightning from the heavens, and is applying it to military communications.

Branch Colors: Orange piped with white. Orange - 65004 cloth; 67110 yarn; PMS 1655. White - 65005 cloth; 67101 yarn; PMS White.

Orange was selected in 1872 as the Signal Corps branch color. In 1902, the white piping was added to conform to the custom that prevailed of having piping of a different color for all branches except the line branches.

Birthday: 21 June 1860. The Signal Corps was authorized as a separate branch of the Army by act of Congress on 3 March 1863. However, the Signal Corps dates its existence from 21 June 1860 when Congress authorized the appointment of one signal officer in the Army, and a War Department order carried the following assignment: "Signal Department - Assistant Surgeon Albert J. Myer to be Signal Officer, with the rank of Major, June 17, 1860, to fill an original vacancy."

★ Special Forces

Branch Insignia   Enlisted Insignia

Branch Insignia: Two crossed arrows 3/4 inch in height and 13/8 inches in width all gold color.

The Special Forces branch insignia was authorized in 1987 for wear by personnel in the Special Forces branch. It was previously authorized in 1984 for wear by enlisted personnel in Career Management Field 18 (*Special Operations*). Originally (*from 1890 to 1926*), crossed arrows were prescribed for wear by Indian Scouts. During World War II, the crossed arrows were worn as collar insignia by officers and enlisted personnel assigned to the First Special Service Force.

Regimental Insignia: The insignia is a silver color metal and enamel device consisting of a pair of silver arrows in saltire, points up and surmounted at their junction by a silver dagger with black handle point up; all over and between a black motto scroll arcing to base and inscribed "DE OPPRESSO LIBER" (*Liberate From Oppression*) in silver letters.

Regimental Insignia Symbolism: The shield of the Coat of Arms was approved for the First Special Service Force of World War II on 26 February 1943. The knife is of a distinctive shape and pattern and was issued only to the First Special Service Force. The crest is the crossed arrows from the collar insignia worn by the First Special Service Force in World War II but changed from gold to silver for harmony with the shield and to make a difference from the collar insignia. The coat of arms and distinctive unit insignia was approved on 8 July 1960.

Branch Colors: Jungle Green. 80066 cloth; 67191 yearn; PMS 343.

The establishment of jungle green as the branch color was approved by the Deputy Chief of Staff for Personnel on 22 May 1987. Silver Gray is used as a secondary color on flags and guidons.

Birthday: 9 April 1987. The first Special Forces unit in the Army was formed on 11 June 1952, when the 10th Special Forces Group was activated at Fort Bragg, North Carolina. A major expansion of Special Forces occurred during the 1960s, with a total of eighteen groups organized in the Regular Army, Army Reserve, and Army National Guard. As a result of renewed emphasis on special operations in the 1980s, the Special Forces Branch was established as a basic branch of the Army effective 9 April 1987, by General Orders No 35 dated 19 June 1987.

★ Special Services

Branch Insignia   Unauthorized Enlisted
                         Insignia

Special Services was initially set up as a division in the Adjutant Generals office just prior to World War II. The division was responsible for Army sports and morale. In 1946, it became a separate administrative service. The Special Services Division was eliminated in 1950.

Special service officers were in charge of the Army Exchanges, the motion picture service, and all recreational services including athletics.

Branch Insignia: Three jousting lances crossed over a green wreath formed the collar insignia. The lances stood for the three divisions of military sports and recreation. The encircling green wreath represented the honors and awards earned by winners in the sports program.

★ Staff Specialist, ARNG/USAR, Officers

 **Branch Insignia:** A sword 1 3/8 inches in length laid horizontally across the upper part of an open book. Below the sword and across the lower corners of the book, two laurel branches crossed at the stems. Insignia 13/16 inch in height of gold color metal.

Prior to World War II, all officers were assigned to one of the arms or services and had an appropriate branch of service insignia. In November 1941, an insignia was created which consisted of the Coat of Arms of the United States within a ring, for officers who were not members of, or on duty with an arm or service, and the Specialist Reserve. Following World War II, unassigned officers became a part of the Staff and Administrative Reserve Section in the Army National Guard and Organized Reserve Corps.

The Insignia was designed by the Heraldic Section, Office of The Quartermaster General and approved 5 February 1948. On 23 September 1949, the Staff and Administrative Reserve branch insignia was redesignated for the Staff Specialist Reserve branch insignia. The Staff Specialist is still a branch of the U.S. Army Reserve (*formerly the Organized Reserve Corps*) but has no equivalent in the Regular Army. The book represents regulations, while the laurel sprays symbolize the honors received in the administration of military regulations. The sword represents the military nature of the regulations.

Branch Color: Green

Branch Insignia

Enlisted Insignia

1 1/4 inches in height overall consisting of a ship's steering wheel bearing a shield charged with a winged car wheel on a rail, all gold centered upon a brick red spearhead point up, all standing upon a curving gold scroll spanning the lower tips of the spearhead and inscribed "SPEARHEAD OF LOGISTICS" in blue letters. The insignia was approved on 7 March 1986.

Branch Insignia: A ship's steering wheel, superimposed thereon a shield charged with a winged car wheel on a rail, all of gold color metal, 1 inch in height.

In 1919, "a winged car wheel, flanged, on a rail, surrounded by a rim one inch in diameter" was approved as the insignia of the Transportation Corps. The Army Reorganization Act, 4 June 1920, placed all transportation except military railways under the Quartermaster General. The Transportation Corps essentially in its present form was organized on 31 July 1942 as a result of the Army reorganization of 1942 and has functioned since then as one of the services. The present Transportation Corps insignia is based on that of the World War I Corps, with shield and ship's wheel added. The winged car wheel is for rail transportation and the Mariner's helm for transport by water. The U.S. highway marker shield is for land transportation.

Regimental Insignia: A gold color metal and enamel device

Regimental Coat of Arms: There is no coat of arms approved for the Transportation Corps Regiment. The regimental insignia in proper colors is displayed above a designation scroll "TRANSPORTATION CORPS". The background of the flag is brick red and the fringe is yellow.

Symbolism of Regimental insignia: Brick red and golden yellow are the Transportation Corps colors. The traditional insignia of the branch superimposed on the spearhead denotes the spirit of the motto. The branch insignia consists of the car wheel symbolizing rail transportation, the wing symbolizing air transportation, a mariner's helm for water transportation, and a U.S. highway marker shield for land transportation.

Branch Colors: Brick red piped with golden yellow. Brick red - 65020 cloth; 67113 yarn; PMS 202. Golden yellow - 65001 cloth; 67104 yarn; PMS 116. When the Transportation Corps was established in 1942, the brick red piped with golden yellow was assigned as the branch color.

Birthday: 31 July 1942. The historical background of the Transportation Corps starts with World War I. Prior to that time, transportation operations were chiefly the responsibility of the Quartermaster General.

Warrant Officer Branch ✪ (Obsolete 9 July 2004)

Branch Insignia: A distinctive insignia was approved for warrant officers on 12 May 1921 and removed 9 July 2004. It consisted of an eagle rising with wings displayed, adapted from the great seal of the United States. The National eagle is standing on two arrows which symbolize the military arts and sciences. The rising eagle is enclosed within a wreath. Warrant Officers now wear the basic branch insignia and colors based on their primary MOS. Warrant Officer's replaced their "Eagle Rising" hat insignia with the "Coat of Arms of the United States" insignia on their service caps effective 9 July 2004.

Branch Colors: The Army Warrant Officer Corps color was brown. The color emanated from the brown strands from burlap bags used by the Mine Planter Service. Now Warrant Officers wear the basic branch color of their primary MOS.

Warrant Officer Corps: A warrant officer is an officer appointed by warrant by the Secretary of the Army, based on technical and tactical competence. They are highly specialized experts who, operate, maintain, administer and manage the Army's equipment, support activities or technical systems for an entire career. Warrant Officers work in every branch of service as reflected by the needs of the Army. Warrant officers specifically trained as pilots or as other specialists and spend their entire career in the Aviation or other branches. As of 9 July 2004 they wear the insignia of the branch they are serving in.

Women's Army Corps ✪ (Obsolete)

Branch Insignia

Enlisted Insignia

WW II Officer Hat Insignia

WW II Enlisted Insignia

Branch Insignia: The head of Greek goddess Pallas Athene, 1 1/8 inches in height, of gold color metal.

The head of Pallas Athene was approved as the insignia for the Women's Army Auxiliary Corps in 1942. Pallas Athene was a goddess of handicrafts, wise in industries of peace and arts of war, also the goddess of storms and battle, who led through victory to peace and prosperity. The design was retained by the Women's Army Corps when it was established in 1943.

The Women's Army Corps was disestablished as a separate corps of the Army on 20 October 1978.

Branch Colors: Mosstone Green and Old Gold

⭐ U.S. Army Badges and Tabs

Introduction to Badges

1782 Badge of
Military Merit

The Army's purpose for awarding badges and tabs is to recognition of the high degree of skill, proficiency and excellence in test, competition and performance of duty. Although General Washington established the Badge of Military Merit, the Army was very slow to recognize the value of military badges as a matter of personal pride and public recognition for professional military skills.

By the early 1900s, Army regulations began to address the wear of badges but certainly not in the modern sense as we do now. Besides decorations and medals *(which were referred to then as badges)* the badges of military societies and of Civil War corps and division were authorized for wear on the uniform. The lack of official badges led the Army to accept badges to wear on the uniform from various military societies for men who in their own right or right of inheritance were members of the Army during the Revolution, War of 1812, Civil War, Spanish-American War etc. .

Military Aviator
Badge (1913)

It was flying that led the way for the first of the skill badges when the Army authorized the first military aviator badge in the fall of 1913. World War I saw the first cloth badges for military aviators and observers. Badges followed for aviation mechanics and different types of pilots until the new Army Air Service had 13 different badges to reflect their skills.

Between World War I and II, badges for marksmanship began to finally appear as the Army realized the importance of recognizing key professional skills.

World War II saw the introduction of a comprehensive badge system to recognize skills and performance. Today, badges are divided into five types of badges:

(1) Combat and special skill badges which are awarded for proficiency in performance of duty under hazardous conditions and circumstances of extraordinary hardship as well as special qualifications and successful completion of prescribed course of training.

(2) Marksmanship badges and tabs which are awarded to indicate the degree in which an individual has qualified in prescribed weapons firing courses or events.

(3) Identification badges are authorized to be worn as public evidence of deserved honor and distinction and to denote service in specified assignments.

(4) Locally authorized special skill badge authority to Major Commanders was rescinded in September 1986. They are no longer allowed but were popular in Korea.

(5) Badges awarded by other U.S. Services and foreign governments which must be approved before wear.

The following pages show these badges in the order of precedence outlined in DA Pam 670-1.

Combat and Special Skill Badge Wear Today

Combat and special skill badges and tabs authorized for wear on the Army uniform are listed below in order of group precedence:

(1) **Group 1.** Combat Infantryman badges *(three awards)*; Expert Infantryman badge ; Combat Action badge.

(2) **Group 2.** Combat Medical badges *(three awards)*; Expert Field Medical badge.

(3) **Group 3.** Army Astronaut device *(worn attached to any aviation badge or Army Space Badge)*; Army Aviator badges *(three degrees)* ; Flight Surgeon badges (three degrees); Aviation badges *(three degrees)*; Explosive

Ordnance Disposal badges *(three degrees)*.

(4) **Group 4.** Glider badge; Parachutist badges *(three degrees)*; Parachutist badges with combat jump device *(four degrees are shown)*; Pathfinder badge; Military Freefall Parachutist badges *(two degrees)*; Military Freefall Parachutist badges with combat jump device; Air Assault badge; Space badges *(three degrees)*; are Ranger, Special Forces, and Sapper tab metal replicas .

(5) **Group 5.** Diver badges *(six badges)*; Driver and Mechanic badge; Parachute Rigger badge.

(6) **Physical fitness badge.** The physical fitness badge is authorized for wear only on the physical fitness uniform.

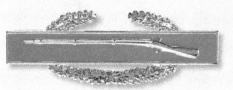

First Award

Second Award

Third Award

Fourth Award

I. **Description:** A silver and enamel badge 1 inch in height and 3 inches in width, consisting of an infantry musket on a light blue bar with a silver border on and over an elliptical oak wreath. Stars are added at the top of the wreath to indicate subsequent awards; one star for the second award, two stars for the third award and three stars for the fourth award.

II. **Symbolism:** The bar is blue, the color associated with the Infantry branch. The musket is adapted from the Infantry insignia of branch and represents the first official U.S. shoulder arm, the 1795 model Springfield Arsenal musket. It was adopted as the official Infantry branch insignia in 1924. The oak wreath symbolizes steadfastness, strength and loyalty.

III. **Award Eligibility:** Awarded to personnel in the grade of Colonel or below with an infantry military occupational specialty who have satisfactorily performed duty while assigned as a member of an infantry unit, brigade or smaller size, after 6 December 1941, when engaged in active ground combat. Expanded to permit award to Command Sergeants Major of infantry battalions or brigades, effective 1 January 1967. Specific criteria for each conflict was also established. Only one award is authorized for service in Vietnam, Laos, Dominican Republic, Korea (*subsequent to 27 July 1954*), Grenada, Panama, and Southwest Asia. The complete criteria for each area and inclusive dates are listed in Army Regulation 600-8-22.

IV. **Date Approved:** The Combat Infantryman Badge *(CIB)* was approved by the Secretary of War on 7 October 1943, and was initially referred to as the Combat Assault Badge; however, the name was changed to the Combat Infantryman Badge as announced in War Department Circular 269 dated 27 October 1943. On 8 February 1952, the Chief of Staff, Army, approved a proposal to add stars to the Combat Infantryman Badge to indicate award of the badge in separate wars. Under this change in policy, the badge was no longer limited to a one-time award, but may now be awarded to eligible individuals for each war in which they participated.

V. **Subdued Badges:** Subdued badges are authorized in metal and cloth. The metal badge has a black finish. The cloth badge has a base cloth with the rifle, wreath, stars and border of the bar embroidered in black.

VI. **Miniature Badges:** A dress miniature badge, 1-1/4 inches in length is authorized for wear on the mess uniforms. A miniature badge, 1 3/4 inches is also authorized in lieu of the regular size badge.

VI. **Remarks:** The CIB is authorized for the following qualifying wars, conflicts, and operations:

(1) World War II *(7 December 1941 to 3 September 1945)*.
(2) The Korean War *(27 June 1950 to 27 July 1953)*.
(3) Republic of Vietnam Conflict *(2 March 1961 to 28 March 1973)*, combined with qualifying service in Laos *(19 April 1961 to 6 October 1962)*.
(4) Dominican Republic *(28 April 1965 to 1 September 1966)*.
(5) Korea on the DMZ *(4 January 1969 to 31 March 1994)*.
(6) El Salvador *(1 January 1981 to 1 February 1992)*.
(7) Grenada *(23 October to 21 November 1983)*.
(8) Joint Security Area, Panmunjom, Korea *(23 November 1984)*.
(9) Panama *(20 December 1989 to 31 January 1990)*.
(10) Southwest Asia Conflict *(17 January to 11 April 1991)*.
(11) Somalia *(5 June 1992 to 31 March 1994)*.
(12) Afghanistan *(Operation Enduring Freedom, 5 December 2001 to a date to be determined)*.
(13) Iraq *(Operation Iraqi Freedom, 19 March 2003 to a date to be determined)*.

Second Award

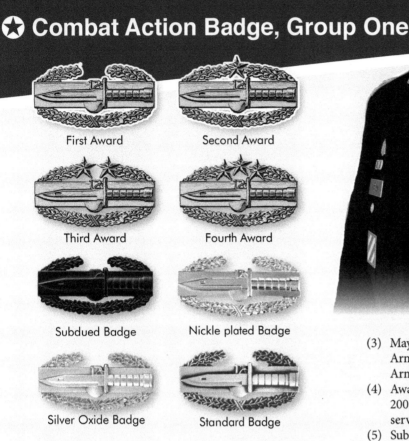

First Award Second Award

Third Award Fourth Award

Subdued Badge Nickle plated Badge

Silver Oxide Badge Standard Badge

I. **Description:** A silver badge 2 inches *(5.08cm)* in width overall consisting of an oak wreath supporting a rectangle bearing a bayonet surmounting a grenade, all silver. Stars are added at the top to indicate subsequent awards; one star for the second award, two stars for the third award and three stars for the fourth award.

II. **Symbolism:** In keeping with the spirit of the Warrior Ethos, the Combat Action Badge provides special recognition to Soldiers who personally engage the enemy, or are engaged by the enemy during combat operations. The bayonet and grenade are associated with active combat. The oak wreath symbolizes strength and loyalty.

III. **Award Eligibility:** The Combat Action Badge *(CAB)* may be awarded by any commander delegated authority by the Secretary of the Army during wartime or the Commanding General, U.S. Army Human Resources Command and will be announced in permanent orders.

(1) The requirements for award of the CAB are Branch and MOS immaterial. Assignment to a Combat Arms unit or a unit organized to conduct close or offensive combat operations, or performing offensive combat operations is not required to qualify for the CAB. However, it is not intended to award all soldiers who serve in a combat zone or imminent danger area.

(2) Specific Eligibility Requirements:
   a. May be awarded to any soldier.
   b. Soldier must be performing assigned duties in an area where hostile fire pay or imminent danger pay is authorized.
   c. Soldier must be personally present and actively engaging or being engaged by the enemy, and performing satisfactorily in accordance with the prescribed rules of engagement.
   d. Soldier must not be assigned/attached to a unit that would qualify the soldier for the CIB/CMB.

(3) May be awarded to members from the other U.S. Armed Forces and foreign soldiers assigned to a U.S. Army unit, provided they meet the above criteria.

(4) Award of the CAB is authorized from 18 September 2001 to a date to be determined. Award for qualifying service in any previous conflict is not authorized.

(5) Subsequent awards:
   a. Only one CAB may be awarded during a qualifying period.
   b. Second and third awards of the CAB for subsequent qualifying periods will be indicated by superimposing one and two stars respectively, centered at the top of the badge between the points of the oak wreath.

(6) Retroactive awards for the CAB are not authorized prior to 18 September 2001, applications *(to include supporting documentation)* for retroactive awards of the CAB will be forwarded through the first two star general in the chain of command to CG, U.S. Army Human Resources Command.

(7) Wear policy is contained in Army Regulation 670-1.

(8) Soldiers may be awarded the CIB, CMB and CAB for the same qualifying period, provided the criteria for each badge is met. However, subsequent awards of the same badge within the same qualifying period are not authorized.

IV. **Date Approved:** On 2 May 2005, the Chief of Staff, Army, approved the creation of the CAB to provide special recognition to soldiers who personally engage, or are engaged by the enemy. HQDA Letter 600-05-1, dated 3 June 2005, announced the establishment of the Combat Action Badge.

V. **Subdued Badge:** Subdued badges are authorized in metal and cloth. The metal badge has a black finish. The cloth badge has a base cloth with the bayonet, grenade, oak wreath and border of the bar embroidered in black.

VI. **Miniature Badges:** A dress miniature badge, 1 1/4 inches *(3.18 cm)* in length is authorized for wear on the mess uniforms. A miniature badge, 1 3/4 inches *(4.45 cm)* is also authorized in lieu of the regular size badge.

I. **Description:** A silver and enamel badge 7/16 inch in height and 3 inches in width, consisting of an Infantry musket on a light blue bar with a silver border.

II. **Symbolism:** The bar is blue, the color associated with the Infantry branch. The musket is adapted from the Infantry insignia of branch and represents the first official U.S. shoulder arm, 1795 model Springfield Arsenal musket. It was adopted as the official Infantry branch insignia in 1924.

III. **Award Eligibility:** Personnel must meet Department of the Army established testing requirements and must possess a military occupational specialty within Career Management Field 11 (Infantry).

IV. **Date Approved:** The Expert Infantryman Badge was approved by the Secretary of War on 7 October 1943, and announced in War Department Circular 269 dated 27 October 1943.

V. **Subdued Badge:** The subdued badge is authorized in metal and cloth. The metal badge has a black finish. The cloth badge has a base cloth with the rifle and border of the bar embroidered in black.

VI. **Miniature Badge:** A miniature badge, 1 3/4 inches in length and 3/8 inch in height, is authorized in lieu of the regular size badge. A dress miniature badge, 1 1/4 inches in length and 3/16 inch in height is also authorized.

Combat Medical Badges, Group Two ★

| First Award | Second Award | Third Award | Fourth Award |

I. **Description:** An oxidized silver badge 1 inch in height and 1 1/2 inches in width, consisting of a stretcher crossed by a caduceus surmounted at top by a Greek cross, all on and over an elliptical oak wreath. Stars are added to indicate subsequent awards; one star at top for the second award, one star at top and one at bottom for the third award, one star at top and one at each side for the fourth award.

II. **Symbolism:** The Medical Corps insignia of branch, modified by the addition of a Greek cross suggesting the Geneva Convention between the wings and the entwined serpents, signifies the recipient's skills and expertise. It is superimposed upon a stretcher alluding to medical field service. The oak wreath symbolizes steadfastness, strength and loyalty.

III. **Award Eligibility:** Awarded to members of the Army Medical Department, Naval Medical Department or Air Force Medical Service who are in the grade of Colonel or below while assigned or attached to a medical unit of company or smaller size organic to an infantry unit during any period the infantry unit was engaged in active ground combat subsequent to 6 December 1941. Only one award is authorized for service in Vietnam, Laos, the Dominican Republic, Korea (*subsequent to 27 July 1954*), Grenada, Panama, and Southwest Asia, regardless of whether an individual has served in one or more of these areas. Specific eligibility requirements by geographic area are listed in Army Regulation 600-8-22.

IV. **Date Approved:** The Combat Medical Badge was approved on 29 January 1945. In February 1951, the proposal to designate the badge as a one-time award

was rescinded and it was approved for subsequent award during specified periods. The addition of stars to indicate subsequent awards was also approved.

V **Subdued Badges:** Subdued badges are authorized in metal and cloth. The metal badge is black. The cloth badge has a base cloth with the stretcher, caduceus, cross, wreath and stars embroidered in black.

VI. **Miniature Badges:** A dress miniature badge, 19/32 inch in height is authorized.

VII. **Remarks:** The CMB is authorized for award for the following qualifying wars, conflicts, and operations:
1. World War II (*7 December 1941 to 3 September 1945*).
2. The Korean War (*27 June 1950 to 27 July 1953*).
3. Republic of Vietnam Conflict (*2 March 1961 to 28 March 1973*), combined with qualifying service in Laos (*19 April 1961 to 6 October 1962*).
4. Dominican Republic (*28 April 1965 to 1 September 1966*).
5. Korea on the DMZ (*4 January 1969 to 31 March 1994*).
6. El Salvador (*1 January 1981 to 1 February 1992*).
7. Grenada (*23 October to 21 November 1983*).
8. Joint Security Area, Panmunjom, Korea (*23 November 1984*).
9. Panama (*20 December 1989 to 31 January 1990*).
10. Southwest Asia Conflict (*17 January to 11 April 1991*).
11. Somalia (*5 June 1992 to 31 March 1994*).
12. Afghanistan (*Operation Enduring Freedom, 5 December 2001 to a date to be determined*).
13. Iraq (*Operation Iraqi Freedom, 19 March 2003 to a date to be determined*).

✪ Expert Field Medical Badge, Group Two

I. **Description:** An oxidized silver badge 15/16 inch in height and 1-7/16 inches in width consisting of a stretcher crossed by a caduceus surmounted at top by a Greek cross.

II. **Symbolism:** The Medical Corps insignia of branch, modified by the addition of a Greek cross suggesting the Geneva Convention between the wings and the entwined serpents, signifies the recipient's skills and expertise. It is superimposed upon a stretcher alluding to medical field service.

III **Award Eligibility:** This badge recognizes Army personnel for attaining a high state of technical skill in field medical functions. It is awarded on the basis of proven skill and performance. Prior to being awarded the badge, personnel must successfully pass all test parts prescribed by Army Regulations.

IV. **Date Approved:** The Expert Medical Badge was approved on 18 June 1965.

V. **Subdued Badges:** Subdued badges are authorized in metal and cloth. The metal badge is black. The cloth badge has a base cloth with the stretcher, caduceus and cross embroidered in black.

VI. **Miniature Badges:** A dress miniature badge 9/16 inch in height is authorized.

✪ Army Astronaut Badges, Group Three

Army Astronaut

Senior Army Astronaut

Master Army Astronaut

I. **Description:** A gold colored stylized shooting star with three contrails enfiling an elyse saltirewise. The device is placed on the appropriate existing aviation badges.

II. **Symbolism:** The badge design is the same as that for Army Aviation (aviator, flight surgeon, crew member, etc.) with the shooting star and elliptical orbit superimposed over the shield. The shooting star passing through the elliptical orbit implies space and the astronaut's theatre of operations.

III. **Award Eligibility:** The appropriate Astronaut Badge may be awarded to any individual who has been awarded any one of the Army Aviation Badges as specified in AR 600-8-22, and who completes a minimum of one operational mission in space (50 miles above earth). Astronauts who have not been awarded an aviation badge previously will be awarded the crew member badge.

IV. **Date Approved:** The Army Astronaut Badge was approved on 17 May 1983.

V. **Subdued Badges:** Subdued badges are authorized in metal and cloth. The metal badge is black with brown device.

VI. **Miniature Badges:** Dress miniature badges are authorized for each of the aviation badges.

✪ Space Badge with Astronaut Device, Group Three

Basic Space Badge

Senior Space Badge

Master Space Badge

The three degrees of the Space Badge authorized for award are:

(1) **Basic Space Badge.**
(2) **Senior Space Badge.**
(3) **Master Space Badge.**

Basic eligibility criteria for award are completion of the appropriate space-related education and/or training an serving the required number of months in an Army space cadre approved and/or coded position.

Army Astronaut Device

Specific criteria for each level of award and processing procedures are outlined in Army Space Personnel Development Office Procedural Guide.

When awarded with the Astronaut Device the Space Badge becomes a Group Three Badge and worn above Group Four and Five Badges. Normal the Space Badge is ranked in Group Four after the Air Assault Badge according to AR 670-1

Army Aviator

Senior Army Aviator

Master Aviator

I. Description: An oxidized silver badge 3/4 inch in height and 2-1/2 inches in width, consisting of the shield of the coat of arms of the United States on and over a pair of displayed wings. A star is added above the shield to indicate qualification as a Senior Army Aviator. The star is surrounded with a laurel wreath to indicate qualification as a Master Army Aviator.

Center and must have been designated as an Aviator in appropriate orders. Senior Aviator: Have 1,500 flying hours in aircraft or seven years from basic rating date. Master Aviator: Have 3,000 hours in aircraft or 15 years from basic rating date.

IV. Date Approved: The Aviator and Senior Aviator Badges were approved on 27 July 1950, and the Master Aviator Badge was approved on 12 February 1957.

Subdued Badge

Plated Badge

Silver Badge

II. Symbolism: The wings suggest flight and reflect the skills associated with aerial flight. The shield of the coat of arms of the United States signifies loyalty and devotion to duty.

III. Award Eligibility: Army Aviator: The individual must have satisfactorily completed the prescribed training and proficiency tests conducted by the U.S. Army Aviation

V. Subdued Badges: Subdued badges are authorized in metal and cloth. The metal badge is black; the cloth badge is a base cloth with design elements embroidered in black.

VI. Miniature Badges: Dress miniature badges are authorized.

Flight Surgeon

Senior Flight Surgeon

Flight Surgeon

I. Description: An oxidized silver badge 23/32 inch in height and 2 1/2 inches in width, consisting of a shield, its field scored with horizontal lines and bearing the Staff of Aesculapius on and over a pair of displayed wings. A star is added above the shield to indicate the degree of Senior Flight Surgeon and the star is surrounded with a laurel wreath to indicate the degree of Master Flight Surgeon.

II. Symbolism: The wings suggest flight and reflect the skills associated with aerial flight. The Staff of Aesculapius is traditionally and historically associated with healing and medical skills.

III. Award Eligibility: Awarded to any medically qualified Army Medical Corps Officer who satisfactorily completes training and other requirements prescribed in AR 600-105.

IV. Date Approved: The Flight Surgeon Badge (originally

approved as the Aviation Medical Officer Badge) was approved on 28 December 1956. The Senior Flight Surgeon (formerly the Flight Surgeon) and Master Flight Surgeon (formerly the Senior Flight Surgeon) Badges were approved on 12 August 1963. The changes in designations were by message from the Commander, U.S. Army Military Personnel Center, 22 November 1973.

V. Subdued Badges: Subdued badges are authorized in metal and cloth. The metal badge is black. The cloth badge is a base cloth with design elements embroidered in black.

VI. Miniature Badges: Dress miniature badges are authorized in the following sizes: Flight Surgeon: 21/64 inch in height and 1 1/4 inches in width; Senior Flight Surgeon: 13/32 inch in height and 1 1/4 inches in width; Master Fight Surgeon: 15/32 inch in height and 1 1/4 inches in width.

Aircraft Crew Member   Master Aircraft Crew Member   Senior Aircraft Crew Member

Nickle plated Badges

Subdued Badges

I. **Description:** An oxidized silver badge 3/4 inch in height and 2 1/2 inches in width, consisting of a shield with its field scored with horizontal lines and bearing the coat of arms of the United States on and over a pair of displayed wings. A star is added above the shield to indicate the degree of Senior Aircraft Crew Member and the star is surrounded with a laurel wreath to indicate the degree of Master Aircraft Crew Member.

II. **Symbolism:** The badge is the same design as that for Army Aviator with the coat of arms of the United States substituted for the shield of the coat of arms of the United States. The wings suggest flight and reflect the skills associated with aerial flight. The coat of arms of the United States on the shield signifies loyalty and devotion to duty.

III. **Award Eligibility:** The badges are awarded in degrees to personnel who have met the following requirements: Crew Member: Individual must be on flying status as a crew member in a specified position or non-crewmember in the case of observers, medical aidmen, gunners, aircraft maintenance supervisors or technical inspectors. Senior: Be recommended and on flying status as a crewmember or as a non-crewmember, performed 7 years in one of the principal duty assignments above, and attained grade E-4 or higher. Master: Be recommended and on flying status in a specified position or non-crewmember position, have performed 15 years in one or more of the principal duty assignments above and attained the grade of E-6 or higher. Personnel who have met the above requirements at any time since 1 January 1947 are eligible for these badges.

IV. **Date Approved:** Approved by the Deputy Chief of Staff for Military Operations on 16 May 1962.

V. **Subdued Badges:** Subdued badges are authorized in metal and cloth. The metal badge is black. The cloth badge is a base cloth with design elements embroidered in black.

VI. **Miniature Badges:** Dress miniature badges are authorized.

⭐ Explosive Ordnance Disposal Badge, Group Three

Basic   Senior   Master

I. **Description:** A silver badge, 1 3/4 inches in height, consisting of shield charged with a conventional, drop bomb, point down, from which radiates four lightning flashes, all in front of and contained within a wreath of laurel leaves. The Senior Explosive Ordnance Disposal Badge is the same as the basic badge except the drop bomb bears a 7/32 inch silver star. The Master Explosive Ordnance Disposal Badge is the same as the Senior except a star, surrounded by a laurel wreath, is added above the shield.

II. **Symbolism:** The shield charged with a drop bomb is from the shoulder sleeve insignia approved for the Bomb Disposal School in 1942. The device was subsequently adopted for wear on a brassard to identify bomb disposal personnel. The bomb, with point down, indicates a live bomb and with the shield reflects the functions of ordnance personnel to safely dispose of live ordnance.

III. **Award Eligibility:** The specific criteria for award of the Explosive Ordnance Disposal Badges is included in AR 600-8-22, all badges require assignment to specific TOE/TDA EOD positions and recommended by the commander in addition to the following:

a. **Explosive Ordnance Disposal (EOD) Badge:** Must have MOS 55D (enlisted) or 91E (officer), complete prescribed instruction and perform satisfactorily for 18 months for the award to become permanent.

b. **Senior Explosive Ordnance Disposal Badge:** Must have been awarded the basic EOD Badge and served 36 months in an EOD position following award of the basic badge.

c. **Master Explosive Ordnance Disposal Badge:** Must have been awarded the Senior EOD Badge and served 60 months in a TOE/TDA officer of NCO EOD position, since award of the senior badge.

IV. **Date Approved:** The Chief of Staff, U.S. Army, approved the Explosive Ordnance Disposal Specialist and the Explosive Ordnance Disposal Supervisor Badges on 31 July 1957. In June 1969, the Master EOD Badge was authorized. At the same time, the designation of the supervisor's badge was changed to Senior EOD Badge and the EOD Specialist Badge was changed to EOD Badge.

V. **Subdued Badge:** The subdued badge is authorized in metal and cloth. The metal badges have a black finish

Subdued Badge

VI. **Miniature Badges:** A dress miniature badge, 7/8 inch wide, is authorized.

I. **Description:** An oxidized silver badge 11/16 inch in height and 1 1/2 inches in width consisting of a glider, frontal view, superimposed upon a, pair of stylized wings displayed and curving inward.

II. **Symbolism:** The wings suggest flight and together with the glider symbolize individual skills and qualifications in aerial flight utilizing the glider.

III. **Award Eligibility:** The Glider Badge is no longer awarded. At the time authorization of the badge was announced, personnel must have been assigned or attached to a glider or airborne unit or to the Airborne Department of the

Glider Badge, Group Four ⭐

Infantry School; satisfactorily completing a course of instruction or participated in at least one combat glider landing into enemy-held territory.

IV. **Date Approved:** Authorization of the Glider Badge was announced in War Department Circular No. 220, 2 June 1944.

V. **Subdued Badges:** A subdued badge in black metal finished of the same design is authorized.

VI. **Miniature Badges:** A dress miniature badge, 13/32 inch in height and 7/8 inch in width is authorized.

Parachutists Badge, Group Four ⭐

Basic

Senior

Master

I. **Description:** An oxidized silver badge 1 13/64 inches in height and 1 1/2 inches in width, consisting of an open parachute on and over a pair of stylized wings displayed and curving inward. A star and wreath are added above the parachute canopy to indicate the degree of qualification. A star above the canopy indicates a Senior Parachutist; the star surrounded by a laurel wreath indicates a Master Parachutist. Small stars are superimposed on the appropriate badge to indicate combat jumps as shown below under combat Parachutist Badges:

II. **Symbolism:** The wings suggest flight and, together with the open parachute, symbolize individual proficiency and parachute qualifications.

III. **Award Eligibility:** Basic, Senior and Master Parachutist badges are awarded to individuals rated excellent in character and efficiency who have met the following requirements:

Basic Parachutist: Completed the proficiency test assigned to an airborne unit or the Airborne Department of the Infantry School or having one combat parachute jump.

Senior Parachutist: A minimum of 30 jumps to include 15 jumps with combat equipment; two night jumps, one as jumpmaster of a stick; two mass tactical jumps which culminate in an airborne assault problem; graduated from the Jumpmaster Course; and served on jump status with an airborne unit or other organization authorized parachutists for at least 24 months.

Master Parachutist: 65 jumps to include 25 jumps with combat equipment; four night jumps, one as a jumpmaster of a stick; five mass tactical jumps which culminate in an airborne assault problem with a battalion or larger; separate company/battery or organic staff of a regiment size or larger; graduated from the Jumpmaster Course; and served in jump status with an airborne unit or other organization authorized parachutists for a total of at least 36 months.

⭐ Combat Parachutist Badges, Group Four

| One Jump | Two Jumps | Three Jumps | Four Jumps | Five Jumps |

A bronze service star is authorized to be worn on the parachute badge to denote a soldiers participation in a combat parachute jump. Orders are required to confirm award of the combat parachute badge. A soldier's combat parachute jump credit is tied directly to the combat assault credit decision for the unit to which the soldier is attached or assigned at the time of the assault. Each soldier must physically exit the aircraft to receive the combat parachute jump credit and the parachutist badge with bronze service star. *(Note: award of the combat parachutist badge qualifies the recipient to wear the bronze arrowhead for a combat assault on the campaign medal awarded for that service.)*

One jump: A bronze star centered on the shroud lines 3/16 inch below the canopy.

Two jumps: A bronze star on the base of each wing.

Three jumps: A bronze star on the base of each wing and one star centered on the shroud lines 3/16 inch below the canopy.

Four jumps: Two bronze stars on the base of each wing.

Five jumps: A gold star centered on the shroud lines 5/16 inch below the canopy.

Stars are shown on a master parachutist badge but would be placed on an individual's badge *(Basic, Senior or Master)*.

⭐ Pathfinder Badge, Group Four

I. **Description:** A gold color metal and enamel badge 1 3/16 inches in height and 1 1/2 inches in width, consisting of a gold sinister wing displayed on and over a gold torch with red and gray flames.

II. **Symbolism:** The wing suggests flight and airborne capabilities; the torch symbolizes leadership and guidance implying pathfinder combat skills.

III. **Award Eligibility:** The Commandant of the U.S. Army Infantry School may award the Pathfinder Badge for successfully completion of the Pathfinder Course.

IV. **Date Approved:** The badge was originally approved on 22 May 1964 in felt and replaced as a metal and enamel item on 11 October 1968.

V. **Subdued Badges:** A subdued badge in black metal finish of the same design is authorized.

VI. **Miniature Badges:** A dress miniature badge, 11/16 inch in height and 7/8 inch in width is authorized.

⭐ Military Free Fall Parachute Badge, Group Four

| Basic MFF Wings | Jumpmaster MFF Wings |

I. **Description:** An oxidized silver badge consisting of a Free Fall parachute, frontal view, superimposed upon a pair of stylized wings displaying the fighting knife of the 1st Special Service force, a World War II special operations unit.

II. **Symbolism:** The wings suggest flight and together with the Free Fall parachute symbolize individual skills and qualifications in high altitude, low opening insertion of special operations forces flight utilizing the glider.

III. **Award Eligibility:** The Military Free Fall Parachutist badges identify Special Operations Forces *(SOF)* Personnel who have qualified in one of the military's most demanding and hazardous skills, Military Free Fall Parachuting. Badges authorized: two degrees of the Military Free Fall Badges are authorized for award: Basic and Jumpmaster. *(1)* To be eligible for the basic badge, an individual must meet one of the following criteria: *(A)* Have satisfactorily completed a prescribed program of instruction in Military Free Fall approved by U.S. Army John F. Kennedy Special Warfare Center & School or *(B)* have executed a Military Free Fall combat jump which would authorized a bronze star in the center of the badge. *(2)* Military Free Fall Parachutist Badge, Jumpmaster. To be eligible for the Jumpmaster Badge, an individual must have satisfactorily completed a prescribed Military Free Fall Jumpmaster program approved by USAJFKSWC&S.

IV. **Date approved:** Effective 7 Jul 1997, the Military Free Fall Parachutist Badges are authorized for permanent wear. Retroactive award. Special operations forces personnel who qualified in military free fall prior to 1 Oct 1994 must obtain approval in writing from the Commander, U.S. Army John F. Kennedy Special Warfare Center and School.

V. **Subdued Badges:** A subdued badge in black metal finished of the same design is authorized.

VI. **Miniature Badges:** A dress miniature badge is authorized.

Master Parachutist and Pathfinder Badges

I. **Description:** An oxidized silver badge 3/4 inch in height and 1 17/32 inches in width, consisting of a helicopter, frontal view, superimposed upon a pair of stylized wings displayed and curving inward

II. **Symbolism:** The wings suggest flight and together with the helicopter symbolize individual skills and qualifications in assault landings utilizing the helicopter.

III. **Award Eligibility:** Awarded by commanders of divisions and separate brigades to individuals who satisfactorily complete an air assault training course in accordance with the U.S. Army Training and Doctrine Command's Standardized Air Assault Core Program of Instruction. Also authorized for any individual who has satisfactorily completed the Standard Air Assault Course when assigned or attached to the 101st Airborne Division *(Air Assault)* since 1 April 1974.

IV. Date Approved: The Air Assault Badge was approved by the Chief of Staff, Army, on 18 January 1978, for Army-wide wear by individuals who successfully completed Air Assault training after 1 April 1974. The badge had previously been approved as the Airmobile Badge authorized for local wear by the Commander of the 101st Airborne Division, effective 1 April 1974.

V. Subdued Badge: Subdued badges are authorized in metal and cloth. The metal badge is black. The cloth badge is a base cloth with design elements embroidered in black.

VI. Miniature Badges: A miniature badge, 7/16 inch in height and 7/8 inch in width is authorized.

Master Parachutist and Free Fall badges

| Basic Space Badge | Senior Space Badge | Master Space Badge |

The three degrees of the Space Badge authorized for award are:

(1) **Basic Space Badge.**
(2) **Senior Space Badge.**
(3) **Master Space Badge.**

Basic eligibility criteria for award are completion of the appropriate space-related education and/or training and serving the required number of months in an Army space cadre approved and/or coded position.

Specific criteria for each level of award and processing procedures are outlined in Army Space Personnel Development Office Procedural Guide #1 located on the Army Space Personnel Development Office. Note if the Space Badge is awarded with the Army Astronaut device it is ranked in Group three.

The Space Badge may be revoked by the approval authority. Once revoked, the badges will not be reinstated except by the Commander, U.S. Army Space and Missile Defense Command/Army Forces Strategic Command, when fully justified

Ranger Qualification Tab

Ranger
Qualification Patch

Description: The ranger qualification tab for the Army green uniform is 2 3/8 inches wide with a yellow embroidered border and letters over a black background. A subdued version with black letters and border on an olive drab background is authorized on battle dress uniforms.

Symbolism: The colors reflect the previously authorized ranger shoulder sleeve insignia which was diamond shaped with yellow border and letters and a deep blue background.

Award Eligibility:

a. The Commandant of the U.S. Army Infantry School awards the Ranger Tab to any person who successfully completed a Ranger Course conducted by that school.

b. The Commander, U.S. Total Army Personnel Command *(PERSCOM)* and the Commander, U.S. Total Army Reserve Personnel Center *(AR-PERSCOM)* may award the Ranger Tab to any person who was awarded the Combat Infantryman Badge while serving during World War II as a member of a Ranger Battalion *(1st Bn - 6th Bn inclusive)* or in the

World War II
Ranger Diamond

5307th Composite Unit, Provisional *(Merrill's Maurauders)*; to any person who was awarded the Combat Infantryman Badge while serving during the Korean Conflict with the 8th Army Ranger Company *(11 October 1950 to 27 March 1951)*; or to any person who successfully completed a Ranger Course conducted by the Ranger Training Command at Fort Benning, GA.

Date Approved: The cloth tab was approved by HQDA on 6 November 1950. Authorization to wear the tab was included in Change 2, AR 600-70, dated 23 January 1953. On 25 November 1984, the Army Chief of Staff approved a metal replica of the embroidered tab for wear on the dress mess uniforms.

Subdued Tab: The subdued tab is embroidered on a cloth background and bordered with black letters. The tab is not authorized in subdued metal.

Miniature Badges: The metal badge authorized for wear on the Army blue or white uniform and green shirt is 1 5/32 inches wide with a black enameled background and gold letters and border. The dress miniature for wear on the mess/dress uniforms is 13/16 inch wide.

Description: The Special Forces qualification tab for wear on the Army uniform is 3 1/4 inches wide with a teal blue embroidered background and border and yellow embroidered letters. A subdued version with olive drab background and borders and black letters is authorized for combat uniforms. A metal Special Forces Badge is authorized for wear on the mess/dress uniforms and green shirt.

Symbolism: The colors of the tab are the same colors as the shoulder sleeve insignia authorized for Special Forces Groups.

Award Eligibility:

a. The Commander, U.S. Army John F. Kennedy Special Warfare Center (USAJFKSWC), Fort Bragg, NC, may award the Special Forces Tab to any individual who has successfully completed the Special Forces Qualification Course or the Special Forces Officer Course.

b. The Special Forces Tab may be awarded to any person on active duty, active status in the Reserve Components, in retired status, or honorably discharged who meets the appropriate criteria listed in AR 600-8-22.

The cloth tab was approved 17 June 1983, On 25 November 1984, the Army Chief of Staff approved a metal replica of the embroidered tab for wear on the mess/dress uniforms.

Subdued Tab: The subdued tab is embroidered with olive drab background and border with black letters. The tab is not authorized in subdued metal.

Miniature Badges: The metal badge authorized for wear on the Army blue or white uniform and green shirt is 1 9/16 inches wide with a teal blue enameled background and gold letters and border. The dress miniature for wear on the mess/dress uniforms is 1 inch wide.

Embroidered Tab

Embroidered Tab

Embroidered Tab

Metal Badge For Dress Uniforms

Sapper Tab: On 28 June 2004 then Army Chief of Staff General Peter Schoomaker approved the creation of a new skill badge: the "Sapper" tab. This new tab is worn by soldiers

Sapper Tab, Group Four ⭐

who successfully complete the twenty-eight day Sapper Leader Course (SLC) given by the U.S. Army Engineer School at Fort Leonard Wood, Missouri and is retroactive to 14 June 1985 for soldiers who had previously completed the course.

Several tabs are worn unofficially by soldiers. Often these tabs were worn on the underside of pocket flaps so as not to violate uniform regulations. These include tabs containing the words "SNIPER", "AIR ASSAULT", "FISTER", "SCOUT", and "RECON" or "RECONDO." The "SAPPER" tab was one of these unofficial tabs until 2004 when it became an official special skill badge/tab of the U.S. Army.

President's Hundred Tab ⭐

President's Hundred Tab: The Presidents Hundred Tab can is awarded to each person who qualifies among the top 100 successful contestants in the President's Match held annually at the National Rifle matches.

The Jungle Expert Patch ⭐

The Jungle Expert Patch was often worn by graduates of the Jungle Operations Training Center (JOTC) until the school became inactive in 1999. The patch may have been authorized for wear by soldiers assigned to U.S. Army South who graduate from JOTC but the patch was never recognized Army-wide.

In 2014, the JOTC was reopened in Hawaii and the Jungle Expert Patch was revitalized as a tab authorized for soldiers who complete the course and are assigned to the U.S. Army Pacific.Other graduates receive the tab as a souvenir.

Current Jungle Expert Tab

Former Jungle Expert Patch

⭐ Diver Badges, Group Five

Scuba (Obsolete)

Salvage

Second Class

First Class

Master

The Army has two different types of diver badges, one for engineer divers and one for special operations divers. Army engineer diver badges are awarded in four degrees *(second-class diver, salvage diver, first-class diver, and master diver)* while Army special operations diver badges are awarded in two degrees *(diver and diving supervisor)*. The second-class and first-class diver badges are identical to those issued by U.S. Navy. Navy-awarded Diving Officer Insignia, Diving Medical Officer Insignia, and Diving Medical Technician Insignia are authorized for wear on Army uniforms with written approval from the United States Army Human Resources Command.[6][7][8]

On 17 September 2004, the Scuba Diver Insignia/Badge was discontinued and replaced by the new Special Operations Diver Badge with an additional grade, the Special Operations Diving Supervisor Badge. Prior to this change, the Scuba Diver Insignia/Badge was the same for all of the U.S. armed forces. The new design includes sharks, symbolizing speed, stealth, and lethal efficiency, and two Fairbairn-Sykes Fighting Knives in saltire, representing the heritage of OSS operational swimmers during World War II. The Army Combat Diver Qualification Course and Army Combat Diving Supervisors Course are taught by Company C, 2nd Battalion, 1st Special Warfare Training Group at the Special Forces Underwater Operations School, Naval Air Station Key West

Scuba: A 1 inch high silver badge consisting of a scuba diver's hood with face mask, mouthpiece, and breathing tubes. The width is 31/32 inch. The distinctive equipment of the scuba diver represents the skills and abilities required to qualify for the basic diver rating.

Salvage: A silver diving helmet, 1 inch in height, with the letter "S" 3/8 inch in height, superimposed on the chest plate. The width is 23/32 inch. The diver's helmet is the basic equipment and the letter "S" is superimposed on the design to reflect salvage activities such as harbor clearance, rock and concrete blasting, steel and timber removal and the removal of propellers for replacement.

Second Class: A silver diving helmet 1 inch in height. The width is 23/32 inch. The diver's helmet is the basic equipment used in diving operations.

First Class: A silver diving helmet 15/16 inch in height, between two dolphins, 1 inch high. The width is 1 3/32 inches. The badge includes the design of the diver's helmet to reflect diving operations and includes the dolphins to suggest the function of diving, without the helmet required of a deep sea diver.

Master: A silver diving helmet 7/8 inch in height in front of a trident 1 1/4 inches in height between two dolphins. The width is 1 3/32 inches. The trident is added to the design of the First Class badge which is symbolic of a marine spearhead and stands for valor and strength.

The Second Class, Salvage, First Class and Master Diver Badges were approved on 15 February 1944.

Subdued Badges: Subdued badges are authorized in metal and cloth. The metal badge for all designs is black.

Miniature Badges: Dress miniature badges are authorized for the following:

a. *Scuba:* 19/32 inch
b. *Second Class:* 7/16 inch
c. *S alvage:* 7/16 inch
d. *First Class:* 11/16 inch.
e. *Master:* 11/16 inch
f. *Special Operations*
g. *Special Operations Supervisor*

⭐ Combat Operations Diver Badges

Special Operations
Diver Badge

Special Operations
Diving Supervisor Badge

The Scuba Diver Badge has been renamed the Special Operations Diver Badge. The Special Operations Diver Badge replaced the Army Diver badge for U.S. Army Special Forces and Special Operations Soldiers.

Changes to the insignia went into effect July 20, 2005 and will effect active duty Army, Army National Guard, and Army Reserve Soldiers.

In addition to the new badge, an additional skill level known as the Special Operations Diving Supervisor's Badge was created.

The Special Operations Diver Badge is awarded to graduates of the U.S. Army John F. Kennedy Special Warfare Center and School *(USAJFKSWCS)* Combat Diver Qualification Course *(CDQC)*, Special Forces Underwater Operations, Key West, Florida or any other United States Army Special Operations Command *(USASOC)* approved combat diver qualification course. The prerequisite for obtaining the Special Operations Diving Supervisor's Badge is the Special Operations Diving Badge.

The Special Operations Diving Badge and Special Operations Diving Supervisor's Badge may be awarded retroactively to soldiers who successfully complete the SWCS Combat Diver's Qualification course on or following October 1, 1964.

Driver and Mechanic Badges *(6 clasps)* ⭐

I. **Description:** An oxidized silver cross pattee with a disk wheel and tire placed in the center. At the bottom of the cross are two rings for attaching qualification bars

II. **Symbolism:** The cross stands for achievement in operations and the wheel symbolizes skill area.

III. **Award Eligibility:** The Driver and Mechanics Badge is awarded to soldiers who successfully complete the prescribed requirements:

Driver; have a U.S. Government motor operators card and 12 months or 8000 miles of accident free driving.

Mechanic; must pass standard mechanics course and demonstrated mechanical skills to justify such a rating.

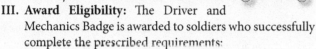

Operator; a soldier whose primary duty is to operate Army material handling equipment or mechanical equipment for 12 months or 500 hours.

IV. **Date Approved:** This badge was authorized during World War II.

V. **Subdued Badge:** No subdued badge is authorized.

VI. **Miniature Badge:** No miniature badge is authorized.

Parachute Rigger Badge, Group Five ⭐

I. **Description:** A silver winged hemispherical canopy with conically arrayed cords, 1-3/4 inches wide, with a band centered on the badge inscribed "RIGGER".

II. **Symbolism:** The winged parachute represents the functions of rigging of supplies for air drop as well as packing and repair of parachutes used for personnel and cargo.

III. **Award Eligibility:** The Parachute Rigger Badge is awarded to soldiers who successfully complete the prescribed course of instruction conducted by the U.S. Army Quartermaster School and have been awarded MOS 43E *(enlisted)* or 401A *(warrant)*. Officers may be awarded the badge upon completion of a course of instruction prescribed by AR 600-8-22.

IV. **Date Approved:** The Parachute Rigger Badge was approved

by the Chief of Staff, U.S. Army, on 9 June 1968. This approval was retroactive to include personnel who completed the prescribed course of instruction subsequent to May 1951.

V. **Subdued Badge:** The subdued badge is authorized in metal and cloth. The metal badges have a black finish. The cloth badge is on a base cloth with the wings, canopy, ropes and letters embroidered in black. The designation band and background between the ropes are embroidered in olive drab.

VI. **Miniature Badge:** A dress miniature badge, 7/8 inch wide, is authorized.

Nuclear Reactor Operator Badges *(Obsolete)* ⭐

The Army no longer conducts nuclear reactor operations nor nuclear reactor training. Current Army recipients may continue to wear them on the Army uniform. AR 672-5-1, dated 1 October 1990, terminated award of the badges.

I. **Description:** The badges are described as follows:

   a. *Basic:* On a 7/8 inch square centered on two horizontal bars each 1/8 inch in width separated by a 3/32 inch square and protruding 1/8 inch from each side of the square, a disc 3/4 inch in diameter bearing the symbol of the planet Uranus all silver colored metal 7/8 inch in height overall.

   b. *Second Class Operator:* The basic badge reduced in size partially encircled at the base by an open laurel wreath,

   c. *First Class Operator:* The basic badge reduced in size and entirely encircled by a closed laurel wreath all silver.

   d. *Shift Supervisor:* The design of the Shift Supervisor Badge is the same as the First Class Operator Badge, except it is gold colored metal.

II. **Symbolism:** The square *(cube)* is used to represent a nuclear reactor, the two bars representing control rods and thus alluding to nuclear reactor operations. The disc is symbolic of completeness and refers to the knowledge and training required of all nuclear reactor operators. The disc is also a

symbol of the sun, the source of all energy and power. The symbol of the planet Uranus from which the term "uranium" is derived refers to nuclear energy and power. Addition of the laurel wreaths signifies further achievement and

Basic   Second Class Operator

First Class Operator   Shift Supervisor

qualification. The gold color for the shift supervisor signifies the highest degree of achievement and qualification.

III. **Award Eligibility:** This badge is no longer awarded.

IV. **Date Approved:** The badges were approved by the Department of the Army on 18 June 1965.

V. **Subdued Badges:** Subdued badges are authorized in metal and cloth. The metal badges are black except the Shift Supervisor Badge, which is brown enamel.

VI. **Miniature Badges:** Dress miniature badges for all designs are authorized. The dress miniature badges are 1 inch wide.

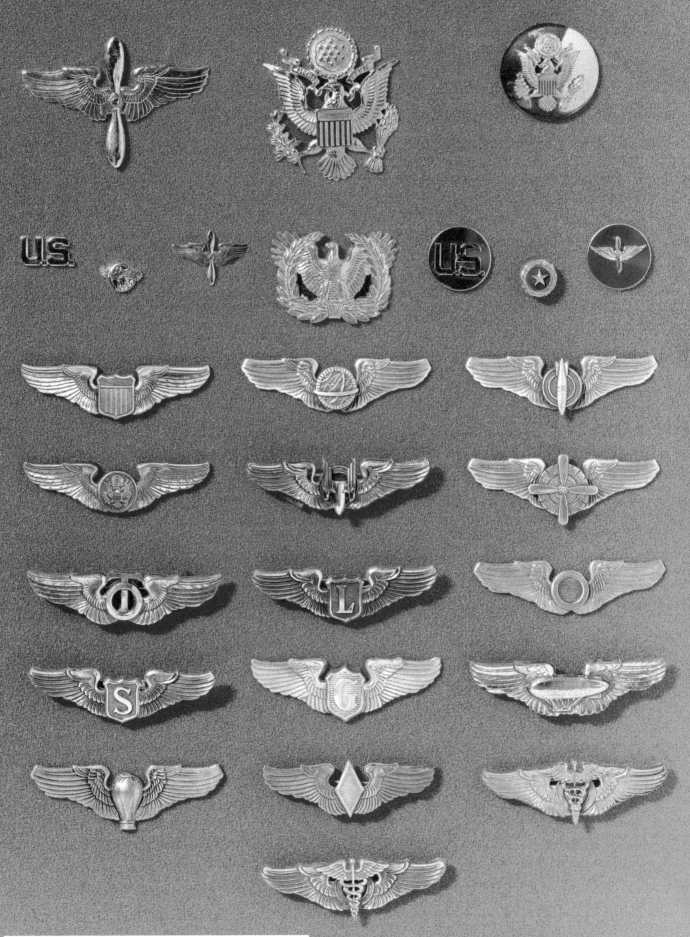

Pilot Wings

The standard design of pilot wings that remains in the U.S. Air Force today was introduced on January 25, 1919, as the "Airplane Pilot Badge."

Senior Pilot Wings

This rating was instituted in 1941 as "Military Airplane Pilot."

Command Pilot Wings

This rating was authorized on November 10, 1941, just after the Senior Pilot Badge.

Navigator Wings

Established on September 4, 1942, the navigator rating was awarded to graduates of the AAF aerial navigation course.

Bombardier Wings

Authorized on September 4, 1942, it depicts a bomb falling on a target, the same emblem used on earlier "Annual Distinguished Bomber" Awards.

Enlisted Aircrew Member Wings

Authorized on Sept. 4, 1942, and initially given to various aircrew positions including gunners, flight engineers, aerial photographers, and other positions.

Aerial Gunner Badge Wings

Authorized on April 29, 1943, for qualified gunners who were regular members of a combat crew.

Flight Engineer Wings

Authorized on June 19, 1945, these wings were awarded to those crew members who performed the flight engineer function.

Technical Observer Wings

Authorized on November 10, 1941, this badge was awarded to officers who were rated as a pilot or balloon pilot and who were certified by their commander as qualified to perform technical observation duty.

Liaison Pilot Wings

This badge with a "L" in the center of the wing was established on September 4, 1942, and was dropped by the AAF shortly thereafter.

Combat Observer (Aircraft Observer) Wings

This badge was established on October 14, 1921, and was discontinued on July 26, 1949. It was redesignated as "Aircraft Observer" on November 10, 1941.

Senior Aircraft Observer Wings

Combat Observer (Aircraft Observer) with 5 years experience.

Service Pilot Wings

Service pilots were qualified civilian pilots to fly transport, liaison in non-combat aircraft.

Glider Pilot Wings

Established 4 Sept. 1942, these wings were awarded to graduates of Advanced Glider Training.

Balloon Pilot Wings

This badge was awarded for completion of the balloon pilot's course in military airships or motorized balloons.

Senior Balloon Pilot Wings

This rating was awarded to balloon pilots who had attained at least 1000 hours of airship or motorized balloon flying and ten years service in air units.

Balloon Observer Wings

Balloon observer wings were authorized in 1941 when the original "balloon observer" wings became "balloon pilot" wings.

Airship Pilot Wings

This badge was authorized in 1921 and was awarded to graduates of the Air Corps Balloon and Airship School who had not less than 200 hours of flying time and had at least 75 hours solo.

Women's Air Force Service Pilots (WASP) Wings

These wings became the official wings presented to graduates of the WASP school from 1943 onward.

Flight Surgeon Wings

The flight surgeon rating was introduced in 1942, and was officially authorized in 1943 for the AAF.

Flight Nurse Wings

Flight nurse wings were established on December 15, 1943, and were awarded to women in the Army Nurse Corps who served at least six months in an AAF hospital.

First Army Marksmanship Badge

Army Expert Rifleman Badge *(obsolete)*

Awarded to Army and Army Reserve personnel who qualified as expert on set rifle courses. The badge has crossed 1903 Springfield rifles over a wreath of laurel leaves. The straight suspension bar has decorative ends. The word Expert Riflemen appear within the bar. While this bar was obsolete by World War II many soldiers who had earned it earlier still wore it since it was considered such a handsome award.

Army Sharpshooter Badge *(obsolete)*

Awarded to Army and Army Reserve personnel who qualified Sharpshooter on set rifle courses. The badge in silver, consisted of maltese like cross with the inner arms pebbled. The center of the cross is a target. The cross is suspended by rings from a suspension bar with rounded ends. The word Sharpshooter is in raised letters within the bar.

Army Marksmanship Badge *(obsolete)*

Awarded to Army and Army Reserve personnel who qualified as marksman with the rifle on set courses. The badge consists

of a silver frame bar with rounded ends. Within the bar appeared the word "marksman", and at both ends of the word are raise targets. The background is pebbled.

Distinguished International Shooter Badge

Awarded by the National Board for the Promotion of Rifle Practice for outstanding performance in major international

competition. It may be awarded to any US citizen who places first, second, or third in rifle, pistol, or shotgun competition (individual or team). Also awarded to members of U.S. international teams who place in the top 15 percent of all competitions in the Olympic Games, International Shooting Union, World Championship, Pan American Games, or the Championship of the Americas. The reverse is blank engraving of the recipient's name and date of award

Army Distinguished Rifleman Badge

Awarded to Army personnel in recognition for outstanding achievement in competitive target practice firing with the military service rifle; the award requires a specified number of points (30) attained from

competition matches, basically this meant winning three team badges. Badge is gold, shield-shaped with a black and white target in the center; the shield is attached to a suspension bar that contains the words "U.S. Army." The reverse is blank engraving of the recipient's name and date of award.

Distinguished Pistol Shot Badge

Army personnel are recognized for outstanding achievement in competitive target practice firing with the military service pistol with the Distinguished Pistol Shot Badge; the award requires a specified number of points (30) attained from competition matches. Usually awarded to a winner of three team badges. It is a gold, shield-shaped badge with a black and white target in the center and the words "U.S. Army" on the suspension bar.

Team Marksmanship Badges *(Obsolete)*

This badge was awarded to members of Army marksmanship teams. There are three parts to this badge; pendant, clasp, and top bar. The pendant has a bow with arrows within the annulet with thirteen stars encircled by an oak wreath. The team disk is bronze with the annulet enameled in the appropriate branch color such as blue for the infantry, yellow for the cavalry etc. Team clasps are in the form of rifles, pistols or automatic rifles. Clasps are in gold, silver or bronze. Different bars could be used to indicate Corps level or Army level.

For U.S. Army Awardees Excellence-In-Competition Badge —Rifle (Bar and Pendant)

Gold　　Silver　　Bronze

Army Bar

Corps Area Bar

Clasps

Rifle Team Bronze

Pistol Team Gold

Automatic Rifle Teams Silver

The current *expert* qualification badges are authorized qualified personnel of the Army, Army Reserve, and National Guard is made of oxidize silver. World War II versions are made of sterling silver but today it is a white metal *(silver, nickel and rhodium)*, 1.17 inches in height, a cross patee with the representation of a target placed on the center and enclosed by a wreath of laurel leaves tied at the bottom with a knot. It has two rings at the bottom for attaching a bar naming the weapon with which the recipient qualified.

Sharpshooter qualification badge is authorized qualified personnel of the Army, Army Reserve, and National Guard. World War II versions are made of sterling silver but today it is a white metal *(silver, nickel, and rhodium)*, 1 inch in height, a cross patee with the representation of a target placed on the center. It has two rings at the bottom for attaching a bar naming the weapon with which the recipient qualified.

Marksman qualification badge is authorized qualified personnel of the Army, Army Reserve, and National Guard. World War II versions are made of sterling silver but today it is a white metal *(silver, nickel, and rhodium)*, 1 inch in height, a cross patee. It has two rings at the bottom for attaching a bar naming the weapon with which the recipient qualified.

Weapons qualification bars: Originally of sterling silver these bars of white metal have rings at the top for attaching to the Expert, Sharpshooter and Marksmanship qualification badge or to the last previously earned bar. Qualification Bars:

RIFLE	PISTOL	ROCKET LAUNCHER	FIELD ARTY
RECOILLESS RIFLE	FLAMETHROWER	SUBMACHINE GUN	AA ARTILLERY
AUTO.RIFLE	SMALL BORE PISTOL	GRENADE	MISSILE
SMALL BORE RIFLE	TANK WEAPON	CARBINE	AEROWEAPONS
BAYONET	MACHINE GUN	MORTAR	

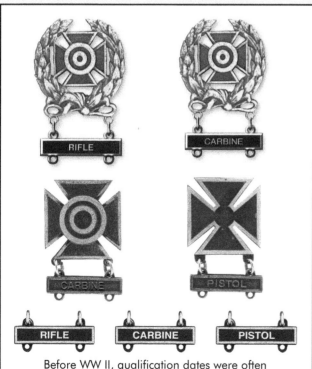

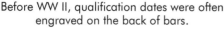

Before WW II, qualification dates were often engraved on the back of bars.

Bars with the following inscriptions are currently authorized for display on the badges:

- Rifle, Machine Gun, Submachine Gun, Rocket Launcher, Small Bore Pistol, Pistol, Field Artillery, Grenade, Mortar, Missile, AA Artillery, Tank Weapons, Carbine, Bayonet, Aeroweapons, Auto Rifle, Flamethrower, Recoilless Rifle and Small Bore Rifle.

Inscription formerly authorized on qualification bars:
- 1941 Deleted Sword, added Small Bore Rifle, Small Bore Pistol, Submachine Gun and Small Bore MG.
- 1944 added Carbine, Antitank, 81mm Mortar, 60 mm Mortar, TD 75mm, TD 57mm and TD 3 inch.
- 1948 added Recoilless Rifle, Mortar. Deleted Pistol D, Pistol M, Mines, C.W.S. Weapons, Aerial Gunner, Aerial bomber, Small Bore MG, Antitank, 81mm Mortar, 60mm Mortar, TD *(all types)*.
- 1951 added Submarine Mines.
- 1972 added Aeroweapons.

Prior to 1951 regulation, the titles of the badges were Marksman and 2d Class Gunner; Sharpshooter and First Class Gunner and Expert.

Presidential Service Identification Badge

The Presidential Service Badge was established on September 1, 1964. It replaced the White House Service Badge which had been established on June 1, 1960. A replica of the Presidential Coat of Arms is superimposed on a dark blue enameled disk surrounded by 27 gold rays radiating from the center. It is given by the President to Armed Forces personnel assigned to duty in the White House office or to military units and support facilities under the administration of the Military Assistant to the President for a period of at least one year, after January 20, 1961, as recognition, in a permanent way, of their contribution in the service of the President. Once earned, the badge becomes a permanent part of the recipient's uniform, and may be worn after the recipient leaves Presidential service.

Presidential
Service Badge

Vice-Presidential Service Identification Badge

Old Vice Presidential
Service Badge

Current Vice Presidential
Service Badge

The Vice-Presidential Service Badge was established on July 8, 1970. The seal of the Vice-President of the United States is superimposed on a white enameled disc surrounded by 27 gold rays radiating from the center. The badge is awarded in the name of the Vice-President to members of the armed forces who have been assigned to duty in the Office of the Vice-President for a period of at least one year after January 20, 1969. Once earned, the badge becomes a permanent part of the uniform.

Office of the Secretary of Defense Identification Badge

The Office of the Secretary of Defense Identification Badge is a military badge issued to members of the United States armed forces who are permanently assigned to the Office of the Secretary of Defense (OSD) and its subordinate offices, and in addition, to some of the Defense Agencies and Department of Defense Field Activities.

The badge was first created in 1949 and was referred to as the "National Military Establishment Identification Badge." In 1950, the badge was renamed as "Department of Defense Identification Badge." On December 20, 1962 the badge was given its current name. It is issued as a permanent decoration and is to be worn for the remainder of an individual's military career, provided that a service member served at least one year (two years for Reserve personnel not on active duty) in or in support of OSD. Army personnel are awarded the badge when they are assigned on a permanent basis to any of the The Offices of the Secretary of Defense The badge, 2 inches in diameter, consists of an eagle with wings grasping three crossed arrows on its breast a shield paleways of thirteen pieces argent and gules a chief azure, a gold annulet passing behind the wing tips bearing thirteen gold stars above the eagle and a wreath of laurel and olive in green enamel below the eagle, the whole superimposed on a silver sunburst of 33 rays.

Joint Chiefs of Staff
Identification Badge
Miniature

The Office of the Joint Chiefs of Staff Identification Badge is a United States military badge authorized members of the Joint Chiefs of Staff upon appointment to position as either a Service Head, Vice Chairman, or Chairman of the Joint Chiefs of Staff. The badge is also authorized staff and support personnel assigned to the Office of the Chairman and the Joint Staff. Individuals may qualify for permanent wear of this badge after being assigned for one year on active duty or two years as a reservist. The badge is an oval silver metal wreath of laurel, 2 1/4 inches in height and 2 inches in width overall, the shield of the United States *(the chief in blue enamel and the 13 stripes alternating white and red enamel)* superimposed on four gold metal unsheathed swords, two in pale and two in saltire with points to chief, the points and pommels resting on the wreath, the blades and grips entwined with a gold metal continuous scroll surrounding the shield with the word JOINT at the top and the words CHIEFS OF STAFF at the bottom, all in blue enamel letters. Laurel is symbolic of achievement, courage, and victory. The four unsheathed swords refer to the armed might of the Army, Navy, Air Force, and Marine Corps and their combined constant vigilance and readiness in the defense of the United States.

The Office of the Joint Chiefs of Staff Identification Badge was first approved in February 1963 and has remained unchanged in appearance since then.

U.S. Army Combat Service Identification Badge

The Combat Service Identification Badge uniquely identifies a Soldier's combat service with a specific major U.S. Army unit. The CSIB is authorized on the blue Army Service Uniform, Class A, Army Service Uniform Class B, and the transitioning *new pinks and green* uniform. The CSIB cannot be worn on the Army Combat Uniform *(ACU)* or the Army Green Uniform. Soldiers will continue to wear the Shoulder Sleeve Insignia-Former Wartime Service *(full-color unit patch denoting service with a specific U.S. Army unit)* on their right sleeve of the ACU and Army Green Uniform to denote combat service. The CSIB is worn centered on the right breast pocket for male Soldiers and on the right side - parallel to the waistline - for female Soldiers. The CSIB is ranked fifth in the order of precedence for identification badges outlined in Army Regulation 670-1.

Army Staff Identification Badge

The Army Staff Identification Badge is a badge worn by personnel who serve at the Office of the Secretary of the Army and the Army Staff at Headquarters, Department of the Army (HQDA) and its agencies. The badge is a distinguishing emblem of service. Initially issued as a temporary badge, officers and enlisted personnel demonstrating outstanding performance of duty and meeting all eligibility requirements can be processed after one complete year (365 days cumulative) of assignment and receive a certificate authorizing permanent wear of the badge.

General Douglas MacArthur first proposed an Army General Staff Badge in 1931, but it was not until 1933 that the United States War Department authorized it. The name was changed in 1982 from the Army General Staff Identification Badge to the Army Staff Identification Badge.

On the Army uniform, the Badge is worn centered on the right breast pocket; however, wear of the Badge is authorized on the left breast pocket when worn in conjunction with a deployment CSIB (Combat Service Identification Badge).

The Guard of the Unknown Soldier identification badge is authorized by the Commanding Officer, First Battalion, Third Infantry, for wear by each member of the Guard, Tomb of the Unknown Soldier, during their assignment of duty. Effective 17 December, 1963, the Commanding Officer, First Battalion, Third Infantry, may authorize the wearing of the badge as a permanent badge for soldiers who have served honorably a minimum of nine months and who are recommended by the Commander of the Honor Guard company, First Battalion *(Reinforced),* Third Infantry *(the Old Guard).* The Identification Badge, Guard of the Tomb of the Unknown Soldier is a beautifully designed silver metal badge for wear on the right breast pocket of the uniform. It is made of frosted and cut silver with the highlights polished. The design is an inverted wreath of laurel and olive leaves intertwined at the top of the badge. In the center of the wreath is

a replica of the of the tomb of the Unknown Soldier resting on a platform with the words Honor Guard. This award is retroactive to 1 February 1958 for personnel on active duty.

Drill Sergeant Identification Badge

Award of the the Drill Sergeant identification badge is successful completion of the Drill Sergeant course and assignment as a drill sergeant to a training command.

The Commandant of the Drill Sergeant school can authorize the permanent wear of the badge to eligible personnel by letter. Officers are authorized to wear this badge if it was permanently awarded to them while in an enlisted status. It is worn on the lower part of the right side breast pocket of the Class A uniform.

The badge may be revoked if the recipient is removed from the position of a Drill Sergeant for cause, regardless of the amount of time the individual has served in the position in a satisfactory manner. Authority to revoked the badge is delegated to Commanders of U.S. Army Training Centers and Commandant of the drill sergeant schools. Commanders of U.S. Army Training Centers may further delegate the revocation authority to commanders in the grade of Colonel or higher who have the authority to remove soldiers from Drill Sergeant duties and withdraw the skill qualification identifier.

U.S. Army Recruiter Identification Badge

The U.S. Army Basic Recruiter Badge is authorized for wear by military personnel assigned to Recruiting Commands designated by the Commanding General, U. S. Army Recruiting Command. Officers are authorized to wear this badge if it was permanently awarded to them while in an enlisted status.

Gold Achievement Stars: 1, 2 or 3 gold achievement stars may be awarded for meeting the criteria set by Recruiting Command. The stars will be affixed to the basic badge.

The Commanding General, Recruiting Command may authorize the wear of the basic recruiter's badge as a permanent part of the uniform for qualified enlisted personnel and commanders who honorably completed their tour of duty in recruiting on or after 1 July 1980.

U. S. Army Gold Recruiter Badge and sapphire achievement stars are authorized by Recruiting Command for wear by eligible members to meet established criteria. This award is retroactive to January 1975 for personnel on active duty. The Gold Recruiter's Badge can be authorized as a permanent part of the uniform for eligible personnel by the Commanding General, U.S. Army Recruiting Command.

Basic Recruiter Badge

Master Recruiter's Badge

After the Vietnam War, the Army's Surgeon General requested a unique recruiter badge be authorized for wear by Army medical recruiters to help distinguished them from regular Army recruiters. In November 1991, the Army Deputy Chief of Staff for Personnel approved the creation of the Army Medical Department Recruiter Identification Badge which was in use until June 2001 when it was replaced by the Army Recruiter Identification Badges.

Career Counselor Badge

Old Basic in silver,
Senior in gold

The Career Counselors Badge may be authorized for wear by enlisted personnel assigned to authorized duty positions which require the military occupational specialty 00E or 79 delta, including personnel assigned to U.S. Army Recruiting Command. The award is retroactive to 1 January 1972. The badge is authorized for temporary wear only and will be withdrawn when the awardee is reassigned or ceases to perform the require duties of MOS 00E or 79 delta satisfactorily.

The Career Counselors Badge may be authorized for wear by enlisted members of the Army Reserve who have successfully completed the Resident or Nonresident Reserve Component Recruiting Course and had been designated as U. S. Army Reserve Reenlistment Noncommissioned Officers. The badge is authorized for temporary wear only and will be withdrawn when the awardee ceases to be a designated a U.S. Army Reserve Reenlistment Noncommissioned Officer.

National Guard Recruiter Badge

The Army National Guard Recruiter's Badge may be authorized for wear by enlisted personnel assigned to authorized National Guard duty positions which require military occupational specialty 00E or 79 delta, including personnel assigned to the United States Army Recruiting Command. Authority to wear this badge is withdrawn when the awardee is released from recruiting duty, although it may be retained as a memento of successful completion of assigned recruiting duties.

New ARNG Recruiting & Retention Badges (Basic, Senior, & Expert)

Master gold
with wreath

U.S. Army Reserve Recruiter Badge

The U.S. Army Reserve Recruiter Badge is authorized for wear by qualified members of the U.S. Army Reserve who had been designated by letter as an Army Reserve Recruiter. Wear of the badge as a uniform item is announced by the Commanders of Army Reserve General Officer Commands. Authority to wear this badge is withdrawn when the awardee is released from recruiting duty, although it may be retained as a memento of successful completion of assigned recruiting duties.

National Defense University Identification Badge

Army personnel assigned to the faculty and the staff of the National Defense University, National War College, Industrial College of the Armed Forces and the Armed Forces Staff College can be authorized to wear the identification badge during their assignment. The badge is normally worn on the right side.

Unified Combat Command Identification Badges

United States Africa Command,	United States Central Command	United States European Command	United States Cyber Command
United States Indo Pacific Command	United States Southern Command	United States Special Operations Command	United States Strategic Command,
United States Northern Command,	United States Transportation Command	United States Joint Forces Command Deactivated 2011	United States Space Command 1985-2002 2018 reactivated

These badges are authorized for military personnel to wear when assigned to the staff of a combatant command and while assigned to subordinate unified command and direct reporting unit. Authorization is determined by the unified combat commander. The identification badge design is unique for each unified combat command. The badge is normally worn on the left side of the Army Class A and B uniform, the Army blue uniform, the mess dress and evening dress uniforms.

Army Instructor Identification Badges

In June 2014, the U.S. Army implemented the Army Instructor Identification Badges. These badges are earned by certified noncommissioned officers (NCOs) who work as instructors in the Noncommissioned Officer Education System.

The Army Instructor Identification Badges are awarded in three levels; basic, senior, and master. To earn the basic badge a NCO must meet the instructor requirements and complete 80 hours of instruction as a primary instructor plus meet two separate evaluations requirements 30 days apart. To earn the senior badge a NCO must meet the same requirements as the basic badge and graduate from the small group instructor training course/intermediate facilitation skills course and the systems approach to training basic course/foundation training developer course. They also must complete 400 hours of instruction as a primary instructor. To earn the master badge a NCO must complete the entire basic and senior badge requirements and graduate from the advanced facilitator skills course or the faculty development program and the evaluating instructor's workshop. These badges can be worn on the Army Combat Uniform, as a subdued badge or patch, and the full-color versions on Army service uniforms. The Army Instructor Identification Badges are permanent awards and can be worn on Army uniforms for the remainder of a soldier's career.

The U.S. Army Military Police Badge is authorized for wear by qualified members of the U.S. Army Military Police who had been designated as Military Police and completed the prescribed course of training. Wear of the badge as a uniform item is announced by the Military Police Commanders. Authority to wear this badge is withdrawn when the awardee is released from Military Police duty. The badge is an official symbol of their office.

Military Police Badge

Physical Fitness Badge

The Secretary of the Army established the Physical Fitness Badge on October 1986 for award to soldiers who obtain a minimum score of 290 points on the Army of physical readiness tests to and meet the weight control requirements in Army Regulation 600-9. Once the badge is awarded, it may be retained as long as a minimum passing score is achieved on subsequent Army physical training tests and the weight control requirements are met. The Army physical fitness scorecard is the document used to certify an individual's entitlement to wear the badge.

Physical Fitness
Excellence Patch

Army ROTC Nurse Cadet Program Identification Badge

The Army ROTC Nurse Cadet Program Identification Badge is authorized for issue to and wear by contract ROTC Cadets enrolled in a program leading to a baccalaureate degree in nursing. This badge was formerly referred to as the Army Student Nurse Program Identification Badge. The badge evolved from the bright red enamel modified Cross of St. John worn on the collar of Army nurses in the Spanish American War. From 1901 to 1907 the Army authorized a green enamel cross for nurses.

Army Nurse
Badge

Overseas Service Bars

The Overseas Service Bar is an Army decoration displayed as an embroidered gold bar worn horizontally on the right sleeve of the U.S. Army Class A uniform. Called an Overseas Chevron in the First World War, it was an inverted chevron sewed on the lower left uniform sleeve. In 1918, the Overseas Chevron design was identical to the Wound Chevron worn on the right sleeve. In World War II, the Overseas Chevron was redesignated as the Overseas Bar and designed as a horizontal bar. Veterans of both the First and Second World Wars wore both the Overseas Bar and Chevron together.

During the Vietnam War, the Overseas Service Bar was worn on the lower right sleeve, instead of the left. Today an Overseas Service Bar is awarded for each 6 months overseas in a combat zone. Overseas time is cumulative, therefore one bar can be awarded for two 3 month deployments. Soldiers can be awarded multiple Overseas Service Bars for several years spent in an overseas combat zone. Multiple Overseas Service Bars are worn vertically on the right sleeve of the uniform. The Overseas Service Bar is a separate decoration from the Overseas Service Ribbon however soldiers can receive both awards for the same period of service.

Overseas
Service Bars

Service Stripes

A service stripe, traditionally called a hash mark by soldiers, is worn by enlisted soldiers to denote length of service. The Army awards each stripe for three years service. The concept of a service stripe goes back to the Civil War where sleeve stripes marked completion of a standard enlistment. Soldiers wear them on the left sleeve and Overseas Service Bars on the right one. Service stripes are only worn on class A uniforms.

A service stripe is presented to an enlisted soldier upon completion of the specified term of service, regardless of the soldier's disciplinary history. A soldier with non-judicial punishments or court-martials will still receive a service stripe for three years service but the Good Conduct Medal would be denied.

Service Stripes

Aides to General of the Army Collar Insignia

Aide to General of the Army

A blue shield, 3/4 inch in height, with five white stars arranged in a circle, inner points touching, surmounted above by a gold color eagle displayed with wings reversed 1/2 inch in height. The insignia for Aides to General of the Army was approved on 15 January 1945.

Aides to General Officers Collar Insignia

A shield, 3/4 inch in height surmounted by a gold color eagle displayed with wings reversed 1/2 inch in height; the chief of the shield is blue with silver stars reflecting the grade of the general officer the aide is serving, and 13 vertical stripes, 7 silver and 6 red. The insignia was approved in 1902.

| General | Lieutenant General | Major General | Brigadier General |

Aide, Secretary of the Army Aide, Under Secretary of the Army Collar Insignia

Aide to the Secretary of the Army — **Aide to the Under Secretary of the Army**

Secretary of the Army: A red shield surmounted by the Coat of Arms of the United States in gold between four white enameled stars, supporting a gold eagle displayed, wings inverted, 1-1/4 inch height overall. Under Secretary of the Army: A white shield surmounted by the Coat of Arms of the United States in gold between four red enameled stars, supporting a gold eagle displayed, wings inverted, 1-1/4 inch height overall. The insignia for aides to the Secretary of the Army was prescribed in Army Regulations of 1948. The insignia for aides to the Under Secretary of the Army was approved in 1962.

Aide, Chief of Staff, Army Aide, Vice Chief of Staff, Army Collar Insignia

Aide to the Chief of Staff

Chief of Staff: A shield 3/4 inch in height divided from lower left to upper right, the upper part red and the lower part white, a silver five-pointed star surmounted by the coat of arms of the United States in gold, between two white five-pointed stars in base, with a gold color eagle with wings reversed, 1/2 inch in height, placed above the shield. Vice Chief of Staff: A shield 3/4 inch in height divided saltirewise, the upper and lower part white and each side red, a silver five-pointed star surmounted by the coat of army of the United States in gold, between two red stars at the top and two red stars at the bottom, with a gold color eagle with wings reversed 1/2 inch in height place above the shield.

Aide, Chief of Staff, Army Aide, Vice Chief of Staff, Army Continued

Aide to the Chief of Staff

Prior to 1963, Aides to the Chief of Staff wore the same insignia as aides to other generals. On 25 April 1963, the present design of insignia for aide to the Chief of Staff was approved. Aides to the Vice-Chief continued to wear the same insignia as aides to other generals. On 10 June 1987, the insignia for aide to the Vice Chief of Staff was approved.

Aide to Secretary of Defense Collar Insignia

Aide to Secretary of Defense

On a blue shield, 3/4 inches in height, surmounted by a gold color eagle displayed with wings reversed 1/2 inch in height, three crossed arrows in gold color between four white enameled stars (two and two). The insignia for Aides to the Secretary of Defense was approved in August 1948. The three crossed arrows are of the style on the Department of Defense Seal. Four stars are commonly used on positional flags for secretarial level positions.

Aides, President of the United States Aides, Vice President of the United States Collar Insignia

Aide to the President

Aide to the Vice President

President of the United States: A blue shield bearing a circle of 13 white stars supporting a gold eagle displayed, wings inverted, 1 1/4 inch height overall. Vice President of the United States: A white shield bearing a circle of 13 blue stars supporting a gold eagle displayed, wings inverted, 1 1/4 inch height overall. Prior to 1946, there was no prescribed insignia for Aides to the President of the United States. In 1946, an insignia was adopted — 48 stars in a ring on a shield surmounted by an eagle. This design was changed in 1953 to 13 white stars on a blue shield surmounted by an eagle. The insignia for Aides to the Vice President of the United States was approved on 24 January 1969.

Aide to Chairman, Joint Chiefs of Staff, Aide to vice Chairman, Joint Chiefs of Staff Collar Insignia

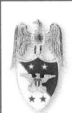

Aide to the Chairman JCS

Aide to the Vice Chairman JCS

Aide to Chairman: On a shield, 3/4 inch in height divided diagonally from upper left to lower right, the upper part blue and the lower part white, a gold color eagle between two white five pointed stars at the top and two blue five pointed stars at the base, with a gold color metal eagle displayed with wings reversed 1/2 inch in height placed above the shield. Aide to Vice Chairman: On a white shield 3/4 inch in height divided diagonally with a blue center stripe from upper left to lower right, a gold color metal eagle between two five pointed stars at the top and two five pointed stars at the base (blue star on white and white star on blue), with a gold color metal eagle with wings reversed, 1/2 inch in height, placed above the shield. The eagle on the shield is of the design of the eagle on the Department of the Defense seal. The background colors are the same as the flag designs for the positions. Light blue is the color normally associated with Department of Defense.

❖ The Aiguillette, Fourragere, Lanyard, and Blue Cord

Aiguillettes - Aides de Camp

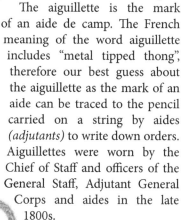

The aiguillette is the mark of an aide de camp. The French meaning of the word aiguillette includes "metal tipped thong", therefore our best guess about the aiguillette as the mark of an aide can be traced to the pencil carried on a string by aides (*adjutants*) to write down orders. Aiguillettes were worn by the Chief of Staff and officers of the General Staff, Adjutant General Corps and aides in the late 1800s.

Today the service aiguillette is a braided gold cord 3/16 of an inch in diameter and 30 1/2 inches long. Aiguillettes are worn by Army officers to identify them as aides to top-ranking government officials and general officers. Aiguillettes are worn with both service and dress uniforms on the right shoulder by aides to the President, Vice-President, foreign heads of state, and White House aides. All others wear the aiguillettes on the left shoulder.

Army attaches, assistant attaches and aides wear the service aiguillette on the Army green and blue uniforms. The dress aiguillette consists of the service aiguillette without the front part and substituting a front part 25 inches in length, with 15 inches of braiding. The aiguillette is worn on the right side by military aides to the president, White House social aides and officers designated aides to foreign heads of state.

Infantry Blue Shoulder Cord

Officers and enlisted men of the Infantry who have been awarded the Combat Infantryman Badge or Expert Infantryman Badge or have completed the basic infantry training courses wear the infantry blue shoulder cord on the right shoulder of the Army dress and full dress uniform. The cord goes under the arm and attaches to a regulation small U.S. Army button attached to the shoulder seam 1/2 inch outside the right collar edge.

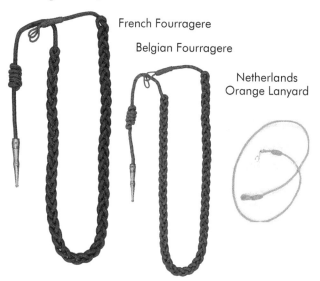

French Fourragere

Belgian Fourragere

Netherlands Orange Lanyard

French Fourragere

The French fourragere is awarded by the French government when a unit has been cited twice for the French Cross of War (*Croix de Guerre*). The fourragere is dark green and red, the colors of the ribbon of the Croix de Guerre. When a unit has been cited four times for the French Cross of War the colors of the fourragere change to those of the French Military Medal (*yellow and green*) since the Medaille Militaire is the ranking decoration. The award of the fourragere requires a specific decree of the French government. The French fourragere may be worn when authorized for either permanent or temporary wear. The fourragere is worn over the left shoulder with the left arm passing through the large loop of the cord; the small loop will engage the button under the shoulder strap. The metal pencil attachment will hang naturally to the front.

Belgian Fourragere

The Belgian fourragere may be awarded by the Belgian government when a unit has been cited twice in the Order of the Day of the Belgian Army. The Belgian fourragere may be worn only when authorized for permanent wear.

Netherlands Orange Lanyard

The Orange Lanyard may be awarded by the Netherlands Government when a unit has been cited and awarded the Netherlands Military Order of William. It may also be awarded independently. The award of the Orange Lanyard is not automatic but must be by specific decree of the Netherlands. The Netherlands orange lanyard may be worn only when authorized for permanent wear.

❖ U.S. Army Shoulder Sleeve Insignia

Since ancient times, the identification of friend or foe has been a battlefield problem. Roman armies often would have the various units wear different colored horse hair in their helmets to provide commanders a quick overall view of their troops disposition. In the Middle Ages, knights would have their family's coat-of-arms painted on their shields or on a banner providing the troops an emblem as a central point to rally around during combat.

During the nineteenth century, the new United States had no real need for battlefield identification until the Civil War (1861-1865). With the massive build-up of armies and the tactics of the time exacerbating the problem, the Union army attempted to resolve the need by assigning each army corps an emblem to be sewn to the tops of caps to provide officers on horseback the ability to identify their respective troops. These emblems were common geometric designs: circle, square, triangle, etc. for the corps. Each division of the corps used the same emblem but in a different color. After the end of hostilities, and the reduction of forces, the custom died out until the last months of World War I.

The rebirth of this concept in the twentieth century was not without controversy. The story is told that when the 81st Infantry Division disembarked in France in 1918, the members of the division were all wearing a "patch" on their left shoulder depicting a black bobcat on an olive-drab background. This was to recall that they had trained on the banks of Bobcat Creek at Camp Jackson, SC. When word of this event reached higher headquarters, there being no regulations to cover this activity, orders were immediately issued to have the offending emblem removed.

The Commanding General of the 81st Division made a personal appeal to General Pershing to permit his troops to continue wearing the patch. General Pershing is reported to have said: "Go ahead. But, be sure that you are worthy of it". General Pershing then not only rescinded the order but, realizing the morale value of this simple piece of cloth, ordered that all other units of the American Expeditionary Force would immediately create similar designs for their troops to wear. It was felt that this would have a positive morale effect on the troops in the trenches and give the members a sense of comradeship and unit cohesion that was necessary for that type of warfare. It permitted the individual to feel that he was a member of a particular group and could take pride in being associated with the accomplishments of that unit. This opened the gates of creativity

13th ENGR. REGIMENT | 5th A.A.A. REGIMENT | CAMOFLAGE CORPS | SEPARATE ARTY. BN. | ANTI-AIRCRAFT DIV. UNITS

and soon the army had designs on everything - uniforms, vehicles, equipment and buildings.

66th Div | 69th Div | 70th Div | 71st Div

Along came World War II and the explosive build-up of the military. New units were mobilized who required insignia. Overnight hundreds of new designs appeared. Designs poured in from all sources; the units themselves, professional designers, Hollywood, and New York.

Since the 1950's, we now have an Institute of Heraldry as part of the Defense Department to create and approve the individual designs. Strict criteria has been put into place to dictate the appearance of the insignia. Examples of this criteria are: There can be nothing in the design to indicate death or destruction to our enemies, no skulls or skeletons and no political signs can be used. The U.S. Army, with all different color combinations can historically catalog over 5,000 patches.

3d Inf CSIB | 3d Inf SSI

The Combat Service Identification Badge (CSIB), a metallic heraldic device worn on the right side of the United States Army's Blue Service Uniform has replaced the Shoulder Sleeve Insignia of Former Wartime Service worn on the Army Green "Class A" Uniform that was discontinued in 2015. CSIB badges are silver or gold-colored metal and enamel devices that are 2 inches in height consisting of a design similar to the unit Shoulder Sleeve Insignia *(SSI)*. The Combat Service Identification Badge is worn on the lower right pocket for male soldiers and on the right side parallel to the waistline for female soldiers. Soldiers wear the CSIB on the blue Army Service Uniform, Class A and Class B. The CSIB is not worn on the Army Combat Uniform *(ACU)* or the discontinued Army Green Uniform. Soldiers continue to wear the subdued Shoulder Sleeve Insignia-Former Wartime Service on their right sleeve of the ACU blouse to denote combat service. However the new Pinks and Greens uniform will bring back the cloth shoulder sleeve insignia as worn in World War II, Korea, and Vietnam.

❖ United States Army Shoulder Sleeve Insignia - World War II

ARMY GROUPS

 First Army Group

 Sixth Army Group

 Twelfth Army Group

 Fifteenth Army Group

ARMIES

 First Army

 Second Army

 Third Army

 Fourth Army

 Fifth Army

 Sixth Army

 Seventh Army

 Eighth Army

 Ninth Army

 Tenth Army

 Fifteenth Army

CORPS

 I Corps

 II Corps

 III Corps

 IV Corps

 V Corps

 VI Corps

 VII Corps

 VIII Corps

IX Corps

X Corps

XI Corps

XII Corps

 XIII Corps

 XIV Corps

 XV Corps

 XVI Corps

 XVIII Corps

 XIX Corps

 XX Corps

XXI Corps

XXII Corps

XXIII Corps

XXIV Corps

XXXVI Corps

INFANTRY, AIRBORNE AND CAVALRY DIVISIONS

 1st Div

 2d Div

 3d Div

 4th Div

5th Div

6th Div

7th Div

8th Div

9th Div

 10th Div

 11th Div

13 th ABN Div

 17th Div

 24th Div

 25th Div

 26th Div

27th Div

28th Div

29th Div

30th Div

31st Div

32d Div

33d Div

34th Div

 35th Div

 36th Div

 37th Div

 38th Div

40th Div

41st Div

42d Div

43d Div

44th Div

45th Div

63d Div

65th Div

 66th Div

 69th Div

 70th Div

 71st Div

75th Div

76th Div

77th Div

78th Div

79th Div

80th Div

81st Div

82d Div

83d Div

 84th Div

 85th Div

 86th Div

 87th Div

88th Div

89th Div

90th Div

91st Div

92d Div

93d Div

94th Div

95th Div

96th Div

 97th Div

 98th Div

 99th Div

 100th Div

101st ABN Div

102d Div

103d Div

104th Div

106th Div

 1st Cav Div

 2d Cav Div

❖ United States Army Shoulder Sleeve Insignia - World War II

ARMORED DIVISIONS

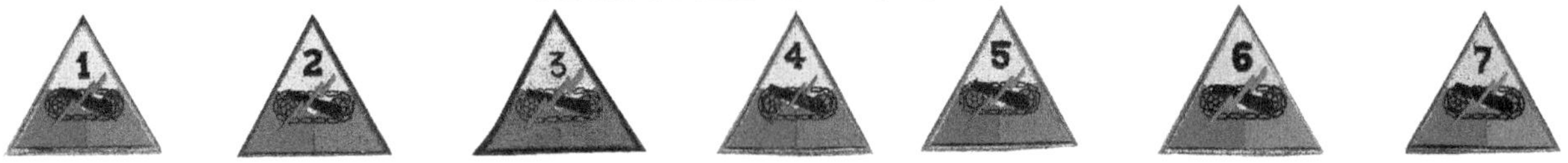

1st Armd Div · 2d Armd Div · 3d Armd Div · 4th Armd Div · 5th Armd Div · 6th Armd Div · 7th Armd Div

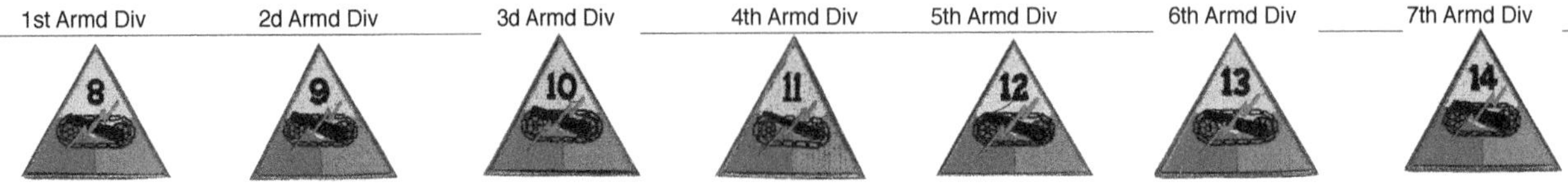

8th Armd Div · 9th Armd Div · 10th Armd Div · 11th Armd Div · 12th Armd Div · 13th Armd Div · 14th Armd Div

ARMY AIR FORCES

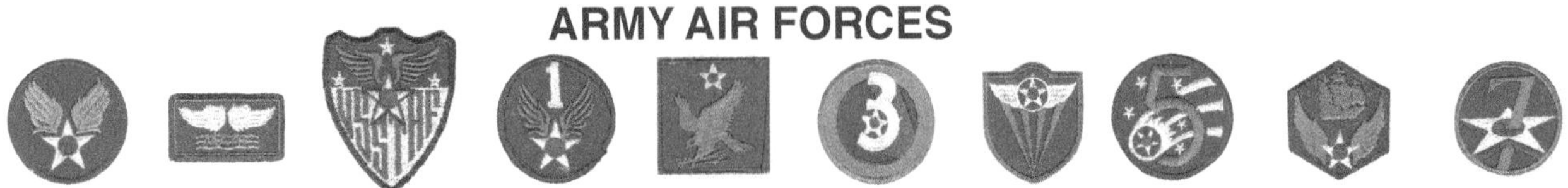

Army Air Forces · Mediterranean Allied Air Force · US Strategic Air Force · First Air Force · Second Air Force · Third Air Force · Fourth Air Force · Fifth Air Force · Sixth Air Force · Seventh Air Force

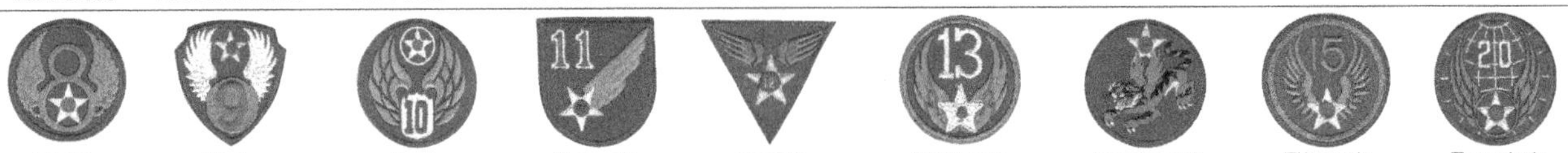

Eighth Air Force · Ninth Air Force · Tenth Air Force · Eleventh Air Force · Twelfth Air Force · Thirteenth Air Force · Fourteenth Air Force · Fifteenth Air Force · Twentieth Air Force

DEFENSE AND BASE COMMANDS

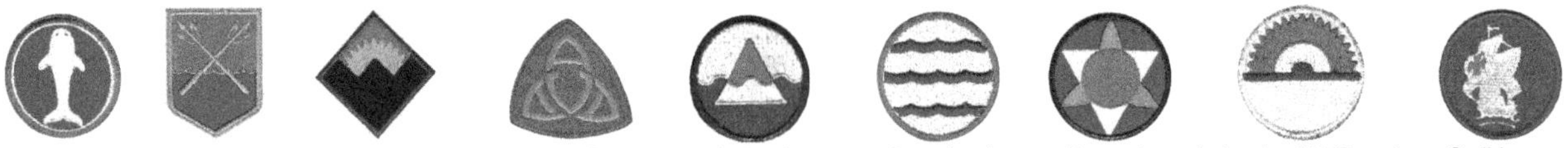

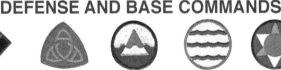

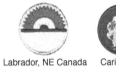

Atlantic Base Comd · Eastern Def Comd · AA Arty Comd Western Def Comd · AA Arty Comd Eastern Def Comd · Iceland Base Comd · Greenland Base Comd · Bermuda Base Comd · Labrador, NE Canada Base Comd · Caribbean Defense Comd

THEATERS

Supreme HQ Allied Expeditionary Force · European Theater of Operations · US Army Forces South Atlantic · HQ SE Asia Command · China-Buma-India Theater · US Army Foces Pacific Ocean Area · US Army Forces Middle East · N. African Theater Of Operations

ARMY GROUND FORCES

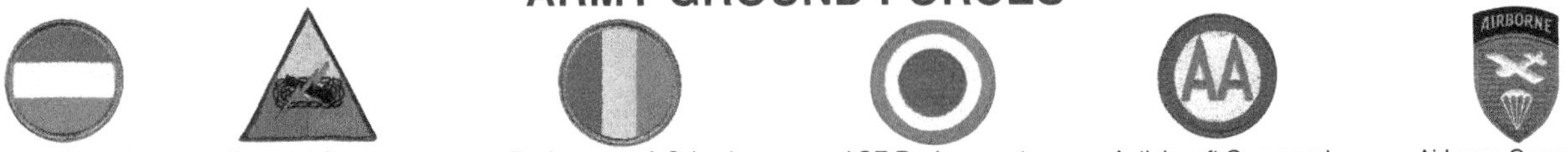

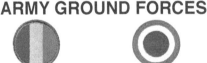

Army Ground Forces · Armored Center · Replacement & School Command · AGF Replacement Depots · Antiaircraft Command · Airborne Command

ARMY SERVICE FORCES

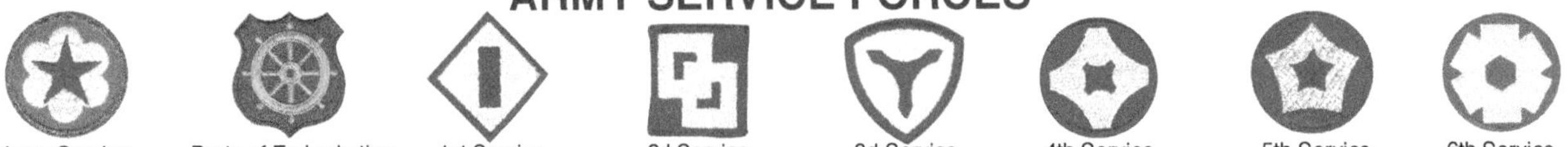

Army Service Forces · Ports of Embarkation · 1st Service Command · 2d Service Command · 3d Service Command · 4th Service Command · 5th Service Command · 6th Service Command

7th Service Command · 8th Service Command · 9th Service Command · NW Service Command · Military District of Washington · ASF Training Center Units · Army Specialized Training Program · Army Specialized Training Program Reserve

SPECIAL INSIGNIA Patches

1st Spc Service Forces · US Military Academy · Allied Force HQ · Combat Team 442 · Tank Destroyer Units · Persian Gulf Service Command · Rangers · AR Personnel Amphibious · AR Personnel w/Veterans Administration

DEPARTMENTS

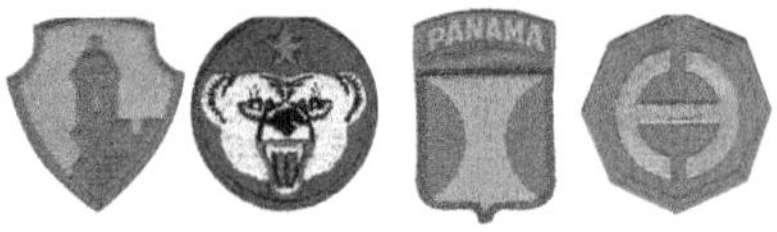

Antilles Dept. · Alaskan Dept. · Panama Canal Dept. · Hawaiian Dept.

❖ Korea, Vietnam, Desert Storm and State Shoulder Sleeve Insignia

KOREA 1950-1953

Eighth Army	I Corps	IX Corps	X Corps	1st Cav Div	2d Inf Div	3d Inf

7th Inf Div	24th Inf Div	25th Inf Div	40th Inf Div	45th Inf Div	5th Inf Regt	187th Inf Regt

VIETNAM 1961-1973

MAAG-Vietnam (Mlty Asst Advy Gp)	MACV US Military Asst Cmd, Vietnam	USARPAC US Army Pacific	USARV US Army Vietnam	I Field Force Vietnam	II Field Force Vietnam	Capitol Milty Asst Cmd	XXIV Corps	1st Cav Div	1st Inf Div	4th Inf Div	5th Inf Div

9th Inf Div	23 Inf Div (America)	25th Inf Div	82d Airborne 3d Bde SEP	101st Airborne Div	11th Armd Cav Regt	11th Inf Bde (Light)	173d Abn Bde	196th Inf Bde (Light)	198th Inf Bde	199th Inf Bde	1st Sp Forces

1st Sqdrn 1st Cav Regt	2d Sqdrn 1st Cav Regt	US Army Criminal Inv	US Army Secty Cmd	1st Avn Bde	US Army Eng Cd Vtm	18th Engr Bde	20th Engr Bde	18th Military Police Bde	1st Sig Bde	USASTRATCOM (US AR Strg Comm Cmd)

1st Med Bde	US Army Health Srv Cmd	1st Logistical Cmd	15TH Support Bde	4th Trans Cmd	5th Tran Cmd	124th Tran Cmd	125th Trans Cmd	US Army Combat Devlpt Cmd	US Army Mtl Cmd	US Army Milt Trf Mgt & Trml Srv

DESERT STORM

III Corps Arty	1st Armd Div	1st Cav Div	1st Inf Div	2d Armd Div	2d Corps Support Cmd	2d Armd Cav Regt	3d Armd Cav Regt	3d Armd Div	3d Inf Div	7th Med Bde

11 Air Def Arty Bde	11 Combat Avn Bde	12 Combat Avn Bde	13th Corps Spt Cmd	24th Inf	82d Abn Div	101st Abn Div	196th Inf Bgde	HQ 3d Army	HQ, VII Corps	HQ, XVIII	7th Med Cmd

5th Spc Fce Gp	513th Mil Intel Bde	44th Med Bde	14th MP Bde	1st Corp Spt Cmd	16th MP Bde	18th Avn Bde	20th Eng Bde

STATE AREA COMMANDS

Alabama	Alaska	Arizona	Arkansas	California	Colorado	Connecticut	Delaware	Dist of Columbia	Florida	Georgia

Guam	Hawaii	Idaho	Illinois	Indiana	Iowa	Kansas	Kentucky	Louisiana	Maine	Maryland	Massachusetts

❖ Army National Guard Shoulder Sleeve Insignia

STATE AREA COMMANDS CONTINUED

Michigan · Minnesota · Mississippi · Missouri · Montana · Nebraska · Nevada · New Hampshire · New Jersey · New Mexico · New York · North Carolina

North Dakota · Ohio · Oklahoma · Oregon · Pennsylvania · Puerto Rico · Rhode Island · South Carolina · South Dakota · Tennessee

Texas · Utah · Vermont · Virgin Islands · Virginia · Washington · West Virginia · Wisconsin · Wyoming

DIVISIONS

26th Inf Div MA, CT, RI · 28th Inf Div PA · 29th Inf Div VA, MD · 35th Inf Div KS, NE, KY, MO, CO · 38th Inf Div IN, MI · 40th Inf Div CA, NV · 42d Inf Div NY · 47th Inf Div MN, IA, IL · 49th Armd Div TX · 50th Armd Div NJ, VT

BRIGADES

27th Inf Bde NY · 29th Inf Bde HI · 30th Inf Bde NC · 30st Armd Bde TN · 31st Armd Bde AL · 32d Inf Bde WI · 33d Inf Bde IL · 39th Inf Bde AK · 41st Inf Bde OR

45th Inf Bde OK · 48th Inf Bde GA · 53d Inf Bde FL · 73d Inf Bde OH · 81st Inf Bde WA · 92d Inf Bde PR · 155th Inf Bde MS · 218th Inf Bde SC · 256 Inf Bde LA

ARMORED CAVALRY REGIMENTS

107th Armd Cav Regt - OH, WV · 116th Armd Cav Regt - ID, OR, MS · 163d Armd Cav Regt - MT, TX · 278th Armd Cav Regt - TN

FIELD ARTILLERY BRIGADES

57th Fld Arty Bde - WI · 103d Fld Arty Bde - RI · 113th Fld Arty Bde - NC · 115th Fld Arty Bde - WY · 118th Fld Arty Bde - GA · 135th Fld Arty Bde - MO · 138th Fld Arty Bde - KY · 142d Fld Arty Bde - AK · 151st Fld Arty Bde - SC

153dth Fld Arty Bde - AZ · 169th Fld Arty Bde - CO · 196th Fld Arty Bde - TN · 197th Fld Arty Bde - NH · 209th Fld Arty Bde - NY · 227th Fld Arty Bde - FL · 631st Fld Arty Bde - MS

MAJOR COMMANDS

I Corps Arty UT · 16th Engr Bde OH · 19th SF Gp UT 20th SF Gp - AL · 30th Engr Bde NC · 35th Engr MO · 43d MP Bde RI · 49th MP Bde CA · 53d Sig Bde FL · 111th AD Bde NM · 112th Med Bde OH

142d Sig Bde AL · 167th Spt Cmd AL · 175th Med Bde CA · 184th Trans Bde MS · 194th Eng Bde TN · 213th Med MS · 228th Sig Bde SC · 260th Milt Pol Bde DC · 261st Sig Cmd DE

Liberation of Iraq

I Corps

III Corps

V Corps

XVIII Corps

1st Cav Div

1st Div

2d Div

3d Div

4th Div

25th Div

30th Div

36th Div

42d Div

82d Div

101st ABN Div

1st Armd

2d Armd

2d Armd Cav Regt

3d Armd Cav Regt

11th ArmdCav Regt

29th Inf Bde

76st Inf Bde

81st Inf Bde

173d Abn Bde

Special Forces

278th Armd Cav Regt

256 Inf Bde

116th Armd Cav Regt

155th Armd Bde

103rd FA Bde

197rd FA Bde

20th MI Bde

22d Signal Bde

44th Medical Bde

130th Eng Bde

18th MP Bde

Examples of new Combat Service Identification Badge (CSIB) on Blue uniform

I Corps

I Corps CSIB

V Corps

CSIB

XVIII Corps

CSIB

1st Div

CSIB

2d Div

CSIB

3d Div

CSIB

4th Div

CSIB

25th Div

CSIB

Examples of Other Current Combat Service Identication Badges (CSIB)

❖ Types of Medals, Ribbons and Attachments

Decoration - An award conferred on an individual for a specific act of gallantry or for meritorious service.

Medal - An individual award presented for performance of certain duties or to those who have participated in designated wars, campaigns, expeditions, etc., or who have fulfilled specified service requirements.

There are two general categories of "medals" awarded by the United States to its military personnel, namely, decorations and service medals.

The terms "decoration" and "medal" are used almost interchangeably today (as they are in this book), but there are recognizable distinctions between them. Decorations, are awarded for acts of gallantry and meritorious service and usually have distinctive (and often unique) shapes such as crosses or stars.

Medals are awarded for good conduct, participation in a particular campaign or expedition, or a noncombatant service and normally come in a round shape. Campaign or service medals are issued to individuals who participate in particular campaigns or periods of service for which a medal is authorized. The fact that some very prestigious awards have the word "medal" in their titles *(e.g.: Medal of Honor)*, can cause some confusion.

Unit Awards & Ribbon Only

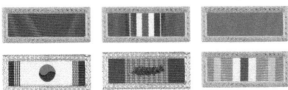

Unit Award - An award made to an operating unit for outstanding performance.

Ribbon Only Award - *An award made to an individual for completion of certain training or specific assignment for which there is no medal.*

Attachments and Devices

Attachment - Any device such as a star, clasp, or other appurtenance worn on a suspension ribbon of a medal or on the ribbon bar *(also called device)*.

Bronze and Silver Service Stars

A bronze star is worn on suspension ribbons of large and miniature medals and ribbon bars to indicate a second or subsequent award or to indicate major engagements in which an individual participated. Silver Stars - A silver star is worn on suspension ribbons of large and miniature medals and ribbon bars in lieu of five bronze stars.

Letter "V"

A bronze letter "V" is worn on specific combat decorations if the award is approved for valor (heroism). Only one "V" is worn and oak leaf clusters are used to indicate additional awards.

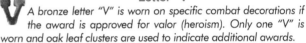

Army Occupation Service Medal Clasp

The bronze Army of Occupation Medal clasp marked "GERMANY" and or "JAPAN" is worn on suspension ribbons of large and miniature Army of Occupation Medals to denote service in those areas.

Oak Leaf Cluster

A bronze Oak Leaf Cluster denotes a second or subsequent award of a personal decoration. A silver Oak Leaf Cluster is worn in lieu of five bronze Oak Leaf Clusters.

Hour Glass

A bronze hour glass device denotes ten years service on the Armed Forces Reserve Medal. Upon the completion of the ten year period, reservists are awarded the Armed Forces Reserve Medal with a bronze hourglass device. Silver and gold hourglass devices are awarded at the end of twenty and thirty years of reserve service, respectively.

Letter "M"

A bronze letter "M" on the Armed Forces Reserve Medal denotes reservists mobilized and called to active duty.

Airplane

The Berlin Airlift Device, a three-eighths inch gold C-54 airplane, is authorized to be worn on the ribbon bar and suspension ribbon of the Army Occupation Service Medal by Personnel who served 90 consecutive days in support of the Berlin Airlift (1948-1949).

Bronze Numerals	Bronze Arrowhead
Denotes total number of awards of the Air Medal and other awards.	Denotes participation in parachute, glider or amphibious landing or assault.

Good Conduct Medal Clasp

Number of loops and color denote number of awards of Good Conduct Medal. Bronze, 2nd - 5th; silver, 6th - 10th; gold, 11th - 15th.

Regulation Ribbon Bar

Enamel Lapel Pins

Miniature Medals

Enamel Hat Pins (unofficial)

Full Size Medals

Miniature Medals Anodized or Gold-Plated

Miniature Ribbons (unofficial)

Bronze

Anodized or Gold-Plated

VIETNAM SERVICE

Brass Plates

Announcement of the decoration is published in official orders.

Decorations are announced in official military orders. The orders are filed in an individual's military record jacket and retired to a records holding area when the individual is discharged or retired. A decoration usually comes with a citation, certificate and boxed medal with ribbon and lapel pin.

Authorization for service medals are noted in an individual's official military records. They are generally issued in a small cardboard box. Ribbon-only awards and unit citations are sometimes issued but generally the individual has to purchase them. Foreign medals, such as the Republic of Vietnam Campaign Medal are generally required to be purchased by individual service members.

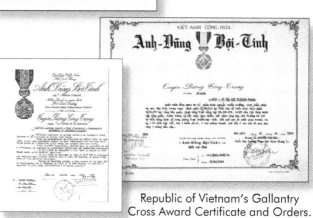

Republic of Vietnam's Gallantry Cross Award Certificate and Orders.

U.S. Army
Military Ribbon & Medal
Wear Guide

Order of Precedence and Attachments of U.S. Army Medals and Ribbons

The Army awards system has evolved into a highly structured program often called the "Pyramid of Honor." The system is designed to reward services ranging from heroism on the battlefield to superior performance of non combat duties.

Since World War II the Army has generally embraced Napoleon's concept of liberally awarding medals and ribbons to enhance morale and esprit de corps. Over the years an expanded and specifically-tailored awards program became generally very popular in the all-volunteer Army and has played a significant part in improving morale, job performance, recruitment and reenlistments among junior officers and enlisted personnel.

The various ways of wearing decorations and awards by active duty, reserve and veterans are shown on the following pages. These awards paint a wonderful portrait of the American soldier whose dedication to the ideals of freedom represent the rich United States Army military heritage.

Ribbon Chart Showing the Complete History of U.S. Army Awards

This one of a kind chart on page 108, reads left to right and shows the ribbon for every Army award since the Civil War with many of the variations used. The chart is a colorful walk through the U.S. Army Military awards history and was originally developed by the late Lonny Borts, America's expert on military ribbons.

Army Order of Precedence Ribbon Chart

On page 109 the current correct order of precedence for Army ribbons is shown going back to World War II. Authorized attachments for each ribbon are displayed below the ribbon and a reference bar on the right side of the page provides guides to a detailed device graphic.

Next is the Army Order of Precedence Chart for Multi service awards. Veterans who have service in multiple branches of the Armed Forces can determine their military ribbon order of precedence beginning on page112.

Army Ribbon Devices (*Appurtenances*) start on page114 and all Army ribbon devices are shown as correctly mounted to ribbons and medals. All Army ribbon devices are shown in alphabetical order starting with the Gold Airplane. For those who desire even more detail charts for proper placement of Army Ribbon Devices (*Appurtenances*) are on pages 116

Ribbons are centered 1/8" over the left breast pocket, normally three to a row but up to four to a row. Ribbons are mounted with no space or 1/8" between rows. The rows may be adjusted so the ribbons are not cover by the uniform lapel. See examples below.

Ribbons examples mounted with no space.

Shown 1/8" between rows, up to four ribbons across and stagger to keep out from under the lapel.

Afghanistan service with campaign star or stars missing from Afghanistan ribbon.

Liberation of Kuwait service with campaign stars on SWA ribbon.

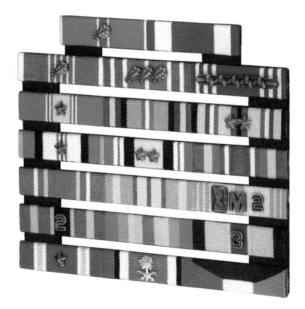

Same ribbons shown mounted three to a row with 1/8" between rows and centered over the left breast pocket.

Vietnam service with silver campaign star (5 campaigns) on Vietnam Service ribbon.

U.S. Army Decorations, Unit Awards & Service Ribbons from 1861

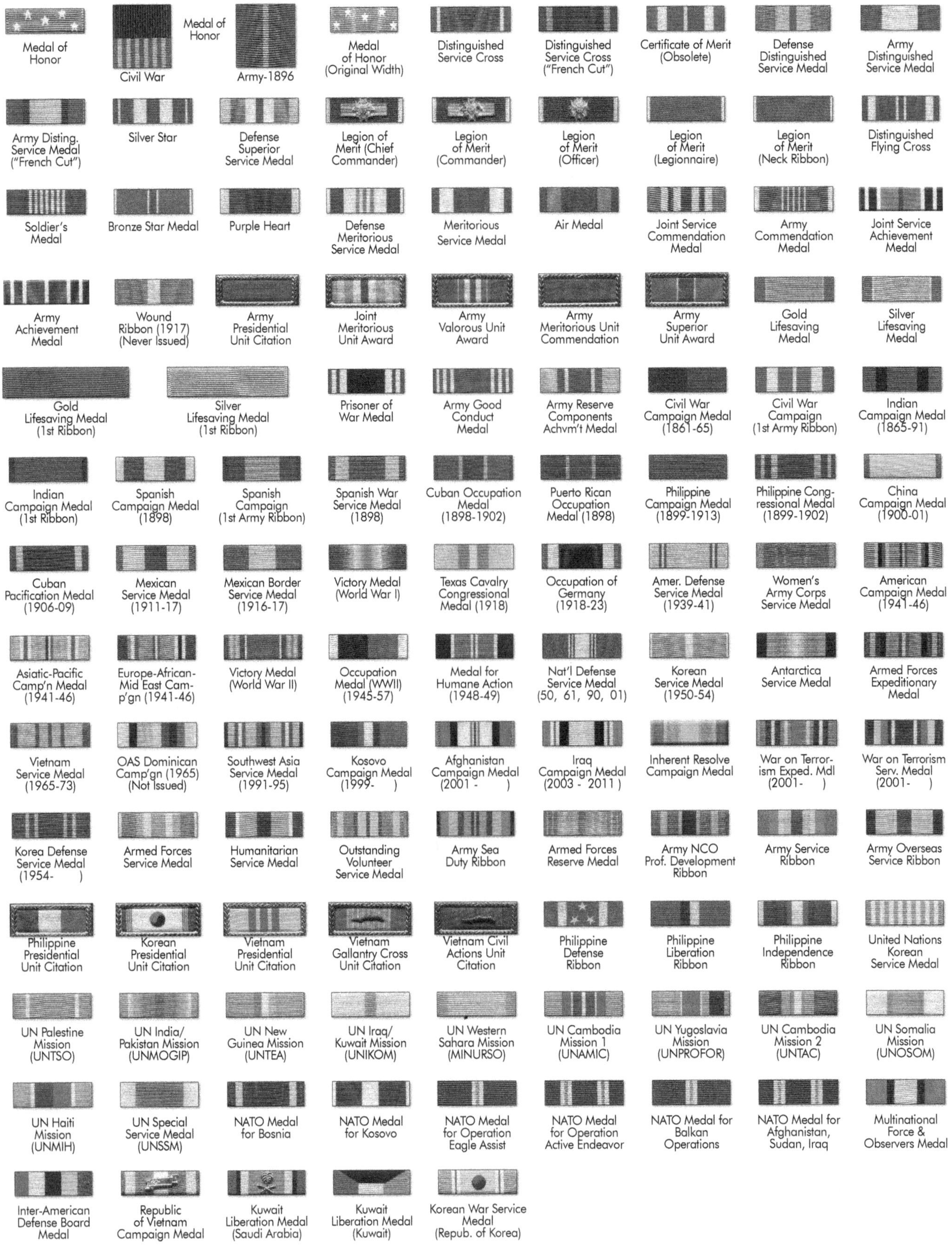
Medal of Honor
Civil War
Medal of Honor
Army-1896
Medal of Honor (Original Width)
Distinguished Service Cross
Distinguished Service Cross ("French Cut")
Certificate of Merit (Obsolete)
Defense Distinguished Service Medal
Army Distinguished Service Medal
Army Disting. Service Medal ("French Cut")
Silver Star
Defense Superior Service Medal
Legion of Merit (Chief Commander)
Legion of Merit (Commander)
Legion of Merit (Officer)
Legion of Merit (Legionnaire)
Legion of Merit (Neck Ribbon)
Distinguished Flying Cross
Soldier's Medal
Bronze Star Medal
Purple Heart
Defense Meritorious Service Medal
Meritorious Service Medal
Air Medal
Joint Service Commendation Medal
Army Commendation Medal
Joint Service Achievement Medal
Army Achievement Medal
Wound Ribbon (1917) (Never Issued)
Army Presidential Unit Citation
Joint Meritorious Unit Award
Army Valorous Unit Award
Army Meritorious Unit Commendation
Army Superior Unit Award
Gold Lifesaving Medal
Silver Lifesaving Medal
Gold Lifesaving Medal (1st Ribbon)
Silver Lifesaving Medal (1st Ribbon)
Prisoner of War Medal
Army Good Conduct Medal
Army Reserve Components Achvm't Medal
Civil War Campaign Medal (1861-65)
Civil War Campaign (1st Army Ribbon)
Indian Campaign Medal (1865-91)
Indian Campaign Medal (1st Ribbon)
Spanish Campaign Medal (1898)
Spanish Campaign (1st Army Ribbon)
Spanish War Service Medal (1898)
Cuban Occupation Medal (1898-1902)
Puerto Rican Occupation Medal (1898)
Philippine Campaign Medal (1899-1913)
Philippine Cong-ressional Medal (1899-1902)
China Campaign Medal (1900-01)
Cuban Pacification Medal (1906-09)
Mexican Service Medal (1911-17)
Mexican Border Service Medal (1916-17)
Victory Medal (World War I)
Texas Cavalry Congressional Medal (1918)
Occupation of Germany (1918-23)
Amer. Defense Service Medal (1939-41)
Women's Army Corps Service Medal
American Campaign Medal (1941-46)
Asiatic-Pacific Camp'n Medal (1941-46)
Europe-African-Mid East Cam-p'gn (1941-46)
Victory Medal (World War II)
Occupation Medal (WWII) (1945-57)
Medal for Humane Action (1948-49)
Nat'l Defense Service Medal (50, 61, 90, 01)
Korean Service Medal (1950-54)
Antarctica Service Medal
Armed Forces Expeditionary Medal
Vietnam Service Medal (1965-73)
OAS Dominican Camp'gn (1965) (Not Issued)
Southwest Asia Service Medal (1991-95)
Kosovo Campaign Medal (1999-)
Afghanistan Campaign Medal (2001 -)
Iraq Campaign Medal (2003 - 2011)
Inherent Resolve Campaign Medal
War on Terror-ism Exped. Mdl (2001-)
War on Terrorism Serv. Medal (2001-)
Korea Defense Service Medal (1954-)
Armed Forces Service Medal
Humanitarian Service Medal
Outstanding Volunteer Service Medal
Army Sea Duty Ribbon
Armed Forces Reserve Medal
Army NCO Prof. Development Ribbon
Army Service Ribbon
Army Overseas Service Ribbon
Philippine Presidential Unit Citation
Korean Presidential Unit Citation
Vietnam Presidential Unit Citation
Vietnam Gallantry Cross Unit Citation
Vietnam Civil Actions Unit Citation
Philippine Defense Ribbon
Philippine Liberation Ribbon
Philippine Independence Ribbon
United Nations Korean Service Medal
UN Palestine Mission (UNTSO)
UN India/ Pakistan Mission (UNMOGIP)
UN New Guinea Mission (UNTEA)
UN Iraq/ Kuwait Mission (UNIKOM)
UN Western Sahara Mission (MINURSO)
UN Cambodia Mission 1 (UNAMIC)
UN Yugoslavia Mission (UNPROFOR)
UN Cambodia Mission 2 (UNTAC)
UN Somalia Mission (UNOSOM)
UN Haiti Mission (UNMIH)
UN Special Service Medal (UNSSM)
NATO Medal for Bosnia
NATO Medal for Kosovo
NATO Medal for Operation Eagle Assist
NATO Medal for Operation Active Endeavor
NATO Medal for Balkan Operations
NATO Medal for Afghanistan, Sudan, Iraq
Multinational Force & Observers Medal
Inter-American Defense Board Medal
Republic of Vietnam Campaign Medal
Kuwait Liberation Medal (Saudi Arabia)
Kuwait Liberation Medal (Kuwait)
Korean War Service Medal (Repub. of Korea)

❖ U.S. Army Ribbons & Devices 1941-2019 Correct Order of Ribbon Wear

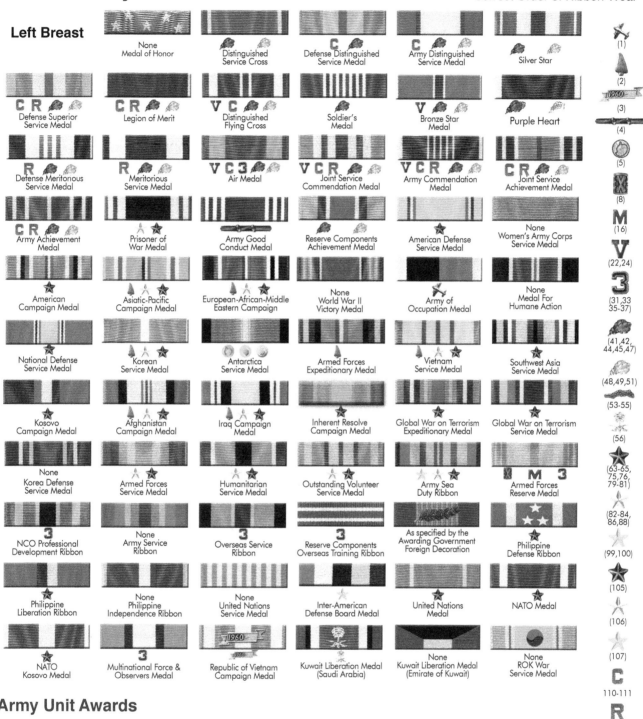

Left Breast

None Medal of Honor	Distinguished Service Cross	Defense Distinguished Service Medal	Army Distinguished Service Medal	Silver Star
Defense Superior Service Medal	Legion of Merit	Distinguished Flying Cross	Soldier's Medal	Bronze Star Medal / Purple Heart
Defense Meritorious Service Medal	Meritorious Service Medal	Air Medal	Joint Service Commendation Medal	Army Commendation Medal / Joint Service Achievement Medal
Army Achievement Medal	Prisoner of War Medal	Army Good Conduct Medal	Reserve Components Achievement Medal	American Defense Service Medal / None Women's Army Corps Service Medal
American Campaign Medal	Asiatic-Pacific Campaign Medal	European-African-Middle Eastern Campaign	None World War II Victory Medal	Army of Occupation Medal / None Medal For Humane Action
National Defense Service Medal	Korean Service Medal	Antarctica Service Medal	Armed Forces Expeditionary Medal	Vietnam Service Medal / Southwest Asia Service Medal
Kosovo Campaign Medal	Afghanistan Campaign Medal	Iraq Campaign Medal	Inherent Resolve Campaign Medal	Global War on Terrorism Expeditionary Medal / Global War on Terrorism Service Medal
None Korea Defense Service Medal	Armed Forces Service Medal	Humanitarian Service Medal	Outstanding Volunteer Service Medal	Army Sea Duty Ribbon / Armed Forces Reserve Medal
NCO Professional Development Ribbon	None Army Service Ribbon	Overseas Service Ribbon	Reserve Components Overseas Training Ribbon	As specified by the Awarding Government Foreign Decoration / Philippine Defense Ribbon
Philippine Liberation Ribbon	None Philippine Independence Ribbon	None United Nations Service Medal	Inter-American Defense Board Medal	United Nations Medal / NATO Medal
NATO Kosovo Medal	Multinational Force & Observers Medal	Republic of Vietnam Campaign Medal	Kuwait Liberation Medal (Saudi Arabia)	None Kuwait Liberation Medal (Emirate of Kuwait) / None ROK War Service Medal

(1)
(2)
(3)
(4)
(5)
(8)
M (16)
V (22,24)
3 (31,33 35-37)
(41,42, 44,45,47)
(48,49,51)
(53-55)
(56)
(63-65, 75,76, 79-81)
(82-84, 86,88)
(99,100)
(105)
(106)
(107)
C 110-111
R

Army Unit Awards

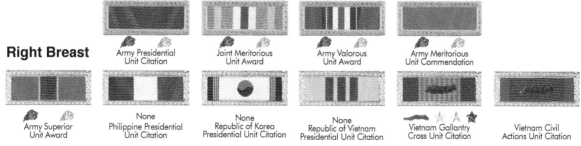

Right Breast

Army Presidential Unit Citation	Joint Meritorious Unit Award	Army Valorous Unit Award	Army Meritorious Unit Commendation
Army Superior Unit Award	None Philippine Presidential Unit Citation	None Republic of Korea Presidential Unit Citation	None Republic of Vietnam Presidential Unit Citation / Vietnam Gallantry Cross Unit Citation / Vietnam Civil Actions Unit Citation

Note: Per Army regulations, no row may contain more than four ribbons or three (3) unit awards. The display is arranged solely to conserve space on the page.

Left Breast

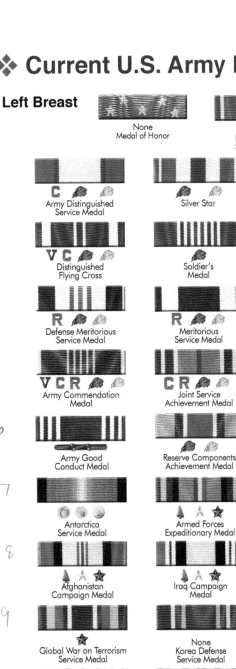

None
Medal of Honor

Distinguished
Service Cross

C
Defense Distinguished
Service Medal

C
Army Distinguished
Service Medal

Silver Star

C R
Defense Superior
Service Medal

C R
Legion of Merit

V C
Distinguished
Flying Cross

Soldier's
Medal

V
Bronze Star
Medal

Purple Heart

R
Defense Meritorious
Service Medal

R
Meritorious
Service Medal

V C 3
Air Medal

V C R
Joint Service
Commendation Medal

V C R
Army Commendation
Medal

C R
Joint Service
Achievement Medal

C R
Army Achievement
Medal

Prisoner of
War Medal

Army Good
Conduct Medal

Reserve Components
Achievement Medal

Army of
Occupation Medal

National Defense
Service Medal

Antarctica
Service Medal

Armed Forces
Expeditionary Medal

Southwest Asia
Service Medal

Kosovo
Campaign Medal

Afghanistan
Campaign Medal

Iraq Campaign
Medal

Inherent Resolve
Campaign Medal

Global War on Terrorism
Expeditionary Medal

Global War on Terrorism
Service Medal

None
Korea Defense
Service Medal

Armed Forces
Service Medal

Humanitarian
Service Medal

Outstanding Volunteer
Service Medal

Army Sea
Duty Ribbon

M 3
Armed Forces
Reserve Medal

3
NCO Professional
Development Ribbon

None
Army Service Ribbon

3
Overseas Service
Ribbon

3
Reserve Components
Overseas Training Ribbon

Foreign Decoration as
specified by the
Awarding Government

Inter-American
Defense Board Medal

United Nations
Medal

NATO Medal for
Meritorious Service

NATO Medal for Bosnia

NATO Medal for
Kosovo

NATO Medal for
Operation Eagle Assist

NATO Medal for Operation
Active Endeavor

NATO Medal for
Balkan Operations

NATO Medal for
Afghanistan, Sudan, Iraq

3
Multinational Force &
Observers Medal

Kuwait Liberation Medal
(Saudi Arabia)

None
Kuwait Liberation Medal
(Emirate of Kuwait)

(1)
(2)
(3)
(4)
(5)
(8)
M (16)
V (22,24)
3 (31,33 35-37)
(41,42, 44,45,47)
(48,49,51)
(53-55)
(56)
★ (63-65, 75,76, 79-81)
(82-84, 86,88)
(99,100)
★ (105)
(106)
(107)
C
110-111
R

The basic UN and NATO medal is defined as the first UN or NATO medal awarded to a Soldier for meeting eligibility criteria for a specific operation. A bronze service star will denote subsequent awards of the UN or NATO medal for service in a different UN or NATO operation. Only one UN or NATO service ribbon is authorized for wear.

Note: Per Army regulations, no row may contain more than four ribbons or three (3) unit awards.

❖ Right Breast Displays on Blue and Green Uniforms

The Army prescribe the wear of "Unit Awards" on the right breast of the dress uniform except when miniature medals are worn on the mess dress formal uniform. They are worn over the right pocket when medals are worn. The Army unit awards are aligned from the wears right to left as shown below.

Army Unit Awards

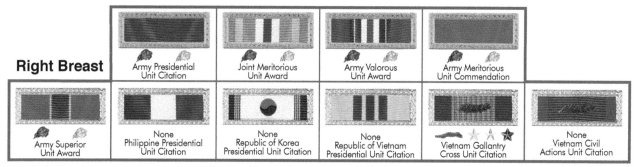

Right Breast

Army Presidential Unit Citation	Joint Meritorious Unit Award	Army Valorous Unit Award	Army Meritorious Unit Commendation
Army Superior Unit Award	None Philippine Presidential Unit Citation	None Republic of Korea Presidential Unit Citation	None Republic of Vietnam Presidential Unit Citation	Vietnam Gallantry Cross Unit Citation	None Vietnam Civil Actions Unit Citation

Note: Per Army regulations, no row may contain more than four ribbons or three (3) unit awards. The display is arranged solely to conserve space on the page.

All unit citations are centered over the right breast pocket the bottom edge 1/8 inch above the top of the pocket.

Correct Order for Multi Service Awards on the U.S. Army Uniform

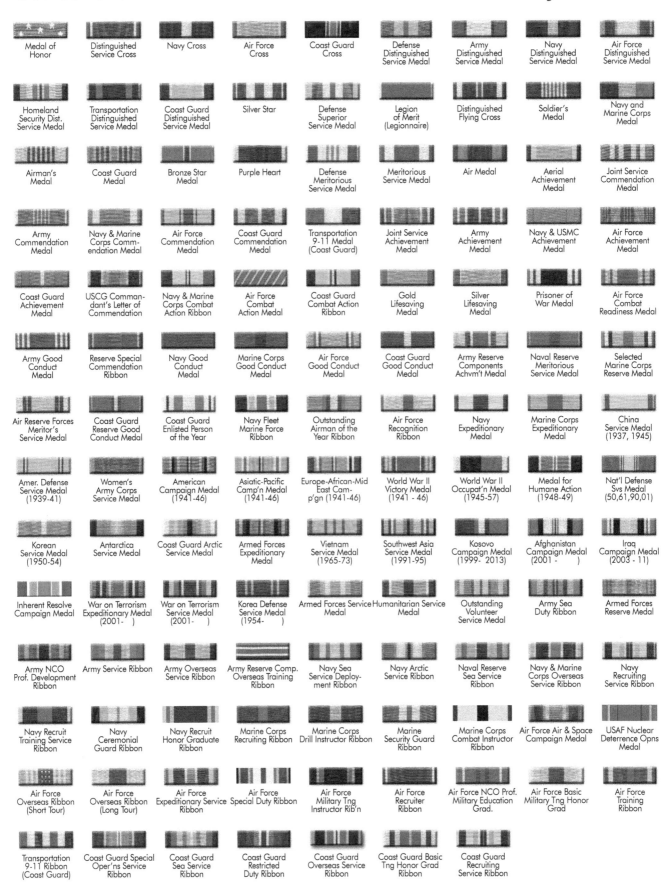

Medal of Honor	Distinguished Service Cross	Navy Cross	Air Force Cross	Coast Guard Cross	Defense Distinguished Service Medal	Army Distinguished Service Medal	Navy Distinguished Service Medal	Air Force Distinguished Service Medal
Homeland Security Dist. Service Medal	Transportation Distinguished Service Medal	Coast Guard Distinguished Service Medal	Silver Star	Defense Superior Service Medal	Legion of Merit (Legionnaire)	Distinguished Flying Cross	Soldier's Medal	Navy and Marine Corps Medal
Airman's Medal	Coast Guard Medal	Bronze Star Medal	Purple Heart	Defense Meritorious Service Medal	Meritorious Service Medal	Air Medal	Aerial Achievement Medal	Joint Service Commendation Medal
Army Commendation Medal	Navy & Marine Corps Commendation Medal	Air Force Commendation Medal	Coast Guard Commendation Medal	Transportation 9-11 Medal (Coast Guard)	Joint Service Achievement Medal	Army Achievement Medal	Navy & USMC Achievement Medal	Air Force Achievement Medal
Coast Guard Achievement Medal	USCG Commandant's Letter of Commendation	Navy & Marine Corps Combat Action Ribbon	Air Force Combat Action Medal	Coast Guard Combat Action Ribbon	Gold Lifesaving Medal	Silver Lifesaving Medal	Prisoner of War Medal	Air Force Combat Readiness Medal
Army Good Conduct Medal	Reserve Special Commendation Ribbon	Navy Good Conduct Medal	Marine Corps Good Conduct Medal	Air Force Good Conduct Medal	Coast Guard Good Conduct Medal	Army Reserve Components Achvm't Medal	Naval Reserve Meritorious Service Medal	Selected Marine Corps Reserve Medal
Air Reserve Forces Meritor's Service Medal	Coast Guard Reserve Good Conduct Medal	Coast Guard Enlisted Person of the Year	Navy Fleet Marine Force Ribbon	Outstanding Airman of the Year Ribbon	Air Force Recognition Ribbon	Navy Expeditionary Medal	Marine Corps Expeditionary Medal	China Service Medal (1937, 1945)
Amer. Defense Service Medal (1939-41)	Women's Army Corps Service Medal	American Campaign Medal (1941-46)	Asiatic-Pacific Camp'n Medal (1941-46)	Europe-African-Mid East Campaign (1941-46)	World War II Victory Medal (1941 - 46)	World War II Occupat'n Medal (1945-57)	Medal for Humane Action (1948-49)	Nat'l Defense Svs Medal (50,61,90,01)
Korean Service Medal (1950-54)	Antarctica Service Medal	Coast Guard Arctic Service Medal	Armed Forces Expeditionary Medal	Vietnam Service Medal (1965-73)	Southwest Asia Service Medal (1991-95)	Kosovo Campaign Medal (1999- 2013)	Afghanistan Campaign Medal (2001 -)	Iraq Campaign Medal (2003 - 11)
Inherent Resolve Campaign Medal	War on Terrorism Expeditionary Medal (2001-)	War on Terrorism Service Medal (2001-)	Korea Defense Service Medal (1954-)	Armed Forces Service Medal	Humanitarian Service Medal	Outstanding Volunteer Service Medal	Army Sea Duty Ribbon	Armed Forces Reserve Medal
Army NCO Prof. Development Ribbon	Army Service Ribbon	Army Overseas Service Ribbon	Army Reserve Comp. Overseas Training Ribbon	Navy Sea Service Deployment Ribbon	Navy Arctic Service Ribbon	Naval Reserve Sea Service Ribbon	Navy & Marine Corps Overseas Service Ribbon	Navy Recruiting Service Ribbon
Navy Recruit Training Service Ribbon	Navy Ceremonial Guard Ribbon	Navy Recruit Honor Graduate Ribbon	Marine Corps Recruiting Ribbon	Marine Corps Drill Instructor Ribbon	Marine Security Guard Ribbon	Marine Corps Combat Instructor Ribbon	Air Force Air & Space Campaign Medal	USAF Nuclear Deterrence Opns Medal
Air Force Overseas Ribbon (Short Tour)	Air Force Overseas Ribbon (Long Tour)	Air Force Expeditionary Service Ribbon	Air Force Special Duty Ribbon	Air Force Military Tng Instructor Rib'n	Air Force Recruiter Ribbon	Air Force NCO Prof. Military Education Grad.	Air Force Basic Military Tng Honor Grad	Air Force Training Ribbon
Transportation 9-11 Ribbon (Coast Guard)	Coast Guard Special Oper'ns Service Ribbon	Coast Guard Sea Service Ribbon	Coast Guard Restricted Duty Ribbon	Coast Guard Overseas Service Ribbon	Coast Guard Basic Tng Honor Grad Ribbon	Coast Guard Recruiting Service Ribbon		

❖ Correct Order of Wear for Foreign Awards on the U.S. Army Uniform

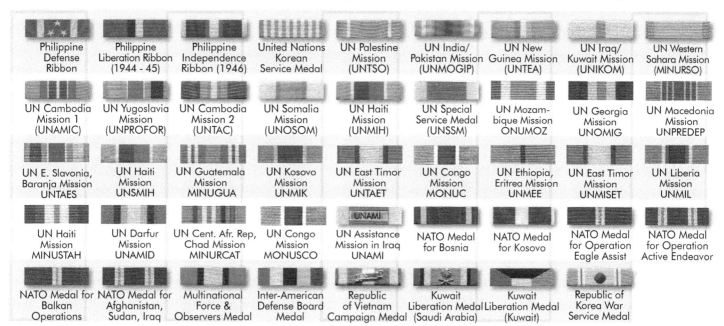

Philippine Defense Ribbon — Philippine Liberation Ribbon (1944 - 45) — Philippine Independence Ribbon (1946) — United Nations Korean Service Medal — UN Palestine Mission (UNTSO) — UN India/Pakistan Mission (UNMOGIP) — UN New Guinea Mission (UNTEA) — UN Iraq/Kuwait Mission (UNIKOM) — UN Western Sahara Mission (MINURSO)

UN Cambodia Mission 1 (UNAMIC) — UN Yugoslavia Mission (UNPROFOR) — UN Cambodia Mission 2 (UNTAC) — UN Somalia Mission (UNOSOM) — UN Haiti Mission (UNMIH) — UN Special Service Medal (UNSSM) — UN Mozambique Mission ONUMOZ — UN Georgia Mission UNOMIG — UN Macedonia Mission UNPREDEP

UN E. Slavonia, Baranja Mission UNTAES — UN Haiti Mission UNSMIH — UN Guatemala Mission MINUGUA — UN Kosovo Mission UNMIK — UN East Timor Mission UNTAET — UN Congo Mission MONUC — UN Ethiopia, Eritrea Mission UNMEE — UN East Timor Mission UNMISET — UN Liberia Mission UNMIL

UN Haiti Mission MINUSTAH — UN Darfur Mission UNAMID — UN Cent. Afr. Rep, Chad Mission MINURCAT — UN Congo Mission MONUSCO — UN Assistance Mission in Iraq UNAMI — NATO Medal for Bosnia — NATO Medal for Kosovo — NATO Medal for Operation Eagle Assist — NATO Medal for Operation Active Endeavor

NATO Medal for Balkan Operations — NATO Medal for Afghanistan, Sudan, Iraq — Multinational Force & Observers Medal — Inter-American Defense Board Medal — Republic of Vietnam Campaign Medal — Kuwait Liberation Medal (Saudi Arabia) — Kuwait Liberation Medal (Kuwait) — Republic of Korea War Service Medal

Wear of Multi Service Unit Citations (Right Breast) on the U.S. Army Uniform

Personnel may wear U.S. and foreign unit award emblems on the service uniforms.

All permanent and temporary unit award emblems, with or without frames, are worn in the order of precedence from the wearer's right to left. Award emblems are worn in rows containing no more than three emblems per row, with no space between emblems, and with up to 1/8 inch space between rows, depending upon the size of emblems with frames. The emblems are worn as follows:

(1) **Male personnel.** Emblems with or without frames are worn centered with the bottom edge of the emblem 1/8 inch above the right breast pocket flap.

(2) **Female personnel.** Emblems with or without frames are worn centered on the right side of the uniform, with the bottom edge 1/2 inch above the top edge of the nameplate.

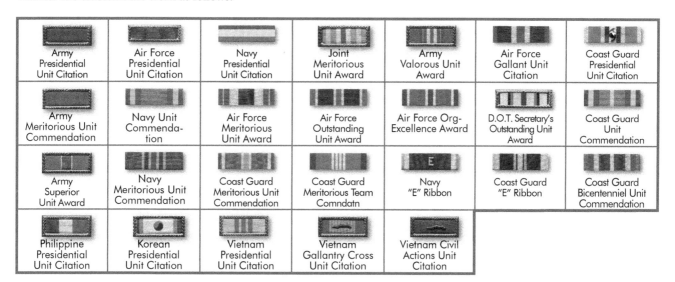

Army Presidential Unit Citation	Air Force Presidential Unit Citation	Navy Presidential Unit Citation	Joint Meritorious Unit Award	Army Valorous Unit Award	Air Force Gallant Unit Citation	Coast Guard Presidential Unit Citation
Army Meritorious Unit Commendation	Navy Unit Commendation	Air Force Meritorious Unit Award	Air Force Outstanding Unit Award	Air Force Org-Excellence Award	D.O.T. Secretary's Outstanding Unit Award	Coast Guard Unit Commendation
Army Superior Unit Award	Navy Meritorious Unit Commendation	Coast Guard Meritorious Unit Commendation	Coast Guard Meritorious Team Comndatn	Navy "E" Ribbon	Coast Guard "E" Ribbon	Coast Guard Bicentenniel Unit Commendation
Philippine Presidential Unit Citation	Korean Presidential Unit Citation	Vietnam Presidential Unit Citation	Vietnam Gallantry Cross Unit Citation	Vietnam Civil Actions Unit Citation		

The following awards may not be worn on the Army uniform.

USAF Longevity Service Award — Navy Dist. Marksman & Pistol Shot — Navy Rifle Marksmanship Ribbon — Navy Pistol Marksmanship Ribbon — Coast Guard Dist. Marksman & Pistol Shot — Coast Guard Rifle Marksmanship Ribbon — Coast Guard Pistol Marksmanship Ribbon — USAF Small Arms Expert

❖ Army Ribbon Devices

1. Airplane, C-54, Gold

Services: All
Worn on: World War II Occupation Medals
Denotes: Service during Berlin Airlift *(1948-49)*

2. Arrowhead, Bronze

Services: Army, Air Force
Worn on: Campaign awards since World War II
Denotes: Combat assault or invasion

3. Bar, Date, Silver

Services: All
Worn on: Republic of Vietnam Campaign Medal
Denotes: Worn upon initial issue; has no significance

4a. Bar, Knotted, Bronze

Services: Army
Worn on: Army Good Conduct Medal
Denotes: Additional periods aof service *(awards 2 through 5)*

4b. Bar, Knotted, Silver

Services: Army
Worn on: Army Good Conduct Medal
Denotes: Additional periods of service *(awards 6 through 10)*

4c. Bar, Knotted, Gold

Services: Army
Worn on: Army Good Conduct Medal
Denotes: Additional periods of service *(awards 11 through 15)*

5a. Disk, Bronze

Services: All
Worn on: Antarctica Service Medal
Denotes: Wintered over on the Antarctic continent

5b. Disk, Gold

Services: All
Worn on: Antarctica Service Medal
Denotes: Wintered over twice on the Antarctic continent

5c. Disk, Silver

Services: All
Worn on: Antarctica Service Medal
Denotes: Wintered over three times on the Antarctic continent

8a. Hourglass, Bronze

Services: All
Worn on: Armed Forces Reserve Medal
Denotes: 10 Years of service in the Reserve Forces

8b. Hourglass, Silver

Services: All
Worn on: Armed Forces Reserve Medal
Denotes: 20 Years of service in the Reserve Forces

8c. Hourglass, Gold

Services: All
Worn on: Armed Forces Reserve Medal
Denotes: 30 Years of service in the Reserve Forces

16. Letter "M", Block, Bronze

Services: All
Worn on: Armed Forces Reserve Medal
Denotes: Mobilization for active military service

22. Letter "V", Serif, Bronze

Services: All *(Except Marine Corps)*
Worn on: Personal decorations
Denotes: Valorous actions in combat

24. Letter "V", Serif, Bronze

Services: All
Worn on: Joint Service Commendation Medal
Denotes: Valorous actions in combat

29a. Medal, Miniature, Gold

Services: Foreign military personnel
Worn on: Legion of Merit
Denotes: Level of award *(Chief Commander)*

29b. Medal, Miniature, Silver

Services: Foreign military personnel
Worn on: Legion of Merit
Denotes: Level of award *(Commander)*

29c. Medal, Miniature, Gold

Services: Foreign military personnel
Worn on: Legion of Merit
Denotes: Level of award *(Officer)*

32. Numeral, Block, Bronze

Services: All *(Except Coast Guard)*
Worn on: Humanitarian Service Medal
Denotes: Number of additional awards *(Obsolete)*

33. Numeral, Block, Bronze

Services: All
Worn on: Armed Forces Reserve Medal
Denotes: Number of times mobilized for active duty

35. Numeral, Block, Bronze

Services: Army
Worn on: Overseas Service and Reserve Components Overseas Training Ribbons
Denotes: Total number of awards

36. Numeral, Block, Bronze

Services: All
Worn on: Multinational Force & Observers Medal
Denotes: Total number of awards

37a. Numeral "2", Block, Bronze

Services: Army
Worn on: NCO Professional Development Ribbon
Denotes: Level of professional training achieved *(Basic)*

37b. Numeral "3", Block, Bronze

Services: Army
Worn on: NCO Professional Development Ribbon
Denotes: Level of professional training achieved *(Advanced)*

37c. Numeral "4", Block, Bronze

Services: Army
Worn on: NCO Professional Development Ribbon
Denotes: Level of professional training achieved (Senior)

37d. Numeral "5", Block, Bronze

Services: Army
Worn on: NCO Professional Development Ribbon
Denotes: Completion of Sergeants-Major Academy *(Obsolete)*

41. Oak Leaf Cluster, Bronze

Services: Army, Air Force
Worn on: Personal Decorations
Denotes: One (1) additional award

42. Oak Leaf Cluster, Bronze

Services: Army, Air Force
Worn on: Unit Awards
Denotes: One (1) additional award

44. Oak Leaf Cluster, Bronze

Services: Army
Worn on: Reserve Components Achievement Medal
Denotes: One (1) additional award

45. Oak Leaf Cluster, Bronze

Services: All
Worn on: Joint Service Decorations and Joint Meritorious Unit Award
Denotes: One (1) additional award

❖ Army Ribbon Devices

47. Oak Leaf Cluster, Bronze

Services: Army
Worn on: National Defense Service Medal
Denotes: One (1) additional award *(Obsolete)*

48. Oak Leaf Cluster, Silver

Services: Army, Air Force
Worn on: Personal Decorations
Denotes: Five (5) additional awards

49. Oak Leaf Cluster, Silver

Services: Army, Air Force
Worn on: Unit Awards
Denotes: Five (5) additional awards

51. Oak Leaf Cluster, Silver

Services: All
Worn on: Joint Service decorations and Joint Meritorious Unit Award
Denotes: Five (5) additional awards

54. Palm, Bronze

Services: All
Worn on: Vietnam Civil Actions Unit Citation
Denotes: No significance, worn upon initial issue

55. Palm, Bronze

Services: Army
Worn on: Vietnam Gallantry Cross Unit Citation
Denotes: Level of Award *(Cited before the Army)*

56. Palm & Swords Device, Gold

Services: All
Worn on: Kuwait Liberation Medal *(Saudi Arabia)*
Denotes: No significance, worn upon initial issue

63. Star 3/16" dia., Bronze

Services: All
Worn on: Campaign awards since World War II
Denotes: Battle participation *(one star per major engagement)*

65. Star 3/16" dia., Bronze

Services: All
Worn on: Prisoner of War and Humanitarian Service Medals
Denotes: One (1) additional award

67. Star 3/16" dia., Bronze

Services: All
Worn on: Service Awards
Denotes: One (1) star per each additional award

72. Star 3/16" dia., Bronze

Services: All
Worn on: World War I Victory Medal
Denotes: One (1) star for each campaign clasp earned

75. Star 3/16" dia., Bronze

Services: All
Worn on: American Defense Service Medal
Denotes: Overseas service prior to World War II

76. Star 3/16" dia., Bronze

Services: All
Worn on: National Defense Service Medal
Denotes: Additional awards *(one star per designated period)*

79. Star 3/16" dia., Bronze

Services: All
Worn on: Philippine Defense and Liberation Ribbons
Denotes: Additional battle honors

80. Star 3/16" dia., Bronze

Services: All *(Except Army)*
Worn on: Philippine Presidential Unit Citation
Denotes: Additional award

81. Star 3/16" dia., Bronze

Services: All
Worn on: United Nations and NATO mission medals
Denotes: One (1) star for each additional mission

82. Star 3/16" dia., Silver

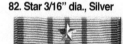

Services: All
Worn on: Campaign awards since World War II
Denotes: Battle participation in five (5) major engagements

83. Star 3/16" dia., Silver

Services: All
Worn on: Expeditionary Medals
Denotes: Five (5) additional expeditions

84. Star 3/16" dia., Silver

Services: All
Worn on: Prisoner of War and Humanitarian Service Medals
Denotes: Five (5) additional awards

86. Star 3/16" dia., Silver

Services: All
Worn on: Service Awards
Denotes: Five (5) additional Awards

88. Star 3/16" dia., Silver

Services: Army
Worn on: Campaign medals up to World War I
Denotes: Citation for Gallantry

99. Star 5/16" dia., Gold

Services: All
Worn on: Inter-American Defense Board Medal
Denotes: One (1) additional award

100. Star 5/16" dia., Gold

Services: Army
Worn on: Army Sea Duty Ribbon
Denotes: 10th (final) award

104. Star 5/16" dia., Silver

Services: Navy
Worn on: World War II Campaign Medals
Denotes: Five (5) major campaigns *(Obsolete)*

105. Star 3/8" dia., Bronze

Services: Army
Worn on: Vietnam Gallantry Cross Unit Citation
Denotes: Level of award *("Cited before the Regiment")*

106. Star 3/8" dia., Silver

Services: Army
Worn on: Vietnam Gallantry Cross Unit Citation
Denotes: Level of award *(Cited before the Division)*

107. Star 3/8" dia., Gold

Services: Army
Worn on: Vietnam Gallantry Cross Unit Citation
Denotes: Level of award *(Cited before the Corps)*

110. Letter "C", Serif, Bronze

Services: New for all
Worn on: Personal decorations
Denotes: award was earned in a combat setting

111. Letter "R", Serif, Bronze

Services: New for All
Worn on: Personal decorations
Denotes: Recognize remote combat action.

Copyright
Medals of America

Placement of the Letter "V" on the Ribbon and Medal

No. of Awards	Army V Device

Legend:
- V = Bronze Letter V
- = Silver Oak Leave Cluster
- = Bronze Oak Leaf Cluster

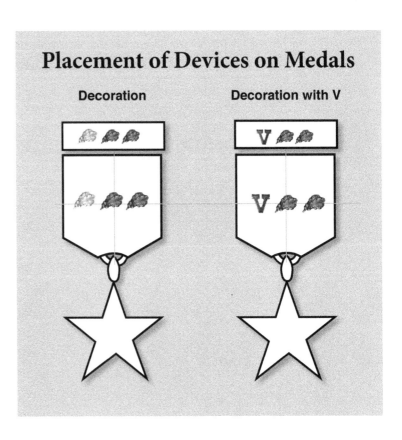

Placement of Devices on Medals

Decoration	Decoration with V

Placement of Oak Leaf Cluster Devices on the Ribbon

No. of Awards	All Services	No. of Awards	
1		6	
2		7	
3		8	
4		9	
5		10	SEE NOTE 1

NOTE 1

1. Army and Air Force regulations limit the number of devices which may be worn on a single ribbon to a maximum of four (4). If more than four devices are authorized, a second ribbon is worn containing the excess devices.

Legend:
- = Bronze Oak Leaf Cluster
- = Silver Oak Leaf Cluster

Placement of Devices on the Armed Forces Reserve Medal

WITH NO CALL UP TO ACTIVE SERVICE

After 10 years of reserve service

After 20 years of reserve service

After 30 years of reserve service

After 40 years of reserve service

WITH CALL-UP TO ACTIVE SERVICE PRIOR TO 10 YEAR PERIOD

With 1 mobilization

With 2 mobilizations

With 3 mobilizations

With 4 mobilizations

WITH CALL-UP TO ACTIVE SERVICE AFTER INITIAL 10 YEAR PERIOD

After 10 years of reserve service and 1 mobilization

After 10 years of reserve service and 2 mobilizations

After 10 years of reserve service and 3 mobilizations

Legend:

= Bronze Hourglass

= Silver Hourglass

= Gold Hourglass

M = Bronze Letter "M"

3 = Bronze Block Numeral

Note:
The M device always goes in the center of the ribbon except for USCG.

Placement Campaign Stars on the Ribbon

No. of Campaigns	All Service	No. of Campaigns	Army & Air Force
1	★	5	⚜
2	★★	6	⚜★
3	★★★	7	⚜★★
4	★★★★	8	⚜★★★
5	⚜	9	SEE NOTE 1

NOTE:
1. Army and Air Force regulations limit the number of devices which may be worn on a single ribbon to a maximum of four. If more than four devices are authorized, a second ribbon is worn containing the excess devices.
2. Campaign stars are often referred to as "Battle Stars".

Legend:
★ = 3/16" Bronze Star
⚜ = 3/16" Silver Star

C Combat & R Remote Device Placement on the Ribbon

No. of Awards	Army C Device		No. of Awards	Army R Device
1	C		1	R
2	C🍃		2	R🍃
3	C🍃🍃		3	R🍃🍃
4	C🍃🍃🍃		4	R🍃🍃🍃
5	SEE NOTE 1		5	SEE NOTE 1

When both C and R device are awarded the C goes before the R and the V before both.

❖ The United States Army Pyramid of Honor

The Pyramid of Honor

As mentioned earlier the Army award system has evolved into a highly structured program which is called the "Pyramid of Honor." The system is designed to reward services ranging from heroism on the battlefield to superior performance of noncombatant duties and even includes the completion of entry level basic training.

Since World War II the Army has generally embraced Napoleon's concept of liberally awarding medals and ribbons to enhance morale and esprit de corps. The large number of Air Medals awarded in World War II is an example of this policy. Army Air Force losses were second only to the Infantry and the leadership wanted an immediate way to recognize the extraordinary service of the air crews. Over the years an expanded and specifically-tailored awards program became generally very popular in the all-volunteer Army and has played a significant part in improving morale, job performance, recruitment and reenlistments among junior officers and enlisted personnel.

On the facing page is a chart showing all United States Military Medals for the five services; Army, Navy, Marines, Air Force and Coast Guard. Some of these decorations and medals apply to all branches of the Armed Forces others just apply to the Army or Naval forces or the Air Force.

The decorations and awards which apply specifically to the Army and represent the rich United States Army military heritage are presented on the following pages. The details of these awards tell the story of the dedication to the ideals of freedom and sacrifices required to earn them.

The color plates display multiple versions of each medal and describe the Service or Services to which the award is authorized, the date instituted and the criteria for award along with appropriate attachments and in some cases examples of how they were earned. Generally every variation, official and unofficial, of the medal, miniature, ribbon and pin is shown. This is probably the only publication in the world that does that.

The medals and ribbons are presented in the Army order of precedence beginning with the Medal of Honor and ending with the commonly awarded foreign medals and ribbons. The foreign section also includes an expanded area on the awards which may have been received by Army personnel from the Republic of South Vietnam.

The Army issues and presents all decorations and many of the service medals. With the exception of the Medal of Honor all of the medals and ribbons presented in this book can be purchased by veterans, their family, active-duty, Guard and Reserve. *Make no mistake, it is against the law to buy or sell a United States Medal of Honor.*

The Stolen Valor Act

The Stolen Valor Act of 2005, was a statute that addressed the unauthorized wear, manufacture or sale of certain military decorations and medals. The law made it a federal misdemeanor to falsely represent oneself as having received any U.S. military decoration or medal. In United States v. Alvarez the U.S. Supreme Court ruled in 2012, that the Stolen Valor Act was too restrictive. In 2013, a new bill was introduced in Congress and the Stolen Valor Act of 2013 was signed into law by the President on June 3, 2013.

United States and Foreign Awards

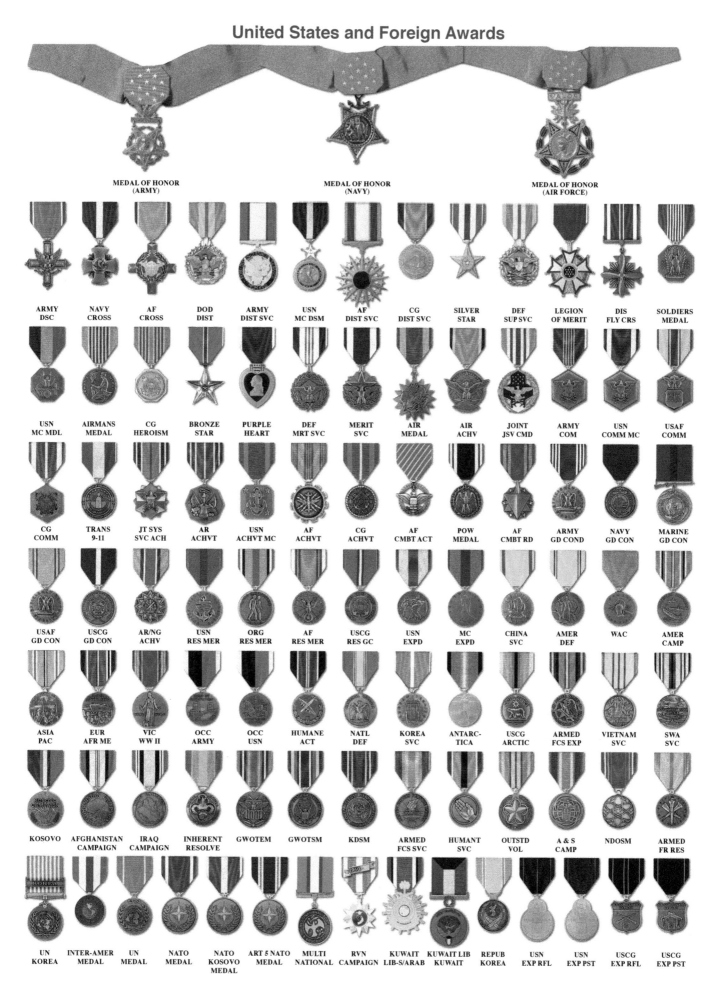

MEDAL OF HONOR (ARMY)

MEDAL OF HONOR (NAVY)

MEDAL OF HONOR (AIR FORCE)

ARMY DSC	NAVY CROSS	AF CROSS	DOD DIST	ARMY DIST SVC	USN MC DSM	AF DIST SVC	CG DIST SVC	SILVER STAR	DEF SUP SVC	LEGION OF MERIT	DIS FLY CRS	SOLDIERS MEDAL
USN MC MDL	AIRMANS MEDAL	CG HEROISM	BRONZE STAR	PURPLE HEART	DEF MRT SVC	MERIT SVC	AIR MEDAL	AIR ACHV	JOINT JSV CMD	ARMY COM	USN COMM MC	USAF COMM
CG COMM	TRANS 9-11	JT SYS SVC ACH	AR ACHVT	USN ACHVT MC	AF ACHVT	CG ACHVT	AF CMBT ACT	POW MEDAL	AF CMBT RD	ARMY GD COND	NAVY GD CON	MARINE GD CON
USAF GD CON	USCG GD CON	AR/NG ACHV	USN RES MER	ORG RES MER	AF RES MER	USCG RES GC	USN EXPD	MC EXPD	CHINA SVC	AMER DEF	WAC	AMER CAMP
ASIA PAC	EUR AFR ME	VIC WW II	OCC ARMY	OCC USN	HUMANE ACT	NATL DEF	KOREA SVC	ANTARC-TICA	USCG ARCTIC	ARMED FCS EXP	VIETNAM SVC	SWA SVC
KOSOVO	AFGHANISTAN CAMPAIGN	IRAQ CAMPAIGN	INHERENT RESOLVE	GWOTEM	GWOTSM	KDSM	ARMED FCS SVC	HUMANT SVC	OUTSTD VOL	A & S CAMP	NDOSM	ARMED FR RES
UN KOREA	INTER-AMER MEDAL	UN MEDAL	NATO MEDAL	NATO KOSOVO MEDAL	ART 5 NATO MEDAL	MULTI NATIONAL	RVN CAMPAIGN	KUWAIT LIB-S/ARAB	KUWAIT LIB KUWAIT	REPUB KOREA	USN EXP RFL	USN EXP PST	USCG EXP RFL	USCG EXP PST

President Barack Obama presents the Medal of Honor to Staff Sgt. Salvatore Giunta of the 173rd Airborne Brigade in the East Room of the White House.

U.S. Army Photo

In the United States, a totally democratic society, it is fitting that the first medal to reward valor on the battlefield should be for private soldiers and seamen *(later extended to officers)*.

The Congressional Medal of Honor *(referred to universally as the Medal of Honor in all statutes, awards and uniform regulations)* was born in conflict and steeped in controversy during its early years until emerging as one of the world's premier awards for bravery.

Although there are three separate medals representing America's highest reward for bravery, there is only a single set of directives governing the award of the most coveted of all U.S. decorations.

Many Americans are confused by the term: "Congressional Medal of Honor" when, in fact, the proper term is "Medal of Honor". Most confusion comes from a July 1918 law that authorizes the President to present the medal" … in the name of Congress".

The fact that all Medals of Honor recipients belong to the Congressional Medal of Honor Society, an official organization chartered by Congress, adds to the confusion. The medal is referred to universally as the "Medal of Honor".

The Medal of Honor

Medal of Honor

The **Medal of Honor** is the highest military award for bravery that can be given to an individual in the United States of America. Conceived in the early 1860's and first presented in 1863, the medal has a colorful and inspiring history which has culminated in the standards applied today for awarding this respected honor.

To judge whether a soldier is entitled to the Medal of Honor, all of the Army regulations permit no margin of doubt or error: (1) The deed of the person must be proved by incontestable evidence of at least two eyewitnesses (2) It must be so outstanding that it clearly distinguishes gallantry beyond the call of duty from lesser forms of bravery and (3) It must involve the risk of life. However, until passage of Public Law 88-77, the Navy awarded Medals of Honor for bravery in saving lives, and deeds of valor performed in submarine rescues, boiler explosions, turret fires and other types of disasters unique to the naval profession.

A recommendation for the Army Medal must normally be made within 2 years of the date of the deed and award of the medal should be made within 3 years after the date of the deed. The recommendations can and do go back in time depending on an Army Review Board or new material.

The Medal of Honor was the result of group thought and action in the winter of 1861-62, following the beginning of hostilities in the Civil War. There was much thought in Washington concerning the necessity for recognizing the deeds of the American soldiers, sailors and marines who were distinguishing themselves in the fighting. The United States, which had given little thought to its Armed Forces during times of peace, now found them to be the focal point of attention. The serviceman was not just fighting, but was fighting gallantly, sometimes displaying a sheer heroism which a grateful Nation desired to reward in a meaningful and dignified manner.

In this spirit a bill was introduced in the Senate to create a Navy Medal of Honor. It was passed and approved by President Abraham Lincoln on December 21, 1861 establishing the Medal of Honor for enlisted men of the Navy and Marine Corps - The first decoration formally authorized by the American Government to be worn as a badge of honor. Action for the Army medal followed on February 17, 1862, when a Senate resolution was introduced providing for presentation of "medals of honor" to enlisted men of the Army and Voluntary Forces who "shall most distinguish themselves by their gallantry in action and other soldier like qualities." President Lincoln's approval made the resolution law on July 12, 1862 which later included Army officers as well as enlisted men and made retroactive to the beginning of the Civil War. Navy and Marine Corps officers were not authorized award of the Medal of Honor until 1915.

There were some sincere men who believed that the idea of a Medal of Honor would not prove popular with Americans. But after the Civil War and in succeeding years, the medal turned out to be too popular and the honors conferred upon its recipients had the effect of inspiring the human emotion of envy. A flood of imitators, including a number by prestigious veteran and patriotic organizations, sprang up following the Civil War and had the effect of causing Congress, eventually, to take steps to protect the dignity of the original medal. This took the form of major changes to the medal and ribbon and over the years, resulted, depending on the source, in seventeen Medal of Honor variations (*six Army, ten Navy and one Air Force*).

On April 27, 1916, Congress approved an act which created a "Medal of Honor Roll" upon which the names of honorably discharged recipients who had earned the Medal of Honor in combat were to be recorded. The purpose of the act was to provide a special pension of $10 per month for life and to give medal recipients the same recognition shown to holders of similar British and French decoration for valor. Unfortunately, the act had some unforeseen consequences since not all of the awards seemed to be for combat actions. Given these doubts, the Secretary of War appointed a board of five retired general officers for the purpose of "investigating and reporting upon past awards of the Medal of Honor by the War Department to see, if any, had been awarded or issued for any cause other than distinguished conduct involving actual conflict with an enemy."

By October 16, 1916, the Board had met, gathered all records on the 2,625 Medals of Honor which had been awarded up to that time, prepared statistics, organized evidence and began its deliberations. On February 15, 1917, all of the pertinent documentation had been examined and considered by the Board and 910 names were stricken from the list.

Of these 910 names, 864 were involved in one group, the 27th Maine Volunteer Infantry. The regiment's enlistment was to have expired in June of 1863 but, to keep the regiment on active duty during the Battle of Gettysburg, President Lincoln authorized Medals of Honor for any members who volunteered for another tour of duty. It was felt that the 309 men who volunteered for extended duty in the face of possible death, were certainly demonstrating "soldier like" qualities and as such were entitled to the Medal under the original law. But their act in no way measured up to the 1916 standards and a clerical error compounded the abuse. Not only did the 309 volunteers receive the medal, but the balance of the regiment, which had gone home also received the award.

In that case, as well as in the remaining 46 scattered instances, the Board felt that the medal had not been properly awarded for distinguished services by the definition of the act of June 3, 1916. Among the 46 others who lost their medals were William F. (*"Buffalo Bill"*) Cody, Dr. Mary Walker, the only female medal recipient and the 29 members of the special Honor Guard that had accompanied the body of Abraham Lincoln from Washington, DC to its final resting place in Springfield, Illinois. There have been no instances of cancellation of Medal of Honor awards within the Naval services due to failure to meet the 1916 award criteria.

Army Medals of Honor

Army Medal of Honor
(1862-1896)

Army Medal of Honor
(1896-1904)

Army Medal of Honor
(1904-1944)

Rosette

Army Medal of Honor
(1944-Present)

Ribbon

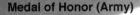

Army Medal of Honor

The Army Medal of Honor was first awarded in 1862 but, owing to extensive copying by veterans groups, was redesigned in 1904 and patented by the War Department to ensure the design exclusivity.

The present medal, a five pointed golden star, lays over a green enamelled laurel wreath.

Medal of Honor (Army)

Awarded to members of the Army Air Force and United States Air Force until May 1954.

The center of the star depicts Minerva, Goddess of righteous war and wisdom, encircled by the words: "United States of America".

Establishing Authority:
The Army Medal of Honor was established by Joint Resolution of Congress, July 12, 1862 *(as amended)*

Effective Date: April 15, 1861

Criteria: Awarded for conspicuous gallantry and intrepidity at the risk of one's own life, above and beyond the call of duty. This gallantry must be performed either while engaged in action against an enemy of the United States, while engaged in military operations involving conflict with an opposing foreign force or while serving with friendly foreign forces engaged in an armed conflict against an opposing armed force in which the United States is not a belligerent party. Recommendation must be submitted through the soldiers chain of command to the Secretary of Defense for approval by the President.

The current Army Medal of Honor was designed by the firm of Arthus Bertrand, Beranger & Magdelaine of Paris, France and is based on the original design of the Medal of Honor created in 1862 by William Wilson & Son Company of Philadelphia, Pennsylvania.

The Medal of Honor is a five-pointed gold-finished star *(point down)* with each point ending in a trefoil. Every point of the star has a green enamel oak leaf in its center and a green enamel laurel wreath surrounds the center of the star, passing just below the trefoils. In the center of the star is a profile of the Goddess Minerva encircled by the inscription, "UNITED STATES OF AMERICA", with a small shield at the bottom. The star is suspended by links from a bar inscribed, "VALOR", topped by a spread winged eagle grasping laurel leaves in its right talon and arrows in the left. The star represents each State in the United States. The oak leaf represents strength and the laurel leaf represents achievement. The head of Minerva represents wisdom with the shield from the Great Seal of the United States representing lawful authority. The laurel leaves clasped in the right claw of the Federal eagle offer peace while the arrows represent military might if the country's offer of peace is rejected. The back of the bar holding the star is engraved, "THE CONGRESS TO." The rest of the medal is smooth to permit engraving the recipient's name. The ribbon is a light blue moiré patterned silk neck band one and three sixteenths inches wide and twenty four inches long, with a square pad in the center of the same ribbon. Thirteen white stars are woven into the pad.

Army Medal of Honor
(July 12, 1862 to May 1, 1896)

The first Army Medal of Honor had the same five-pointed star and flag ribbon as the Navy. The only differences were in the means of suspension. While the Navy medal was suspended by a fouled anchor, the Army's was suspended from an American eagle with outstretched wings with a stack of eight cannon balls and a saber in front of crossed cannon. The cannon, shot and saber represent the artillery and cavalry with the eagle as the national symbol. The top of the ribbon was held by a shield derived from the Great Seal of the United States flanked by two cornucopia, symbolizing America as the land of plenty. The reverse of the medal was engraved with the words, THE CONGRESS TO but was otherwise blank to permit engraving the recipient's name.

Army Medal of Honor
(May 2, 1896 to April 23, 1904)

In the years following the Civil War, many veteran's organizations and other patriotic societies adopted membership badges and insignia which were thinly-disguised replicas of the Medal of Honor. To protect the sanctity of the Medal of Honor, Congress authorized a new ribbon for the Army Medal of Honor in 1896 to clearly distinguish it from veterans association's badges. The basic colors of the original ribbon were not changed, but simply altered.

Army Medal of Honor
(April 23, 1904 to 1944)

Unfortunately, the Army Medal of Honor continued to be widely copied and its design criticized. On April 23, 1904 a new design was approved and was granted Patent Number 197,369. In addition to the new planchet, the redesigned award was suspended from the now familiar light blue moire ribbon symbolic of the loyalty and vigilance, containing 13 embroidered white stars representing the 13 original states. This new version of the Medal of Honor is the design that is still used to the present day. The only change that has taken place since its adoption in 1904 is the suspension which was modified in 1942 from a pin on breast ribbon to a neck ribbon.

❖ Old Distinguished Service Cross

Regulation Ribbon Bar

Enamel Lapel Pin

Full Size Bronze Medal

Captain Eddie Rickenbacker
was awarded nine
Distinguished
Service Crosses.

Medal Reverse

Service	Army
Instituted	1918
Criteria	Extraordinary heroism in action against an enemy of the U.S. while engaged in military operations involving conflict with an opposing foreign force or while serving with friendly foreign forces.
Devices	Bronze, Silver Oak Leaf Cluster

Gen. John J. Pershing (second from left) decorates Brig. Gen. Douglas MacArthur (third from left) with the Distinguished Service Cross. (US Army photo)

The first 100 Distinguished Service Crosses were manufactured in the Philadelphia Mint and numbered on the right side of the lower arm. The arms of the cross were embossed with oak leaves with an American Eagle in the center of a diamond shape with stars on the corner of the diamond. Below the eagle was a scroll reading" E Pluribus Unum". The reverse of the medal had the words "For Valor" surrounded by a laurel wreath. The overall medal was influenced by the art deco design of the period and was soon replaced by a second design with decorative, fluted edges and a small ornamental scroll topped by a ball at the end of each arm. The diamond and stars design was replaced by a wreath behind an enlarged eagle. Several variations of the first type DSC were made in France and are generally thinner and slightly smaller in size. None of the French made DSCs were numbered.

❖ Distinguished Service Cross

Bronze

Anodized or Gold-Plated

Regulation Ribbon Bar

Enamel Lapel Pin

Miniature Medals

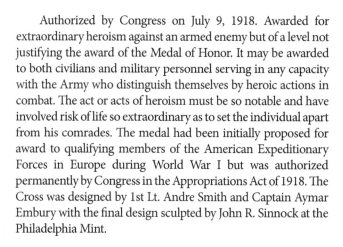

Medal Reverse

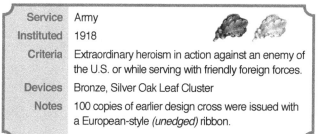

Mini Ribbon (unofficial)

Hat Pin

Authorized by Congress on July 9, 1918. Awarded for extraordinary heroism against an armed enemy but of a level not justifying the award of the Medal of Honor. It may be awarded to both civilians and military personnel serving in any capacity with the Army who distinguish themselves by heroic actions in combat. The act or acts of heroism must be so notable and have involved risk of life so extraordinary as to set the individual apart from his comrades. The medal had been initially proposed for award to qualifying members of the American Expeditionary Forces in Europe during World War I but was authorized permanently by Congress in the Appropriations Act of 1918. The Cross was designed by 1st Lt. Andre Smith and Captain Aymar Embury with the final design sculpted by John R. Sinnock at the Philadelphia Mint.

While DSCs were originally numbered, the practice was discontinued during World War II. In 1934 the DSC was authorized to be presented to holders of the Certificate of Merit which had been discontinued in 1918 when the Distinguished Service Medal was established. The medal is a cross with an eagle with spread wings centered on the cross behind which is a circular wreath of laurel leaves. The cross has decorative fluted edges with a small ornamental scroll topped by a ball at the end of each arm. The laurel wreath is tied at its base by a scroll which upon which are written the words, "FOR VALOR." The eagle represents the United States and the laurel leaves surrounding the eagle representing victory and achievement. The reverse of the cross features the same decorations at the edges that appear on the front. The eagle's wings, back and tips also show. Centered on the reverse of the cross is a laurel wreath. In the center of the wreath is a decorative rectangular plaque for engraving the soldier's name. The ribbon has a one inch wide center of national blue edged in white and red. The national colors taken from the flag stand for sacrifice (red), purity *(white)* and high purpose *(blue)*.

Service	Army
Instituted	1918
Criteria	Extraordinary heroism in action against an enemy of the U.S. or while serving with friendly foreign forces.
Devices	Bronze, Silver Oak Leaf Cluster
Notes	100 copies of earlier design cross were issued with a European-style *(unedged)* ribbon.

173rd, 2-503 SSG Erich R. Phillips Awarded Distinguished Service Cross for Battle at Ranch House

General William "Billy" Mitchell is shown wearing the Distinguished Service Cross and Distinguished Service Medal among other medals at the end of WW I. He enlisted as an Army private early in the Spanish-American war and was later commissioned. He was the first American officer to fly over German lines in World War I. Promoted to Colonel in 1917, by September 1918 he planned and led an allied air force of over 1000 planes in the battle of St. Mihiel, the first coordinated air ground offense in the history of modern warfare.

The display to the right shows award of the Distinguished Service Cross as well as two awards of the Silver Star, Purple Heart and Combat Infantry Badge to an Infantry Colonel during his service in World War II and Vietnam. The Good Conduct Medal shows he also enlisted as a private and was later commissioned as an Infantry Officer.

❖ DOD Distinguished Service Medal

Bronze

Anodized or Gold-Plated

Regulation Ribbon Bar

Enamel Lapel Pin

Medal Reverse

Miniature Medals

Mini Ribbons
(unofficial)

Enamel Hat Pin
(unofficial)

Authorized on July 9, 1970 and awarded to military officers for exceptionally meritorious service while assigned to a Department of Defense joint activity. The Secretary of Defense is the awarding authority for the medal, which is usually awarded to very senior officers. Examples of assignments that may allow qualification for this medal are: Chairman, Joint Chiefs of Staff; Chiefs and Vice Chiefs of the Military Services, including the Commandant and Assistant Commandant of the Marine Corps and Commanders and Vice Commanders of Unified and Specified Commands. It may also be awarded to other senior officers who serve in positions of great responsibility or to an officer whose direct and individual contributions to national security or defense are also recognized as being so exceptional in scope and value as to be equivalent to contributions normally associated with positions encompassing broader responsibilities. Subsequent awards are denoted by bronze and silver oak leaf clusters.

Service	All Services (by Sec. of Defense)
Instituted	9 July 1970
Criteria	Exceptionally meritorious service to the United States while assigned to a Joint Activity in a position of unique and great responsibility.
Devices	C Devices and Oak Leafs Cluster

The medal depicts an American bald eagle with wings spread and the United States shield on its breast; the eagle is superimposed on a medium blue pentagon (which represents the five services) and is surrounded by a gold circle that has thirteen stars in the upper half and a laurel and olive wreath in the lower half. On the reverse of the medal is the inscription, "FROM THE SECRETARY OF DEFENSE TO...FOR DISTINGUISHED SERVICE." Space is provided between the TO and FOR for engraving of the recipient's name. The ribbon has a central stripe of red flanked by stripes of gold and blue. The red represents zeal and courageous action, the gold denotes excellence and the medium blue represents the Department of Defense.

The Defense Distinguished Service Medal was designed by Mildred Orloff and sculpted by Lewis J. King, Jr., both of the Institute of Heraldry.

The Defense Distinguished Service Medal is the top of the senior officer's awards for meritorious service.

❖ Distinguished Service Medal *(Army)*

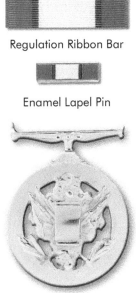

Regulation Ribbon Bar

Enamel Lapel Pin

Medal Reverse

Miniature Medals

Mini Ribbons
(unofficial)

Bronze

Anodized or Gold-Plated

Enamel Hat Pin
(unofficial)

Authorized by Congress on July 9, 1918 for exceptionally meritorious service to the United States while serving in a duty of great responsibility with the U.S. Army. It was originally intended for qualifying actions during wartime only but was later authorized during both wartime or peacetime. As this country's highest award for meritorious service or achievement, it has been awarded to both military and civilians, foreign and domestic. In 1918 the first American to receive this medal was General John J. Pershing, Commanding General of the American Expeditionary Forces during World War I. Individuals who had received the Certificate of Merit before its disestablishment in 1918 were authorized to receive

Service	Army *(Army Air Service)*
Instituted	1918
Criteria	Exceptionally meritorious service to the United States Government in a duty of great responsibility.
Devices	C Devices and Bronze & Silver Oak Leaf Cluster
Notes	Originally issued with European *(unedged)* ribbon *(French Cut)*

the DSM. The Army DSM is seldom awarded to civilians and personnel below the rank of Brigadier General.

The medal is a circular design containing the U.S. Coat of Arms encircled by a blue ring with the inscription, "FOR DISTINGUISHED SERVICE MCMXVII". Subsequent awards are denoted by the attachment of a bronze oak leaf cluster to the medal and ribbon. In the center of the reverse of the medal, amidst several flags and weapons, is a blank scroll for engraving the awardees name.

The ribbon has a central wide white stripe edged with blue and an outer red band representing the colors of the U.S. flag. The Army Distinguished Service Medal was designed by Captain Aymar E. Embury III and sculpted by Private Gaetano Cecere.

General Curtis Scaparrotti was the Supreme Allied Commander, Europe in late spring of 2016, and is shown wearing the Army DSM with a cluster for the second award.

❖ Silver Star

Bronze

Anodized or Gold-Plated

Regulation Ribbon Bar

Enamel Lapel Pin

Medal Reverse

Miniature Medals

Mini Ribbons
(unofficial)

Enamel Hat Pin
(unofficial)

Notes: *Derived from the 3/16" silver "Citation Star" previously worn on Army campaign medals.*

Awarded for gallantry in action against an enemy of the United States or while engaged in military operations involving conflict against an opposing armed force in which the United States is not a belligerent party. The level of gallantry required, while of a high degree, is less than that required for the Medal of Honor, Army, Air Force or Navy Cross. The Silver Star is derived from the Army's "Citation Star", a 3/16" dia. silver star device which was worn on the ribbon bar and suspension ribbon of the "appropriate Army campaign medal" by any soldier cited in orders for gallantry in action. Although most applicable to the World War I Victory Medal, it was retroactive to all Army campaign medals dating back to the Civil War.

The Silver Star Medal was instituted in 1932 with the first award presented to General Douglas MacArthur, the Army's then-Chief-of-Staff. The Silver Star was designed by Rudolf Freund of the firm of Bailey, Banks and Biddle. On August 7, 1942, the award was extended to Navy personnel and, later that year, authorized for civilians serving with the armed forces who met the stated criteria specified in the initial regulation.

The medal is a five-pointed star finished in gilt-bronze. In the center of the star is a three-sixteenths inch silver five-pointed star within a wreath of laurel, representing the silver [citation] star prescribed by the original legislation. The rays of both stars align. The top of the medal has a rectangular-shaped loop for the suspension ribbon. The laurel wreath signifies achievement and the larger gilt-bronze star represents military service. The reverse contains the inscription, "FOR GALLANTRY IN ACTION" with a space to engrave the name of the recipient.

The ribbon, based on the colors of the National flag, has a center stripe of red flanked by a stripes of white which are flanked by blue bands with borders of white edged in blue. Additional awards are denoted by a bronze or silver oak leaf clusters or gold and silver stars depending on the recipient's Branch of Service.

Service	All Services *(Originally Army only)*
Instituted	1932
Criteria	Gallantry in action against an armed enemy of the United States or while serving with friendly foreign forces.
Devices	Army/Air Force: Bronze, Silver Oak Leaf Cluster; Navy/Marine Corps/Coast Guard: Gold, Silver Star
Notes	Derived from the 3/16" silver "Citation Star" previously worn on Army campaign medals.

Sgt. 1st Class Earl D. Plumlee, assigned to 1st Special Forces Group (Airborne), is presented the Silver Star Medal by Maj. Gen. Kenneth R. Dahl. SFC Plumlee was awarded the Silver Star for his actions in Afganistan, August 2013.

❖ Defense Superior Service Medal

Bronze

Anodized

Regulation Ribbon Bar

Enamel Lapel Pin

Medal Reverse

Miniature Medals

Mini Ribbon
(unofficial)

Enamel Hat Pin
(unofficial)

Authorized on February 6, 1976 by an executive order signed by President Gerald R. Ford. Awarded by the Secretary of Defense to any member of the armed forces for superior meritorious service after February 6, 1976 in a position of significant responsibility while assigned to a DOD joint activity, including the Office of the Secretary of Defense, the Joint Chiefs of Staff, and specified and unified commands. The medal was created to provide recognition to those assigned to joint duty on a level equivalent to that recognition provided by the Legion of Merit. Prior to establishment of the Defense Superior Service Medal, the Office of the Secretary of Defense had to provide recognition through equivalent awards that were approved through individual service channels. Although it was established as equivalent to the Legion of Merit, its precedence is before the Legion of Merit when

Service	All Services *(by Secretary of Defense)*	CR 🍂 🍂
Instituted	6 February 1976	
Criteria	Superior meritorious service to the United States while assigned to a Joint Activity in a position of significant responsibility.	
Devices	C and R Devices, Bronze & Silver Oak Leaf Cluster	

both are worn. Oak leaf clusters denote additional awards.

The medal depicts a silver American bald eagle with wings spread and the United States shield on its breast; the eagle is superimposed on a medium blue pentagon *(which represents the five services)* and is surrounded by a silver circle that has thirteen stars in the upper half and a laurel and olive wreath in the lower half. On the reverse of the medal is the inscription, "FROM THE SECRETARY OF DEFENSE TO...FOR SUPERIOR SERVICE." Space is provided between the TO and FOR for engraving of the recipient's name. The ribbon consists of a central stripe of red, flanked on either side by stripes of white, blue and gold.

DID YOU KNOW?

At the time of its creation it was decided that this medal would be obtained at the lowest possible cost and "with as little involvement as possible." For these reasons and because it would rank just below the Defense Distinguished Service Medal for similar service, it was decided to use the same design as the Defense Distinguished Service Medal, except that it would be finished in silver rather than gold and the inscription on the reverse would be modified.

❖ Legion of Merit

Regulation Ribbon Bar

Enamel Lapel Pin

Miniature Medals

Mini Ribbon
(unofficial)

Enamel
Hat Pin
(unofficial)

Bronze   Anodized or Gold-Plated   Medal Reverse

Authorized by Congress on July 20, 1942 for award to members of the Armed Forces of the United States for exceptionally meritorious conduct in the performance of outstanding service. Superior performance of normal duties will not alone justify award of this decoration. It is not awarded for heroism but rather for service and achievement while performing duties in a key position of responsibility. It may be presented to foreign personnel but is not authorized for presentation to civilian personnel. There are four degrees of this decoration that are awarded to foreign personnel only (*Chief Commander, Commander, Officer and Legionnaire*). The first two degrees are comparable in rank to the Distinguished Service Medal and are usually awarded to heads of state and to commanders of armed forces, respectively. The last two degrees are comparable in rank to the award of the Legion of Merit to U.S. service members. The Medal was designed by Colonel Robert Townsend Heard and sculpted by Katharine W. Lane .

The name and design of the Legion of Merit was strongly influenced by the French Legion of Honor. The medal is a white enameled five-armed cross with ten points, each tipped with a gold ball and bordered in red enamel. In the center of the cross, thirteen stars on a blue field are surrounded by a circle of heraldic clouds. A green enameled laurel wreath circles behind the arms of the cross. Between the wreath and the center of the medal and in between the arms of the cross are two crossed arrows pointing outward. The blue circle with thirteen stars surrounded by clouds is taken from the Great Seal of the United States and is symbolic of a "new constellation," as the signers of the Declaration of Independence called our new republic. The laurel wreath represents achievement, while the arrows represent protection of the nation. The reverse of the cross is a gold colored copy of the front with blank space to be used for engraving The raised inscription, "ANNUIT

Service	All Services
Instituted	1942 *(retroactive to 8 Sept 1939)*
Criteria	Exceptionally meritorious conduct in the performance of outstanding services to the United States.
Devices	C and R Devices and Bronze, Silver Oak Leaf Cluster; Letter "V" *(for valor)* not authorizedCluster
Notes	Issued in four degrees *(Legionnaire, Officer, Commander & Chief Commander)* to foreign nationals.

COEPTIS MDCCLXXXII" with a bullet separating each word encircles the area to be engraved. The words, "UNITED STATES OF AMERICA" and "ANNUIT COEPTIS" *(He [God] Has Favored Our Undertaking)* come from the Great Seal of the United States and the date, "MDCCLXXXII" *(1782)* refers to the year General Washington established the Badge of Military Merit. The ribbon is a purple-red called American Beauty Red which is edged in white. The color is a variation of the original color of the Badge of Military Merit.

President Franklin D. Roosevelt, established the rules for the Legion of Merit and required the President's approval for the award. However, in 1943, at the request of General George C. Marshall, approval authority for U.S. personnel was delegated to the War Department.

Executive Order 10600, dated March 15, 1955, by President Dwight D. Eisenhower, revised approval authority. Current provisions are contained in Title 10, United States Code 1121.

❖ Legion of Merit for Foreign Military Personnel

Chief Commander
Legion of Merit

Commander
Legion of Merit

Officer
Legion of Merit

Legionnaire
Legion of Merit

The Legion of Merit is awarded to members of armed forces of foreign nations in four degrees according to the level of responsibility, rank and position of the receiver of the award.

The degrees of Chief Commander, Commander, Officer, and Legionnaire are awarded only to members of armed forces of foreign nations under the criteria outlined in Army Regulation 672-7 and is based on the relative rank or position of the recipient as follows:

Chief Commander: Head of state or government. However this degree was awarded by President Roosevelt to some Allied World War II theater commanders usually for joint amphibious landings or invasions. (The President had this power under Executive Order 9260 of October 29, 1942 paragraph 3b.[6])

Commander: Equivalent of a U.S. military chief of staff or higher position, but not to a head of state.

Officer: General or flag officer below the equivalent of a U.S. military chief of staff; colonel or equivalent rank for service in assignments equivalent to those normally held by a general or flag officer in U.S. military service; or military attachés.

Legionnaire: All recipients not included above. When the Legion of Merit is awarded to members of the uniformed services of the United States it is awarded without reference to degree.

The degrees and the design of the decoration were clearly influenced by the French Legion of Honor (Légion d'honneur) The Chief Commander Degree of the Legion of Merit Medal overall width is 2 15/16 inches *(75 mm)*. The words "UNITED STATES OF AMERICA" are engraved in

the center of the reverse. A miniature of the decoration in gold on a horizontal gold bar is worn on the service ribbon.

The Commander Degree of the Legion of Merit Medal overall width is 2 1/4 inches *(57 mm)*. A gold laurel wreath in the v-shaped angle at the top connects an oval suspension ring to the neck ribbon that is 1 15/16 inches (49 mm) in width. The reverse of the five-pointed star is enameled in white, and the border is crimson. In the center, a disk for engraving the name of the recipient surrounded by the words "ANNUIT COEPTIS MDCCLXXXII." An outer scroll contains the words "UNITED STATES OF AMERICA." A miniature of the decoration in silver on a horizontal silver bar is worn on the service ribbon.

The Officer Degree of the Legion of Merit Medal is similar to the degree of Commander except the overall width is 1 7/8 inches *(48 mm)* and the pendant has a suspension ring instead of the wreath for attaching the ribbon. A gold replica of the medal, 3/4 inch (19 mm) wide, is centered on the suspension ribbon.

The Legionnaire Degree of the Legion of Merit Medal and the Legion of Merit Medal issued to U.S. personnel are basically the same as the degree of Officer, except the suspension ribbon does not have the medal replica. The date "MDCCLXXXII" *(1782)*, which is the date of America's first decoration, the Badge of Military Merit, now known as the Purple Heart. The ribbon design also follows the pattern of the Purple Heart ribbon.

The degrees and the design of the decoration were clearly influenced by the French Legion of Honor (Légion d'honneur)

❖ Distinguished Flying Cross

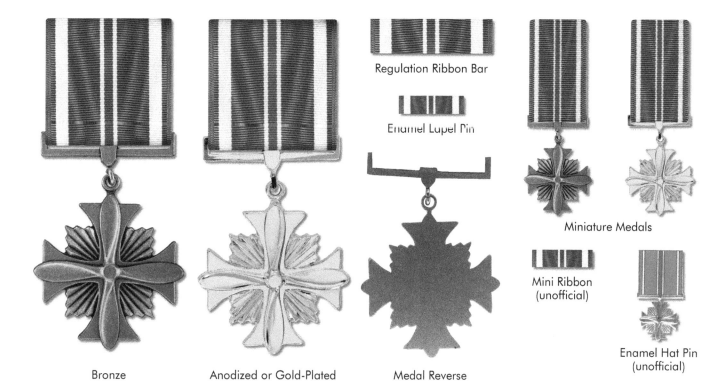

Regulation Ribbon Bar

Enamel Lapel Pin

Medal Reverse

Miniature Medals

Mini Ribbon
(unofficial)

Enamel Hat Pin
(unofficial)

Bronze

Anodized or Gold-Plated

The Distinguished Flying Cross was authorized on July 2, 1926 and implemented by an executive order signed by President Calvin Coolidge on January 28, 1927. It is awarded to United States military personnel for heroism or extraordinary achievement that is clearly distinctive involving operations during aerial flight that are not routine. It is the first decoration authorized in identical design and ribbon to all branches of the U.S. Armed Forces. Captain Charles A. Lindbergh was the first recipient of the Distinguished Flying Cross for his solo flight across the Atlantic. The Wright Brothers were awarded the DFC by an Act of Congress for their first manned flight at Kitty Hawk, North Carolina in 1903. Amelia Earhart became the only female civilian to be awarded the DFC when it was presented to her by the United States Army Air Corps for her aerial exploits. Such awards to civilians were prohibited on March 1, 1927 by Executive Order 4601.

While the Distinguished Flying Cross was never intended to be an automatic award, the Army Air Force did use it in that capacity many times during World War II by awarding DFCs for specific number of sorties and flying hours in a combat theater.

The front of the medal is a four-bladed propeller contained within a bronze cross suspended from a straight bar attached to the medal drape. The reverse is blank and provides space for the recipient's name and date of the award. The ribbon is blue with a narrow stripe of red bordered by white in the center. The ribbon edges are outlined with bands

Service	All Services
Instituted	1926 (retroactive to 6 April 1917)
Criteria	Heroism or extraordinary achievement while participating in aerial flight.
Devices	Letter "V" and C Devices: Bronze, Silver Oak Leaf Cluster

of white inside blue. Additional awards are denoted by bronze and silver oak leaf clusters or gold and silver stars depending on the recipient's Service Branch.

Capt. Brendan P. Murphy, of Company B, 2nd Battalion, 3rd Aviation Brigade, distinguished himself as the air mission command and pilot in command of a CH-47D helicopter, Sept. 5, 2010, during Operation Enduring Freedom X, in Afghanistan. (Army Photo)

❖ Distinguished Flying Cross

Distinguished Flying Cross Tie

This display of a 20th Army Air Force World War II veteran shows his awards of the Distinguished Flying Cross, Purple Heart, four Air Medals, American Campaign Medal, the Asiatic Pacific Campaign Medal with four battle stars, the World War II Victory Medal, the Philippine Liberation Medal, and the Philippine Independence Medal. The final medals are 2 World War II Victory Commemoratives.

This display of a Vietnam Warrant Officer Pilot shows his awards of the Distinguished Flying Cross, Bronze Star, Purple Heart Medal ,Multiply Air Medals, the Army Commendation Medal, National Defense Service Medal, the Vietnam Service Medal, the RVN Cross of Gallantry and the RVN Campaign Medal.

This display of a Vietnam Senior NCO Air crewman veteran of the First Cavalry Division and the 11th Armored Calvary shows his awards of the Distinguished Flying Cross, Bronze Star, Purple Heart Medal ,Meritorious Service Medal, Multiple Air Medals, the Army Commendation Medal, Good Conduct Medal, the Army Achievement Medal, National Defense Service Medal, the Vietnam Service Medal and the RVN Campaign Medal.

❖ Soldier's Medal *(Heroism)*

Bronze

Anodized or Gold-Plated

Regulation Ribbon Bar

Enamel Lapel Pin

Medal Reverse

Miniature Medals

Mini Ribbon
(unofficial)

Enamel Hat Pin
(unofficial)

Authorized by Congress on July 2, 1926 to any member of the Army, National Guard or Reserves for heroism not involving actual conflict with an armed enemy.

The bronze octagonal medal has, as its central feature, a North American bald eagle with raised wings representing the United States. The eagle grasps an ancient Roman fasces symbolizing the State's lawful authority and conveys the concept that the award is to a soldier from the Government. There are seven stars on the eagle's left side and six stars and a spray of leaves to its right. The octagonal shape distinguishes the Soldier's Medal from other decorations. The stars represent the thirteen original colonies that formed the United States. The laurel spray balances the groups of stars and represents achievement. The reverse has a U.S. shield with sprays of laurel and oak leaves representing achievement and strength in front of a scroll. The words, "SOLDIER'S MEDAL" and "FOR VALOR" are inscribed on the reverse.

The ribbon contains thirteen alternating stripes of white *(seven)* and red *(six)* in the center, bordered by blue and are taken from the United States flag. The thirteen red and white stripes are arranged in the same manner as the thirteen vertical stripes in the U.S. Coat of Arms shield and also represent the thirteen original colonies.

Gaetano Cecere designed and sculpted the Soldier's Medal *(the art deco influence of the 1920's can certainly be seen in this medal more than in any other Army award.)* The Soldier's

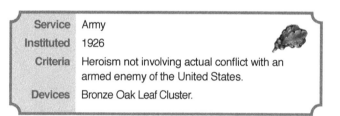

Service	Army
Instituted	1926
Criteria	Heroism not involving actual conflict with an armed enemy of the United States.
Devices	Bronze Oak Leaf Cluster.

Medal is one of four decorations for which an enlisted soldier may increase his retirement by ten percent. The increase is not automatic, however; recipients of the Soldier's Medal must petition the Army Decorations Board for the bonus. Additional awards are denoted by oak leaf clusters.

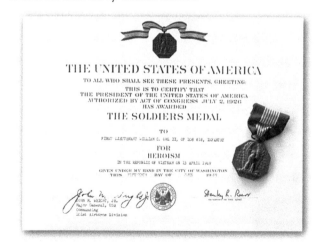

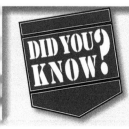

DID YOU KNOW? The Soldier's Medal is awarded for risking one's life to save another's. The medal is awarded in peacetime for actions of heroism held to be equal to or greater than the level which would have justified an award of the Distinguished Flying Cross if the act had taken place in combat and involved actual conflict with an enemy. Any American Service Member who is eligible for retirement pay will receive an increase of 10 percent in retirement pay, if the level of valor was equal to that which would earn the Distinguished Service Cross.

❖ Bronze Star Medal

Bronze   Anodized or Gold-Plated

Regulation Ribbon Bar

Enamel Lapel Pin

Medal Reverse

Miniature Medals

Mini Ribbons
(unofficial)

Enamel Hat Pin
(unofficial)

Notes: *Awarded to World War II holders of Army Combat Infantryman Badge or Combat Medical Badge.*

Authorized on February 4, 1944, retroactive to December 7, 1941. It is awarded to individuals who, while serving in the United States Armed Forces in a combat theater, distinguish themselves by heroism, outstanding achievement or by meritorious service not involving aerial flight.

The Bronze Star was originally conceived by the U.S. Navy as a junior decoration comparable to the Air Medal for heroic or meritorious actions by ground and surface personnel. The level of required service would not be sufficient to warrant the Silver Star if awarded for heroism or the Legion of Merit if awarded for meritorious achievement. In a strange twist of fate, the Bronze Star Medal did not reach fruition until championed by General George C. Marshall, the Army Chief of Staff during World War II. Marshall was seeking a decoration that would reward front line troops, particularly infantrymen, whose ranks suffered the heaviest casualties and were forced to endure the greatest danger and hardships during the conflict. Once established, the Bronze Star Medal virtually became the sole province of the Army in terms of the number of medals awarded.

Although Marshall wanted the Bronze Star Medal to be awarded with the same freedom as the Air Medal, it never came close to the vast numbers of Air Medals distributed during the war. The only exception was the award of the Bronze Star Medal to every soldier of the 101st Airborne Division who had fought in the Normandy invasion, Operation Market Garden in Holland, the Battle of the Bulge or were wounded.

After the war, when the ratio of Air Medals to airmen was compared to the numbers of Bronze Star Medals awarded to

Service	All Services
Instituted	1944 (retroactive to 7 Dec. 1941)
Criteria	The Bronze Star Medal is awarded to individuals who, while serving in the United States Armed Forces in a combat theater, distinguish themselves by heroism, outstanding achievement or by meritorious service not involving aerial flight.
Devices	Letter "V" *(for Valor)* Devices Army/Air Force: Bronze, Silver Oak Leaf Cluster.

combat soldiers, it became clear that a huge disparity existed and many troops who deserved the award for their service had not received it. *Therefore, in September 1947, the Bronze Star Medal was authorized for all personnel who had received either the Combat Infantryman's Badge (CIB) or the Combat Medical Badge (CMB) between December 7, 1941 to September 2, 1945. In addition, personnel who had participated in the defense of the Philippine Islands between December 7, 1941 and May 10, 1942 were awarded the Bronze Star Medal if their service was on the island of Luzon, the Bataan Peninsula or the harbor defenses on Corregidor Island and they had been awarded the Philippine Presidential Unit Citation.*

The Bronze Star Medal is a five-pointed bronze star with a smaller star in the center (similar in design to the Silver Star Medal); the reverse contains the inscription, "HEROIC OR MERITORIOUS ACHIEVEMENT" in a circular pattern. The ribbon is red with a white-edged blue band in the center and white edge stripes. The Bronze Star Medal was designed by Rudolf Freund of Bailey, Banks and Biddle. *Continued.....*

❖ Bronze Star Medal

PENNSYLVANIA
0000 SAMPLE B V
BRONZE STAR FOR VALOR

❖ Purple Heart

Bronze

Anodized or Gold-Plated

Regulation Ribbon Bar

Enamel Lapel Pin

Enamel Hat Pin
(unofficial)

Mini Ribbon
(unofficial)

Miniature Medals

Medal Reverse

Early Purple Hearts were numbered on the edge of the medal.

The Purple Heart is America's oldest military decoration. It was originally established on August 7, 1782 by General George Washington who designed the original award called the "Badge of Military Merit." The Badge of Military Merit was awarded for singularly meritorious action to a deserving hero of the Revolutionary War. There were only three known recipients of the award, all of whom were noncommissioned officers of the Continental Army. The Badge of Military Merit was intended by Washington to be a permanent decoration but was never used again after the three initial presentations until it was reestablished as the Purple Heart Medal on February 22, 1932 *(the 200th anniversary of Washington's birth)* by the Army War Department.

During the First World War, War Department General Order No.134 of October 12, 1917 authorized a red ribbon with a narrow white center stripe to be worn on the right breast for wounds received in action. However, the order was rescinded 32 days later and the ribbon never became a reality. Instead the Army authorized wound chevrons which were worn on the lower right sleeve of the tunic.

On July 21, 1932, General Douglas MacArthur, who was a key figure in its revival, received the first Purple Heart after it was reestablished. President Franklin D. Roosevelt signed an executive order on December 3, 1942 that expanded the award to members of the Navy, Marine Corps and Coast Guard as well. Although the Purple Heart was awarded for meritorious service between 1932 and 1943, the primary purpose of the award has always been to recognize those who received wounds while in military service.

Service	All Services *(Originally Army Only)*
Instituted	1932; The Purple Heart is retroactive to 5 April 1917; however, awards for qualifying prior to that date have been made.
Criteria	Awarded to any member of the Armed Forces of the United States or to any civilian national of the United States who, while serving under competent authority in any capacity with one of the U.S. Armed Forces, since 5 April 1917 has been wounded, killed, or who has died or may die of wounds received from an opposing enemy force while in armed combat or as a result of an act of international terrorism or being a Prisoner of War.
Devices	Army/Air Force: Bronze, Silver Oak Leaf Cluster

Later Presidential Executive Orders extended eligibility for the Purple Heart to military and civilian personnel who received wounds from a terrorist attack or while performing peace keeping duties. Currently, it is awarded for wounds received while serving in any capacity with one of the U.S. Armed Forces after April 5, 1917; it may be awarded to civilians as well as military personnel. The wounds may have been received while in combat against an enemy, while a member of a peacekeeping force, while a Prisoner of War, as a result of a terrorist attack or as a result of a friendly fire incident in hostile territory. The 1996 Defense Authorization Act extended eligibility for the Purple Heart to prisoners of war before 25 April 1962; 1962 legislation had only authorized the medal to POWs after 25 April 1962.

Wounds that qualify must have required treatment by a medical officer or must be a matter of official record.

The Purple Heart was designed by the Army's Institute of Heraldry from a design originally submitted by General Douglas MacArthur and modeled by John Sinnock, Chief Engraver at the Philadelphia Mint. The medal is a purple heart with a bronze gilt border and a bronze profile of George Washington in the center. Above the heart is a shield from George Washington's Coat of Arms between two sprays of green enameled leaves. On the back of the medal, below the Coat of Arms and leaves, there is a raised bronze heart with the raised inscription FOR MILITARY MERIT and room to inscribe the name of the recipient. Initially the medals were numbered, but this practice was discontinued in July 1943 as a cost-cutting measure. The ribbon is purple edged in white. Additional awards are denoted by Bronze and Silver Oak Leaf clusters.

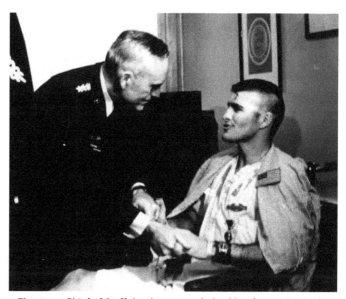

The Army Chief of Staff thanks a wounded soldier for service to the nation at Walter Reed Army Hospital in Washington, D.C.

Kuwait. Refurbished, many of these Purple Hearts continued to be awarded to veterans. The World War II Purple Hearts are generally identified by the high quality of workmanship and a single white stitch under the left and right edge of the ribbon bar of the medal drape. It is not improbable for an Iraq or an Afghanistan veteran to receive the Purple Heart medal that was originally manufactured for his grandfather's generation.

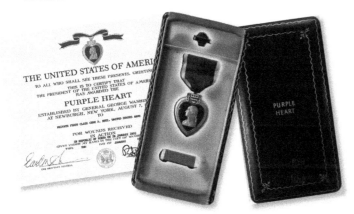

World War II Purple Heart Presentation Case

Purple Heart License Plate

Purple Heart Tie

Purple Heart Stamp

The Purple Heart medal has always been highly respected by military personnel since it was earned by giving one's life or being wounded while in military service of our country. Shown above is a World War II Purple Heart and its WW II period presentation box. The presentation came with the medal, a ribbon and a lapel pin. During World War II contracts were issued for over a million and a half Purple Heart medals with the largest number being produced in anticipation of the invasion of Japan.

The Japanese Armed Forces determination to fight to the death during the Pacific campaign led everyone, especially the Navy and Marines to anticipate heavy casualties. The government requested so many Purple Hearts be manufactured that it was not until almost 1947 that all the contracts were completed. Meanwhile the Air Force bombing campaign and the use of the first atomic bombs lead to the capitulation of Japan and ended the requirement for the huge order of Purple Heart medals.

Approximately a half million Purple Hearts went into the military inventories after World War II. Even with many of these medals presented during the Korean and Vietnam eras there were over 100,000 World War II Purple Heart medals still in the military supply chain during the Liberation of

Vietnam Veteran's awards with Purple Heart Medal

❖ Defense Meritorious Service Medal

Bronze

Anodized or Gold-Plated

Regulation Ribbon Bar

Enamel Lapel Pin

Medal Reverse

Miniature Medals

Mini Ribbon
(unofficial)

Enamel Hat Pin
(unofficial)

Authorized on November 3, 1977. The Defense Meritorious Service Medal is awarded to any active member of the U.S. Armed Forces who distinguishes him/herself by noncombat meritorious achievement or service while serving in a Joint Activity after November 3, 1977. Examples of Joint assignments that may allow qualification for this medal are: Office of the Secretary of Defense, Office of the Joint Chiefs of Staff, Unified or Specified Commands, Joint billets in NATO or NORAD, Defense Agencies, National Defense University, National War College, Industrial College of the Armed Forces, Armed Forces Staff College and the Joint Strategic Target Planning Staff.

Service	All Services (by Secretary of Defense)
Instituted	3 November 1977
Criteria	Noncombat meritorious achievement or service while assigned to a Joint Activity.
Devices	Bronze, Silver Oak Leaf, Bronze Letter "R"

The bronze medal has an eagle with spread wings in the center superimposed on a pentagon in the center of a laurel wreath. The reverse is inscribed with the words, "DEFENSE MERITORIOUS SERVICE" and "UNITED STATES OF AMERICA". The ribbon has a wide white center stripe with three light blue stripes in the middle. The white stripe is flanked by ruby red and white. The ruby red and white are copied from the ribbon of the Meritorious Service Medal with the blue stripes representing the Department of Defense. Subsequent awards are denoted by bronze and silver oak leaf clusters. The Defense Meritorious Service Medal was designed by Lewis J. King, Jr. of the Institute of Heraldry.

Marine Corps Non Commissioned Officer's display case with Defense Meritorious Service Medal after the Bronze Star Medal and before the Meritorious Service Medal.

❖ Meritorious Service Medal

Regulation Ribbon Bar

Enamel Lapel Pin

Miniature Medals

Mini Ribbon
(unofficial)

Bronze   Anodized or Gold-Plated   Medal Reverse

Enamel Hat Pin
(unofficial)

Authorized on January 16, 1969 and awarded to members of the Armed Forces for noncombat meritorious achievement or meritorious service after that date. The Meritorious Service Medal evolved from an initial recommendation in 1918 by General John J. Pershing, the Commander of the American Expeditionary Forces during World War I. He suggested that an award for meritorious service be created to provide special recognition to deserving individuals by the U.S. government. Although the request by General Pershing was disapproved, it was revisited several more times during World War II and afterwards. During the Vietnam War the proposal to create the medal received significant attention and was eventually approved when President Lyndon B. Johnson signed the executive order on January 16, 1969. The Meritorious Service Medal cannot be awarded for service in a combat theater. It has often been the decoration of choice for both end of tour and retirement recognition for field grade officers and senior enlisted personnel.

The MSM is a bronze medal with six rays rising from the top of a five-pointed star with beveled edges with two smaller stars outlined within. On the lower part of the medal in front of the star there is an eagle with its wings spread. It is standing on two curving laurel branches tied between the

Service	All Services
Instituted	16 January 1969
Criteria	Outstanding noncombat meritorious achievement or service to the United States.
Devices	Bronze, Silver Oak Leaf, Bronze, Silver Oak Leaf, Bronze Letter "R"

eagle's talons. The eagle, symbol of the nation, holds laurel branches representing achievement. The star represents military service with the rays symbolizing individual efforts to achieve excellence. The reverse of the medal has the inscription, "UNITED STATES OF AMERICA" at the top and "MERITORIOUS SERVICE" at the bottom; the space inside the circle formed by the text is to be used for engraving the recipient's name. The ribbon is ruby red with two white stripes and is a variation of the Legion of Merit ribbon. Jay Morris and Lewis J. King of the Institute of Heraldry designed and sculpted the Meritorious Service Medal. Additional awards are indicated by bronze and silver oak leaf clusters or gold and silver stars depending on the recipient's Service Branch.

The Meritorious Service Medal was designed to provide appropriate recognition for non-combat achievement or service comparable to the Bronze Star for combat achievement or service. Today, most MSM recipients are field grade officers, pay grade (O-4 to O-6), senior warrant officers (W-3 to W-5), senior noncommissioned officers (E-7 to E-9) and individuals who have displayed a level of service that warrants an award of such magnitude. Normally, the acts or services rendered must be comparable to that required for the Legion of Merit but in a duty of lesser, though considerable, responsibility.

DID YOU KNOW?

❖ Air Medal

Bronze   Anodized or Gold-Plated

Regulation Ribbon Bar

Enamel Lapel Pin

Medal Reverse

Miniature Medals

Mini Ribbon *(unofficial)*

Enamel Hat Pin *(unofficial)*

Authorized on May 11, 1942. Awarded for single acts of achievement after September 8, 1939, to individuals who distinguish themselves by heroism, outstanding achievement or by meritorious service while participating in aerial flight. In WW II the Air Medal was to be awarded for a lesser degree of heroism or achievement than required for the DFC. Many AAF units began to award the Air Medal on a quota basis, e.g. 20 missions equaled one Air Medal or an Air Medal for every enemy aircraft shot down. Some commands carried this to extremes by awarding a DFC for every 5 Air Medals. By the end of WW II, over a million Air Medals were awarded *(many of which were, of course, oak leaf clusters)*. While some will say this was extreme, in truth the generous award of the Air Medal provided combat aircrews a visible sign that their devotion and determination were appreciated by the country. The Air Medal helped keep morale up in a force that suffered the highest casualty rate of the war after the Infantry. The Bronze Star was meant to be the equivalent of the Air Medal for the infantry but it was not until after WW II that it was awarded in bulk to honor combat infantry and medics.

The AAF used oak leaf clusters to indicate additional awards while the Army uses numerals since 1968.

The Air Medal was often awarded in Vietnam to combat arms soldiers for a certain number of helicopter assaults and Army helicopter pilots were often awarded numerous air medals reflecting their huge number of combat missions. The medal is a bronze sixteen point compass rose suspended by a Fleur-de-lis. In the center there is an diving eagle carrying a lighting bolt in each talon. The compass rose represents the global capacity of American air power. The lightning bolts show the United States' ability to wage war from the air. The Fleur-de-lis represents the high ideals of American airmen. The reverse of the compass rose is plain with

Service	All Services
Instituted	1942 *(Retroactive to 8 September 1939)*
Criteria	Heroic actions or meritorious service while participating in aerial flight, but not of a degree that would justify an award of the Distinguished Flying Cross.
Devices	Bronze, Silver Oak Leaf, Bronze "V", "C" & numerals
Notes	During World War II, the Army Air Corps and U.S. Army Air Force employed bronze and silver oak leaf clusters as additional award devices on all decorations including the Air Medal. The same devices were used by the Army until the establishment of the bronze numeral as its unique additional award device for the Air Medal during the Vietnam War.

an area for engraving the recipient's name. The ribbon is ultramarine blue with two golden orange stripes representing the colors of the Army Air Force. The Air Medal was designed and sculpted by Walker Hancock.

U.S. Army Photo

❖ Joint Service Commendation Medal

Bronze

Anodized or Gold-Plated

Regulation Ribbon Bar

Enamel Lapel Pin

Medal Reverse

Miniature Medals

Mini Ribbons
(unofficial)

Enamel Hat Pin
(unofficial)

Authorized on June 25, 1963, this was the first medal specifically authorized for members of a Joint Service organization. Awarded to members of the Armed Forces for meritorious achievement or service while serving in a Joint Activity after January 1, 1963. The "V" device is authorized if the award is made for direct participation in combat operations.

The medal consists of four conjoined green enameled hexagons edged in gold which represent the unity of the Armed Forces. The top hexagon has thirteen gold five-pointed stars *(representing the thirteen original states)* and the lower hexagon has a gold stylized heraldic device *(for land, air and sea)*. An eagle with spread wings and a shield on its breast is in the center of the hexagons. The eagle is grasping three arrows in its talons. The hexagons are encircled by a laurel wreath bound with gold bands *(representing achievement)*. On the reverse there is a plaque for engraving the recipient's name. Above the plaque are the raised words, "FOR MILITARY" and below, "MERIT" with a laurel spray below. The words and laurel spray are derived from the Army

Service	All Services *(by DOD)*
Instituted	June 25, 1963
Criteria	Meritorious service or achievement while assigned to a Joint Activity.
Devices	Bronze Letter "V" *(for valor)*, Bronze, Silver Oak Leaf, Bronze Letter "V", "C", "R"

and Navy Commendation Medals. The ribbon is a center stripe of green flanked by white, green, white and light blue stripes. The green and white are from the Army and Navy Commendation ribbons and the light blue represents the Department of Defense.

The Joint Service Commendation Medal was designed by the Institute of Heraldry's Stafford F. Potter. Oak leaf clusters denote additional awards.

❖ Army Commendation Medal

Bronze

Anodized or Gold-Plated

Regulation Ribbon Bar

Enamel Lapel Pin

Medal Reverse

Miniature Medals

Mini Ribbon
(unofficial)

Enamel Hat Pin
(unofficial)

Authorized on December 18, 1945 as a commendation ribbon and awarded to members of the Army and Army Air Force for heroism, meritorious achievement or meritorious service after December 6, 1941. It was meant for award where the Bronze Star Medal was not appropriate, i.e., outside of operational areas.

The Army Commendation Medal, commonly called the ARCOM, is unique as it is the first and only Army award that started as a ribbon only award and then became a medal. After World War II, it became the only award created for the express purpose of peacetime and wartime meritorious service as well as the only award designed expressly for presentation to junior officers and enlisted personnel.

In short, the ARCOM became the peacetime version of the Bronze Star Medal to recognize outstanding performance and boost morale. Subsequent to World War II, retroactive awards of the Commendation Ribbon were authorized for any individual who had received a Letter of Commendation from a Major General or higher before January 1, 1946.

In 1947, the rules were changed allowing the ARCOM to be awarded in connection with military operations for which the level of service did not meet the requirements for the Bronze Star or Air Medal. In 1949 the change from a ribbon-only award to a pendant was approved. Anyone who received the ribbon could apply for the new medal. The Army redesignated the Commendation Ribbon With Metal Pendant as the Army Commendation Medal in 1960. In 1962, it was authorized for award to a member of the Armed Forces of a friendly nation for the same level of achievement or service which was mutually beneficial to that nation and the United States. The next big change occurred on February 29, 1964 with the approval of the "V" device to denote combat heroism of a degree less than that

Service	Army
Instituted	1945 (retroactive to 1941)
Criteria	Heroism, meritorious achievement or meritorious service
Devices	Bronze letter "V" (for valor), Bronze, Silver Oak Leaf, Bronze Letter "V", "C", "R"
Notes	Originally a ribbon-only award then designated "Army Commendation Ribbon with Metal Pendant "Redesignated: "Army Commendation Medal" in 1960

required for the Bronze Star Medal. Additionally, the ARCOM continued to be awarded for acts of courage not qualifying for the Soldier's Medal. Award is not authorized General Officers.

The medal, a bronze hexagon, depicts the American bald eagle with spread wings on the face. The eagle has the U.S. shield on its breast and is grasping three crossed arrows in its talons. On the reverse of the medal are inscriptions "FOR MILITARY" and "MERIT" with a plaque for engraving the recipient's name between the two inscriptions. A spray of laurel, representing achievement is at the bottom. The ribbon is a field of myrtle green with five white stripes in the center and white edges. The Army Commendation Medal was designed and sculpted by Thomas Hudson Jones of the Institute of Heraldry.

❖ Joint Service Achievement Medal

Bronze

Anodized or Gold-Plated

Regulation Ribbon Bar

Enamel Lapel Pin

Medal Reverse

Miniature Medals

Mini Ribbon
(unofficial)

Enamel Hat Pin
(unofficial)

The Joint Service Achievement Medal was established in 1983 specifically to complete the Department of Defense awards hierarchy and thereby provide a system of decorations for meritorious achievement comparable to those of the separate services. In so doing, the integrity of the more senior Joint Service medals was protected and the opportunity to earn recognition while assigned to a Joint Activity was provided.

It is awarded for meritorious service or achievement while serving in a Joint Activity after August 3, 1983 to military personnel below the rank of colonel. Oak leaf clusters denote additional awards.

The medal features an American eagle with the United States coat of arms on its breast holding three arrows in the center of the bronze medal which consists of a star of twelve points chosen to make it distinctive. The eagle was taken from the Seal designed for the National Military Establishment in 1947 by the President and the arrows were adapted from the seal of the Department of Defense. This is the same design seen on the Army and Navy Commendation Medals.

The reverse of the medal contains the inscriptions, "JOINT SERVICE" and "ACHIEVEMENT AWARD" in a circle. There is space in the center for inscribing the recipient's name. The ribbon consists of a center stripe of red flanked on either side by stripes of light blue, white, green, white and blue.

The Joint Service Achievement Medal was designed by Jay Morris and sculpted by Donald Borja, both of the Institute of Heraldry.

Service	All Services
Instituted	1983
Criteria	Meritorious service or achievement while serving with a Joint Activity
Devices	Bronze, Silver Oak Leaf Cluste Bronze Letter "C", "R"

DID YOU KNOW?

The JSAM may not be awarded for any act or period of service for which a Military Department medal was awarded, and it should not be awarded for retirement. Bronze oak-leaf clusters are used to denote the 2nd through 5th award. No more than four bronze oak-leaf clusters can be worn. Bronze oak-leaf clusters may be worn with one or more silver oak-leaf clusters to denote 7 or more awards.

❖ Army Achievement Medal

Bronze

Anodized or Gold-Plated

Regulation Ribbon Bar

Enamel Lapel Pin

Medal Reverse

Miniature Medals

Mini Ribbon
(unofficial)

Enamel Hat Pin
(unofficial)

Key elements of the Department of the Army Seal are centered in a bronze octagon one and a half inches in diameter. The medal shape was chosen to distinguish it from other Army decorations. The Army Seal represents the authority under which the award is given.

On the reverse are three lines in the upper half reading, "FOR MILITARY ACHIEVEMENT". At the bottom of the medal there is a double spray of laurel which represents achievement. The ribbon has a central stripe of blue with a white center stripe. The blue is bordered by white, green, white and is edged in green.

The Army Achievement Medal is awarded for significant achievement deserving recognition but not considered adequate to qualify for an award of the Army Commendation Medal. Award authority rests with commanders in the grade of Lieut. Colonel and above. The Army Achievement Medal was limited to noncombat achievement before the C device. Members of other branches of the Armed Forces may be eligible for the medal under certain circumstances. Award authority rests with local commanders, granting a broad discretion of when and for what action the Achievement Medal may be awarded.

The Combat C Device may be attached if awarded in a combat area and the R device may be attached if awarded for remote operations. The V device is not authorized.

At the same time the Secretary of the Army approved the Army Achievement medal he also approve the Overseas Service Ribbon, the NCO Academy Ribbon (renamed the NCO Professional Development Ribbon) and the Army Service Ribbon. Additional awards of the Army Achievement Medal are denoted by oak leaf clusters. The Army Achievement Medal was designed by Jay Morris and sculpted by Donald Borja of the Institute of Heraldry.

Service	Army
Instituted	1981
Criteria	Meritorious service or achievement
Devices	Bronze, Silver Oak Leaf Cluste Bronze Letter "C", "R"

❖ Army Presidential Unit Citation

The Army Presidential Unit Citation (PUC) was established on February 26, 1942 as the "Distinguished Unit Badge" or the "Distinguished Unit Citation" and redesignated as the Presidential Unit Citation in 1966. It is awarded to Army units that display the same degree of heroism in combat as would warrant the Distinguished Service Cross for an individual. Like all Army unit awards, the PUC is worn above the pocket on the right breast of the uniform.

The gold-colored frame around the ribbon is worn with the open end of the "V" of the laurel leaf pattern pointing upward. The badge may only be worn permanently by those individuals who were assigned to the unit for the period for

Service	Army
Instituted	1942, Redesignated in 1966
Criteria	Awarded to Army units for extraordinary heroism in action against an armed enemy.
Devices	Bronze, Silver Oak Leaf Cluster
Notes	Original designation: Distinguished Unit Citation. Redesignated to present name in 1966.

which it was cited. Current members of the unit who were not assigned to the unit for the award period are entitled to wear the ribbon but only for the duration of their assignment with the cited unit. Personnel must remove it from their uniform upon reassignment. Additional awards are denoted by bronze oak leaf clusters.

❖ Joint Meritorious Unit Award

The Joint Meritorious Unit Award was authorized by the Secretary of Defense on June 10, 1981 *(retroactive to January 23, 1979)* and was originally called the Department of Defense Meritorious Unit Award. It is awarded in the name of the Secretary of Defense for meritorious service, superior to that which would normally be expected during combat, a declared national emergency or under extraordinary circumstances that involve national interest.

The service performed by the unit would be similar to that performed by an individual awarded the Defense Superior Service Medal. The ribbon is similar to the Defense

Service	All Services
Instituted	1981 *(Retroactive to 1979)*
Criteria	Awarded to Joint Service units for superior meritorious achievement or service
Devices	Bronze, Silver Oak Leaf Cluster

Superior Service Medal ribbon with a gold metal frame with laurel leaves. Like the Defense Superior Service Medal, the ribbon consists of a central stripe of red flanked on either side by stripes of white, blue and yellow, but with blue edges. Additional awards are denoted by oak leaf clusters.

❖ Army Valorous Unit Award

The Army Valorous Unit Award was approved and established by the Army Chief of Staff on January 12, 1966. It is awarded to units of the Armed Forces of the United States for extraordinary heroism in action against an armed enemy of the United States while engaged in conflict with an opposing foreign force on or after August 3, 1963. The Valorous Unit Award requires a lesser degree of gallantry than that required for the Presidential Unit Citation. Nevertheless, the unit must have performed with marked distinction under difficult and hazardous conditions so as to set it apart from the other units participating in the same conflict. The degree of heroism

Service	Army
Instituted	1963
Criteria	Awarded to U.S. Army units for outstanding heroism in armed combat against an opposing armed force.
Devices	Bronze, Silver Oak Leaf Cluster

required is the same as that which would warrant award of the Silver Star to an individual. This award will normally be earned by units that have participated in single or successive actions covering relatively brief time spans but only on rare occasions will a unit larger than a battalion qualify for this award. Additional awards are denoted by bronze oak leaf clusters

❖ Army Meritorious Unit Commendation

The Army Meritorious Unit Commendation is awarded to units for exceptionally meritorious conduct in performance of outstanding services for at least six continuous months of military operations against an armed enemy occurring on or after January 1, 1944. Service in a combat zone is not required but must be directly related to the combat effort. Units based in the continental U.S. or outside the combat area of operation are excluded.

Service	Army and Army Air Force
Instituted	1944
Criteria	Awarded to U.S. Army units for exceptionally meritorious conduct in the performance of outstanding service.
Devices	Bronze, Silver Oak Leaf Cluster
Notes	Originally a golden wreath worn on the lower sleeve.

❖ Army Superior Unit Award

The Army Superior Unit Award was approved in April, 1985 (modified in July, 1986) and is awarded for outstanding meritorious performance of a unit during peacetime in a difficult and challenging mission under extraordinary circumstances. The unit must display such outstanding devotion and superior performance of exceptionally difficult tasks to set it apart from and above other units with similar missions. For the purpose of this award, peacetime is defined as any period during which wartime or combat awards are not authorized in the geographical area in which the mission was executed. The award may be given for operations of a humanitarian nature. The award is designed for battalion-size and smaller or comparable units, but,

Service	Army
Instituted	1985
Criteria	Awarded to U.S. Army units for meritorious performance in difficult peacetime missions.
Devices	Bronze, Silver Oak Leaf Cluster

under most circumstances, headquarters type units would not be eligible. Awards to units larger than battalion size would be infrequent. As with other Army unit citations, it has a gold frame surrounding the ribbon; the open end of the "V" shaped design on the frame points upward and is worn with other unit citations on the right side of the uniform. Additional awards are denoted by bronze and silver oak leaf clusters.

❖ Prisoner of War Medal

Bronze

Anodized or Gold-Plated

Regulation Ribbon Bar

Enamel Lapel Pin

Medal Reverse

Miniature Medals

Mini Ribbon
(unofficial)

Enamel Hat Pin
(unofficial)

The Prisoner of War Medal is awarded to any person who was taken prisoner of war and held captive after April 5, 1917. It was authorized by Public Law Number 99-145 in 1985 and may be awarded to any person who was taken prisoner or held captive while engaged in an action against an enemy of the United States, while engaged in military operations involving conflict with an opposing armed force or while serving with friendly forces engaged in armed conflict against an opposing armed force in which the United States is not a belligerent party. The recipient's conduct while a prisoner must have been honorable.

The Prisoner of War Medal is worn after all unit awards (*after personal decorations in the case of the Army*) and before the various Armed Service Good Conduct Medals (*before the Combat Readiness Medal in the case of the Air Force*).

Service	All Services
Instituted	1985
Criteria	Awarded to any member of the U.S. Armed Forces taken prisoner during any armed conflict dating from World War I.
Devices	Bronze, Silver Star

The Prisoner of War Medal was designed by the Institute of Heraldry. The medal is a circular bronze disc with an American eagle centered and completely surrounded by a ring of barbed wire and bayonet points. The reverse of the medal has a raised inscription, "AWARDED TO" with a space for the recipient's name and, "FOR HONORABLE SERVICE WHILE A PRISONER OF WAR" set in three lines. Below this is the shield of the United States and the words, "UNITED STATES OF AMERICA." The ribbon is black with thin border stripes of white, blue, white and red. Additional awards are denoted by three-sixteenth inch bronze stars.

❖ Army Good Conduct Medal

Bronze   Anodized or Gold-Plated

Regulation Ribbon Bar

Enamel Lapel Pin

Medal Reverse

Miniature Medals

Mini Ribbon
(unofficial)

Enamel Hat Pin
(unofficial)

Authorized on June 28, 1941 for exemplary conduct, efficiency and fidelity and awarded to Army enlisted personnel who, on or after August 27, 1940, had honorably completed three years of active Federal military service. The medal could also be awarded for one year of service after December 7, 1941 while the U.S. was at war. The award was not automatic and required certification by a commanding officer (usually a battalion commander or higher).

The Army Good Conduct Medal was designed by Joseph Kiselewski with an eagle perched on a roman sword atop a closed book. Around the outside are the words, "EFFICIENCY, HONOR, FIDELITY." The reverse of the medal has a five pointed star just above center with a blank scroll for engraving the soldier's name. Above the star are the words, "FOR GOOD" and below the scroll is the word, "CONDUCT." A wreath of half laurel leaves, denoting accomplishment and half oak leaves, denoting bravery surrounds the reverse design.

The ribbon was designed by Arthur E. DuBois, the legendary Director of the Army Institute of Heraldry, and is scarlet with three narrow white stripes on each side. The ribbon is divided by the white stripes so as to form thirteen stripes representing the thirteen original colonies of the United States. During the Revolutionary War, the color scarlet symbolized the mother country and the white stripe symbolized the virgin land separated by force from the mother country.

Unlike other additional award devices, e.g., oak leaf clusters, bronze, silver, or gold clasps with knots *(or loops)* are used to indicate the ***total*** number of awards of the Army Good Conduct Medal. For instance, two awards of the medal are indicated by two bronze knots, three by three, etc. Six total awards are indicated by one silver knot, seven by two

Service	Army
Instituted	1941
Criteria	Exemplary conduct, efficiency and fidelity during three years of active enlisted service with the U.S. Army *(1 year during wartime).*
Devices	Bronze, Silver, Gold Knotted clasp

silver knots, etc. Eleven total awards are indicated by one gold knot, twelve by two gold knots, etc. While all regulations since World War II only authorize a clasp to be worn after the second award or higher; it was not unusual to see veterans with a clasp having a single bronze knot on their Army Good Conduct Medal or ribbon; this may have indicated either a single or second award and seems to have been an earlier unofficial practice.

Although the Good Conduct Medal was officially instituted by executive order in 1941, it really goes back to the American Revolution. When General George Washington established the Badge of Military Merit in 1782 he also created an award called the Honorary Badge of Distinction. This was the first good conduct award since it was to be conferred on veteran noncommissioned officers and soldiers of the Army who served more than three years with bravery, fidelity and good conduct. However, just as the Badge of Military Merit disappeared after the Revolution so did the Honorary Badge of Distinction.

Vietnam Veteran with Good Conduct Medal and basic Vietnam service medals.

When President Roosevelt signed executive order 9323 on March 31, 1943 he officially changed the policy so that the Army Good Conduct Medal could be awarded after one year. Additional awards of the Good Conduct Medal cannot be given for each additional year of service in World War II but required completion of a subsequent additional three-year period.

During the Korean War, President Eisenhower approved a first award only which could be presented for service after June 27, 1950 with less than three years but more than one year service.

Soldiers Cold War awards include the Good Conduct Medal.

Army Reserve Components Achievement Medal

Authorized by the Secretary of the Army on March 3, 1971 and amended by Dept. of the Army General Order 4, 1974, this medal is awarded to any person in the rank of Colonel or below for exemplary behavior, efficiency and fidelity while serving as a member of the Army National Guard (ARNG), a United States Army Reserve troop program unit (TPU) or as an individual augmentee.

The medal is 1-1/4 inches in diameter. In the center is a flaming torch symbolizing the vigilance of the Guard and the Reserve and their readiness to come to the Nation's aid. Two crossed swords in front of and behind the torch represent the history of the Guard and Reserve forged in combat. Left and right of the torch are five pointed stars and the entire design is surrounded by a laurel wreath symbolizing accomplishment. Around these symbols is a twelve pointed star superimposed over a smaller twelve-pointed star indicating the Guard and Reserve's ability to travel where needed in the United States or the world. In between the points of the larger star are laurel leaves and a berry representing achievement.

On the reverse side of the medal in the upper center is a miniature breast plate taken from the Army seal. Above this, the outside edge of the medal is inscribed either, "UNITED STATES ARMY RESERVE" or "ARMY NATIONAL GUARD." Along the bottom edge of the medal are the words, "FOR ACHIEVEMENT."

The ribbon has a wide center stripe of red flanked by narrow stripes of white and blue, reflecting our national colors and patriotism. The outside gold stripes are symbolic of merit. Additional awards are denoted by bronze and silver oak leaf clusters.

Service: Army

Instituted: 1971

Criteria: Exemplary conduct, efficiency and fidelity during 3 years of service with the U.S. Army Reserve or National Guard.

Devices:

❖ American Defense Service Medal

Bronze   Anodized or Gold-Plated

Regulation Ribbon Bar

Enamel Lapel Pin

Medal Reverse

Service	All Services
Instituted	1941
Dates	1939-41
Criteria	12 months of active duty service during the above period
Devices	All Services: Bronze Star *(denotes bars)*
Bars	Army: Foreign Service for service outside the continental United States *(CONUS)*

Authorized June 28, 1941 for military service during the limited emergency ordered by President Roosevelt on September 8, 1939 or the unlimited emergency proclaimed on May 27, 1941 until December 7, 1941 for 12 months or longer. active duty for A Foreign Service Clasp was issued for Army military service outside the continental limits of the United States, including Alaska. It is a Bronze bar 1/8 inch in width and 1-1/2 inches in length with the words FOREIGN SERVICE and a star at each end. A bronze star is worn on the ribbon to denote receipt of a bar.

On the front the female Grecian figure, Columbia, representing America or Liberty is holding a shield and sword while standing on an oak branch, symbolic of strength. The oak leaves represent the strength of the Army, Navy, Marine Corps and Coast Guard. The inscription, "American Defense," is around the outside upper edge. The reverse of the medal carries the inscription, "For Service During the Limited Emergency Proclaimed By the President on September 8, 1939 or During the Unlimited Emergency Proclaimed By the President on May 27, 1941."

The golden yellow color of the ribbon symbolizes the golden opportunity of United States youth to serve the nation, represented by the blue, white and red stripes on both sides of the ribbon. The medal was approved by the Commission of Fine Arts on May 5, 1942.

❖ Women's Army Corps Service Medal

Bronze

Regulation Ribbon Bar

Medal Reverse

Service	Army
Instituted	1943
Dates	1942-45
Criteria	Service with both the Women's Army Auxiliary Corps and Women's Army Corps during the above period.
Devices	None
Notes	Only U.S. award authorized for women only.

Authorized on July 29, 1943 for service in both the Women's Army Auxiliary Corps *(WAAC)* between July 10, 1942 and August 31, 1943 and the Women's Army Corps *(WAC)* between September 1, 1943 and September 2, 1945. After 1945, members of the WAC received the same medals as other members of the Army. No attachments are authorized.

The front of the medal contains the head of Pallas Athena, goddess of victory and wisdom, superimposed on a sword crossed with oak leaves and a palm branch. The sword represents military might; the oak leaves represent strength and the palm branch represents peace. The reverse contains thirteen stars, an eagle and a scroll along with the words, "FOR SERVICE IN THE WOMEN'S ARMY AUXILIARY CORPS," and the dates "1942-1943." The dates on the medal, 1942-1943, remained the same even after the WAAC became the WAC. The ribbon is moss green with old gold edges, the branch colors of the Women's Army Corps. Green indicates merit and gold refers to achievement. *This is the only U.S. service medal specifically created and authorized for women in the military.*

❖ American Campaign Medal

Bronze   Anodized or
Gold-Plated

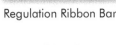

Regulation Ribbon Bar

Enamel Lapel Pin

Medal Reverse

For service during World War II within the American Theater of Operations. The American Campaign Medal was established by Executive Order on November 6, 1942 and amended on March 15, 1946, which established a closing date. The medal is awarded to any member of the Armed Forces who served in the American Theater of Operations during the period from December 7, 1941 to March 2, 1946 or was awarded a combat decoration while in combat against the enemy. The service must have been an aggregate of one year within the continental United States, thirty consecutive days outside the continental United States, or sixty nonconsecutive days outside the continental United States, but within the American Theater of Operations. Maps of the three theaters of operations during World War II were drawn on November 6, 1942 to include the American Theater, European- African - Middle Eastern Theater and Asiatic-Pacific Theater.

Service	All Services
Instituted	1942
Criteria	Service outside the U.S. in the American theater for 30 days, or within the continental United States (CONUS) for one year.
Devices	All Services: Bronze star

The American Campaign Medal was designed by the Army's Institute of Heraldry. The medal is a circular bronze disc showing a Navy cruiser, a B-24 bomber and a sinking enemy submarine above three waves. Shown in the background are buildings representing the United States. Above is the raised inscription, "AMERICAN CAMPAIGN." The reverse of the medal shows an American eagle standing on a rock. On the left of the eagle are the raised inscribed dates, "1941-1945" and on the right, "UNITED STATES OF AMERICA." The ribbon is azure blue with three narrow stripes of red, white and blue (United States) in the center and four stripes of white, red (Japan), black and white (Germany) near the edges. Three-sixteenth inch bronze stars indicated participation in specialized antisubmarine, escort or special operations. The American Campaign Medal is worn after the Women's Army Corps Service Medal by Army & Air Force personnel.

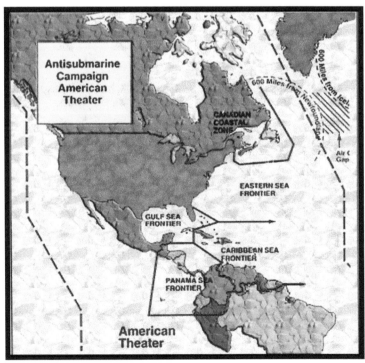

❖ Asiatic-Pacific Campaign Medal

Bronze

Anodized or
Gold-Plated

Regulation Ribbon Bar

Enamel Lapel Pin

Medal Reverse

Authorized on November 6, 1942 and amended on March 15, 1946. Awarded to members of the U.S. Armed Forces for at least 30 consecutive *(60 nonconsecutive)* days service *(less if in combat)* within the Asiatic-Pacific Theater between December 7, 1941 and March 2, 1946.

The front of the medal shows a palm tree amidst troops with an aircraft overhead and an aircraft carrier, battleship and submarine in the background. The reverse has the American eagle, symbolizing power, on a rock, symbolizing stability, with the inscription, "UNITED STATES OF AMERICA" on the eagle's back. The orange yellow of the ribbon represents Asia while the white and red stripes toward each edge represent Japan. The center blue, white and red thin stripes are taken from the American Defense Service Medal, referring to America's continued defense preparedness after Pearl Harbor.

A bronze star denoted participation in a campaign. A silver star attachment is used to represent five bronze stars. An

Service	All Services
Instituted	1942
Dates	7 December 1941 to 2 March 1946
Criteria	Service in the Asiatic-Pacific theater for 30 days or receipt of any combat decoration.
Devices	All Services: Bronze, Silver Star; Army/Air Force: Bronze arrowhead

arrowhead attachment is authorized by the Army and Air Force for participation in a combat parachute jump, combat glider landing or amphibious assault landing *(only one arrowhead may be worn on the medal/ribbon despite the number of qualification events)*. The ribbon is worn with the center blue stripe on the wearer's right.

Designated Army & AAF campaigns for the Asiatic-Pacific Campaign Medal are:

Burma, 1941-1942
Philippine Islands, 1941-1942
Central Pacific, 1941-1943
East Indies, 1942
Aleutian Islands, 1942-1943
Guadalcanal, 1942-1943
Papua, 1942-1943

Air Offensive, Japan, 1942-1945
China Defensive, 1942-1945
India-Burma, 1942-1945
Bismark Archipelago, 1943-1944
New Guinea, 1943-1944
Northern Solomons, 1943-1944
Eastern Mandates (Air), 1943-1944
Eastern Mandates (Ground), 1944
Leyte, 1944-1945

Luzon, 1944-1945
Western Pacific, 1944-1945
Central Burma, 1945
China Offensive, 1945
Ryukyus, 1945
Southern Philippines, 1945
Air Combat, 1941-1945
Antisubmarine, 1941-1945
Ground Combat, 1941-1945

❖ European-African-Middle Eastern Campaign Medal

Bronze

Anodized or
Gold-Plated

Regulation Ribbon Bar

Enamel Lapel Pin

Medal Reverse

Authorized on November 6, 1942, as amended on March 15, 1946. Awarded to members of the U.S. Armed Forces for at least 30 days of consecutive *(60 days nonconsecutive)* service within the European Theater of Operations between December 7, 1941 and November 8, 1945 *(lesser periods qualify if individual was in actual combat against the enemy during this period).*

The front of the bronze medal shows a Landing Ship, Tank *(LST)* unloading troops while under fire with an airplane overhead. The reverse has the American eagle, symbol of power, standing on a rock, symbol of stability, with the inscription, "UNITED STATES OF AMERICA" and dates, "1941-1945."

Three-sixteenth inch diameter bronze and silver stars denoted participation in the specific campaigns described below. A bronze arrowhead indicated participation in a combat parachute jump, combat glider landing or amphibious assault landing. The ribbon's central blue, white

Service	All Services
Instituted	1942
Dates	7 December 1941 to 2 March 1946
Criteria	Service in the European-African-Middle Eastern theater for 30 days or receipt of any combat decoration.
Devices	All Services: Bronze, Silver Star; Army/Air Force: Bronze Arrowhead

and red stripes represent the United States. The wide green stripes represent the green fields of Europe, the brown edges represent the African desert sands, the thin green, white, and red stripes represent Italy and the thin black and white stripes represent Germany.

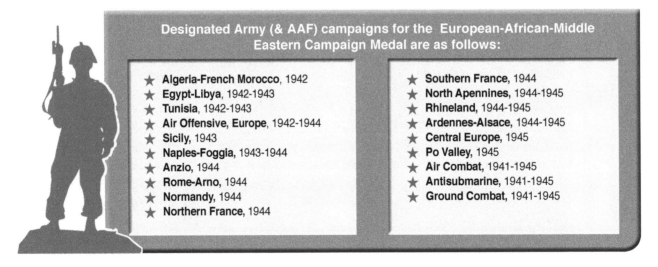

Designated Army (& AAF) campaigns for the European-African-Middle Eastern Campaign Medal are as follows:

- ★ **Algeria-French Morocco**, 1942
- ★ **Egypt-Libya**, 1942-1943
- ★ **Tunisia**, 1942-1943
- ★ **Air Offensive, Europe**, 1942-1944
- ★ **Sicily**, 1943
- ★ **Naples-Foggia**, 1943-1944
- ★ **Anzio**, 1944
- ★ **Rome-Arno**, 1944
- ★ **Normandy**, 1944
- ★ **Northern France**, 1944

- ★ **Southern France**, 1944
- ★ **North Apennines**, 1944-1945
- ★ **Rhineland**, 1944-1945
- ★ **Ardennes-Alsace**, 1944-1945
- ★ **Central Europe**, 1945
- ★ **Po Valley**, 1945
- ★ **Air Combat**, 1941-1945
- ★ **Antisubmarine**, 1941-1945
- ★ **Ground Combat**, 1941-1945

❖ World War II Victory Medal

Bronze

Anodized or Gold-Plated

Medal Reverse

Regulation Ribbon Bar

Enamel Lapel Pin

Does the Victory Medal appear slightly larger than the other medals? Well it is. The bronze World War II Victory medal is 1 3/8 inches in width while the regular campaign medals are 1 1/4 inches wide.

Authorized by an Act of Congress on July 6, 1945 and awarded to all members of the Armed Forces who served at least one day of honorable, active federal service between December 7, 1941 and December 31, 1946, inclusive. The World War II Victory Medal was initially issued as a service ribbon called the "Victory Ribbon." Not until after the war in 1946 was a full medal designed and struck with a new title: World War II Victory Medal.

The front of the medal depicts the Liberty figure resting her right foot on a war god's helmet with the hilt of a broken sword in her right hand and the broken blade in her left hand. The reverse contains the words, "FREEDOM FROM FEAR AND WANT, FREEDOM OF SPEECH AND RELIGION, and UNITED STATES OF AMERICA 1941-1945." The red center stripe of the ribbon is symbolic of Mars, the God of War, representing both courage and fortitude. The twin rainbow stripes, suggested by the World War I Victory Medal, allude to the peace following a storm. A narrow white stripe separates the center red stripe from each rainbow pattern on both sides of the ribbon. The World War II Victory Medal provides deserving recognition to all of America's veterans who served during World War II.

No attachments are authorized although some veterans received the

Service	All Services
Instituted	1945
Dates	7 December 1941 to 31 December 1946
Criteria	Awarded for service in the U.S. Armed Forces during the above period.
Devices	None

ribbon with an affixed bronze star which, according to rumors at the time, was to distinguish those who served in combat from those who did not. No official documentation has ever been found to support this supposition. Although eligible for its award, many World War II veterans never actually received the medal since many were discharged prior to the medal's institution.

❖ Army of Occupation Medal

Service	Army/Air Force
Instituted	1946
Dates	1945-55 (Berlin: 1945-90)
Criteria	30 consecutive days of service in occupied territories of former enemies during above period.
Devices	Gold Airplane
Bars	"Germany", "Japan"

Regulation Ribbon Bar

Enamel Lapel Pin

Medal Reverse

Bronze

Anodized or Gold-Plated

Authorized on June 7, 1946 for both Army and Army Air Force personnel who serviced at least 30 consecutive days in formerly enemy territories, including Germany *(1945-1955)*, Berlin *(1945-1990)*, Austria *(1945-1955)*, Italy *(1945-1947)*, Japan *(1945-1952)* and Korea *(1945-1949)*.

The front of the medal depicts the Remagen Bridge on the Rhine River with the inscription, "ARMY OF OCCUPATION" at the top. The reverse depicts Mount Fujiyama in Japan with two Japanese junks in front of the mountain. Although not specifically authorized by regulations, many veterans received Occupation Medals with reversed medallions, apparently to indicate the theater of occupation service, i.e., if occupation

service was in Japan, the reverse side showing Mount Fujiyama became the front of the medal. The white and black colors of the ribbon represent Germany and the white and red colors represent Japan.

A gold-colored C-54 airplane device is authorized to denote participation in the Berlin Airlift. Medal clasps inscribed: Germany and Japan are authorized for the suspension ribbon of the medal for occupation service in those respective territories. An individual who performed occupational service in both areas is authorized to wear both clasps with the upper clasp representing the area where occupation was first performed. No attachment is authorized for the ribbon bar.

Italy, May 9, 1945 - Sept. 15, 1947

Germany *(except West Berlin),* May 9, 1945 - May 5, 1955

Austria, May 9, 1945 - Jul. 27, 1945 - Oct. 2, 1990

Germany *(West Berlin),* May 9, 1945 - Oct. 2, 1990

Korea, Sept. 3, 1945 - Jun. 29, 1949

Japan, Sept. 3, 1945 - Apr. 27, 1952

❖ Medal for Humane Action

Service	All Services
Instituted	1949
Dates	1948-49
Criteria	120 consecutive days of service participating in, or in support of the Berlin Airlift.
Devices	None

Regulation Ribbon Bar

Enamel Lapel Pin

Medal Reverse

Bronze

Anodized or Gold-Plated

Authorized for members of the U.S. Armed Forces on July 20, 1949 for at least 120 days of service while participating in or providing direct support for the Berlin Airlift during the period June 26, 1948 and September 30, 1949. The prescribed boundaries for qualifying service include the area between the north latitudes of the 54th and the 48th parallels and between the 14th east longitude and the 5th west longitude meridians. Posthumous award may be made to any person who lost his/her life while, or as a direct result of, participating in the Berlin Airlift, without regard to the length of such service.

Continued on next page.

Medal for Humane Action continued

Authorized for members of the U.S. Armed Forces on July 20, 1949 for at least 120 days of service while participating in or providing direct support for the Berlin Airlift during the period June 26, 1948 and September 30, 1949.Posthumous award may be made to any person who lost his/her life while, or as a direct result of, participating in the Berlin Airlift, without regard to the length of such service.

The front of the medal depicts the C-54 aircraft, which was the primary aircraft used during the airlift, above the coat of arms of Berlin which lies in the center of a wreath of wheat. The reverse has the American eagle with shield and arrows and bears the inscriptions, "FOR HUMANE ACTION and TO SUPPLY NECESSITIES OF LIFE TO THE PEOPLE OF BERLIN GERMANY." On the ribbon, the black and white colors of Prussia refer to Berlin, capital of Prussia and Germany. Blue alludes to the sky and red represents the fortitude and zeal of the personnel who participated in the airlift.No attachments are authorized. However, instances have been noted where the gold C-54 airplane device was incorrectly placed on this award rather than its proper usage, the Occupation Medal.

❖ National Defense Service Medal

Bronze

Anodized or Gold-Plated

Regulation Ribbon Bar

Enamel Lapel Pin

Medal Reverse

Miniature Medals

Mini Ribbon *(unofficial)*

Hat Pin *(unofficial)*

Initially authorized on April 22, 1953. It is awarded to members of the U.S. Armed Forces for any honorable active federal service during the Korean War *(June 27, 1950 - July 27, 1954)*, Vietnam War *(January 1, 1961- August 14, 1974)*, Desert Shield/Desert Storm *(August 2, 1990 - November 30, 1995)* and/or Operations Iraqi Freedom and Enduring Freedom *(Afghanistan) (September 11, 2001 to a date TBD)*. Executive Order 12776 on October 8, 1991 authorizied award of the medal to all members of the Reserve forces whether or not on active duty during the designated period of the Gulf War.

The latest award dated April 2, 2002, from the Office of the Deputy Secretary of Defense, authorizes the award to all U.S. Service Members on duty on or after September 11, 2001 to a date TBD. Today, there are probably more soldiers authorized this medal than any other award in U.S. history. Circumstances not qualifying as active duty for the purpose of this medal include: (1) Members of the Guard and Reserve on short tours of active duty to fulfill training obligations; (2) Service members on active duty to serve on boards, courts, commissions, and like organizations; (3) Service members on active duty for the sole purpose of undergoing a physical examination; and (4) Service members on active duty for purposes other than extended active duty. Reserve personnel who have received the Armed Forces Expeditionary Medal or the Vietnam Service Medal are eligible for this medal. The National Defense Service Medal is also authorized to those individuals serving as cadets or midshipmen at the Air Force,

Service	All Services
Instituted	1953
Dates	1950-54, 1961-74, 1990-95, 2001-TBD
Criteria	120 consecutive days of service participating in, or any honorable active duty service during any of the above periods.
Devices	Bronze Star, Bronze Oak Leaf Cluster
Notes	Reinstituted in 1966, 1991 and 2001 for Vietnam, Southwest Asia *(Gulf War)* and Iraq/Afghanistan actions respectively.

Army or Naval Academies. The front shows the American bald eagle with inverted wings standing on a sword and palm branch and contains the words, "NATIONAL DEFENSE"; the reverse has the United States shield amidst an oak leaf and laurel spray. Symbolically, the eagle is the national emblem of the United States, the sword represents the Armed Forces and the palm is symbolic of victory. The reverse contains the shield from the great seal of the United States flanked by a wreath of laurel and oak representing achievement and strength. The ribbon has a broad center stripe of yellow representing high ideals. The red, white and blue stripes represent the national flag. Red for hardiness and valor, white for purity of purpose and blue for perseverance and justice.

Only one medal is awarded to an individual and today a three-sixteenth inch diameter bronze star denotes an additional award of the medal in lieu of the bronze oak leaf used earlier.

❖ Korean Service Medal

Bronze

Anodized or Gold-Plated

Regulation Ribbon Bar

Enamel Lapel Pin

Medal Reverse

Miniature Medals

Mini Ribbon
(unofficial)

Hat Pin
(unofficial)

Authorized by executive order on November 8, 1950 and awarded for service between June 27, 1950 and July 27, 1954 in the Korean theater of operations. Members of the U.S. Armed Forces must have participated in combat or served with a combat or service unit in the Korean Theater for 30 consecutive or 60 nonconsecutive days during the designated period. Personnel who served with a unit or headquarters stationed outside the theater but in direct support of Korean military operations are also entitled to this medal. The combat zone designated for qualification for the medal encompassed both North and South Korea, Korean waters and the airspace over these areas.

The first campaign began when North Korea invaded South Korea and the last campaign ended when the Korean Armistice cease-fire became effective. The period of Korean service was extended by one year from the cease fire by the Secretary of Defense; individuals could qualify for the medal during this period if stationed in Korea but would not receive any campaign credit. An award of this medal qualifies personnel for award of the United Nations (Korean) Service Medal and the Republic of Korea War Service Medal *(approved 1999)*.

A Korean gateway is depicted on the front of the medal along with the inscription, "KOREAN SERVICE" and on the

Service	All Services
Instituted	1950
Dates	1950-54
Criteria	Participation in military operations within the Korean area during the above period.
Devices	All Services: Bronze, Silver Star, Army, Air Force: Bronze Arrowhead

reverse are the "Taeguk" symbol from the Korean flag that represents unity and the inscription: "UNITED STATES OF AMERICA." A spray of oak and laurel line the bottom edge. The suspension ribbon and ribbon bar are both blue and white representing the United Nations. Bronze and silver stars are affixed to the suspension drape and ribbon bar to indicate participation in any of the 10 designated campaigns in the Korean War *(see below)*. Army and Air Force personnel who participated in an amphibious assault landing are entitled to wear the arrowhead attachment.

Campaigns designated by the Army for the Korea Service Medal are:

★ **UN Defensive,** 27 June - 15 Sept, 1950
★ **UN Offensive,** 16 Sept - 2 Nov, 1950
★ **CCF Intervention,** 3 Nov, 1950 - 24 Jan, 1951
★ **1st UN Counteroffensive,** 25 Jan - 21 Apr, 1951
★ **CCF Spring Offensive,** 22 Apr - 8 July, 1951

★ **UN Summer-Fall Offensive,** 9 July - 27 Nov, 1951
★ **Second Korean Winter,** 28 Nov, 1951 - 30 Apr, 1952
★ **Korea, Summer-Fall,** 1 May - 30 Nov, 1953
★ **Third Korean Winter,** 1 Dec, 1952 - 30 Apr, 1953
★ **Korea, Summer,** 1 May - 27 July, 1953

Different displays of an Engineer, an Infantry Sgt. and an Artillery Corporal whose bottom row of medals are commemoratives.

❖ Antarctica Service Medal

Regulation Ribbon Bar

Mini Ribbon
(unofficial)

Miniature Medals

Bronze   Anodized or Gold-Plated   Medal Reverse

Service	All Services
Instituted	July 7, 1960
Dates	1946 to Present
Criteria	30 calendar days of service on the Antarctic Continent
Devices	All Services: Bronze, Gold, Silver disks
Bars	Wintered Over" in Bronze, Gold, Silver

Authorized on July 7, 1960 and awarded to any member of the Armed Forces who, from January 2, 1946, as a member of a U.S. Antarctic expedition, participates in, or performs services in direct support of scientific or exploratory operations on the Antarctic Continent. Qualifying service includes personnel who participate in flights or naval operations supporting operations in Antarctica. The medal may also be awarded to any U.S. citizen who participates in Antarctic expeditions under the same conditions as Service personnel.

The front of the medal depicts a figure appropriately clothed in cold weather gear with his hood thrown back, arms extended and legs spread, symbolizing stability, determination, courage and devotion. The reverse depicts a map of the Antarctic continent in polar projection across which are three centered lines containing the inscription, "COURAGE SACRIFICE DEVOTION."

A clasp containing the raised inscription, "WINTERED OVER" is worn on the medal and a disc of the same metal, containing the outline of the Antarctic Continent is worn on the ribbon bar if the individual remains on the continent during the winter months. For the first stay, the disc and bar are made of bronze, for the second stay, they are gold-colored and for the third and all subsequent winter tours, the devices are silver. The Coast Guard alone specifies the small three-sixteenths inch diameter bronze star as an additional award device.

❖ Armed Forces Expeditionary Medal

Bronze   Anodized or Gold-Plated

Regulation Ribbon Bar

Enamel Lapel Pin

Medal Reverse

Miniature Medals

Mini Ribbon
(unofficial)

Hat Pin
(unofficial)

President John F. Kennedy characterized the post World War II period as: "a twilight that is neither peace nor war." During the period commonly referred to as the Cold War, the Armed Services agreed to one medal to recognize major actions not otherwise covered by a specific campaign medal.

The Armed Forces Expeditionary Medal was authorized on December 4, 1961 to any member of the United States Armed Forces for U.S. military operations, U.S. operations in direct support of the United Nations and U.S. operations of assistance to friendly foreign nations after July 1, 1958. Operations that qualify for this medal are authorized in specific orders. Participating personnel must have served at least 30 consecutive *(60 nonconsecutive)* days in the qualifying operation or less if the operation was less than 30 days in length. The medal may also be authorized for individuals who do not meet the basic criteria but who do merit special recognition for their service in the designated operation.

The first qualifying operation was Operation Blue Bat, a peacekeeping mission in Lebanon from July 1 to November 1, 1958. This medal was initially awarded for Vietnam service between July 1, 1958 and July 3, 1965; an individual awarded the medal for this period of Vietnam service may elect to keep the award or request the Vietnam Service Medal in its place. However, both awards may not be retained for the same period of Vietnam service. Many personnel received this medal for continuing service in Cambodia after the Vietnam cease-fire. The medal was also authorized for those serving in the Persian Gulf area who previously would have qualified for the Southwest Asia

Service	All Services
Instituted	1961
Dates	July 1, 1968 to Present
Criteria	Participation in military operations not covered by specific war medal.
Devices	All Services: Bronze, Silver Star
Notes	Authorized for service in Vietnam until establishment of Vietnam Service Medal.

Service Medal and the National Defense Service Medal whose qualification periods for that area terminated on November 30, 1995. Individuals who qualify for both the Southwest Asia Service Medal and the Armed Forces Expeditionary Medal must elect to receive the Expeditionary medal.

The front of the medal depicts an American eagle with wings raised, perched on a sword. Behind this is a compass rose with rays coming from the angles of the compass points. The words "ARMED FORCES EXPEDITIONARY SERVICE" encircle the design. The reverse of the medal depicts the Presidential shield with branches of laurel below and the inscription, "UNITED STATES OF AMERICA." The American national colors are located at the center position or honor point of the ribbon. The light blue sections on either side suggest water and overseas service, while various colors representing areas of the world where American troops may be called upon to serve run outward to the edge.

The qualifying campaigns:

- ★ **Lebanon,** Jul. 1, 1958 - Nov. 1, 1958

- ★ **Taiwan Straits,** Aug. 23, 1958 - Jan. 1, 1959

- ★ **Quemoy & Matsu Islands,** Aug. 23, 1958 - Jun. 1, 1963

- ★ **Vietnam,** Jul. 1, 1958 - Jul. 3, 1965

- ★ **Congo,** Jul. 14, 1960 - Sep. 1, 1962

- ★ **Laos,** Apr. 19, 1961 - Oct. 7, 1962

- ★ **Berlin,** Aug. 14, 1961 - Jun. 1, 1963

- ★ **Cuba,** Oct. 24, 1962 - Jun. 1, 1963

- ★ **Congo,** Nov. 23-27, 1964

- ★ **Dominican Republic,** Apr. 23. 1965 - Sep. 21, 1966

- ★ **Korea,** Oct. 1, 1966 - Jun. 30, 1974

- ★ **Cambodia,** Mar. 29, 1973 - Aug. 15, 1973

- ★ **Thailand,** Mar. 29, 1973 - Aug. 15, 1973
  (Only those in direct support of Cambodia)

- ★ **Operation Eagle Pull -** Cambodia,
  Apr. 11-13, 1975 *(Includes evacuation)*

- ★ **Operation Frequent Wind -**
  Vietnam, Apr. 29-30, 1975

- ★ **Mayaquez Operation,** May 15, 1975

- ★ **El Salvador,** Jan. 1 , 1981 - Feb. 1, 1992

- ★ **Lebanon,** Jun. 1, 1983 - Dec. 1, 1987

- ★ **Operation Urgent Fury -** Grenada,
  Oct. 23, 1983 - Nov. 21, 1983

- ★ **Eldorado Canyon - Libya,**
  Apr. 12-17, 1986

- ★ **Operation Earnest Will -** Persian Gulf,
  Jul. 24, 1987 - Aug. 1, 1990
  (Only those participating in, or in direct support)

- ★ **Operation Just Cause -** Panama,
  Dec. 20, 1989 - Jan. 31, 1990
  (USS Vreeland & other SVS-designated aircrew mbrs.
  outside the Conus in direct support)

- ★ **United Shield -** Somalia,
  Dec. 5, 1992 - Mar. 31, 1995

- ★ **Operation Restore Hope -** Somalia,
  Dec. 5, 1992 - Mar. 31, 1995

- ★ **Operation Uphold Democracy -** Haiti,
  Sept. 1994 - Mar. 31, 1995

- ★ **Operation Joint Endeavor -** Bosnia,
  Croatia, the Adriatic Sea & Airspace,
  Nov. 20, 1995 - Dec. 19, 1996

- ★ **Operation Vigilant Sentinel -** Iraq, Saudi Arabia, Kuwait,
  & Persian Gulf
  Dec. 1, 1995 - Sep. 1, 1997

- ★ **Operation Southern Watch -** Iraq, Saudi
  Arabia, Kuwait, Persian Gulf, Bahrain,
  Qatar, UAE, Oman, Gulf of Oman W of
  62° E Long., Yemen, Egypt, & Jordan

- ★ **Operation Maritime Intercept -** Iraq, Saudi
  Arabia, Kuwait, Red Sea, Persian Gulf,
  Gulf of Oman W of 62° E Long., Bahrain,
  Qatar, UAE, Oman, Yemen, Egypt & Jordan
  Dec. 1, 1995 - Open

- ★ **Operation Joint Guard -** Bosnia, Herzegovina, Croatia,
  Adriatic Sea & Airspace,
  Dec. 20, 1996 - Jun. 20, 2008

- ★ **Operation Northern Watch -** Iraq, Saudi Arabia, Kuwait,
  Persian Gulf of W of 56° E Long., and Incirlik AB, Turkey
  (Only pers. TDY to ONW), Jan. 1, 1997 - 18 March 2003

- ★ **Operation Joint Forge -** Bosnia-Herzegovina, Croatia,
  Adriatic Sea & Airspace,
  Jun. 21, 1998 - Open

- ★ **Operation Desert Thunder -** Iraq, Saudi Arabia, Kuwait, Bahrain,
  Qatar, UAE, Omar, Yemen, Egypt, Jordan, Persian Gulf,
  Gulf of Oman, Red Sea support,
  Nov. 11, 1998 - Dec. 22, 1998

- ★ **Operation Desert Fox -** Iraq, Saudi Arabia, Kuwait, Bahrain,
  Qatar, UAE, Oman, Yemen, Egypt, Jordan,
  Persian Gulf, Gulf of Oman,
  USN Red Sea support,
  16 Dec. -22 Dec. 1998

- ★ **Operation Desert Spring -** Haiti, Southwest Asia,
  31 Dec.1998-18 Mar. 2003

- ★ **Operation Secure Tomorrow -**
  29 Feb. 2004 - 15 Jun. 2004

The Defense Department announced the transition of the Kosovo Campaign Medal to the Armed Forces Expeditionary Medal, effective Jan. 1, 2014.

As smaller contingencies of U.S. forces continue to support Operation Joint Guardian and NATO headquarters in Sarajevo, the AFEM will be awarded to recognize that support of operations in the Balkans.

The AFEM area of eligibility mirrors that of the KCM with the addition of Bosnia-Herzegovina, Croatia and Hungary. The eligible area also encompasses Serbian land and airspace including Vojvodina, Montenegro, Albania, Macedonia.

The Department of Defense Manual 1348.33, Volume 2, "Manual of Military Decorations and Awards" contains specific eligibility criteria.

❖ Vietnam Service Medal

Bronze

Anodized or Gold-Plated

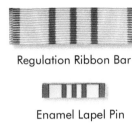

Regulation Ribbon Bar

Enamel Lapel Pin

Medal Reverse

Miniature Medals

Mini Ribbon
(unofficial)

Hat Pin (unofficial)

Authorized by executive order on July 8, 1965 for U.S. military personnel serving in the Vietnam Theater of Operations after July 3, 1965 through March 28, 1973. Personnel must have served in Vietnam on temporary duty for at least 30 consecutive/60 nonconsecutive days or have served in combat with a unit directly supporting a military operation in Southeast Asia. Military personnel serving in Laos, Cambodia or Thailand in direct support of operations in Vietnam are also eligible for this award. The Armed Forces Expeditionary Medal was awarded for earlier service in Vietnam from July 1, 1958 to July 3, 1965, inclusive; personnel receiving that award may be awarded the Vietnam Service Medal but are not authorized both awards for Vietnam service. The front of the medal depicts an oriental dragon behind a grove of bamboo trees; below the base of the trees is the inscription, "REPUBLIC OF VIETNAM SERVICE." The reverse of the medal depicts a crossbow with a torch through the center and contains the inscription, "UNITED STATES OF AMERICA" along the bottom edge. The colors of the suspension drape and ribbon suggest the flag of the Republic of Vietnam (*the red stripes represent the three ancient Vietnamese empires of Tonkin, Annam, and Cochin China*) and the green represents the Vietnamese jungle. Bronze and silver stars are authorized to signify participation in any of the 17 designated campaigns during the inclusive period.

Service	All Services
Instituted	1965
Dates	1965-73
Criteria	Service in Vietnam, Laos, Cambodia or Thailand during the above period.
Devices	Bronze, Silver star

Campaigns Designated by the Army for the Vietnam Service Medal

1. **Vietnam (VN) Advisory -** Mar 15, 1962 to Mar 7, 1965
2. **VN Defense -** Mar 8, 1965 to Dec 24, 1965
3. **VN Counteroffensive -** Dec 25, 1965 to Jun 30, 1966
4. **VN Counteroffensive Phase II -** July 1, 1966 to May 31, 1967
5. **VN Counteroffensive Phase III -** Jun 1, 1967 to Jan 29, 1968
6. **TET Counteroffensive -** Jan 30, 1968 to Apr 1, 1968

7. **VN Counteroffensive Phase IV -** Apr 2, 1968 to Jun 30, 1968
8. **VN Counteroffensive Phase V -** July 1, 1968 to Nov 1, 1968
9. **VN Counteroffensive Phase VI -** Nov 2, 1968 to Feb 22, 1969
10. **TET69 Counteroffensive -** Feb 23, 1969 to Jun 8, 1969
11. **Vietnam Summer -** Fall 1969 - Jun 9, 1969 to Oct 31, 1969
12. **Vietnam Winter-** Spring 1970 - Nov 1, 1969 to Apr 30, 1970

13. **Sanctuary Counteroffensive -** May 1, 1970 to Jun 30, 1970
14. **VN Counteroffensive Campaign Phase VII -** Jul 1, 1970 to Jun 30, 1971
15. **Consolidation I -** Jul 1, 1971 to Nov 30, 1971
16. **Consolidation II -** Dec 1, 1971 to Mar 29, 1972
17. **Vietnam Cease-fire -** Mar 30, 1972 to Jan 28, 1973

❖ Southwest Asia Service Medal

Bronze

Anodized or Gold-Plated

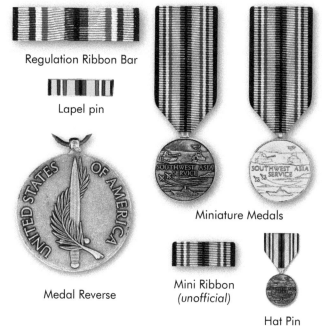

Regulation Ribbon Bar

Lapel pin

Medal Reverse

Miniature Medals

Mini Ribbon
(unofficial)

Hat Pin
(unofficial)

Awarded to members of the United States Armed Forces who participated in, or directly supported, military operations in Southwest Asia or in surrounding areas between August 2, 1990 and November 30, 1995 *(Operations Desert Shield, Desert Storm and follow-up)*. The medal was established by an executive order signed by President George Bush on March 15, 1991.

The front of the medal depicts the tools of modern desert warfare, i.e., aircraft, helicopter, tank, armored personnel carrier, tent and troops, battleship, in both desert and sea settings along with the inscription, "SOUTHWEST ASIA SERVICE" in the center. The reverse of the medal contains a sword entwined with a palm leaf representing military preparedness and the maintenance of peace and the inscription "UNITED STATES OF AMERICA" around the periphery. The ribbon is predominately tan, symbolizing the sands of the desert and contains thin stripes of the U.S. national colors towards each edge. The green and black center stripes and the black edges, along with the red and white, suggest the flag colors of most Arab nations in the region of Southwest Asia.

Service	All Services
Instituted	1992
Dates	1991-1995
Criteria	Active participation in, or support of, Operations Desert Shield, Desert Storm and/or subsequent follow-on operations in southwest Asia.
Devices	All Services: Bronze Star
Notes	Recipients of this medal are usually entitled to the Saudi Arabian Medal for the Liberation of Kuwait and the Emirate of Kuwait Medal for the Liberation of Kuwait.

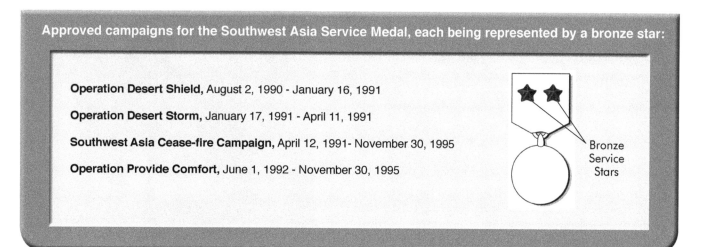

Approved campaigns for the Southwest Asia Service Medal, each being represented by a bronze star:

Operation Desert Shield, August 2, 1990 - January 16, 1991

Operation Desert Storm, January 17, 1991 - April 11, 1991

Southwest Asia Cease-fire Campaign, April 12, 1991- November 30, 1995

Operation Provide Comfort, June 1, 1992 - November 30, 1995

Bronze Service Stars

❖ Kosovo Campaign Medal

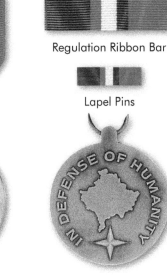

Bronze   Anodized or Gold-Plated

Regulation Ribbon Bar

Lapel Pins

Medal Reverse

Miniature Medals

Mini Ribbon
(unofficial)

Hat Pin
(unofficial)

For participation in, or in direct support of Kosovo operations. The Kosovo Campaign Medal is worn after the Southwest Asia Service Medal and before the Afghanistan Campaign Medal. The Kosovo Campaign Medal was established by executive order on May 15, 2000. The medal is awarded to all members of the Armed Forces who participated in or provided direct support to Kosovo operations within established areas of eligibility *(AOE)* from March 24, 1999 to December 31, 2013. The service member must have been a member of a unit participating in, or engaged in support of one or more of the following operations for 30 consecutive days or 60 nonconsecutive days.

Service	All Services
Instituted	2000
Dates	24 March1999 - 31 December 2013
Criteria	Active participation in, or direct support of, Kosovo operations.
Devices	Bronze Star

HUMANITY" across the top. There are two bronze service stars authorized for the Kosovo Campaign Medal. The Armed Forces Expeditionary Medal is now awarded for service in Kosovo.

Allied Force - March 24, 1999 through June 10, 1999
Joint Guardian - June 11, 1999 to December 31, 2013
Allied Harbour - April 4, 1999 through September 1, 1999
Sustain Hope, Shining Hope - April 4, 1999- July 10, 1999;
Noble Anvil - March 24, 1999 through July 20, 1999
Kosovo Task Forces
Hawk - April 5, 1999 through June 24, 1999
Saber - March 31, 1999 through July 8, 1999 and,
Falcon - June 11, 1999 through November 1, 1999 and
Hunter - April 1, 1999 through November 1, 1999
Kosovo Air Campaign - 24 March 1999 to 10 June 1999
Kosovo Defense Campaign - 11 June 1999 to 31 Dec. 2013

The Kosovo Campaign Medal was designed by the Institute of Heraldry. The medal is a circular bronze disk depicting rocky terrain, a fertile valley and sunrise behind a mountain pass in Kosovo. Above the scene, on two lines, are the words, "KOSOVO CAMPAIGN." At the lower edge is a stylized wreath of grain reflecting the agricultural nature of the area. The reverse shows an outline of the province of Kosovo with the curved inscription, "IN DEFENSE OF

❖ Afghanistan Campaign Medal

Bronze

Anodized or Gold-Plated

Regulation Ribbon Bar

Enamel Lapel Pin

Medal Reverse

Miniature Medals

Mini Ribbon
(unofficial)

Enamel Hat Pin
(unofficial)

The Afghanistan Campaign Medal is awarded to Service members who have served in direct support of Operation Enduring Freedom on or after Oct. 24, 2001 until 31 December 2014. Effective 1 January 2015, Operation Freedom's Sentinel *(OFS)* is an approved operation for award of the ACM. The area of eligibility encompasses all land areas of the country of Afghanistan and all air spaces above the land.

Service members must have been assigned, attached or mobilized to units operating in these areas of eligibility for 30 consecutive days or for 60 non-consecutive days or meet one of the following criteria:

a. Be engaged in combat during an armed engagement, regardless of the time in the area of eligibility; or
b. While participating in an operation or on official duties, is wounded or injured and requires medical evacuation from the area of eligibility; or
c. While participating as a regularly assigned air crewmember flying sorties into, out of, within or over the area of eligibility in direct support of the military operations; each day of operations counts as one day of eligibility.

Service members qualified for the Global War on Terrorism Expeditionary Medal for service between Oct. 24, 2001, and April 30, 2005, in an area for which the Afghanistan Campaign Medal is authorized and between March 19, 2003, remain qualified for the medal. Upon application, any such service member may be awarded the Afghanistan Campaign Medal in lieu of the Global War on Terrorism Expeditionary Medal for such service but no one shall be entitled to both medals for the same act, achievement or period of service. The medal may be awarded posthumously.

Service	All Services
Instituted	2004
Dates	2001 to 31 Dec. 2014, 1 Jan. 2015 until a date TBD
Criteria	Active service in direct support of Operation ENDURING FREEDOM, and FREEDOM'S SENTINEL.
Devices	Bronze Star, Silver Star

Only one award of the Afghanistan Campaign Medal is authorized. A bronze service star is worn on the suspension and campaign ribbon for one or more days of participation in each designated campaign phase. The Afghanistan Campaign Medal shall be positioned after the Kosovo Campaign Medal and before the Iraq Campaign Medal.

On the front of the medal, above a range of mountains is a map of Afghanistan in the center with the inscription, "AFGHANISTAN CAMPAIGN" around the top. On the reverse side on top is a radiating demi-sun superimposed by an eagle's head. Inscribed on the bottom half of the reverse side are three lines, "FOR SERVICE IN AFGHANISTAN" all enclosed by a laurel wreath symbolizing victory.

Phase 1: **Liberation of Afghanistan**	September 11, 2001	November 30, 2001
Phase 2: **Consolidation I**	December 1, 2001	September 30, 2006
Phase 3: **Consolidation II**	October 1, 2006	November 30, 2009
Phase 4: **Consolidation III**	December 1, 2009	June 30, 2011
Phase 5: **Transition I**	July 1, 2011	December 31, 2014
Phase 6: **Transition II**	January 1, 2015	Present

❖ Iraq Campaign Medal

Bronze

Anodized or Gold-Plated

Regulation Ribbon Bar

Enamel Lapel Pin

Medal Reverse

Miniature Medals

Mini Ribbon
(unofficial)

Enamel Hat Pin
(unofficial)

Presidential Executive Order 13363 established the Iraq Campaign Medal. Those authorized the Iraq Campaign Medal must have served in direct support of Operation Iraqi Freedom on or after March 19, 2003 to 31 December 2011. The area of eligibility encompasses all land area of the country of Iraq and the contiguous water area out to 12 nautical miles and all air spaces above the land area of Iraq and above the contiguous water area out to 12 nautical miles.

Service members must have been assigned, attached or mobilized to units operating in these areas of eligibility for 30 consecutive days or for 60 non-consecutive days or meet one of the following criteria:

a. Be engaged in combat during an armed engagement, regardless of the time in the area of eligibility; or
b. While participating in an operation or on official duties, is wounded or injured and requires medical evacuation from the area of eligibility; or
c. While participating as a regularly assigned air crewmember flying sorties into, out of, within or over the area of eligibility in direct support of the military operations; each day of operations counts as one day of eligibility.

Service members qualified for the Global War on Terrorism Expeditionary Medal by reasons of service between Oct. 24, 2001 and April 30, 2005, in an area for which the Iraq Campaign Medal was subsequently authorized, shall remain qualified for the medal.

Upon application, any such service member may be awarded the Iraq Campaign Medal in lieu of the Global War on Terror Expeditionary Medal for such service. No service member shall be entitled to both medals for the same act, achievement or period of service. Medals may be awarded posthumously.

Service	All Services
Instituted	2004
Dates	2003 to 31 December 2011
Criteria	Active service in direct support of Operation IRAQI FREEDOM.
Devices	Bronze Star, Silver Star

Only one award of the Iraq Campaign Medal may be authorized for any individual. Individuals may receive both the medals if they meet the requirement of both awards; however, the qualifying period of service used to establish eligibility for one award cannot be used to justify eligibility for the other.

The Iraq Campaign Medal shall be positioned after the Afghanistan Campaign Medal and before the Global War on Terrorism Expeditionary Medal.

The medal's obverse features a relief map of Iraq displaying two irregular lines representing the Tigris and Euphrates Rivers surmounting a palm wreath. Above is the inscription, "IRAQ CAMPAIGN". The Statue of Freedom is shown on the reverse surmounting a sunburst, encircle by two scimitars, points down, crossed at the tips of the blades, all above the inscription, "FOR SERVICE IN IRAQ".

A bronze star is worn on the suspension and campaign ribbon for one or more days of participation in each designated campaign phase.

The designated Iraqi Freedom campaigns are:

Liberation of Iraq: 19 March 2003 - 1 May 2003
Transition of Iraq: 2 May 2003 - 28 June 2004
Iraqi Governance: 29 June 2004 - 15 December 2005
National Resolution: 16 December 2005 - 9 January 2008
The Surge: 10 January 2008 - 31 December 2008
Iraqi Sovereignty: 1 January 2009 - 31 August 2010
New Dawn: 1 Sepember. 2010 - 15 Decemberr 2011

Iraq Campaign Medal

Iraq Campaign Medal

❖ Inherent Resolve Campaign Medal

Regulation Ribbon Bar

Enamel Lapel Pin

Bronze   Medal Reverse

Service	All Services
Instituted	30 March 2016
Dates	15 June, 2014 to TBD
Criteria	Active service in direct support of Operation Inherent Resolve.
Devices	Bronze Star, Silver Star

The Inherent Resolve Campaign Medal was established 30 March, 2016. It provides special recognition for members of the Armed Forces serving, or having served, 30 consecutive days or 60 nonconsecutive days in Iraq, Syria, or contiguous waters or airspace on or after 15 June, 2014 to a future date to be determined by the Secretary of Defense. Personnel are also authorized the medal regardless of the time criteria if they were engaged in combat during an armed engagement or while participating in an operation or official duties and were killed or wounded. Aircrew members accrue one day of eligibility for each day they fly into, out of, with in, or over the area of engagement.

Previously the Global War on Terror Expeditionary Medal was authorized for service in Iraq and Syria for operation INHERENT RESOLVE, however, that award is now terminated. Service members who were awarded a GWOT–EM for their Inherent Resolve Campaign Medal qualifying service in Iraq or Syria during the period of 15 June, 2014 to 30 March, 2016 remain qualified for the GWOT–EM. However, service members, may apply to be awarded the

IRCM in lieu of the GWOT–EM. Service members can not be awarded both medals for the same qualifying periods.

The Inherent Resolve Campaign Medal is worn after the Iraq Campaign Medal and before the GWOT–EM. The medal is only presented upon initial award and a separate bronze campaign star is worn on the suspension and campaign ribbon to recognize each designated campaign phase in which a member participated for one or more days.

The scorpion, symbolic for treachery and destruction, is found on most major land masses. The dagger alludes to swiftness and determination. The eagle represents the United States and is symbolic of might and victory. The decorated star panels are common in the Arabian and Moorish styles of ornamentation.

The ribbon is blue, teal, sand and orange. This color combination is inspired by the colors of the Middle East landscape and the Ishtar Gate, the eighth gate leading to the historic inner city of Babylon.

Designated Inherent Resolve campaigns are:

Abeyance 15 June 2014 - 24 November 2015
Intensification: 25 November 2015 - TBD

❖ Global War on Terrorism Expeditionary Medal

Bronze

Anodized or Gold-Plated
(Original size)

Medal Reverse

Regulation Ribbon Bar

Enamel Lapel Pin

The medal has been
redesigned and is slightly
smaller in diameter and
word medal has been
removed from the reverse.
Original first medals are
still official.

Miniature Medals

Mini Ribbon
(unofficial)

Enamel Hat Pin
(unofficial)

Awarded for deployed service abroad in support of Global War on Terrorism operations on, or after September 11, 2001. The Global War on Terrorism Expeditionary Medal is worn after the Iraq Campaign Medal and before the Global War on Terrorism Service Medal.

The Global War on Terrorism Expeditionary Medal was authorized by executive order. The medal is awarded to any member of the Armed Forces who is deployed in an approved operation, such as ENDURING FREEDOM. The Chairman of the Joint Chiefs of Staff has designated the specific area of deployed eligibly per qualifying operation. To be eligible personnel must have participated in the operation by authority of written order. Qualification includes at least 30 consecutive days or 60 nonconsecutive days, or be engaged in actual combat *(hostile weapons fire is exchanged),* or duty that is equally as hazardous as combat duty, or wounded or injured requiring evacuation from the operation, or while participating as a regularly assigned air crewmember flying sorties into, out of, within or over the area of eligibility in direct support of the military operations.

Personnel may receive both the Global War on Terrorism Expeditionary Medal and the Global War on Terrorism Service Medal if they meet the requirements of both awards; however, service eligibility for one cannot be used to justify service eligibility for the other.

The Global War on Terrorism Expeditionary Medal was designed by the Institute of Heraldry. The medal is a circular bronze disc which displays a shield adapted from the Great Seal of the United States surmounting two sword hilts enclosed within a wreath of laurel; overall an eagle, wings displayed, grasping a serpent in its claws. The reverse of the medal displays the eagle, a serpent and swords from the front of the medal within the encircling inscription, "WAR ON TERRORISM EXPEDITIONARY." The ribbon is scarlet, white and blue representing the United States; light blue refers to worldwide cooperation against terrorism; gold denotes excellence. *Effective 2005, the GWOTEM is no longer authorized to be awarded for service in Afghanistan and/or Iraq.*

Service	2003
Instituted	2001 to present
Criteria	Active participation in, or support of, Operations ENDURING FREEDOM, IRAQI FREEDOM, NOMAD SHADOW or follow-on operations while deployed abroad for service in the Global War on Terrorism.
Devices	Bronze and Silver Star

To date, the Areas of Eligibility associated with the operations ENDURING FREEDOM, IRAQI FREEDOM and NOMAD SHADOW are:

Afghanistan	Saudi Arabia
Bahrain	Somalia
Bulgaria	Syria
Crete	Tajikistan
Cyprus	Turkey *(east of*
Diego Garcia	*35 degrees east lat.)*
Djibouti	Turkmenistan
Egypt	United Arab Emirates
Eritrea	Uzbekistan
Ethiopia	Yemen
Iran	*That portion of the Arabian Sea north of*
Iraq	*10 degrees north latitude and west of*
Israel	*68 degrees longitude*
Jordan	Bab el Mandeb
Kazakhstan	Gulf of Aden
Kenya	Gulf of Aqaba
Kuwait	Gulf of Oman
Kyrgyzstan	Gulf of Suez
Lebanon	*That portion of the Mediterranean Sea*
Oman	*east of 28 degrees east longitude*
Pakistan	Persian Gulf
Philippines	Red Sea
Qatar	Strait of Hormuz
Romania	Suez Canal

The six approved operations and effective dates for the award of the Global War on Terrorism Expeditionary Medal are:
- *Enduring Freedom, Sept. 11, 2001 – to be determined.*
- *Iraqi Freedom, March 19, 2003-Aug. 31, 2010.*
- *Nomad Shadow, Nov. 5, 2007 – to be determined*
- *New Dawn, Sept.1, 2010-Dec. 31, 2011.*
- *Inherent Resolve, June 15, 2014 – to be determined*
- *Freedom's Sentinel, Jan. 1, 2015 – to be determined.*

❖ Global War on Terrorism Service Medal

Bronze

Anodized or Gold-Plated

Regulation Ribbon Bar

Enamel Lapel Pin

Medal Reverse

Miniature Medals
Original Design

Mini Ribbon
(unofficial)

Enamel Hat Pin
(unofficial)

Awarded to members of the United States Armed Forces who participated in, or served in support of operations relating to the Global War on Terrorism between September 11, 2001 and a date to be determined at a later date. The medal was established by an executive order signed by President George W. Bush on October 28, 2003. Initial award of the Global War on Terrorism Service Medal was limited to Airport Security Operations from September 27, 2001 until May 31, 2002 and to Service members who supported Operations ENDURING FREEDOM, NOBLE EAGLE and IRAQI FREEDOM.

Qualifying Air Force members must be assigned, attached or mobilized to a unit participating in or service in direct support of designated for 30 consecutive days or 60 nonconsecutive days. It is to be noted that eligibility for the Global War on Terrorism Service Medal is defined as support for the War on Terrorism in a non-deployed status, whether stationed at home or overseas. By contrast, service in an operationally deployed status abroad within a designated area of eligibility merits primary eligibility for the Global War on Terrorism Expeditionary Medal. Personnel may receive both the Global War on Terrorism Service and Expeditionary Medals if they meet the requirements of both awards. However, the qualifying period for one cannot be used to justify eligibility for the other. Establishing the award of the GWOTSM for general support of the war on terror makes the medal similar to the award of the National Defense Service Medal. The major difference between the National Defense Service Medal and GWOTSM is that the NDSM is authorized when an individual joins the Armed Forces and the GWOTSM is only authorized after 30 days of active service or 60 days non consecutive service for reserve forces.

Although qualifying circumstances would be extremely rare, Battle Stars may be applicable for personnel who were engaged in actual combat against the enemy under circumstances involving grave danger of death or serious bodily injury from enemy action.

Service	All Services
Instituted	2004
Dates	2001 to Present
Criteria	Active participation in, or service in support of Global War on Terrorism operations on or after 11 September, 2001.
Devices	Bronze Star *(not authorized to date)*

The Global War on Terrorism Service Medal was designed by the Institute of Heraldry. The medal is a circular bronze disc which displays an eagle, wings displayed, with a stylized shield of thirteen vertical bars on its breast and holding in dexter claw an olive branch and in sinister claw three arrows, all in front of a terrestrial globe with the inscription above, "WAR ON TERRORISM SERVICE." The reverse of the medal displays a laurel wreath on a plain field. The ribbon is scarlet, white and blue representing the United States; gold denoting excellence.

The Original Medal

The new version of the medal has been redesigned and is slightly smaller in diameter and word "medal" has been removed from the front. The original issued medals are still official and are issued until the current stock is exhausted.

❖ Korea Defense Service Medal

Bronze

Anodized or Gold-Plated

Regulation Ribbon Bar

Enamel Lapel Pin

Medal Reverse

Miniature Medals

Mini Ribbon
(unofficial)

Enamel Hat Pin
(unofficial)

The Korea Defense Service Medal is authorized for Armed Forces members who served in support of the defense of the Republic of Korea after the signing of the Korean Armistice Agreement. To qualify a service member must serve at least 30 consecutive days in the Korean theater. The medal is also awarded for 60 non-consecutive days of service to include reservists on annual training in Korea.

Exceptions are made for the time requirement if a service member participated in a combat armed engagement, was wounded or injured in the line of duty requiring medical evacuation, or participated as a regularly assigned aircrew member in flying sorties which totaled more than 30 days of duty in Korean airspace. In such cases, the KDSM is authorized regardless of time served in theater.

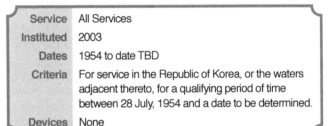

Service	All Services
Instituted	2003
Dates	1954 to date TBD
Criteria	For service in the Republic of Korea, or the waters adjacent thereto, for a qualifying period of time between 28 July, 1954 and a date to be determined.
Devices	None

The medal is retroactive to the end of the Korean War and is granted for any service performed after July 28, 1954. An official exception to policy entitles military personnel to both the Armed Forces Expeditionary Medal, and the KDSM for being in operations in Korea between October 1, 1966 - June 30, 1974. Only one award of the Korea Defense Service Medal is authorized, regardless of the time served in the Korean theater. The Korea Defense Service Medal is worn after the Global War on Terrorism Service Medal and before the Armed Forces Service Medal.

Designed by John Sproston of the Institute of Heraldry, the medal is a bronze disc with a Korean circle dragon within a scroll inscribed, "KOREA DEFENSE SERVICE" with two sprigs of laurel at the base. The four-clawed dragon is a traditional Korean symbol representing intelligence and strength of purpose. The sprig of laurel denotes honorable endeavor and victory, the bamboo refers to the land of Korea. The reverse displays two swords placed over a map of Korea to signify defense of freedom and the readiness to engage in combat. The enclosing circlet represents the five-petal symbols common in Korean armory.

The dark green ribbon represents the land of Korea, blue indicates overseas service and commitment to achieving peace. Gold denotes excellence, white symbolizes idealism and integrity. Light blue with a thin white stripe in the center and narrow white stripes at the edges.

The Original Medal

The Institute of Heraldry changed the specifications for the Korea Defense Service Medal. At first glance you might not notice the change, but the new medals being manufactured have a slightly different look and the word medal has been removed from the front of the medallion. The original medal is still authorized for wear and may still be issued as long as they are in the supply system.

❖ Armed Forces Service Medal

Bronze
New Design

Anodized or
Gold-Plated Old Design

Regulation Ribbon Bar

Enamel lapel Pin

Medal Reverse

Miniature Medals

Mini Ribbon
(unofficial)

Enamel Hat Pin
(unofficial)

Authorized on January 11, 1996 for U.S. military personnel who, on or after June 1, 1992, participate in a U.S. military operation deemed to be a significant activity in which no foreign armed opposition or imminent hostile action is encountered and for which no previous U.S. service medal is authorized. The medal can be awarded to service members in

Service	All Services
Instituted	1995
Dates	1995 to Present
Criteria	Participation in military operations not covered by a specific war medal or the Armed Forces Expeditionary Medal.
Devices	All Services: Bronze, Silver Star

The Original Medal

The Institute of Heraldry redesigned the Armed Forces Service Medal to conform to changes made to three other medals. Unless you compare the original medal first authorized in 1995 with the new ones being struck you might not notice the change. The new medals being manufactured have a slightly different look and the word "Medal" has been removed from the front of the medallion. The change to the AFSM is one of 4 medals: GWOT Exp, GWOT Service and the Korea Defense Service Medal that the Institution of Heraldry has made minor modifications to and removed the word "Medal". The original medal is still authorized for wear and may still be issued as long as they remain in the supply system.

direct support of the United Nations or North Atlantic Treaty Organization and for assistance operations to friendly nations. The initial awards of this medal were for operations that have occurred in the Balkans since 1992. Qualifications include at least one day of participation in the designated area. Direct support of the operation and aircraft flights within the area also qualify for award of this medal as long as at least one day is served within the designated area. Recent operations that qualify for the medal are *Provide Promise, Joint Endeavor, Able Sentry, Deny Flight, Maritime Monitor and Sharp Guard.*

The front of the medal contains the torch of liberty within its center and contains the inscription "ARMED FORCES SERVICE" around its periphery. The reverse of the medal depicts the American eagle with the U.S. shield in its chest and spread wings clutching three arrows in its talons encircled by a laurel wreath and the inscription, "IN PURSUIT OF DEMOCRACY." Bronze and silver service stars are worn to denote additional awards.

The Armed Forces Service Medal was originally intended to complement the Armed Forces Expeditionary Medal. The primary difference between the two is that the Armed Forces Service Medal is awarded for actions "through which no foreign armed opposition or imminent threat of hostile action was encountered". This definition separates the two medals in that the Armed Forces Expeditionary Medal is normally awarded for combat operations and other combat support missions.

DID YOU KNOW?

❖ Humanitarian Service Medal

Bronze

Anodized or Gold-Plated

Regulation Ribbon Bar

Enamel Lapel Pin

Medal Reverse

Miniature Medals

Mini Ribbon
(unofficial)

Enamel Hat Pin
(unofficial)

Authorized on January 19, 1977 and awarded to Armed Forces personnel *(including Reserve components)* who, after April 1, 1975, distinguish themselves by meritorious direct participation in a DOD-approved significant military act or operation of a humanitarian nature. According to regulations, the participation must be "hands-on" at the site of the operation; personnel assigned to staff functions geographically separated from the operation are not eligible for this medal. Service members must be assigned and/or attached to participating units for specific operations by official orders. Members who were present for duty at specific qualifying locations for the medal but who did not make a direct contribution to the action or operation are specifically excluded from eligibility. It should be noted that some of the earliest recipients of the Humanitarian Service Medal, e.g., for the evacuations of Laos, Cambodia and Vietnam, would more likely be awarded the Armed Forces Service Medal in today's environment.

The medal was designed by Jim Hammond and sculptured by Jay Morris of the Institute of Heraldry. The front of the medal depicts a human right hand with open palm within a raised circle. At the top of the medal's reverse is the raised inscription, "FOR HUMANITARIAN SERVICE" set in three lines. In the center is an oak branch with three acorns and leaves and, below this, is the raised circular inscription, "UNITED STATES ARMED FORCES" around the lower edge of the medal. The ribbon is medium blue with a wide center stripe of navy blue. It is edged by a wide stripe of purple which is separated from the light blue field by a narrow white stripe. Bronze and silver stars are authorized for additional awards.

Note: *All branches now use Coast Guard placement of stars.*

Service	All Services
Instituted	1977
Dates	1975 to Present
Criteria	Direct participation in specific operations of a humanitarian nature.
Devices	Bronze, Silver Star, Bronze Numeral

This Cold War Engineer Sgt. displays his Joint Achievement Medal, Good Conduct Medal, National Defense Service and Humanitarian Medal along with a Cold War Victory, Airborne and Honorable Service Commemorative Medals. The P38 C ration can opener between his dogtags is a bit of GI humor.

❖ Outstanding Volunteer Service Medal

Bronze

Anodized or Gold-Plated

Regulation Ribbon Bar

Enamel Lapel Pin

Medal Reverse

Miniature Medals

Mini Ribbon
(unofficial)

Enamel Hat Pin
(unofficial)

The Outstanding Volunteer Service Medal was authorized in 1993 to members of the U.S. Armed Forces and reserve components and is awarded for outstanding and sustained voluntary service to the civilian community after December 31, 1992. It may be awarded to active duty and reserve members who perform outstanding volunteer service over time as opposed to a single event. The service performed must have been to the civilian community and must be strictly voluntary and not duty-related. The volunteerism must be of a sustained and direct nature and must be significant and produce tangible results while reflecting favorably on the Armed Forces and the Department of Defense. There are no specific time requirements as to how many hours must be spent on the volunteer activity, but the activity should consist of significant action and involvement rather than, for example, simply attending meetings as a member of a community service group. An individual would normally be considered for only one award during an assignment. Group level commanders, including commanders of provisional and composite groups, have approval authority for the medal.

Service	All Services
Instituted	1993
Dates	1993 to Present
Criteria	Awarded for outstanding and sustained voluntary service to the civilian community.
Devices	All Services: Bronze, Silver Star

The front of the bronze medal has a five-pointed star with a circular ring over each point; the star, a symbol of the military and representing outstanding service, is encircled by a laurel wreath which represents honor and achievement. The reverse has an oak leaf branch, symbolic of strength and potential, with three oak leaves and two acorns along with the inscriptions, "OUTSTANDING VOLUNTEER SERVICE," and "UNITED STATES ARMED FORCES." Bronze and silver stars are authorized to denote additional awards.

❖ Army Sea Duty Ribbon

The Army Sea Duty Ribbon is awarded to those members of the Active United States Army, United States Army Reserve and Army National Guard for completion of sea duty on class A or B United States Army vessels. To be awarded the ribbon, active duty members must complete two years of cumulative sea duty aboard class A or B vessels. For members for the Army Reserve, and National Guard, soldiers must have two credible years in a U.S. Army watercraft unit. In addition to being assigned to a qualifying unit, reserve component soldiers must spend at least 25 days during each of the qualifying years underway, along with two annual training exercises on a class A or B vessel. A ninety day deployment on board a

Service: Army
Instituted: 2006

Criteria: Completion of two (2) years of cumulative sea duty aboard Class A or B vessels.
Devices: ⭐ (67) ⭐ (86) ⭐(100)

class A or B vessel also qualifies. Additional awards of the Army Sea Duty Ribbon are denoted by bronze and silver stars while the tenth and final award is indicated by a five-sixteenth inch diameter gold star.

❖ Armed Forces Reserve Medal

Bronze

Anodized or Gold-Plated

Medal Reverse

Regulation Ribbon Bar

Enamel Lapel Pin

Mini Ribbon
(unofficial)

Enamel Hat Pin
(unofficial)

Miniature Medals

Authorized in 1950 for 10 years of honorable and satisfactory service within a 12 year period as a member of one or more of the Reserve Components of the Armed Forces of the United States.

An executive order of Aug. 8, 1996 authorized the award of a bronze letter "M" mobilization device to U.S. reserve component members who were called to active-duty service in support of designated operations on or after August 1, 1990 *(the M device was not authorized for any operations prior to August 1, 1990 although it had been previously proposed)*. Units called up in support of Operations Desert Storm/Desert Shield were the first units to be authorized the "M" device. If an "M" is authorized, the medal is awarded even though service might be less than 10 years. Previous to this change, only bronze hourglasses were awarded at each successive 10 year point *(first hourglass at the 20 year point)*.

The front of the medal depicts a flaming torch placed vertically between a crossed bugle and powder horn; thirteen stars and thirteen rays surround the design. The front of the

Service	All Services
Instituted	1950
Criteria	10 years of honorable service in any reserve component of the United States Armed Forces Reserve or award of "M" device.
Devices	Bronze, Silver and Gold Hourglass, Bronze Letter "M", Bronze Numeral

medal is the same for all services; only the reverse design is different *(see designs below)*. Bronze numerals beginning with "2" are worn to the right of the bronze "M" on the ribbon bar and below the "M" on the medal, indicating the total number of times the individual was mobilized. Bronze, silver and gold hourglasses are awarded for 10, 20 and 30 years service, respectively.

The different services medal reverses are shown here:

Army
has a Minuteman in front of a circle with 13 stars represening the original colonies.

Navy
has a sailing ship with an anchor on its front with an eagle with wings spread superimposed upon it.

Marine Corps
has the USMC emblem, eagle, globe and anchor.

Coast Guard
has the Coast Guard emblem, crossed anchor with the Coast Guard shield in the center.

National Guard
has the National Guard insignia on the reverse, an eagle with crossed fasces in its center.

Army N.C.O. Professional Development Ribbon

The Non-Commissioned Officer Professional Development Ribbon was established by the Secretary of the Army on April 10, 1981 and is awarded to members of the U.S. Army, Army National Guard and Army Reserve who successfully complete designated NCO professional development courses. To indicate completion of specific levels of subsequent courses, a bronze numeral is affixed to the center of the ribbon.

The basic ribbon itself represents the Primary Level, the numeral "2" indicates the Basic Level course, the numeral "3" denotes the Advanced Level course and the numeral "4" indicates the Senior Level (*Sergeants Major*

Service: Army

Instituted: 1981

Criteria: Successful completion of designated NCO professional development courses.

Devices:  (37)

Academy) course. At one time, the numeral "5" signified completion of the Sergeants Major Academy but this was later rescinded.

Army Service Ribbon

The Army Service ribbon was established on April 10, 1981 by the Secretary of the Army and is awarded to members of the Army, Army Reserve and Army National Guard for successful completion of initial-entry training. It may also be awarded retroactively to those personnel who completed the required training before August 1, 1981. Officers will be awarded this ribbon upon successful completion of their basic/orientation or higher level course.

Enlisted soldiers will be awarded the ribbon upon successful completion of their initial MOS-producing course.

Service: Army

Instituted: 1981

Criteria: Successful completion of initial entry training.

Devices: None

Officer or Enlisted personnel assigned to a specialty, special skill identifier or MOS based on civilian or other service acquired skills, will be awarded the ribbon upon honorable completion of four months active service. Since only one award is authorized, no devices are worn with this ribbon.

Army Overseas Service Ribbon

The Army Overseas Service Ribbon was established by the Secretary of the Army on April 10, 1981. Effective August 1, 1981, the Army Overseas Service Ribbon is awarded to all members of the Active Army, Army National Guard and Army Reserve in an active Reserve status for successful completion of overseas tours if the tour is not recognized by the award of another service or campaign medal.

The ribbon may be awarded retroactively to personnel who were credited with a normal overseas tour completion before August 1, 1981, provided they had an Active Army status on or after August 1, 1981. Subsequent tours will

Service: Army

Instituted: 1981

Criteria: Successful completion of normal overseas tours not recognized by any other service award.

Devices:  (35)

be indicated by the use of numerals with the basic ribbon representing the first tour, the bronze numeral "2" denoting the second tour, the numeral "3" the third, etc.

Army Reserve Components Overseas Training Ribbon

The Reserve Components Overseas Training Ribbon was established on July 11, 1984 and is awarded to members of the Army Reserves or Army National Guard for successful completion of annual training or active duty for training for a period of not less than ten consecutive duty days on foreign soil (*outside the 50 states, District of Columbia, and U.S. possessions and territories*), in the performance of duties in conjunction with Active Army, Joint Services, or Allied Forces. The ribbon may be awarded retroactively to personnel who successfully completed annual training or active duty for training on foreign soil in a Reserve status

Service: Army

Instituted: 1984

Criteria: Successful completion of annual training or active duty training for 10 consecutive duty days on foreign soil.

Devices: (35)

prior to July 11, 1984, provided they had an active status in the Reserve Components on or after July 11, 1984. Bronze numerals are used to denote second and subsequent awards.

Authorized foreign decorations for wear by United States Armed Forces are military decorations *(as opposed to service medals)* which have been approved for wear by the Department of Defense but whose awarding authority is a foreign government. French, British and other Allies decorations were presented to U.S. service members extensively during World War I and World War II. In World War I and II the French and Beligium Croix de Guerre were the most commonly awarded decorations to United States service members of all ranks.

Republic of Vietnam military awards *(South Vietnam decorations)* were first awarded to United States service members beginning around 1964. The Vietnamese Gallantry Cross and the Vietnamese Civil Actions Medal were awarded to many U.S. servicemen for heroism and meritorious service.

Foreign campaign *(service)* medals and Unit Awards have also been awarded U.S. military Personel. Those that were commonly awarded to U.S. military personnel are covered in the following pages.

While each service has its own order of precedence, these general rules typically apply to all services when wearing foreign awards:

- U.S. military personal decorations
- U.S. military unit awards
- U.S. non-military personal decorations
- U.S. non-military unit awards
- U.S. military campaign and service medals
- U.S. military service and training awards *(ribbon-only awards)*
- U.S. Merchant Marine awards and non-military service awards
- Foreign military personal decorations
- Foreign military unit awards
- International decorations & service medals *(United Nations, NATO, etc.)*
- Foreign military service awards
- Marksmanship awards *(Air Force, Navy & Coast Guard)*
- State awards of the National Guard *(Army & Air Force only)*

Croix de Guerre
Country: France
Instituted: 1915 (1939- 1945 version shown)
Criteria: Individual feats of arms as recognized by mention in dispatches.
Devices:

Notes: *The ribbon for the Croix de Guerre awarded during WW I is green.*

Croix de Guerre
Country: Belgian
Instituted: 1915 (WW I ribbon shown)
Criteria: Individual feats of arms as recognized by mention in dispatches.
Devices: a bronze lion, cited at the regiment level a silver lion, cited at the brigade level a gold lion, cited at the division level a bronze palm, cited at the army level. A silver palm for five bronze ones and a gold one for five silver ones.

Notes: *The ribbon for the WW I I Belgian Croix de Guerre is different.*

Republic of Vietnam Gallantry Cross

Country: Republic of Vietnam

Instituted: 1950

Criteria: Deeds of valor and acts of courage/heroism while fighting the enemy.

Devices:

    (55)

    (105)

    (106)

    (107)

Republic of Vietnam Armed Forces Honor Medal

Country: Republic of Vietnam

Instituted: 1953

Criteria: For outstanding contributions to the training and development of RVN Armed Forces.

Devices: None

Notes: *1st Class for officers is shown; the 2nd Class medal is in silver and ribbon does not have the yellow edge stripes.*

Republic of Vietnam Staff Service Medal

Country: Republic of Vietnam

Instituted: 1964

Criteria: Awarded for staff service to the Armed Forces evidencing outstanding initiative and devotion to duty.

Notes: *Occasionally called Staff Service Honor Medal. First class has green edge, 2d class for enlisted has blue ribbon edge.*

First Class

Second Class

Republic of Vietnam Technical Service

Country: Republic of Vietnam

Instituted: 1964

Criteria: Awarded to military servicemen and civilians working as military technicians who have shown outstanding professional capacity, initiative, and devotion to duty.

Notes: *Second Class medal ribbon awarded to NCOs and enlisted men does not have 2 center red stripes. Occasionally called Technical Services Honor Medal.*

First Class

Republic of Vietnam Training Medal

Country: Republic of Vietnam

Instituted: 1964

Criteria: Awarded to instructors and cadres at military schools and training centers and civilians and foreigners who contribute significantly to training.

Notes: First Class medal is awarded to officers and is occasionally referred to as the Training Service Honor Medal. Second Class medal ribbon awarded to NCOs and enlisted men does not have 2 center pink stripes.

Republic of Vietnam Civil Actions Medal

Country: Republic of Vietnam

Instituted: 1964

Criteria: For outstanding achievements in the field of civic actions.

Devices: None

Notes: *1st Class for officers is shown; the 2nd Class ribbon has no center red stripes. Also awarded as a unit award. Sometimes called Civic Actions Honor Medal.*

❖ Commonly Awarded Foreign Unit Awards

Philippine Republic Presidential Unit Citation

Service: All Services

Instituted: 1948

Criteria: Awarded to units of the U.S. Armed Forces for service in the war against Japan and/or for 1970 and 1972 disaster relief.

Devices: (80) (except Army)

The Philippine Republic Presidential Unit Citation was awarded to U.S. Armed Forces personnel for services resulting in the liberation of the Philippines during World War II. The award was made in the name of the President of the Republic of the Philippines. It was also awarded to U.S. Forces who participated in disaster relief operations in 1970 and 1972. The ribbon has three equal stripes of blue, white and red enclosed in a rectangular gold frame with laurel leaves identical to U.S. unit awards. A three-sixteenth inch bronze star denotes receipt of an additional award.

Korean Republic Presidential Unit Citation

Service: All Services

Instituted: 1951

Criteria: Awarded to certain units of the U.S. Armed Forces for services rendered during the Korean War.

Devices: None

Awarded by the Republic of Korea for service in a unit cited in the name of the President of the Republic of Korea for outstanding performance in action. The Republic of Korea Presidential Unit Citation was awarded to units of the United Nations Command for service in Korea during the Korean Conflict from 1950 to 1954. The ribbon is white bordered with a wide green stripe and thin stripes of white, red, white, red, white and green. In the center is an ancient oriental symbol called a Taeguk (the top half is red and the bottom half is blue). The ribbon is enclosed in a rectangular gold frame with laurel leaves identical to U.S. unit awards. No devices are authorized.

Republic of Vietnam Presidential Unit Citation

Service: Army/Navy/ Marine Corps/Coast Guard

Instituted: 1954

Criteria: Awarded to certain units of the U.S. Armed Forces for humanitarian service in the evacuation of civilians from North and Central Vietnam.

Devices: None

Awarded by the Republic of Vietnam for service in a unit cited in the name of the President of the Republic of Vietnam for outstanding performance in action. The Republic of Vietnam Presidential Unit Citation referred to as the "Friendship Ribbon" and was awarded to members of the United States Military Assistance Advisory Group in Indochina for services rendered during August and September 1954. The ribbon is yellow with three narrow red stripes in the center. The ribbon is enclosed in a rectangular gold frame with laurel leaves identical to U.S. unit awards. No devices are authorized.

Republic of Vietnam Gallantry Cross Unit Citation

Service: All Services

Instituted: 1966

Criteria: Awarded to certain units of the U.S. Armed Forces for valorous combat achievement during the Vietnam War, 1 March 1961 to 28 March 1974.

Devices: ☆

　　　　　　(55)　　(105)　(106)　(107)

The Republic of Vietnam Gallantry Cross Unit Citation was established on August 15, 1950 and awarded by the Republic of Vietnam to units of the U.S. Armed Forces in recognition of valorous achievement in combat during the Vietnam War. The Republic of Vietnam Gallantry Cross Unit Citation ribbon is red with a very wide yellow center stripe which has eight very thin double red stripes. The ribbon bar is enclosed in a gold frame with laurel leaves identical to U.S. unit awards.

Republic of Vietnam Civil Actions Unit Citation

Service: All Services

Instituted: 1966

Criteria: Awarded to certain units of the U.S. Armed Forces for meritorious service during the Vietnam War, 1 March 1961 to 28 March 1974.

Devices: (54)

Awarded by the Republic of Vietnam to units in recognition of meritorious civil action service. The Republic of Vietnam Civil Actions Unit Citation was widely bestowed on American forces in Vietnam and recognizes outstanding achievements made by units in the field of civil affairs. The Republic of Vietnam Civil Actions Unit Citation ribbon is dark green with a very thin double red center stripe narrow red stripes near the edges. The ribbon is enclosed in a rectangular one-sixteenth inch gold frame with laurel leaves identical to U.S. unit awards and is awarded with a bronze laurel leaf palm attachment.

❖ World War II Philippine Military Medals

The **Philippine Defense Medal** was authorized to any WW II veteran of either the Philippine military or an allied armed force, to recognize the initial resistance against Japanese invasion between 8 December 1941 and 15 June 1942. The award was first created in December 1944, and was issued as the Philippine Defense Ribbon. A full-sized medal was authorized and added in July, 1945.

The **Philippine Liberation Medal** was established by the Commonwealth Army of the Philippines on 20 December 1944, and first issued as a Ribbon. The medal was presented to Philippine Commonwealth and allied forces, who participated in the liberation of the Philippine Islands between t 17 October 1944, and 2 September 1945. A full-sized medal was authorized and added on 22 July 1945 and authorized by the United States in 1948.

To be authorized the Philippine Liberation Medal, a service member must have participated in at least one of the following actions:

- Participation in the initial landing operation of Leyte and adjoining islands from 17 October to 20 October 1944.
- Participation in any engagement against hostile Japanese forces on Leyte and adjoining islands during the Philippine Liberation Campaign of 17 October 1944, to 2 September 1945.
- Participation in any engagement against hostile Japanese forces during the Philippine Liberation Campaign of 17 October 1944, to 2 September 1945.
- Served in the Philippine Islands or on ships in Philippine waters for not less than 30 days during the period.
- World War II veterans awarded the medal for participation in any of the above-mentioned operations are authorized a bronze 3/16" service star to the Philippine Liberation

The **Philippine Independence Medal** was established by the Philippine Army 3 July 1946 as the Philippine Independence

Ribbon. The medal was added in 1968. The medal's criteria effectively awarded the medal to anyone who had participated in both the initial resistance against Japanese invasion and also in the campaigns to liberate the Philippines from Japanese occupation in 1945. The medal was also authorized for award to the United States personnel in the Philippines up to 1948.

Philippine Defense Medal

Country: Republic of the Philippines
Instituted: 1945 (Army: 1948)
Criteria: Service in defense of the Philippines between 8 December 1941 and 15 June 1942.
Devices:

Philippine Liberation Medal

Country: Republic of the Philippines
Instituted: 1945 (Army: 1948)
Criteria: Service in the liberation of the Philippines between 17 October 1944 and 3 September 1945.
Devices:

Philippine Independence Medal

Country: Republic of the Philippines
Instituted: 1946 (Army: 1948)
Criteria: Receipt of both the Philippine Defense and Liberation Medals/Ribbons. Originally presented to those present for duty in the Philippines on 4 July 1946.
Devices: None

United Nations Service Medal (Korea)

Service: All Services
Instituted: 1951
Criteria: Service on behalf of the United Nations in Korea between 27 June 1950 and 27 July 1954.
Devices: None

Notes: *Above date denotes when award was authorized for wear by U.S. military personnel.*

Originally, U.S. military personnel serving with United Nations Missions were permitted to wear only two UN medals, the United Nations Korean Service Medal and the United Nations Medal *(shown to the right)*. However, changes in Department of Defense policy in 1996 authorized the wear of the ribbons of 11 missions on the U.S. military uniform.

In 2011 sixteen more missions were added to the list, which, along with the United Nations Special Service Medal, brought the total to 28. However, only one ribbon (or medal) may be worn on the U.S. military uniform and awards for any subsequent missions are denoted by the three-sixteenth inch bronze stars.

United Nations Medal

Service: All Services
Instituted: 1964
Criteria: 6 months service with any authorized UN mission.
Devices:

Notes: *Medal worn with appropriate mission ribbon. (See below for complete list).*

UNTSO United Nations Truce Supervision Organization Country/Location: **Israel, Egypt** Dates: **1948 - Present**	**UNMOGIP** United Nations Military Observer Group in India/Pakistan Country/Location: **India, Pakistan** Dates: **1949 - Present**	**UNOGIL** United Nations Observer Group in Lebanon Country/Location: **Lebanon** Dates: **1958**

UNSF/UNTEA United Nations Security Force in West Guinea (West Irian) Country/Location: **West New Guinea (West Irian)** Dates: **1962 - 1963**	**UNIKOM** United Nations Iraq/Kuwait Observation Mission Country/Location: **Iraq/Kuwait** Dates: **1991 - 2003**	**MINURSO** United Nations Mission for the Referendum in Western Sahara Country/Location: **Morocco** Dates: **1991 to Present**

UNAMIC United Nations Advance Mission in Cambodia Country/Location: **Cambodia** Dates: **1991 -1992**	**UNPROFOR** United Nations Protection Force Country/Location: **Former Yoguslavia, (Bosnia, Herzegovina, Croatia, Serbia, Montenegro, Macedonia)** Dates: **1992 - 1995**	**UNTAC** United Nations Transitional Authority in Cambodia Country/Location: **Cambodia** Dates: **1992 - 1993**

ONUMOZ
United Nations Operation in Mozanbique
Country/Location: **Mozambique**
Dates: **1992 - 1994**

UNOSOM II
United Nations Operation in Somalia II
Country/Location: **Somalia**
Dates: **1993 - 1995**

UNOMIG
United Nations Observer
Mission in Georgia
Country/Location: **Georgia (Russia)**
Dates: **1993 - 2009**

UNMIH
United Nations Mission in Haiti
Country/Location: **Haiti**
Dates: **1993 - 1996**

UNPREDEP
United Nations Prevention
Deployment Force
Country/Location: **Former
Yugoslavia; Republic of Macedonia**
Dates: **1995 - 1999**

UNTAES
United Nations Transitional Administration
for Eastern Slavonia, Baranja
and Western Sirmium
Country/Location: **Croatia**
Dates: 1996 - **1998**

UNSMIH
United Nations Support
Mission in Haiti
Country/Location: **Haiti**
Dates: **1996 - 1997**

MINUGUA
United Nations Verification
Mission in Guatemala
Country/Location: **Guatemala**
Dates: **1997-1997**

UNMIK
United Nations Interim
Administration Mission in Kosovo
Country/Location: **Kosovo**
Dates: **1999 - Present**

UNTAET
United Nations Transitional
Administration in East Timor
Country/Location: **Timor (New Guinea)**
Dates: **1999 - 2002**

MONUC
United Nations Organization Mission in
the Democratic Republic of the Congo
Country/Location: **Congo**
Dates: **1999 - 2010**

UNMEE
United Nations Mission to Ethiopia
and Eritrea
Country/Location: **Ethiopia, Eritrea**
Dates: **2000 - 2008**

UNMISET
United Nations Mission of
Support in East Timor
Country/Location: **Timor (New Guinea)**
Dates: **2000 - 2005**

UNMIL
United Nations Mission in Liberia
Country/Location: **Liberia
(West Africa)**
Dates: **2003 - Present**

MINUSTAH
United Nations Stabilization
Mission in Haiti
Country/Location: **Haiti**
Dates: **2004 - Present**

UNAMID
United Nations / African Union Hybrid
Operation in Darfur
Country/Location: **Darfur (East Africa)**
Dates: **2007 - Present**

MINURCAT
United Nations Mission in the Central
African Republic and Chad
Country/Location: **Central African
Republic, Chad (Central Africa)**
Dates: **2007 - 2010**

MONUSCO
United Nations Organization
Stabilization Mission in the Democratic
Republic of the Congo
Country/Location: **Congo**
Dates: **2010 - Present**

| United Nations Special Service Medal UNSSM | UNAMI |

Background: Established in 1994 by the Secretary General of the United Nations, the UNSSM is awarded to military and civilian personnel service in capacities other than established peace-keeping missions or those permanently assigned to UN Headquarters. The UNSSM may be awarded to eligible personnel service for a minimum of ninety (90) consecutive days under the control of the UN in operations or offices for which no other United Nations award is authorized. Posthumous awards may be granted to personnel otherwise eligible for the medal who died while serving under the United Nations before completing the required 90 days of service.

Clasps: Clasps engraved with the name of the country or United Nations organization (e.g.: UNHCR, UNSCOM, UNAMI, etc.) may be added to the medal suspension ribbon and ribbon bar.

Awarded to U.S. military personnel for service under the NATO command and in direct support of NATO operations. Recipients may qualify for such NATO operations as:

(1) Former Yugoslavia: 30 days service inside or 90 days outside the former Republic of Yugoslavia after July 1, 1992 to a date to be determined.

(2) Kosovo: 30 continuous/accumulated days in or around the former Yugoslavian province of Kosovo from October 13, 1998 to a date to be determined.

Multiple rotations or tours in either operational area will only qualify for a single award of that medal.

The NATO Medal, like the United Nations Medal, has a common planchet/pendant but comes with unique ribbons for each operation. As in the case of the United Nations, U.S. Service personnel who qualify for both NATO Medals will wear the first medal/ribbon awarded and a bronze service star on the ribbon bar and suspension ribbon to denote the second award. As before however, the two medal clasps which may accompany the medal. i.e., "FORMER YUGOSLAVIA and KOSOVO" may not be worn on the U.S. military uniform.

The medal is a bronze disk featuring the NATO symbol in the center surrounded by olive branches around the periphery. The reverse contains the inscription, "NORTH ATLANTIC TREATY ORGANIZATION" in English around the top edge and the same wording in French along the lower edge. A horizontal olive branch separates the central area into two areas. Atop this, set in three lines, is the inscription, "IN SERVICE OF PEACE AND FREEDOM" in English. The same text in French on four lines is inscribed in the lower half.

In November, 2002, the NATO Military Committee issued a new NATO Medal Policy in which two classes of service awards will now be issued, namely "Article 5" and "Non-Article 5". The reference is to Article 5 of the original NATO Charter Treaty in which the member nations agreed that an armed attack against any one of them in Europe or North America shall be considered an attack against them all and if such an armed attack occurs, each of them will take such action, including the use of armed force, to restore and maintain the security of the North Atlantic area. Non-Article 5 operations are those conducted as a peace support or crisis operation authorized by the North Atlantic Council.

To date, two Article 5 Medals have been issued by NATO, the first being for Operation "Eagle Assist". Following the 9-11 attacks, NATO Early Warning (NAEW&C) aircraft were deployed from October 12, 2001 to May 16, 2002, to monitor the airspace over the United States to protect against further airborne attack by terrorists.

The second award, is awarded to personnel who took part in Operation "Active Endeavor", the deployment of a NATO Standing Naval Force to patrol the Eastern Mediterranean against hostile forces. That effort began on October 26, 2001 and will be terminated at a date to be announced in the future. In addition, two Non-Article 5 NATO have been authorized for U.S. military personnel. The

NATO Medal

Service: All Services
Instituted: 1992
Criteria: 30 days service in or 90 days outside the former Republic of Yugoslavia and the Adriatic Sea under NATO command in direct support of NATO operations.
Devices: ★

Notes: Above date denotes when award was authorized for wear by U.S. military personnel. "Former Yugoslavia" and "Kosovo" Bars not authorized for wear by U.S. Military personnel.

Article 5 NATO Medal

Service: All Services
Instituted: 2002
Criteria: 30 days service as part of Operation "Eagle Assist" (Medal 1) or Operation Active Endeavor (Medal 2).
Devices:

Notes: As per a memorandum issued by the Deputy Secretary of Defense dated 2 March 2006, the above medals are now authorized for wear on the uniform by U.S. military personnel.

Non-Article 5 NATO Medal and ISAF Medal

Service: All Services
Instituted: 2002
Criteria: 30 days service as part of NATO operations in the Balkans (Medal 3) of Afghanistan (Medal 4).
Devices:

Notes: As per a memorandum issued by the Deputy Secretary of Defense dated 2 March 2006, the above medals are now authorized for wear on the uniform by U.S. military personnel.

qualification period for the NATO Balkans Medal is thirty days of continuous or accumulated service from January 1, 2003 to a date to be determined. The NATO medals for Afghanistan and Iraq are also awarded for 30 days of service in country.

The medal designs are the same as all previous NATO Medals. As in the past, only one NATO Medal may be worn on the uniform with subsequent operations and/or tours indicated by bronze stars affixed to the center of the ribbon bar or suspension ribbons. Also as before, the mission bars depicted above may not be worn on the U.S. military uniform.

The NATO Meritorious Service Medal

The NATO Meritorious Service Medal was established in 2003 for military and civilian personnel commended for providing exceptional or remarkable service to NATO. The Medal is the personal Award of The Secretary General of NATO, who signs each citation. Generally fewer than 50 medals are awarded each year and it is the only significant award for individual effort on the NATO staff. It can be awarded to both Military and Civilian staff. The criteria for the award reflects: the performance of acts of courage in difficult or dangerous circumstances; showing exceptional leadership or personal example; making an outstanding individual contribution to a NATO sponsored program or activity; or enduring particular hardship or deprivation in the interest of NATO.

The ribbon and medal fabric is NATO Blue with white edges, with silver and gold threads centered on the white. The medal disc is of silver color, occasional you will see copies being sold with the regular brass medallion. The NATO Meritorious Service Medal is now authorized for wear on U.S. Military uniforms.

The NATO Meritorious Service Medal

Multinational Force & Observers Medal

The international peacekeeping force known as The Multinational Force and Observers *(MFO)* was established following the ratification of the Camp David Accords and the 1979 peace treaty between Israel and Egypt. Its sole purpose was to monitor the withdrawal of Israeli forces from the occupied portions of the Sinai Peninsula and the return of that territory to the sovereignty of Egypt.

The MFO Medal was established by the Director General on March 24, 1982 to recognize those personnel who served at least 90 days with the Multinational Force and Observers after August 3,1981 *(the requirement was changed to 170 days after March 15, 1985)*. Periods of service on behalf of the MFO outside the Sinai are also counted towards medal eligibility.

The medal is a bronze disk depicting a stylized dove of peace surrounded by olive branches in its center. Around the edge of the medallion are the raised inscriptions, "MULTINATIONAL FORCE" at the top and "OBSERVERS"

Multinational Force and Observers Medal

Service: All Services
Instituted: 1982
Criteria: 6 months service with the Multinational Force & Observers peacekeeping force in the Sinai Desert.
Devices:

on the lower half. The reverse is plain with the inscription, "UNITED IN SERVICE FOR PEACE" set on 5 lines *(all inscriptions are in English)*.

Inter-American Defense Board Medal

The medal and ribbon were authorized on December 11, 1945 by the Inter-American Defense Board, *(IADB)* and were approved by the U.S. Department of Defense for wear by U.S. military personnel on May 12, 1981. The IADB Medal is classified as a foreign service award and is awarded for permanent wear to military personnel who have served on the Inter-American Defense Board for at least one year, either as chairman of the board, delegates, advisors, officers of the staff, as officers of the secretariat or officers of the Inter-American Defense College. The medal is a golden-bronze circular disk with a representation of the globe of the world in the center depicting the Western Hemisphere. Around the periphery of the globe are the arrayed the flags of the member nations of the IADB. The reverse of the medal is plain. A five-sixteenth inch diameter gold star device is worn on the ribbon bar and the suspension ribbon for each five years of service to the IADB.

Inter-American Defense Board Medal

Service: All Services
Instituted: 1981
Criteria: Service with the Inter-American Defense Board for at least 1 year.
Devices:

Notes: *Above date denotes when award was authorized for wear by U.S. military personnel.*

Republic of Vietnam Campaign Medal

The Republic of Vietnam Campaign Medal was established by the Government of the Republic of Vietnam on May 12, 1964 and authorized for award to members of the United States Armed Forces by the Department of Defense on June 20, 1966. To qualify for award, personnel must meet one of the following requirements:

(1) Have served in the Republic of Vietnam for 6 months during the period from March 1, 1961 to March 28, 1973.

(2) Have served outside the geographical limits of the Republic of Vietnam and contributed direct combat support to the Republic of Vietnam and Armed Forces for six months. Such individuals must meet the criteria established for the Armed Forces Expeditionary Medal *(Vietnam)* or the Vietnam Service Medal, during the period of service required to qualify for the Republic of Vietnam Campaign Medal.

(3) Have served for less than six months and have been wounded by hostile forces, captured by hostile forces, but later escaped, was rescued or released or killed in action.

Special eligibility rules were established for personnel assigned in the Republic of Vietnam on January 28, 1973. To be eligible for the medal, an individual must have served a minimum of 60 days in the Republic of Vietnam as of that date or have completed a minimum of 60 days service in the Republic of Vietnam during the period from January 28, 1973 to March 28, 1973, inclusive.

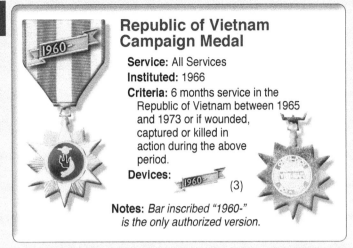

Republic of Vietnam Campaign Medal

Service: All Services
Instituted: 1966
Criteria: 6 months service in the Republic of Vietnam between 1965 and 1973 or if wounded, captured or killed in action during the above period.
Devices: (3)

Notes: *Bar inscribed "1960-" is the only authorized version.*

The Republic of Vietnam Campaign Medal is a white six-pointed star with cut lined, broad gold star points between and a central green disk with a map of Vietnam in silver surmounted with three painted flames in red, signifying the three regions of Vietnam. The reverse contains the inscription, "VIET-NAM" in a lined circle in the center with the name of the medal inscribed in Vietnamese text at the upper and lower edges separated by many short lines. The device, an integral part of the award, is a silver ribbon 28mm long on the suspension ribbon and 15mm long on the service bar inscribed, "1960- " and was evidently intended to include a terminal date for the hostilities. Many examples of this medal are found with devices inscribed with other dates but the only version authorized for U.S. personnel is the one described.

Kuwait Liberation Medal *(Saudi Arabia)*

Established in 1991 by the Government of Saudi Arabia for members of the Coalition Forces who participated in Operation DESERT STORM and the Liberation of Kuwait. In the same year, the U.S. Defense Department authorized the acceptance and wearing of the Kuwait Liberation Medal by members of the Armed Forces of the United States.

To be eligible, U.S. military personnel must have served for at least one day in support of Operation DESERT STORM between January 17 and February 28, 1991 in The Persian Gulf, Red Sea, Gulf of Oman, portions of the Arabian Sea, The Gulf of Aden or the total land areas of Iraq, Kuwait, Saudi Arabia, Oman, Bahrain, Qatar and the United Arab Emirates. The recipient must have been attached to or regularly serving for one or more days with an organization participating in ground and/or shore operations, aboard a naval vessel directly supporting military operations, actually participating as a crew member in one or more aerial flights supporting

Saudi Arabian Medal for the Liberation of Kuwait

Service: All Services
Instituted: 1991
Criteria: Participation in, or support of, Operation Desert Storm. (Jan.-Feb. 1991).
Devices:

(56)

military operations in the areas designated above or serving on temporary duty for 30 consecutive days during this period. That time limitation may be waived for people participating in actual combat operations.

The medal depicts the map of Kuwait in the center with a crown at its top between two encircling palm branches, all of which is fashioned in gold. Above this is a gold palm tree surmounted by two crossed swords. Surrounding the entire design is a representation of an exploding bomb in silver. The reverse is plain. The ribbon bar is issued with a replica of the palm tree with crossed swords found on the medal and is the only authorized attachment.

Kuwait Liberation Medal *(Emirate of Kuwait)*

Established in July, 1994 by the Government of Kuwait for members of the United States military who participated in Operations DESERT SHIELD and DESERT STORM. On March 16, 1995, the Secretary of Defense authorized the acceptance and wearing of the Kuwait Liberation Medal *(Kuwait)* by members of the Armed Forces of the United States. To be eligible, U.S. military personnel must have served in support of Operations DESERT SHIELD and DESERT STORM between August 2, 1990 and August 31, 1993, in The Arabian Gulf, Red Sea, Gulf of Oman, portions of the Arabian Sea , The Gulf of Aden or the total land areas of Iraq, Kuwait, Saudi Arabia, Oman, Bahrain, Qatar and the United Arab Emirates. The recipient must have been attached to or regularly serving for one or more days with an organization participating in ground and/or shore operations, aboard a naval vessel directly supporting military operations, actually participating as a crew member in one or more aerial flights directly supporting military operations in the areas designated above or serving on temporary duty for 30 consecutive days or 60 nonconsecutive days during this period. That time limitation may be waived for people participating in actual combat operations. The Kuwait Liberation Medal *(Kuwait)* follows the Kuwait Liberation Medal from the government of Saudi Arabia in the order of precedence.

The medal is a bronze disk which depicts the Kuwaiti Coat of Arms with the Arabic inscription, "1991 - Liberation Medal." The reverse contains a map of Kuwait with a series of rays

Kuwaiti Medal for the Liberation of Kuwait

Service: All Services
Instituted: 1995
Criteria: Participation in, or support of, Operations Desert Shield and/or Desert Storm (1990-93).
Devices: None

Notes: *Above date denotes when award was authorized for wear by U.S. military personnel.*

emanating from the center out to the edge of the medal - all in bas-relief. The ribbon bar may be one of the most unusual ever displayed on the American military uniform. It consists of three equal stripes of red, white and green with a black, trapezoidal-shaped section silk-screened across the entire upper half. No attachments are authorized for the medal or ribbon.

Did You Know? The Kuwait Liberation Medal was approved by the Kuwait Council of Ministers for award in five classes, generally according to the rank of the recipient. The only version authorized U.S. service personnel is the 5th class award.

Republic of Korea War Service Medal

The Republic of Korea War Service Medal was established in 1951 by the Government of the Republic of Korea for presentation to the foreign military personnel who served on or over the Korean Peninsula or in its territorial waters between June 27, 1950 and July 27, 1953. However, it was not approved for acceptance and wear by the U.S. until 1999. To be eligible for this award, U.S. military personnel must have been on permanent assignment or on temporary duty for 30 consecutive days or 60 non-consecutive days. The duty must have been performed within the territorial limits of Korea, in the waters immediately

adjacent thereto or in aerial flight over Korea participating in actual combat operations or in support of combat operations. The 48 year interval between establishment and its formal acceptance represents the second longest period of time in U.S. history between a significant national and military conflict and the award of an appropriate medal.

Republic of Korea War Service Medal
Service: All Services **Instituted:** 1953
Criteria: Service on the Korean Peninsula between 1950 and 1953
Devices: None

Notes: *Above date denotes when award was authorized for wear by U.S. military personnel.*
Notes: Not accepted by the United States Government for wear on the military uniform until 1999. *Some original 1953 medals had a taeguk in the center of the drape like the ribbon bar.

The medal is a bronze disk containing a map of the Korean Peninsula at top center over a grid of the world and olive branches on either side of the design. Below the map are two crossed bullets. In the center of the ribbon and earlier medal drapes *(1950's)*, is an ancient oriental symbol called a taeguk *(the top half is red and the bottom half is blue)*. The reverse contains the inscription, "FOR SERVICE IN KOREA" in English embossed on two lines with two small blank plaques on which the recipient's name may be engraved.

General Macomb Commemorative Medal

The United States Government, State Governments, Veterans Organizations, private mints and individuals have a long tradition of striking commemorative medals to recognize and honor specific military victories, historical events and military service to our great Republic. Until the 20th Century the United States did not issue military service medals recognizing service by veterans in the different wars, battles, campaigns or other significant military events.

The tradition of honoring U.S. military heroes began when the Continental Congress awarded gold and silver medals to our triumphant commanders of The Revolutionary War. While these were struck as table display medals, General Gates the victor of Saratoga, wasted no time hanging his from a neck ribbon and wearing it for his official portrait. General Washington was awarded the first commemorative medal for driving the British from Boston and the first commemorative to a naval hero was awarded to Captain John Paul Jones. These Congressionally authorized medals were the forerunners of modern combat decorations. Some medals commemorate events such as the Mexican War and the Civil War, with reverse designs depicting famous battle scenes.

During the Mexican War certain states such as South Carolina issued medals to veterans of the state regiment which fought in the war. Other times veterans formed societies and issued medals commemorating their service. Some of the more famous examples are the Grand Army of the Republic reunion medals and the Aztec Club medal struck by veterans of the Mexican War. In some cases commanders during the Civil War issued privately commissioned commemorative medals such as the Kearney Cross.

Grand Army of the Republic Reunion Medal

The U.S. Mint regularly produces commemorative medals typically to celebrate and honor American people, places, events, including medals honoring military heroes, veterans and the Armed Services. For example The Vietnam Veterans National Medal commemorates the courage and dedication of the men and women who served in that conflict. The Missing in Action medal is a 15/16 inch miniature replica of the

3-inch medal authorized for presentation to the next-of-kin of American military and civilian personnel missing or other unaccounted for in Southeast Asia. The 200th anniversaries of the U.S. Army, Navy, Marine Corps and Coast Guard were also celebrated with the striking of national medals and the Persian Gulf National Medal honored Persian Gulf War veterans. Only bronze medals are available for sale to the public. For a complete listing of medals available from the U.S. Mint, call 1-800-872-6468.

While the federal government issues commemorative medals from the U.S. mint, state and county governments who were particularly active after World War I used private mints and contractors to issue hundreds of different commemorative medals honoring World War veterans and providing a visible symbol of gratitude to their returning veterans. All of these

Vietnam Commemorative Medal

medals were especially meaningful to both returning veterans and their families. Veteran's associations such as the American Legion, Veterans of Foreign Wars and even the Daughters of the Confederacy issued commemorative medals. For the past two hundred years these groups coupled with private mints have issued medals honoring historical military events, victories, deeds and service that honor American veterans.

Commemorative medals reflect typical American ingenuity and spirit, where local government, veterans associations and private leadership step forward to facilitate honoring service and deeds the federal government fails to recognize. In recent years the 75th Anniversary of World War I and the 50th Anniversary celebrations of both World War II and the Korea War were the occasions for well-deserved commemorative medals to honor the veterans of these conflicts. The most recent example is the Cold War Victory Commemorative Medal struck to fill the void created when Congress authorized a Cold War Victory Recognition certificate but never funded a medal.

Although unofficial in nature and usually struck by private mints or associations, commemorative medals provide a very tangible memento to honor all veterans and families for their service and sacrifice. On the next page are examples of commemorative medals from the last sixty years.

Cold War Victory Commemorative Medal

U.S. Army
Commemorative Medal©

To honor all Soldiers who for their service on active, guard or Reserve Duty since 1776.

Combat Service
Commemorative Medal©

To honor all Soldiers, Sailors, Marines, Coast Guardsmen and Airmen who served in an overseas combat theater or expeditionary combat operation.

Presidential Citation
Commemorative Medal©

To honor all Soldiers, Sailors, Marines and Airmen who served in a combat theater or expeditionary combat operation in a unit or ship that was awarded the Presidential Unit Citation.

American Defense
Commemorative Medal©

To honor all Soldiers, Sailors, Marines Airmen and Coast Guardsmen who served in the United States for over 30 days.

World War II Victory
Commemorative Medal©

To honor all who served in the United States Armed Forces in WW II. The Goddess of Truth and Freedom raises the sword and laurel crown of Victory over Nazi and Japanese shields.

50th Anniversary Korean Defense
Commemorative Medal©

To honor all military personnel who served in Korea or in direct support anytime from 1950 to present.

Vietnam Service
Commemorative Medal©

To honor all Soldiers, Sailors, Marines and Airmen who served in South Vietnam or in direct support from Thailand, Guam, Okinawa, Philippines or the waters off shore between 1960 and 1975.

The Liberation of Kuwait
Commemorative Medal©

To honor all military personnel who served in the Southwest Asia theater of operations or in support of the Liberation of Kuwait between 1990 - 2000.

Liberation of Afghanistan
Commemorative Medal©

To honor all Soldiers, Sailors, Marines and Airmen who served in Afghanistan or in direct support of the Liberation of Afghanistan.

Operation Iraqi Freedom
Commemorative Medal©

To honor all Soldiers, Sailors, Marines, Coast Guardsmen and Airmen who served in Iraq or in direct support of Operation Iraqi Freedom.

Global War on Terror Service
Commemorative Medal©

To honor all military personnel who served in the Armed Forces during the GWOT in CONUS or overseas.

Cold War Victory
Commemorative Medal©

To recognize all Soldiers, Sailors, Marines and Airmen who served between 2 Sept. 1945 and 26 December 1991.

How Army Medals and Ribbons Are Worn

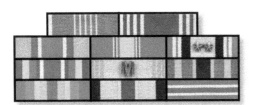

United States Army

Wear of Service Ribbons — Ribbons may be worn on the Army green, blue and white uniform coats. The ribbons are worn in one or more rows in order of precedence with either no space or 1/8 inch between rows, usually three ribbons to a row but no more than four ribbons to a row. The top row is centered or aligned to left edge of the row underneath, whichever looks the best. Unit awards are centered above the right breast pocket with a maximum of three per row.

Wear of Full Size Decorations & Service Medals — Decorations and service medals may be worn on the Army blue or white uniform after retreat and by enlisted personnel on the dress uniform for social functions. The medals are mounted in order of precedence, in rows with not more than four medals in a row. The top row cannot have more medals than the one below. Rows are separated so that the pendants of the lower medals are fully visible. Medals may not overlap (as Navy and Marines do), so normally there are only three to a row due to the size of the coat. The first row of medals is centered 1/8 inch above the right breast pocket. Unit citations are centered over the right breast pocket 1/8 inch above the top of the pocket. Service and training ribbons are not worn with full size medals.

Wear of Miniature Decorations & Service Medals — Miniature medals are scaled down replicas of full size medals. Only miniature medals are authorized for wear on the mess and evening uniform jackets and with the blue and white uniform after retreat on formal occasions. Miniature medals are mounted on bars with the order of precedence from the wearer's right to left. The medals are mounted side by side if there are four or less. They may be overlapped up to 50% when five, six or seven are in a row. Overlapping is equal for all medals with the right one fully displayed. When two or more rows are worn, the bottom pendants must be fully visible.

For information on uniform wear policy, consult DA Pam 670-1, Wear and Appearance of Army Uniforms and Insignia.

Wear of Awards and Insignia on the Uniform

The United States Army is a uniformed service where discipline, esprit de corps and morale is judged by how the individual wears the uniform. Therefore, there are very precise regulations governing the wear of awards, insignia and accoutrements on the uniform. Army regulation 670-1 is the governing military publication. The following pages provide examples of insignia placement on Army uniforms since World War I.

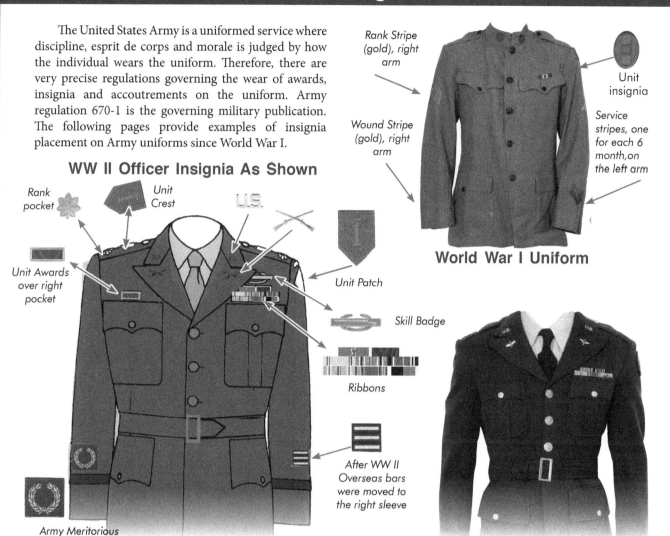

WW II Officer Insignia As Shown

Rank pocket

Unit Crest

U.S.

Unit Awards over right pocket

Unit Patch

Skill Badge

Ribbons

After WW II Overseas bars were moved to the right sleeve

Army Meritorious Unit Commendation - Original Configuration

World War II and Korea Officer
See page 37 for Vietnam Uniform examples

Rank Stripe (gold), right arm

Wound Stripe (gold), right arm

Unit insignia

Service stripes, one for each 6 month, on the left arm

World War I Uniform

WW II & Korea Enlisted Vietnam, SWA and Cold War uniform details page 37

Vietnam Enlisted

WW II Enlisted

Korean War
Uniform shown in an enlisted Ike Jacket

❖ Uniforms - Male Officer

U.S. is worn 5/8" above lapel notch and parallel to the inside edge of the lapel.

Branch insignia is worn 1 1/4" below U.S. insignia. Align so center line of branch insignia bisects the center line of the U.S. and is parallel to the inside edge of the lapel.

Regimental insignia worn centered 1/8" above pocket or 1/4" above unit awards.

Unit awards are centered 1/8" above the right breast. pocket.

Identification badges are centered on the pocket between the bottom of the pocket and the bottom of the pocket flap.

Overseas bars are centered on the bottom half of the right sleeve 1/4" above the braid.

Full size medals may be worn on blue uniform.

Ribbons are centered 1/8" over the left breast pocket, normally three to a row; with no space or 1/8" between rows.

Combat and skill badges are worn 1/4" above ribbons or below top of pocket 1/2" apart.

Blue Uniform

Greens and Pinks Uniform

Regimental insignia worn on right lapel centered 1/2" below notch.

Up to three miniature class 1-5 combat or skill badges may be worn.

Miniature medals are centered 1/2" below notch.

Identification badges are centered between the first and second button

❖ Uniform - Female Officer

On the female blue uniform branch insignia is worn on the both lapels only 1" below the notch. Align parallel to the inside edge of the lapel. A single U.S. is worn on the each lapel aligned with the branch insignia.

Regimental insignia worn centered 1/2" above nameplate or 1/2" above unit awards or foreign badges on new green and blue uniform.

Unit awards are centered 1/2" above nameplate.

Identification badges are centered across from the third button as shown

Overseas bars are centered on the bottom half of the right sleeve 1/4" above the braid.

Women's ribbons and badges are aligned with the plastic nameplate. The plate is adjusted to individual figure differences. The nameplate is centered horizontally on the right side between one and two inches above the top button of the coat. Individual service ribbons are aligned parallel to the bottom of the name plate.

Combat and skill badges are worn 1/4" above ribbons or below 1/2" apart.

Ribbons are centered as shown, normally three to a row; with no space or 1/8" between rows.

Full size medals may be worn on blue uniform.

Green shoulder marks obsolete as of Sept 1992.

U.S. Army Photos

Blue Uniform

Regimental Crest are worn 1/4" above the nameplate or 1/2" above unit awards.

Black shoulder marks.

Up to three miniature class 1-5 combat or skill badges may be worn.

Miniature medals are centered 1/2" below notch.

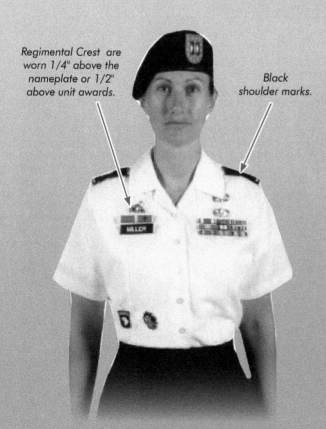

❖ Uniform - Male Enlisted

US is worn 1" above the left lapel notch and parallel to the inside edge of the lapel the branch insignia is worn on the right lapel using the same alignment.

DUI (crest) is centered between button outer edge and inside edge of upper sleeve.

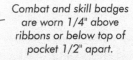

Combat and skill badges are worn 1/4" above ribbons or below top of pocket 1/2" apart.

Regimental insignia worn centered 1/8" above pocket or 1/4" above unit awards.

Unit awards are centered 1/8" above the right breast pocket.

Identification badges are centered on the pocket between the bottom of the pocket and the bottom of the pocket flap.

Ribbons are centered 1/8" over the left breast pocket, normally three to a row; with no space or 1/8" between rows.

Rank is sewn on the sleeve halfway between the shoulder seam and the elbow.

Hashmarks are placed 4" above the bottom of the left sleeve centered on the sleeve.

New Blue Uniform

Full size medals may be worn on blue uniform up to four across as shown below.

New Pinks and Green Uniform

U.S. Army
Photos

Overseas bars are placed 4" above the bottom of right sleeve centered on the sleeve

Old Blue Uniform

❖ Uniform - Female Enlisted

*U.S. is centered on the right collar 5/8"
above lapel notch and parallel to the
inside edge of the lapel.*

*DUI (crest) is centered
between button outer edge
and inside edge of the top of
the sleeve.*

*Branch insignia is centered and
is parallel to the inside edge of
the right lapel.*

*Regimental insignia
worn centered 1/2"
above nameplate
or 1/2" above unit
awards or foreign
badges.*

*Women's ribbons and badges are
aligned with the plastic nameplate.
The plate is adjusted to individual
figure differences. The nameplate is
centered horizontally on the right side
between one and two inches above
the top button of the coat. Individual
service ribbons are aligned parallel to
the bottom of the name plate.*

*Unit awards are
centered 1/2"
above nameplate.*

*Rank is sewn on
the sleeve halfway
between the shoulder
seam and the elbow.*

*Bottom of name tag
lines up with ribbon.*

*Identification badges are
centered across from the
third button as shown.*

*Overseas bars are
placed 4" above
the bottom of right
sleeve centered on
the sleeve.*

*Hashmarks are placed 4"
above the bottom of the
left sleeve centered on
the sleeve. Old style ww
shown.*

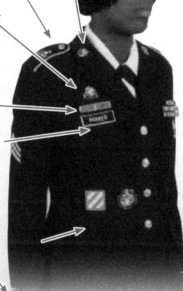

*Regimental Crest are
worn 1/2" above the
nameplate or 1/2"
above unit awards*

U.S. Army Photos

These rules apply to the Blue uniforms

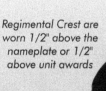

*Black shoulder
marks.*

Green Army uniform.

New Army uniform.

Green uniform

Pwroposed new Pinks and
Green uniform

Examples of wearing full size and miniature medals, ribbons and mini ribbons by veterans.

Introduction

One of the first lessons taught to new recruits is proper wear of the uniform and insignia. The same rules apply to wear of military awards by veterans and retirees on their old uniform. There are many occasions when tradition, patriotism, ceremonies and social occasions call for the wear of military awards.

Civilian Dress

 The most common manner of wearing a decoration or medal is as a lapel pin in the left lapel of a civilian suit jacket. The small enameled lapel pin represents the ribbon bar of a single decoration or medal an individual has received (*usually the highest award or one having special meaning to the wearer*).

 Many well-known veterans such as former Senator Bob Dole, a World War II Purple Heart recipient, wear a lapel pin. Pins are available for all awards and some ribbons such as the Combat Action Ribbon or Presidential Unit Citation. Small miniature wings, parachute badges and Combat Infantry Badges are also worn in the lapel or as a tie tack. Additionally, retirees are encouraged to wear their retired pin and World War II veterans are encouraged to wear their Honorable Discharge Pin (*affectionately referred to as the "ruptured duck"*).

Honorably discharged and retired Armed Forces members may wear full-size or miniature medals on civilian suits on appropriate occasions such as Memorial Day and Armed Forces Day. Female members may wear full-size or miniature medals on equivalent dress. It is not considered appropriate to wear skill or qualification badges on civilian attire.

Formal Civilian Wear

For more formal occasions, it is correct and encouraged to wear miniature decorations and medals. For a black or white tie occasion, the rule is quite simple: if the lapel is wide enough wear the miniatures on the left lapel or, in the case of a shawl lapel on a tuxedo, the miniature medals are worn over the left breast pocket. The center of the holding bar of the bottom row of medals should be parallel to the ground immediately above the pocket. Do not wear a pocket handkerchief. Miniature medals really do make a handsome statement of patriotic service at weddings and other social events.

Miniature medals can also be worn on a civilian suit at veterans' functions, memorial events, formal occasions of ceremony and social functions of a military nature.

Wear of the Uniform by Retired Personnel

On certain occasions, retired Armed Forces personnel may wear either the uniform prescribed at the date of retirement or any of the current active duty authorized uniforms. Retirees should adhere to the same grooming standards as Armed Forces active duty personnel when wearing the uniform (for example, a beard is inappropriate while in uniform). Whenever the uniform is worn, it must be done in such a manner as to reflect credit upon the individual and the service from which he/she is retired. (Do not mix uniform items.)

The occasions for uniform wear by retirees are
- Military ceremonies.

- Military funerals, weddings, memorial services and inaugurals.

- Patriotic parades on national holidays.

- Military parades in which active or reserve units are participating.

- Educational institutions when engaged in giving military instruction or responsible for military discipline.

- Social or other functions when the invitation has obviously been influenced by the member's earlier active service.

Honorably separated wartime veterans may wear the uniform authorized at the time of their service. The occasions are:

- Military funerals, memorial services, and inaugurals.

- Patriotic parades on national holidays.

- Any occasion authorized by law.

- Military parades in which active or reserve units are participating.

Non-wartime service personnel separated (other than retired, Army National Guard and Reserve) are not authorized to wear the uniform but may wear the medals.

How to Determine a Veteran's Medals

Many veterans and their families are unsure of which military medals they were awarded and often for good reasons. Twenty-five, thirty, even fifty years after military service, it is often difficult to remember or clearly identify the awards a veteran may have earned the right to wear or display. Thousands of veterans have been heard to say "I don't want any awards I'm not authorized, but I want everything I am authorized." So the question is, *"What are the medals authorized the veteran for his military service during each conflict?"*

There are a number of reasons besides the passage of time that veterans are not always sure of their military awards. At the end of World War II many campaign medals had not yet been struck and were only issued as ribbons due to the restriction on brass and other metals for the war effort. Many unit awards had not yet been authorized and on the whole, most soldiers, sailors, marines and airmen were more interested in going home than they were in their military records. Other changes such as Congress' decision in the 1947s to authorize a Bronze Star Medal for meritorious service to all recipients of the Combat Infantryman and Combat Medical Badge was not well known. Many veterans never realized that they had earned a Bronze Star Medal. Perhaps the most striking example is the recently-approved Republic of Korea War Service Medal. The Republic of Korea offered the medal to all U.S. Korean War veterans but it was not accepted by our government until 1999. In other cases, veterans came home and stuffed their medals and awards into a cigar box which usually found its way into the hands of children and these magnificent symbols of valor and service from a grateful nation simply disappeared over time.

Today there is a wonderfully renewed interest in wearing and displaying United States military medals, both to honor veterans' patriotic service and to display a family's pride in military service. World War II, Korea and Vietnam veterans now wear their medals at formal social and patriotic events and a display of military medals and insignia is often in the family home place of honor.

As mentioned earlier, military medals are divided into two categories: Decorations awarded for valor or meritorious service and Campaign and Service medals awarded for a particular service or event. Additionally there are Unit Awards which are for unit valor and meritorious service and ribbon-only awards presented for completing special training or recognizing certain service.

Decorations are individual awards which are of such singular significance that most veterans and their family will remember when such awards have been presented. Decorations are noted on a veteran's official discharge papers *(called a DD Form 214)* as well as published in official unit orders. However there are exceptions, such as the Bronze Star Medal issued for meritorious service after World War II and in some cases Purple Heart medals that were never officially presented. Someone who is unsure if they received a decoration can request the National Records Center in St. Louis or other veterans records holding areas to check their records. Home of Heroes at www.homeofheroes.com list all Medal of Honor, Service Crosses and most Silver Star awardees. Bronze Star, Air Medal, Purple Heart, Commendation and Achievement medals are announced in unit orders which are normally found in the individual's military service record.

Campaign and service medals, unit awards and ribbon-only awards are more clearly identifiable. The Army for example, has a campaign register which provides a clear indication of which campaign medals, unit awards, campaign stars and foreign unit awards are authorized a particular unit during certain periods of time. To aid in identifying the campaign medals authorized veterans of different conflicts and to show how they can be displayed, United States and Allied campaign medals authorized since World War II are summarized on the next page. Exact criteria for each medal and the campaigns associated with it are shown in detail later in the book.

Basically there are several ways to identify the military medals a veteran has earned. The early medals such as the Civil War Campaign medal are easy. If an ancestors served during the Civil War then they earned it (see page 125). The other early campaign medals prior to World War I, such as the Spanish-American campaign medals were earned by both 250,000 federal and state volunteers and their records are in the National Archives on microfilm. These files can be found by going to www.familysearch.com.

World War I is fairly straight forward, with few exceptions for all of the soldiers, sailors, marines and airmen who receive the World War I Victory Medal (see page 129). Their campaign bars and any other awards are also available on the government website: www.archives.gov.

World War II and Later

The identification of World War II and later veterans is the information most veterans and families want and that really just comes from two places. The first is the veteran's discharge certificate which has his service history. Early World War II Army versions were an AGO Form 55 which later became the Department of Defense Form 214 (DD 214). While this is the official record it is often incomplete or missing information which was not available at the time of the veteran's discharge. Which of course is the purpose of this book, to bring veterans and their families up to date on their military awards.

So let's start with how you obtain a copy of your DD 214 or for the veteran in your family.

All of the federal government's military records for World War II veterans are stored at the National Personnel Records Center (NPRC) in St. Louis, Missouri. The National Personnel Records Center is part of the National Archives and Records Administration.

There are specific rules for requesting a veterans records because of the privacy act. As long as the veteran is still living, he is the only one who may request his complete military records. However if the veteran is deceased, then the next of kin is entitled to the complete military file. By the next of kin the NRPC means the unmarried widow or widower, son or daughter, father or mother, brother or sister of a deceased veteran. Grandchildren, nieces or nephews are not generally included his next of kin.

So if you are not the next of kin of the deceased veteran you really must have one of the next of kin make the request for the records. One exception is the military files will be provided if you are really the only living relative of a deceased veteran. While the NPRC will provide the complete military files for the purpose of identifying the military awards you are really only interested in the DD 214 record of discharge.

Unfortunately in 1973 there was a huge fire at the NPRC that destroyed nearly 18 million official military personnel records. Eighty per cent of those records destroyed were for Army and Army Air Force personnel that had been discharged between 1912 and 1960. Approximately 75% of Air Force records for personnel who were discharged between 1947 to 1964 beginning with the last name Hubbard through Z were also destroyed. The Air Force became a separate service from the Army in 1947. Even if you're relatively sure that the veterans records may have been burned you should go ahead and send them a request because NPRC has been able to reconstruct some files.

There is a another source for locating a veteran's DD214. Surprisingly a very high percentage of all veterans recorded a copy of their DD 214 in the local county courthouse. At the time of the veterans discharge it was recommended that they do this because it was the single most important document for them to have for applying for any veteran's benefits. By having it recorded at the local County Courthouse they could always obtain a copy. If you are researching a veteran's file you might be very pleasantly surprised to find a copy on file at the county courthouse.

Issue of U.S. Medals to Veterans, Retirees and Their Families

How to Request the DD214

Veterans of any United States military service may request medals never issued (the majority of WW II veterans for example) or replacement of medals which have been lost, stolen, destroyed or rendered unfit through no fault of their own. Requests may also be filed for awards that were earned but, for any reason, were never issued to the veteran. A good example is the Korea Defense Service Medal which was recently approved and back dated to cover everyone who served in Korea after 1954. More than 2 million former service personnel are now authorized this medal. The next-of-kin of deceased veterans may also make the same request for the medals of their veteran family member.

The National Personnel Records Center, Military Personnel Records *(NPRC-MPR)* is the repository of millions of military personnel, health, and medical records of discharged and deceased veterans of all services during the 20th century. Information from the records is made available upon written request *(with signature and date)* to the extent allowed by law. Please note that NPRC holds historical Military Personnel Records of nearly 100 million veterans. The vast majority of these records are paper-based and not available on-line.

There are two ways for those seeking information regarding military personnel records stored at NPRC (MPR). If you are a veteran or next-of-kin of a deceased veteran, you may now use vetrecs.archives.gov to order a copy of your military records. For all others, your request is best made using a Standard Form 180. It includes complete instructions for preparing and submitting requests.

Using the vetrecs.archives.gov Requests for the issuance or replacement of military service medals, decorations, and awards should be directed to the specific branch of the military in which the veteran served. However, for Air Force *(including Army Air Corps)* and Army personnel, the National Personnel Records Center will verify the awards to which a veteran is entitled and forward the request with the verification to the appropriate service department for issuance of the medals.

The Standard Form (SF 180), Request Pertaining to Military Records, is recommended for requesting medals and awards. Provide as much information as possible and send the form to the appropriate address shown on the next page.

1. How to Obtain Standard Form 180 *(SF-180),* Request Pertaining to Military Records

    A. Download and print a copy of the SF-180 in PDF format by going to: **http://www.archives.gov/facilities/mo/ st_louis/military_personnel_records standard_ form_180.html#sf.**

B. Write to **The National Personnel Records Center** 9700 Page Avenue, St. Louis, Missouri 63132.

    The SF 180 may be photocopied as needed. You must submit a separate SF 180 for each individual whose records are being requested.

2. Write a Letter to Request Records

If you are not able to obtain SF-180, you may still submit a request for military records by letter. The letter should indicate if the request is for a specific medal(s), or for all medals earned. It is also helpful to include copies of any military service documents that indicate eligibility for medals, such as military orders or the veteran's report of separation *(DD Form 214 or its earlier equivalent).* Federal law [5 USC 552a(b)] requires that all requests for information from official military personnel files be submitted in writing. Each request must be signed *(in cursive)* by the veteran or his next-of-kin indicating the relationship to the deceased and dated *(within the last year).* For this reason, no requests are accepted over the internet.

Requests must contain enough information to identify the record among the more than 70 million on file at NPRC (MPR). Certain basic information is needed to locate military service records. This information includes:

*   The veteran's complete name used while in service, Service number or social security number
*   Branch of service

If the request pertains to a record that may have been involved in the 1973 fire, also include:
*   Place of discharge
*   Last unit of assignment
*   Place of entry into the service, if known

Submit a separate request *(either SF 180 or letter)* for each veteran whose records are being requested. Response times for records requested from the *(NPRC)* vary greatly depending on the nature of the request. For example, the NPRC Military Records Facility can run a backlog of 180,000 requests and receives approximately 5,000 requests per day. The Center may have a difficult time locating records since millions of records were lost in a fire in 1973. Although the requested medals can often be issued on the basis of alternate records, the documents sent in with the request are sometimes the only means of determining proper eligibility.

Finally, you should exercise extreme patience. It may take several months or, in some cases, a year to determine eligibility and dispatch the appropriate medals. The Center asks that you not send a follow-up request for 90 days. Because of these delays, many veterans simply purchase their medals from a supplier such as **www. usmedals.com.**

Generally, there is no charge for medal or award replacements from the government. The length of time to receive a response or your medals and awards varies depending upon the branch of service sending the medals.

Cold War Recognition Certificate

In accordance with section 1084 of the Fiscal Year 1998 National Defense Authorization Act, the Secretary of Defense approved awarding Cold War Recognition Certificates to all members of the armed forces and qualified federal government civilian personnel who faithfully served the United States during the Cold War era, from Sept. 2, 1945 to Dec. 26, 1991. The application for the certificate is best obtained by doing an internet search for Cold War Recognition Certificate since the site location has changed several times.

ARMY		
If the person served in the Army, the request should be sent to:	**National Personnel Records Center** 1 Archives Drive St. Louis, MO 63138	In case of a problem or an appeal write to: **U.S. Army Human Resources Cmd Awards Division** Attn: AHRC-PDP-A 1600 Spearhead Ave. Fort Knox, KY 40122-5408
AIR FORCE		
The Air Force processes requests for medals through the National Personnel Records Center, which determines eligibility through the information in the veteran's records. Once verified, a notification of entitlement is forwarded to Randolph Air Force Base, Texas, from which the medals are mailed to the requestor. To request medals earned while in the Air Force or its predecessors, the Army Air Corps or Army Air Force veterans or their next-of-kin should write to:	**National Personnel Records Center** 1 Archives Drive St. Louis, MO 63138	In case of a problem or an appeal write to: **Headquarters Air Force Personnel Ctr AFPC/DPPPR** 550 C Street West, Suite 12 Randolph AFB, TX 78150-4714
NAVY		
If the person served in the Navy, the request should be sent to:	**National Personnel Records Center** 1 Archives Drive St. Louis, MO 63138	In case of a problem or an appeal write to: **Department of the Navy Chief of Naval Operations (DNS-35)** 2000 Navy Pentagon Washington, DC 20350-2000
MARINE CORPS		
If the person served in the Marine Corps, the request should be sent to:	**National Personnel Records Center** 1 Archives Drive St. Louis, MO 63138	In case of a problem or an appeal write to: **Commandant of the Marine Corps Military Awards Branch (MMMA)** 2008 Elliot Road Quantico, VA 22134
COAST GUARD		
If the person served in the Coast Guard, the request should be sent to:	**Coast Guard Personnel Center** 4200 Wilson Blvd, Suite 900 (PSC-PSD-MA) STOP 7200 Arlington, VA 20598-7200	In case of a problem or an appeal write to: **Commandant U.S. Coast Guard Medals and Awards Branch (PMP-4)** Washington, DC 20593-0001

❖ World War II Military Medals Records

Many readers of earlier editions ask for detail information about determining a veterans military awards. As mentioned on the previous pages the veterans DD214 or equivalent is the key. Shown below is a typical World War II DD214 with the individuals name removed. It is also a good example of the need to be able to translate the military abbreviations of that period and figure out what may be missing. In this case can you find the clue that tells you the soldier became authorized the Bronze Star medal in 1947, two years after his discharge in 1945?

The key is award of the Combat Medical Badge (Med Badge).

Navy, Marine and Coast Discharges are similar to the ones shown for World War II Army and Army Air Force.

ENLISTED RECORD AND REPORT OF SEPARATION
HONORABLE DISCHARGE

177-92

1. LAST NAME - FIRST NAME - MIDDLE INITIAL	2. ARMY SERIAL NO.	3. GRADE	4. ARM OR SERVICE	5. COMPONENT
— VETERAN'S NAME	37 611 552	Pfc	MD	AUS

6. ORGANIZATION	7. DATE OF SEPARATION	8. PLACE OF SEPARATION
Med Det 194th Gli Inf	16 Nov 45	Jefferson Barracks Mo. Separation Center

9. PERMANENT ADDRESS FOR MAILING PURPOSES	10. DATE OF BIRTH	11. PLACE OF BIRTH
1844 So 12th St St Louis Mo.	16 Jul 1943	Elvins Mo.

12. ADDRESS FROM WHICH EMPLOYMENT WILL BE SOUGHT	13. COLOR EYES	14. COLOR HAIR	15. HEIGHT	16. WEIGHT	17. NO. DEPEND.
See #9	Brown	Brown	6'	161 lbs.	1

18. RACE			19. MARITAL STATUS			20. U.S. CITIZEN		21. CIVILIAN OCCUPATION AND NO.
WHITE X	NEGRO	OTHER (specify)	SINGLE X	MARRIED	OTHER (specify)	YES X	NO	Painter Helper 9-32.21

MILITARY HISTORY

22. DATE OF INDUCTION	23. DATE OF ENLISTMENT	24. DATE OF ENTRY INTO ACTIVE SERVICE	25. PLACE OF ENTRY INTO SERVICE
12 Apr 1943	-----	19 Apr 1943	Jefferson Barracks Mo.

SELECTIVE SERVICE DATA	26. REGISTERED	27. LOCAL S.S. BOARD NO.	28. COUNTY AND STATE	29. HOME ADDRESS AT TIME OF ENTRY INTO SERVICE
	YES X NO	#1	Farmington Mo.	Flat River Mo.

30. MILITARY OCCUPATIONAL SPECIALTY AND NO.	31. MILITARY QUALIFICATION AND DATE (i.e. infantry, aviation and marksmanship badges, etc.)
Truck driver light 345	Parachutist GO 138 Hq 17th AB 27 Jul44

32. BATTLES AND CAMPAIGNS
Rhineland, Ardennes, Central Europe.

33. DECORATIONS AND CITATIONS
Awarded 3 bronze stars for the above Campaign GO 33-40 1945 Good Conduct Medal. Med badge GO#49 Hq 194th Gli Inf 20 May 45. Glider badge GO#59 Hq 194th Gli Inf 26 Jul 44

34. WOUNDS RECEIVED IN ACTION
None

35. LATEST IMMUNIZATION DATES				36. SERVICE OUTSIDE CONTINENTAL U.S. AND RETURN		
SMALLPOX	TYPHOID	TETANUS	OTHER (specify)	DATE OF DEPARTURE	DESTINATION	DATE OF ARRIVAL
20Apr43 30Jul45	20Apr43 4May43	20Apr43 1June43	BT/A	20 Aug 44 19 Aug 45	ETO USA	Aug 41 Aug45

37. TOTAL LENGTH OF SERVICE						38. HIGHEST GRADE HELD
CONTINENTAL SERVICE			FOREIGN SERVICE			
YEARS	MONTHS	DAYS	YEARS	MONTHS	DAYS	
1	6	25	1	0	10	Pfc

39. PRIOR SERVICE
None

40. REASON AND AUTHORITY FOR SEPARATION
AR 615-365 Convenience of the Govt RR 1-1 (Demobilization) 15 Dec 44

41. SERVICE SCHOOLS ATTENDED	42. EDUCATION (Years)		
None	Grammar 8	High School 0	College 0

PAY DATA

43. LONGEVITY FOR PAY PURPOSES			44. MUSTERING OUT PAY		45. SOLDIER DEPOSIT	46. TRAVEL PAY	47. TOTAL AMOUNT, NAME OF DISBURSING OFFICER
YEARS	MONTHS	DAYS	TOTAL	THIS PAYMENT			
2	7		$300	$100		$06.75	J.W. MC MANUS LT COL F.D.

INSURANCE NOTICE

IMPORTANT IF PREMIUM IS NOT PAID WHEN DUE OR WITHIN THIRTY-ONE DAYS THEREAFTER, INSURANCE WILL LAPSE. MAKE CHECKS OR MONEY ORDERS PAYABLE TO THE TREASURER OF THE U.S. AND FORWARD TO COLLECTIONS SUBDIVISION, VETERANS ADMINISTRATION, WASHINGTON 25, D.C.

48. KIND OF INSURANCE			49. HOW PAID		50. Effective Date of Allotment Discontinuance	51. Date of Next Premium Due (One month after 50)	52. PREMIUM DUE EACH MONTH	53. INTENTION OF VETERAN TO
Nat. Serv.	U.S. Govt.	None	Allotment	Direct to V.A. X	31 Oct 45	30 Nov 45	$6.50	Continue / Continue Only / Discontinue X

54.	55. REMARKS (This space for completion of above items or entry of other items specified in W.D. Directives)
	No time lost under AW 107. Lapel button issued. Entitled to wear the Amer Theatre Campaign Ribbon. European-African-Middle Eastern Theatre Campaign Ribbon, 2 overseas bars. Victory Ribbon. Inactive ERC service from the 12 Apr 43 to 19 Apr 43. ASR score 55 (2 Sep 45).

56. SIGNATURE OF PERSON BEING SEPARATED	57. PERSONNEL OFFICER (Type name, grade and organization-signature)
	C.J. DOWNIE 1st LT., SIG., C.

APPLICATION FOR
READJUSTMENT ALLOWANCE
MADE THROUGH
STATE OF MISSOURI
9 20 46

WD AGO Form 53-55
1 November 1944

This form supersedes all previous editions of WD AGO Forms 53 and 55 for enlisted persons entitled to an Honorable Discharge, which will not be used after receipt of this revision.

Interperting the DD 214 for Awards World War II Military Medals

Just below where the veteran's name is in the upper left-hand corner you can see he was assigned to a medical detachment in the 194th Glider Infantry (*An Airborne Regt, assigned to the 17th Airborne Division*)

Box 30 indicates he was a truck driver (*ambulance most likely*) and box 31 shows he was paratrooper qualified.

Box 32 and **33** are the ones that you will always be most interested in as they identify decorations and awards. **Box 32** says he served in three campaigns, Rhineland, Ardennes and Central Europe. **Box 33** indicates the three bronze stars for the above campaigns but does not identify the campaign ribbons/medals until the remarks in **box 35**. It does identify the award of Good Conduct Medal followed by an MED badge citing the general order by which it was awarded. It also notes the award of a glider badge in 1944.

In **box 55,** the remarks section it indicates he was issued the honorable discharge lapel pin (*aka "The Ruptured Duck"*). It also states he is authorized the American Theater Campaign ribbon, European African Middle Eastern Theater Campaign ribbon, 2 overseas bars and a Victory Ribbon. Notice there is no reference to the word medals because many of the medals such as the Victory Medal were not minted until a year or more after the war.

Paratroopers of the 17th Airborne Division to include a medic are honored after Operation VARSITY in World War II.

Ribbons he came home with in August 1945.

Medals actually authorized but probably never received.

So when this veteran was discharged and returned to the United States in August 1945 he received 4 ribbons and an honorable discharge lapel pin. He also had earned the parachute badge, the glider badge and combat medical badge which was referred to during World War II as a Medical badge (*Med. badge*).

What the DD214 does not tell (*and could not know*) is the award of the Medical Badge (*now called the Combat Medical Badge*) authorized him the Bronze Star Medal as of Army General Orders in 1947. He was also authorized the American Theater Campaign Medal, the European – African – Middle Eastern Theater Campaign Medal, the Victory Medal (*which was not struck until 1947*) and the Army of Occupation Medal which was not available until 1947 but was authorized for all military personnel that served at least 30 days in occupied enemy territory. The 194th GIR served in the Army of Occupation of Germany from 2 May - 14 August 1945. Since Germany surrendered in May 1945 and he returned home in August 1945 he is authorized the Army Occupation of Germany Medal. The DD 214 gives you all the clues but knowing the medals that pertain to the period and war fills in the complete picture of his awards.

❖ World War II Campaign Medals

Good Conduct Medals (WW II verison) · **American Defense Service Medal** · **Womens Army Corps Medal** · **American Campaign Medal**

Europe-African-Middle Eastern Campaign · **Asiatic Pacific Campaign** · **WW II Victory** · **WW II Occupation Medal, Army & Navy** · **Philippine Defense Medal** · **Philippine Liberation Medal**

The basic medals of World War II are shown above. The Navy, Marine Corps and Coast Guard had already established Good Conduct Medals while the Army *(which included the Army Air Force)* established a Good Conduct Medal in 1941.

The American Defense Service Medal was authorized for the period of national emergency prior to 7 December 1941. After America declared war, the conflict was divided into (1) the American theater, (2) the European, African, Middle Eastern theater, and the (3) Asiatic Pacific Theater. Examples of the medals awarded are shown above.

American Defense was awarded for service between 1939 and 7 Dec. 1941.

American Campaign was for service in the American Theater, outside the US for 30 days or in the US for a year. Most veterans qualified for this medal.

All WW II veterans qualified for the Victory Medal.

WW II veterans who served 30 days in an occupied country qualify for an Occupation Medal.

Philippine Defense and Liberation Medals for service in the Philippines.

---

32. BATTLES AND CAMPAIGNS
Battle of the Southern Philippines

33. DECORATIONS AND CITATIONS
Asiatic Pacific Theatre Ribbon w/ 1 star   Good Conduct Medal
Philippine Liberation Ribbon w/ 1 star   Combat Infantry Badge

34. WOUNDS RECEIVED IN ACTION
None

35. LATEST IMMUNIZATION DATES

SMALLPOX	TYPHOID	TETANUS	OTHER (specify)
14Oct44	18Oct45	25Nov44	Typhus 21Feb45 Cholera 21Feb45

36. SERVICE OUTSIDE CONTINENTAL U.S. AND RETURN

DATE OF DEPARTURE	DESTINATION	DATE OF ARRIVAL
17 Feb 45	Pacific Theatre	17 Mar 45

38. HIGHEST GRADE HELD
Pfc

37. TOTAL LENGTH OF SERVICE

CONTINENTAL SERVICE			FOREIGN SERVICE		
YEARS	MONTHS	DAYS	YEARS	MONTHS	DAYS
no	4	23	no	8	14

This soldier's DD214 types out 3 of his 5 medals. The 2 medals not shown are the Victory Medal and the 1947 retroactive award of the Bronze Star medal for his award of the Combat Infantry Badge.

The U.S. Government will not issue foreign awards and he or his family will have to purchase the Phillipine Liberation Medal.

26. DATE OF ENTRY ON ACTIVE DUTY	27. MILITARY OCCUPATIONAL SPECIALTY AND NO.	
22 April 1944	Tank Unit Commander 1203	RECORDED
28. BATTLES AND CAMPAIGNS Ardennes Central Europe		The Adjutant General's Office Concord, New Hampshire AUG 12 1947 Date....................................
29. DECORATIONS AND CITATIONS Purple Heart Medal World War II Victory Medal	ETO Service Medal American Theatre Service Medal	
WOUNDS RECEIVED IN ACTION		
Belgium 1 January 1945		

This Army Armor Officer DD214 has a stamp showing it was registered with the New Hampshire Adjutant General's Office. He is authorized 4 medals. Armor soldiers did not qualify for the Combat Infantry Badge so he is not authorized the 1947 retroactive award of the Bronze Star medal .

The European African Middle Eastern Theater Campaign Medal is abbreviated as the ETO Service medal or sometimes the EAME. He would have 2 battle stars on his ETO medal as shown by the 2 listed campaigns.

❖ Korean Campaign Medals 1950-1954

The Armed Forces approved acceptance of the ROK War Service Medal in Oct. 1999 for all Korean War Veterans. The Korea Defense Service Medal for 30 days service in Korea after 27 July 1954 was approved in 2003.

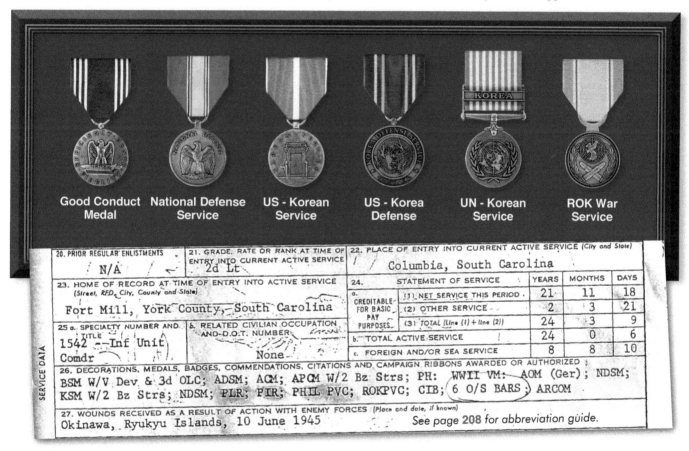

Good Conduct Medal	National Defense Service	US - Korean Service	US - Korea Defense	UN - Korean Service	ROK War Service

20. PRIOR REGULAR ENLISTMENTS	21. GRADE, RATE OR RANK AT TIME OF ENTRY INTO CURRENT ACTIVE SERVICE	22. PLACE OF ENTRY INTO CURRENT ACTIVE SERVICE (City and State)			
N/A	2d Lt	Columbia, South Carolina			
23. HOME OF RECORD AT TIME OF ENTRY INTO ACTIVE SERVICE (Street, RFD, City, County and State)		24.	STATEMENT OF SERVICE	YEARS	MONTHS	DAYS
Fort Mill, York County, South Carolina		a. CREDITABLE FOR BASIC PAY PURPOSES	(1) NET SERVICE THIS PERIOD	21	11	18
			(2) OTHER SERVICE	2	3	21
25 a. SPECIALTY NUMBER AND TITLE	b. RELATED CIVILIAN OCCUPATION AND-D.O.T. NUMBER		(3) TOTAL (line (1) + line (2))	24	3	9
1542 --Inf Unit Comdr	None	b. TOTAL ACTIVE SERVICE		24	0	6
		c. FOREIGN AND/OR SEA SERVICE		8	8	10

26. DECORATIONS, MEDALS, BADGES, COMMENDATIONS, CITATIONS AND CAMPAIGN RIBBONS AWARDED OR AUTHORIZED
BSM W/V Dev & 3d OLC; ADSM; ACM; APCM W/2 Bz Strs; PH: WWII VM: AOM (Ger); NDSM;
KSM W/2 Bz Strs; NDSM; PLR; PIR; PHIL PVC; ROKPVC; CIB; 6 O/S BARS ; ARCOM

27. WOUNDS RECEIVED AS A RESULT OF ACTION WITH ENEMY FORCES (Place and date, if known)
Okinawa, Ryukyu Islands, 10 June 1945   See page **208** for abbreviation guide.

With service in WW II and Korea this Infantry Officer's DD214 is a great example of the many abbreviations you will see. BSM/W/V means a Bronze Star Medal with Valor Device (as opposed for award for meritorious service) and 3 Oak leaf clusters to indicate he was awarded the medal 4 times. ADSM is the American Defense Service Medal; ACM is the American Campaign Medal; APCM W/2BS is the Asiatic Pacific Campaign Medal with 2 Bronze stars: PH is the Purple Heart Medal: WWII VM is the Victory Medal and the AOM (Ger) is the Army Occupation Medal with Germany Bar. His service awards in the Korean War are

indicated by NDSM which is the National Defense Service Medal; the KSM W/2 Bz Strs is the Korean Service Medal with 2 Bronze Stars. PLR is the Philippine Liberation Medal; PIR is the Philippine Independence Medal; PHIL PVC is the Philippine Presidential Unit Citation; ROKPVC is the Republic of Korea Presidential Unit Citation. The CIB is his award of the Combat Infantry Badge but does not indicate if there was a second award for Korea. 6 O/S Bars stand for 6 six months periods in combat and the ARCOM stands for award of the Army Commendation Medal. What is missing is the ROK War Service Medal which was not approved until 1999.

❖ Vietnam Campaign Medals 1965-1973

Good Conduct Medals

National Defense Service Medal

U.S. Vietnam Service Medal

Vietnam Campaign Medal

RVN Gallantry Cross Unit Citation

4. MAILING ADDRESS *(Include ZIP Code)* OSHKOSH GARDEN NEBRASKA 69154		

5. ORIGINAL DD FORM 214 IS CORRECTED AS INDICATED BELOW:	
ITEM NO.	**CORRECTED TO READ**
24	SEPARATION DATE ON DD FORM 214 BEING CORRECTED: 1969/11/07 DELETE: VIETNAM SERVICE MEDAL// ADD: PURPLE HEART//COMBAT INFANTRYMAN BADGE//ARMY GOOD CONDUCT MEDAL//REPUBLIC OF VIETNAM MEDAL W/DEVICE (1960)//REPUBLIC OF VIETNAM GALLANTRY CROSS W/PALM UNIT CITATION//REPUBLIC OF VIETNAM CIVIL ACTIONS HONOR MEDAL FIRST CLASS UNIT CITATION//EXPERT MARKSMANSHIP QUALIFICATION BADGE W/RIFLE BAR (M-14)//SHARPSHOOTER MARKSMANSHIP QUALIFICATION BADGE W/MACHINE GUN BAR (M-60)//MARKSMAN MARKSMANSHIP QUALIFICATION BADGE W/RIFLE BAR (M-16)//VIETNAM SERVICE MEDAL W/TWO BRONZE SERVICE STARS//NOTHING FOLLOWS

Occasionally a DD214 discharge needs to be corrected and this soldier's DD214 is a good example showing the Vietnam Service Medal was deleted and replaced with an entry at the end of the update form showing it was to have 2 campaign stars. This corrected form does an excellent job spelling out his awards and badges.

ITEM NO	CORRECTED TO READ
24	SEPARATION DATE ON DD FORM 214 BEING CORRECTED: 27 OCT 70 DELETE: VSM//BSM//ARCOM ADD: VIETNAM SERVICE MEDAL W/3 BRONZE SERVICE STARS//REPUBLIC OF VIETNAM GALLANTRY CROSS W/PALM UNIT CITATION BADGE//PURPLE HEART//ARMY COMMENDATION MEDAL W/"V" DEVICE//BRONZE STAR MEDAL W/"V" DEVICE AND FIRST OAK LEAF CLUSTER//NOTHING FOLLOWS

This DD214 discharge corrections deletes the abbreviations; VSM//BSM//ARCOM and spells out full name with the appropriate devices. In this case there is a big difference between a BSM and ARCOM with no devices and the corrected verisons that show the awards were for valor as opposed for meritorious service and the that there were 2 awards of the Bronze Star Medal *(Oak Leaf)*

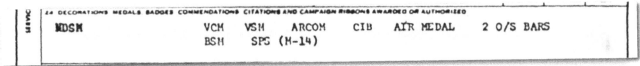

24 DECORATIONS MEDALS BADGES COMMENDATIONS CITATIONS AND CAMPAIGN RIBBONS AWARDED OR AUTHORIZED						
NDSM	VCM	VSM	ARCOM	CIB	AIR MEDAL	2 O/S BARS
	BSM	SPS (M-14)				

This soldier's Vietnam era discharge is typical of abbreviations: NDSM is National Defense Service Medal; the VCM is the RVN Vietnam Campaign Medal; the VSM is the Vietnam Service Medal but missing the campaign stars and it is difficult to tell how many campaign stars he rates on his service medal without knowing when he was there. If you know the dates of his service in Vietnam you can compute the campaign stars from the table listed on the page describing the Vietnam Service Medal. ARCOM is the Army Commendation Medal, CIB, the Combat Infantryman Badge and Air Medal (AM) is correct. The 2 overseas service bars tell you he spent a year in Vietnam so he will have at least 2, up to 4 campaign stars depending on the period. The BSM is the Bronze Star Medal and SPS is for a Sharp Shooters badge. The Vietnamese Cross of Gallantry Unit Citation is missing.

❖ Cold War 1947-1991

Millions of Americans served in the Armed Forces during the Cold War often in dangerous and difficult places. In many cases the current Good Conduct Medals of the Army, Navy, Marines, Air Force and Coast Guard were all they were authorized.

❖ Southwest Asia, Bosnia/Kosovo, Afghanistan & Iraq Campaign Medals

Southwest Asia Service Medal 1991-1995
Bosnia/Kosovo Campaign Medal 1999-2013
Afghanistan Campaign Medal 2001-To a date To Be Determined
Iraq Campaign Medal 2003-2011
Inherent Resolve Campaign Medal 2014-To a date To Be Determined

After Vietnam the Armed Forces began a much better job describing the decorations and awards of honorably discharged personnel. Current DD214s such as shown on the next page clearly spell all authorized awards the veteran has earned. Examples of the campaign medals for the period above are shown below and two examples of the DD214 discharges used today are shown on the next page.

| Good Conduct Medals (Current issue) | National Defense Service Medal | Southwest Asia Service | Saudi Arabia Liberation of Kuwait | Kuwait Liberation of Kuwait | Kosovo Campaign Medal | NATO Bosnia Medal |
| NATO Kosovo Medal | National Defense Service Medal | Afghanistan Campaign | Iraq Campaign | War on Terrorism Expeditionary | War on Terrorism Service | Inherent Resolve Campaign |

13. DECORATIONS, MEDALS, BADGES, CITATIONS AND CAMPAIGN RIBBONS AWARDED OR AUTHORIZED (All periods of service)

PURPLE HEART (2ND AWARD)//ARMY ACHIEVEMENT MEDAL//ARMY GOOD CONDUCT MEDAL//NATIONAL DEFENSE SERVICE MEDAL//AFGHANISTAN CAMPAIGN MEDAL W/ TWO CAMPAIGN STARS//IRAQ CAMPAIGN MEDAL W/ CAMPAIGN STAR//OVERSEAS SERVICE RIBBON (2ND AWARD))//NATO MEDAL//COMBAT INFANTRYMAN BADGE//CONT IN BLOCK 18

14. MILITARY EDUCATION (Course title, number of weeks, and month and year completed)

AIRBORNE COURSE, 3 WEEKS, 2007//INFANTRYMAN COURSE, 8 WEEKS, 2007//WARRIOR LEADER COURSE, 2 WEEKS, 2009//NOTHING FOLLOWS

		YES	X	NO
15a. COMMISSIONED THROUGH SERVICE ACADEMY		YES	X	NO
b. COMMISSIONED THROUGH ROTC SCHOLARSHIP (10 USC Sec. 2107b)		YES	X	NO
c. ENLISTED UNDER LOAN REPAYMENT PROGRAM (10 USC Chap. 109) (If Yes, years of commitment: NA)		YES		NO

16. DAYS ACCRUED LEAVE PAID 12

17. MEMBER WAS PROVIDED COMPLETE DENTAL EXAMINATION AND ALL APPROPRIATE DENTAL SERVICES AND TREATMENT WITHIN 90 DAYS PRIOR TO SEPARATION — YES / NO: X

18. REMARKS

CONTINUOUS HONORABLE ACTIVE SERVICE: 20070206-20120527//ENLISTMENT BONUS PAID: $5000.00, 20070405//SERVED IN A DESIGNATED IMMINENT DANGER PAY AREA//SERVICE IN IRAQ 20071115-20090215//SERVICE IN AFGHANISTAN 20101030-20110917//MEMBER HAS COMPLETED FIRST FULL TERM OF SERVICE//NOT ELIGIBLE FOR SEPARATION PAY; SIGNED DECLINATION FOR CONTINUED SERVICE, DA FORM 4991-R//CONT FROM BLOCK 13: //PARACHUTIST BADGE//NOTHING FOLLOWS

---

13. DECORATIONS, MEDALS, BADGES, CITATIONS AND CAMPAIGN RIBBONS AWARDED OR AUTHORIZED (All periods of service)

ARMY COMMENDATION MEDAL (3RD AWARD)//ARMY ACHIEVEMENT MEDAL (2ND AWARD)//ARMY SUPERIOR UNIT AWARD//ARMY GOOD CONDUCT MEDAL//ARMY RESERVE COMPONENT ACHIEVEMENT MEDAL (2ND AWARD)//NATIONAL DEFENSE SERVICE MEDAL (2ND AWARD)//GLOBAL WAR ON TERRORISM EXPEDITIONARY MEDAL//CONT IN BLOCK 18

14. MILITARY EDUCATION (Course title, number of weeks, and month and year completed)

NONE//NOTHING FOLLOWS

15a. COMMISSIONED THROUGH SERVICE ACADEMY

(Specify the item number of the block continued for each entry.) PROFESSIONAL DEVELOPMENT RIBBON (2ND AWARD)//ARMY SERVICE RIBBON// CONT FROM BLOCK 18: PROFESSIONAL DEVELOPMENT RIBBON (2ND AWARD)//ARMED FORCES RESERVE MEDAL W/ 10-YEAR DEVICE-BRONZE HOURGLASS// OVERSEAS SERVICE RIBBON//ARMED FORCES RESERVE MEDAL W/ M DEVICE//NOTHING FOLLOWS ARMED FORCES RESERVE MEDAL W/ M DEVICE//NOTHING FOLLOWS

DENTAL EXAMINATION AND ALL APPROPRIATE DENTAL SERVICES AND TREATMENT WITHIN 90 DAYS PRIOR TO SEPARATION — YES / NO: X

18. REMARKS

SERVED IN A DESIGNATED IMMINENT DANGER PAY AREA//SERVICE IN UNITED ARAB EMIRATES 20130807-20140505//ITEM 12D ABOVE DOES NOT ACCOUNT FOR ANNUAL AND/OR WEEKEND TRAINING THIS SOLDIER MAY HAVE ACCOMPLISHED PRIOR TO DATE ENTERED IN ITEM 12A//INDIVIDUAL COMPLETED PERIOD FOR WHICH ORDERED TO ACTIVE DUTY FOR PURPOSE OF POST SERVICE BENEFITS AND ENTITLEMENTS//ORDERED TO ACTIVE DUTY IN SUPPORT OF OPERATION ENDURING FREEDOM IAW 10 USC 12302//MEMBER HAS COMPLETED FIRST FULL TERM OF SERVICE//CONT FROM BLOCK 13: //GLOBAL WAR ON TERRORISM SERVICE MEDAL//NON COMMISSIONED OFFICER//SEE ATTACHED CONTINUATION SHEET

Abbreviations

AM	Air Medal	JMUA	Joint Meritorious Unit Citation
ACM	American Campaign Medal	JSAM	Joint Service Achievement Medal
ADSM	American Defense Service Medal	JSCM	Joint Service Commendation Med
ASM	Antarctic Service Medal	KSM	Korean Service Medal
AFEM	Armed Forces Expeditionary Medal	KCM	Kosovo Campaign Medal
AFRM	Armed Forces Reserve Medal	KLM(K)	Kuwait Liberation Medal (Kuwait)
AFSM	Armed Forces Service Medal	KLM(SA)	Kuwait Liberation Medal (Saudi Arabia)
AAM	Army Achievement Medal	LM or LOM	Legion of Merit
ARCOM	Army Commendation Medal	M or M Dev	Letter "M" Device
GCM or AGCM	Army Good Conduct Medal	V or V Dev	Letter "V" Device
AOM	Army of Occupation Medal	MHA	Medal for Humane Action
ARCAM	Army Reserve Components Ach. Medal	MH or MOH	Medal of Honor
ARCOTR	Army Reserve Components Overseas Tng Rib	MSM	Meritorious Service Medal
ASR	Army Service Ribbon	MUC	Meritorious Unit Citation
ASUA	Army Superior Unit Citation	NDSM	National Defense Service Medal
APCM	Asiatic-Pacific Campaign Medal	NPDR	NCO Professional Development Rib
BF	Belgian Fourragere	NOL	Netherlands Orange Lanyard
BA, AH or BAH	Bronze Arrowhead	OLC	Oak Leaf Cluster
OLC or BOLC	Bronze Oak Leaf Cluster	OSR	Overseas Service Ribbon
BSS or BCS	Bronze Service Star	PDR	Philippine Defense Ribbon
BSM	Bronze Star Medal	PIR	Philippine Independence Ribbon
CIB	Combat Infantryman Badge	PLR	Philippine Liberation Ribbon
CMB or MB	Combat Medical Badge	POW	POW Medal
DDSM	Defense Distinguished Service Medal	PU	Presidential Unit Citation
DMSM	Defense Meritorious Service Medal	PH	Purple Heart
DSSM	Defense Superior Service Medal	VCM	Republic of Vietnam Campaign
DFC	Distinguished Flying Cross	SS	Silver Star
DSC	Distinguished Service Cross	SM	Soldier's Medal
DSM	Distinguished Service Medal	SWASM	Southwest Asia Service Medal
EAMECM or EAME or ETO	European-African-Middle Eastern Campaign Medal	UNSM	United Nations Service Medal
EFMB	Expert Field Medical Badge	VUA	Valorous Unit Citation
EIB	Expert Infantryman Badge	VSM	Vietnam Service Medal
FF	French Fourragere	WACSM	Women's Army Corps Service Medal
HSM	Humanitarian Service Medal	WWIVM	World War I Victory Medal

Awards Displays that Honor American Veterans!

The display tells the story of a member of 106th " Golden Lion" Infantry Division which was struck by the full weight of the German Winter Offensive on December 16th,1944. A battle we all know by the name of the "The Battle of the Bulge".

Let No American Veteran Be Forgotten!

The most positive thing a veteran or their family can do to honor and remember their service to our country is to display their military awards for future generations. Many veterans or families are not sure where to start. Sometimes there is an old uniform, a cigar box full of old insignia that children or grandchildren once played with or perhaps some old black and white photographs.

The picture above shows what this book can help you do. The old uniform carries the insignia of an infantry corporal in the 106th "Golden Lion" Infantry Division which took the full weight of Von Rundstedt's Ardennes Campaign in December of 1944. This veteran had been awarded the Combat Infantry Badge, the Bronze Star

medal, the Purple Heart medal, the Good Conduct Medal, the American Campaign Medal and the European-African-Middle Eastern Campaign Medal and the World War Victory Medal.

The Division was assigned occupation duty in Bad Ems after the war which qualifies him for the World War II Occupation Medal and he has personally added the Battle of the Bulge Commemorative Medal to indicate his participation in one of most significant and difficult battles of World War II. The display tells the story of his service with his medals, division, branch insignia and qualification badges even to his World War II Honorable discharge pin. A display of service that will be admired by generations to come.

U.S. Army Award Display World War II

Army Rank

Medals

Campaign Battle Stars

Shooting Badges

Army Insignia

Army Badges

Commemorative Medals

Honorable Discharge Pin AKA "Ruptured Duck"

The soldiers of World War II did not received their campaign medals at the end of the war. They only received the ribbon bars because brass had been restricted for munitions and many of the medals had yet to be struck or approved. In fact, some medals were not approved until 1985.

IN MEMORY OF
SGT. JAMES P. FLAGHERTY
PRESENTED TO HIS SON IN GRATEFUL
RECOGNITION OF HIS FATHER'S SERVICE

Brass Plates

World War II (Europe)

The display shows the awards and insignia that tell the unique story of each veteran's service. Each medal, badge, unit insignia, rank and ribbon recalls an event in the life of the veteran it honors.

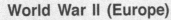
Letters

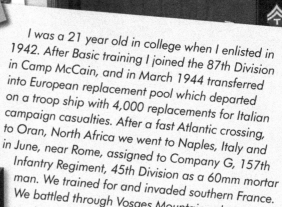

I was a 21 year old in college when I enlisted in 1942. After Basic training I joined the 87th Division in Camp McCain, and in March 1944 transferred into European replacement pool which departed on a troop ship with 4,000 replacements for Italian campaign casualties. After a fast Atlantic crossing, to Oran, North Africa we went to Naples, Italy and in June, near Rome, assigned to Company G, 157th Infantry Regiment, 45th Division as a 60mm mortar man. We trained for and invaded southern France. We battled through Vosges Mountains along western edge of France into Alsace. By Jan. 1945, I was one of 13 survivors from Company G. After Germany surrendered we were alerted for the invasion of Japan. We felt the bomb saved our lives. I was home for Christmas.

U.S. Army Award Display WW II, Europe and Pacific

World War II (Pacific)
This veteran's case shows American and Pacific service with medals and commemoratives reflecting Combat Service, and victory over Japan. Ribbons above Medals. WW II Tech 5 rank with Honorable Discharge Button & Shooting Badges.

World War II (Pacific)
This Staff Sgt. combat veteran case shows Pacific service in the 25th and Americal Division including the Liberation of the Philippines, the Presidential Unit Citation, and shooting badges.

World War II (Europe)
These displays show the awards and insignia that tell the unique story of each veteran's service.

U.S. Army Korean War Award Display Examples (1950-53)

Korean War

Korean War Master Sgt. has picture as focal point and gold plated medals with medal description plates. Shooting badges and ROK Presidential Unit Citation. Korean Service and United Nations Commemoratives round out a magnificent display.

Korean War
This Corporal's display has a ribbon rack flanked by unit awards. Second row of medals are commemoratives, reflecting Combat Service, ROK Presidential unit citation, Korean & UN Service plus Honorable Service. Shooting Badges and Brass plate round out his military story.

DID YOU KNOW? Korean War veterans had to wait 46 years before the ROK War Service Medal was authorized and even longer before the Korean Defense Service medal was approved.

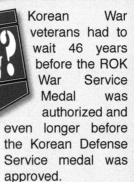

Korean War

This veteran's flag is displayed with a picture in uniform and his Bronze Star and multiple awards of the Purple Heart medal.

Korean War

These two displays tell the story that both men were on Japan occupation duty when the Korean War started and while each have the same medals they are displayed differently. Actually the display on the right was done by the veteran's son after his dad passed on.

Cold War Veteran Displays (1947-1991)

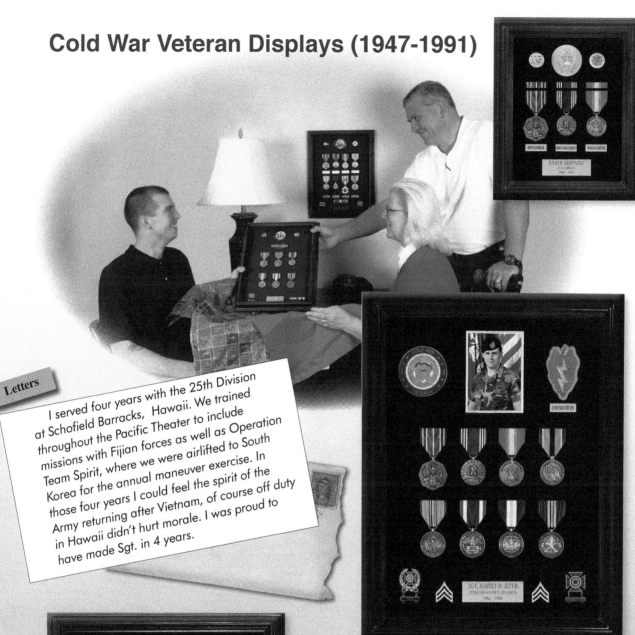

Cold War
This Infantry Sgt. display reflects meritorious service in the Reserve Forces for over 10 years.

Cold War
This Sgt. served in the 4th Infantry Division and in Europe as well as in the Reserve Forces.

U.S. Army Vietnam Display Cases

Vietnam Insignia

Medals

Sharpshooter w/Bar

DANIEL G. WHITE, USCG RETIRED
CHIEF QUARTERMASTER
CGC GALLATIN WHEC - 721
UNITED STATES COAST GUARD
1 AUG 1974 - 1 SEP 1984

Brass Plates

Patches

Campaign Battle Stars

Commemorative Medals

Army Insignia

Display Cases

Vietnam 1965-1975

Over 3,403,000 Americans served in Vietnam during the 10 years of fighting. Their devotion to duty and combat record was extraordinary. Only after the US military withdrew after signing a peace accord did South Vietnam fall to the Communist who ignored the peace accord.

Vietnam
This Patriotic Combat Medic Specialist 5 served 18 months and 5 campaigns (1 Silver star) in Vietnam plus Reserve service.

Vietnam
This II Field Force soldier pictured on the radio personalized his award display case with medallions, his unit patch, his ribbons, skill badges and rank. He added two commemorative medals to represent that he had been in combat action and one to represent his RVN Gallantry Cross Unit Citation.

Vietnam
This Infantry CPL's handsome oak display case shows distinguished service in the First infantry Division, the " Big Red One."

Vietnam
This Artillery Recon Sgt. served in MACV and ARVN units and was decorated by both. Commemorative Medals for Unit awards balance a terrific personal display.

Vietnam
This Transportation Specialist 4 served 18 months and 5 campaigns in Vietnam plus Reserve service.

U.S. Army Vietnam Award Displays

I joined the 5th Infantry "Red Diamond" Division in 67 and was alerted for Vietnam deployment March 1968. We reorganized as 1st Brigade Separate with Colonel Glikes as CO. After intensive training we loaded vehicles on railroad cars and arrived at Quang Tri, in July. August we moved into "Leatherneck Square" bordered by Con Thien, Cam Lo, Dong Ha, Gio Linh. My unit, D Co., 1-11 Inf was patrolling north of Con Thien when we ran into dug-in NVA units and got pinned down. C Company and tanks from 1-77 came charging in and we ran the NVA out of their holes. We conducted battalion-size operations all over the demilitarized zone until November when we moved to AO Marshall Mountain near Quang Tri City doing routine patrols with the 1st ARVN Division. It was a year I will never forget nor the guys I served with!

Vietnam

This Military Intelligence Specialist 5th class served in Korea, Europe and Vietnam and rounds out his decorations and service medals with a 1968 Tet Offensive commemorative medal and RVN Gallantry Cross Unit award.

Vietnam

The First Sgt. served in the First Air Cavalry Division and the 11th Armored Cavalry Regt. in Vietnam. He has Army Aircrew wings and has been awarded the Distinguished Flying Cross.

U.S. Army Gulf War "DESERT STORM" Displays

Army Desert Storm

A classic configuration flanked with "Big Red One" patches and centering the Army medallion above the senior NCO's ribbons. A handsome display for a Master Sgt. and especially nice using individual name plates underneath each medal

Liberation of Kuwait and service in Kosovo

This great young American Infantry Captain earned three foreign awards in Desert Storm and Kosovo and used the Liberation of Kuwait Commemorative Medal to round out his display.

Army Desert Storm

Another classic configuration with the new Combat Action Badge flanked with a 3rd and 4th Infantry Division Patches and medals below. Challenge coins, skill and rank badges flank a brass plate.

Army Desert Storm

This Reserve Sgt served in "Desert Storm" and later was also mobilized for service in Iraq as part of the Global War on Terror.

U.S. Army Afghanistan and Iraq Display Cases

Army "Iraqistan"

This Infantry Captain has been mobilized twice once with the 18th Airborne Corps and with the 3rd Infantry Division and displays his 13 full size medals accented with insignia and badges. The medallion makes for a great centerpiece and the unit challenge coins below show his unit pride in service. The stark black background really allows the color of the ribbons to be visually dominant. The display would be better with a brass nameplate to show dates of service since he has served in Afghanistan, Iraq and Kosov.

Army "Iraqistan"

This former specialist to Major tells his military service with his 14 full size medals accented with insignia and badges. The hat brass makes for a great centerpiece and the coins below show his pride in rank and service. The name plates below the medals and the larger brass name plate provide details of his career as an enlisted man and officer with service in Afghanistan, Iraq, South Korea and Kosov.

Afghanistan and Iraq service

This young Air Defense Sgt. earned 2 decorations and the Combat Action Badge in Afghanistan and Iraq during his military service. His dog tag is a nice touch.

Afghanistan and NATO service with one mobilization with the 33rd Inf. Division

This Artillery Captain adds a non authorized Combat Artillery badge to his display.

Afghanistan and Iraq service

This great young paratrooper Infantry Staff Sgt. with the 173rd Airborne Bde earned the CIB and 3 decorations in Afghanistan and Iraq. Ribbon only awards on bottom.

U.S. Army Iraq Display Cases

Iraq and Desert Storm

A truly awesome display of a paratrooper Sgt. First Class from the 82d and 173rd Airborne. The arrowhead on his Iraq Campaign medal indicates he made a combat parachute jump into Iraq with the 173rd and fought in Desert Storm with the 82d Airborne Division.

Army Iraq

This traditional Army green shadow box features Combat Service Identification Badges in lieu of patches for a modern uniform look. This Master Sgt. has 2 Reserve awards and added unofficial combat engineer and armor badges at the bottom.

Iraq

This Quartermaster Sgt proudly displays his Combat Action badge over his medals. His Wheel Driver qualification badge is displayed over his Expert Rifleman's badge.

Iraq

This Specialist 4th class displays his badges over his ribbons, unit awards and medals. In addition to his CIB he proudly displays his hard earned Expert Infantryman's badge.

Other Army Medal, Miniature Medals and Ribbon Display Cases

Other Types of Displays

Medals mounted with certificates such as the Bronze Star and Distinguished Flying Cross are a very handsome display as well as displays featuring miniature medals mounted for wear. Ribbon and badges make a nice smaller display as well as mounting a single medal with ribbon.

U.S. Army Multi Wars Career Display Cases

BIBLIOGRAPHY

Adjutant General of the Army- American Decorations 1862-1926, 1927

Belden, B.L.- United States War Medals, 1916

Borthwick, D. and Britton, J. - Medals, Military and Civilian of the United States, 1984

Boatner III, Major Mark M. - Military Customs and Traditions

Borts, L.H.- United Nations Medals and Missions, 1997

Crocker, US Army (Ret), LTC Lawrence P. - Army Officer's Guide 42nd Edition

Crocker, US Army (Ret), LTC Lawrence P. - Army Officer's Guide 45th Edition

Dept. of Defense Manual DOD 1348.33M- Manual of Military Decorations & Awards, 1996

Campbell, J. Duncan. Aviation Badges and Insignia of the United States Army, 1913-1946, 1977.

Dorling, H.T. - Ribbons and Medals, 1983

Emmerson, William H., Encyclopedia of the United States Army Insignia and Uniform

Fisher, Jr., Ernest F. - Guardians of the Republic

Fisch, Jr., Arnold and Wright, Jr., Robert K. - The Story of the Noncommissioned Officer corps, The Backbone of the Army

Foster, Frank. Complete Guide to United States Army Medals, Badges and Insignia, 2004.

Foster, Frank. Military Medals of America, 2019.

Foster, Frank. United States Army Medals, Badges and Insignia, 2011.

Foster, Frank and Borts, Lawrence. Military Medals of the United States, 7th Edition 2010.

Foster, Frank and Sylvester, John. The Decorations and Medals of the Republic of Vietnam and Her Allies, 1950-1975, 1995.

Gleim, A.F.- United States Medals of Honor 1862-1989, 1989

Inter-American Defense Board- Norms for Protocol, Symbols, Insignia and Gifts, 1984

Jacobsen, Jr. Jacques Noel - Regulations and Notes for the Uniform of the Army of the Unites States, 1917

Katcher, Philip - The American Soldier - US Armies in Uniform, 1775 to Present

Kerrigan, E.- American Badges and Insignia, 1967

Kerrigan, E.- American Medals and Decorations, 1990

Kerrigan, E.- American War Medals and Decorations, 1971

Kredel, Fritz and Todd, Fredrick P. - Soldiers of the American Army, 1775-1954

Maguire, Jon A. Silver Wings, Pinks and Greens, 1994

Military Service Publishing Co. - The Officer's Guide 1948, April Edition

Morgan, J.L. Pete -United States. Military Patch Guide, 2006

National Geographic Magazine, December, 1919

National Geographic Society- Insignia and Decorations of the U.S. Armed Forces, 1944

Oliver, Ray. "What's In A Name?," 1983.

Rosignoli, Guido. Badges and Insignia of World War II, 1980

Rosignoli, G. - The Illustrated Encyclopedia of Military Insignia of the 20th Century

Rush, USA (Ret), CSM Robert S. - NCO Guide

Simon and Schuster - Official Guide to the Army Air Forces, 1944

Smith, Richard W. Shoulder Sleeve Insignia of the U.S. Armed Forces, 1981.

Strandberg, J.E. and Bender, R.J.- The Call to Duty, 1994

Smith, Richard W. Shoulder Sleeve Insignia of the U.S. Armed Forces, 1981

Spink, Barry L. "A Chronology of the Enlisted Rank Chevron of the United States Air Force," 1992

Thompson, James G. - Decorations, Medals, Ribbons, Badges and Insignia of the United States Marine Corps, 1998

Troiani, Don, Coates, Earl J., and Kochan, James L. - Don Troiani's Soldiers in America

U.S. Army Regulation 670-1- Wear and Appearance of Army Uniforms and Insignia, May, 2000

U.S. Army Regulation 600-8-22- Military Awards, 1995

U.S. Army Regulation 600-35, 1944.

U.S. Army Regulation 672-5 - Military Awards, 1990.

Vietnam Council on Foreign Relations- Awards & Decorations of Vietnam, 1972

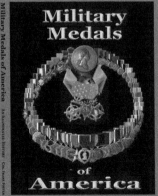

INDEX

Other books in the "No Veterans Forgotten" Series.

Military Medals of America
An Illustrated Guide & History

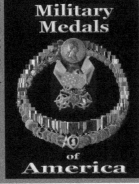

Order @ www.moapress.com

This is the most comprehensive, uptodate and lavishly illustrated guide to all the medals and ribbons of the U.S. Armed Forces from the Revolution to today. To appreciate the scope, detail and incredible illustrations you can look through the book at **www.moapress.com**. In a nut shell this is the most complete book ever written on America awards with :Color plates of all Armed Forces medals and ribbons. All Military decorations and service medals, history and award criteria. Foreign awards and UN medals. Complete displays of Army, Navy, Marine, Air Force and Coast Guard ribbons in correct order with all devices.All military Medals from 1775 to 2019. Their History and how to claim and display them. 232 pages, 8 1/2 x 11 inch trim, all four color.

Code	Book ISBN	Retail
BK 51 Hardcover	978-1-884452-71-0	$34.95
BK 52 Softcover	978-1-884452-72-7	$29.95

United States Military Patch Guide

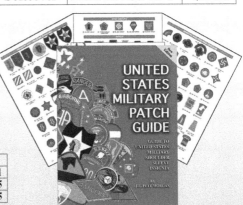

- Over **5000 military** color patches and tabs pictured and identified.
- Guide and Reference on American Military patches.
- Covers World War I, World War II, Korea, Vietnam, Kuwait, Bosnia and Afghanistan.

- Sections on the Army, Marine Corps, Air Forces, National Guard, Special Forces and Civil Air Patrol. United States shoulder sleeve insignia and patches.
- Size: 8¹/₂" x 11"   162 pages

Number of Books		
Code	Book ISBN	Retail
BK 114	HB 978-1-884452-34-5	$29.95
BK 115	SB 978-1-884452-37-6	$24.95

Order @ www.moapress.com

Medals and Ribbons of the United States Air Force A Complete Guide

- Features color plates of all Air Force decorations and ribbons along with award criteria.
- Precedence chart included for all USAF awards and ribbons.
- Attachments for awards and ribbons.
- Army Air Force and USAF Veterans Awards Display examples.

- Includes USAF Devices.
- Explains qualification requirements for all badges worn by Air Force personnel from 1941.
- Display of Air Force how to wear ribbons, medals and miniatures on current USAF uniform.
- Size: 8¹/₂" x 11"   192 pages

Number of Books		
Code	Book ISBN	Retail
BK 29	HB 978-1-884452-60-4	$29.95
BK 30	SB 978-1-884452-55-0	$24.95

Marine Awards and Insignia

- Color plates of all Marine Corps medals and ribbons.
- All Marine decorations and service medals, history and award criteria.
- Foreign awards and UN medals.
- Complete set of Marine ribbons in correct order with all attachments and devices.
- All Marine insignia including officer and enlisted rank insignia 1944 to present World War II shoulder patches.

- Descriptions of service ID badges, aiguillettes shoulder cords, etc.
- Detailed information on marksmanship and trophy badges.
- A guide to correct wear of medals, ribbons, insignia and badges by active duty Marines and veterans.
- Displaying awards and insignia.
- How to claim medals.
- Size: 8¹/₂" x 11"   208 pages

All available at
www.moapress.com.
or AMAZON

Number of Books		
Code	Book ISBN	Retail
BK 35	HB 978-1-884452-29-1	$29.95
BK 36	SB 978-1-884452-41-3	$24.95

CPSIA information can be obtained
at www.ICGtesting.com
Printed in the USA
LVHW071438171120
671941LV00006B/103

9 781884 452628